Torah
Mates

Presented as a gift
from
Oorah/Torah Mates
We hope you will find this book beneficial.

1.877.TORAH123
www.torahmates.org

ArtScroll Series®

Rabbi Nosson Scherman / Rabbi Meir Zlotowitz

General Editors

THROUGH TEHILLIM

RABBI ZELIG PLISKIN

EXPLORING PSALMS
FOR LIFE TRANSFORMING THOUGHTS

GROWTH

Published by

Mesorah Publications, ltd

FIRST EDITION
First Impression ... August 2004
Second Impression ... May 2005
Third Impression ... June 2007
Fourth Impression ... August 2010
Fifth Impression ... February 2018

Published and Distributed by
MESORAH PUBLICATIONS, Ltd.
4401 Second Avenue
Brooklyn, New York 11232

Distributed in Europe by
LEHMANNS
Unit E, Viking Business Park
Rolling Mill Road
Jarrow, Tyne & Wear NE32 3DP
England

Distributed in Israel by
SIFRIATI / A. GITLER — BOOKS
POB 2351
Bnei Brak 51122

Distributed in Australia & New Zealand by
GOLDS WORLD OF JUDAICA
3-13 William Street
Balaclava, Melbourne 3183
Victoria Australia

Distributed in South Africa by
KOLLEL BOOKSHOP
Northfield centre, 17 Northfield Avenue
Glenhazel 2192, Johannesburg, South Africa

Typography by CompuScribe at ArtScroll Studios, Ltd.
4401 Second Avenue / Brooklyn, N.Y. 11232 / (718) 921-9000

Printed in the United States of America by Noble Book Press

Table of Contents

Acknowledgments

I wish to express my profound gratitude to Hashem for giving me life and for making this book possible.

May the thoughts in this book bring us closer to Him.

I thank Rabbi Meir Zlotowitz, Shmuel Blitz, Rabbi Avrohom Biderman, and the entire Artscroll staff for enabling this book to be published.

I am grateful to Rabbi Noah Weinberg, founder and head of Aish HaTorah, for his idealism and intense drive to spread the fire of Torah.

Thank you, Rabbi Kalman Packouz, for your continued friendship and encouragement.

I am deeply grateful to my brother-in-law, Rabbi Hershel Weizberg, for his ongoing kindness and patience. May Hashem bless him in all ways.

INTRODUCTION

Tehillim is a source of great light. The spiritually and emotionally uplifting thoughts are potentially life-transforming. We elevate ourselves when we internalize them and make them an integral part of our worldview. We see what we might not have seen otherwise. We become more aware of the constant kindnesses of our loving Heavenly Father.

In times of darkness and distress, verses of *Tehillim* are a light to our souls. They are an antidote to discouragement and despair. They console and give hope. They raise our sights. Throughout the ages when our ancestors faced challenges, whether relatively minor ones or serious life-threatening challenges, the holy verses have been a source of encouragement and support. They have provided inner strength in the past, and continue to do so in the present.

Tehillim is the ultimate work that connects us experientially with our loving Father and All-powerful King, Creator and Sustainer of the universe. We connect with our loving Eternal Father with our profound appreciation for all of His many kindnesses to us personally and to the entire world.

In *Tehillim* we express many diverse needs: Needs for healing, for being saved from harm, for release from deep emotional pain and distress, and also the need to enrich our positive experiences by realizing that they are gifts from the Source of all Kindness. Thanking Him for those gifts exponentially multiplies the value of those gifts. They are no longer material and temporal. They become spiritual assets that nourish our eternal soul.

While King David himself, author and compiler of *Tehillim*, did not live to see the building of the Holy Temple in Jerusalem, which his son King Solomon built, his words were sung as part of the

Temple service. Together with musical instruments, the sounds and words inspired and raised spirits. They created some of the loftiest emotional states possible for humans to achieve. Each of us in our own way connects with those elevated spiritual feelings as we recited the same words that were sung then, and which will be repeated there, in the future.

There are times in life when a person feels that "nothing can be done" to change a dire situation. But there is always something that we can do: we can connect with our Father and King in heartfelt prayer. We can pray in our own words after we repeat the sublime, uplifting words that were Divinely inspired and sanctified in *Tehillim*. Reciting Psalms elevates us and opens our hearts. The personal prayers we say afterwards follow our greater awareness of our connection with the One Who can answer our prayers.

The three Hebrew words *"ki l'olam chasdo,* for His kindness is forever,"* is a basic theme that is repeated throughout *Tehillim*. The kindness of the Creator is the source of creation and everything that exists. We benefit from His kindness every moment of our lives. But we choose when we will focus on it. The ultimate level to reach is, to focus on this kindness with each breath we take. This is what the Midrash (*Yalkut Shimoni,* 989) on the last verse of *Tehillim,* tells us to do: "Thank Hashem for each and every breath." The more we live with this concept, the more light, gratitude and joy we will experience throughout our lives.

The purpose of every event in our life is to supply us with opportunities to elevate ourselves. As R' Moshe Chaim Luzzatto writes in the first chapter of his classic work, *Mesilas Yesharim,* "All aspects of life are challenges (*nisyonos*) to help us grow. For example, both poverty and wealth are tests. When life goes smoothly, it tests one's character, and so does a life of suffering." Adding *Tehillim* to each situation is a powerful tool. The verses enable us to achieve deeper gratitude to our Creator for the fortunate events and situations that we spontaneously appreciate. They enable us to express ourselves better than we could with our own words, when we have a need to cry out to our Heavenly Father to help us in times of danger when we are experiencing difficulties.

The purpose of the present work is to enrich our experience of reciting *Tehillim*. It is limited in its scope. We will be focusing on a selection of verses with the goal of gaining a greater understanding of what they can mean to us. What we offer here can serve as a model to help the reader gain in even more ways from the same verses and all the other verses of *Tehillim*.

As a young child growing up in Baltimore, I remember visiting my grandparents in Cleveland. My grandmother, of blessed memory, would recite *Tehillim* throughout the day. It was not that she would also recite *Tehillim* in between her involvement in the myriad tasks of cooking and baking for family members and guests. Rather, she would pray and recite *Tehillim* the entire day, and in between verses, she would take care of all the many things that needed her attention. These apparent interruptions were not a break in the immersion of *Tehillim*, rather they were activities that flowed from the words she would constantly recite. The sense of holiness that pervaded all that she did, was a direct product of the *Tehillim* verses that she so fervently said.

My father was a disciple of the saintly Chofetz Chaim in Radin, Poland. He studied there for the last seven years of the Chofetz Chaim's life and for another five years after that. The name of his teacher was frequently mentioned in our house, when I was growing up. The Chofetz Chaim spent a lifetime teaching and spreading the importance of watching the words we say. Great care must be taken not to say anything that might eventually cause distress or pain to another person. The Chofetz Chaim's name, was taken from two Hebrew words from *Tehillim*. In chapter 34, King David gives us a formula for long life: "Who is the person who wants the life (*He'chofetz Chaim*) ...? Guard your tongue from evil and your lips from speaking deceit." This one message from *Tehillim* has the power to totally transform one's life. How many more messages are stored in all the chapters and verses that will have an enlightening and elevating effect on our lives when we integrate and internalize them!

Your thoughts create you, moment by moment. As you continue to grow through *Tehillim*, your own thoughts, words, and actions will be directed on a Heavenward path.

⊰ 1 / א ⊱

א אַשְׁרֵי־הָאִישׁ אֲשֶׁר לֹא הָלַךְ בַּעֲצַת רְשָׁעִים וּבְדֶרֶךְ
חַטָּאִים לֹא עָמָד וּבְמוֹשַׁב לֵצִים לֹא יָשָׁב:
ב כִּי אִם־בְּתוֹרַת יהוה חֶפְצוֹ וּבְתוֹרָתוֹ יֶהְגֶּה יוֹמָם וָלָיְלָה:

¹ *Praiseworthy is the person who walked not in the counsel of the evil, and stood not in the path of the sinful, and sat not in the session of scorners.*

² **But his desire is in the Torah of** HASHEM, **and in his Torah he thinks about day and night.**

The first chapter of *Tehillim* praises the way of the righteous. While the majority of *Tehillim* are expressions of praise of the Almighty, and prayers to be saved from harm and danger, this chapter makes a statement about choosing an elevated path of life. And in the very first verse King David tells us not to associate with those who are on the path of evil. Even before we fill our minds and hearts with Torah and a God-consciousness, we must first make a strong resolution to keep away from negative influences. By clearing our minds of negativity, we are preparing it to receive Hashem's Torah and the elevated thoughts expressed in *Tehillim*.

Some people claim, "I can be around anyone, and I won't be influenced negatively." But the Rambam, whose deep understanding of human nature has withstood the test of time, cited this verse and stated emphatically, "The very nature of a human being is to be influenced in thoughts and actions by his friends and acquaintances, and to behave in the manner of the people of his country" (*Hilchos De'os* 6:1).

Your thoughts are who you are. For example, the difference between a joyful person and a sad person lies in his thoughts. It does not necessarily mean that a joyful person has a much better life situation and a sad person a much worse one. Rather, a joyful person creates joy with the way that he consistently thinks. He enjoys the gifts Hashem constantly bestows upon him. He is full of appreciation and gratitude. He sees the positive and the benefit in situations and circumstances. He sees how he grows from challenges and adversity.

Conversely, people who are consistently sad, angry, frustrated, or miserable, think in ways that are the opposite of the thinking patterns of the person who is consistently joyful, serene, patient, kind, and compassionate. Everyone wants to live a joyful life. The Almighty enables us to do this by giving us free will in our choice of thoughts. As the Rambam states so clearly, we are all influenced by the thoughts and actions of others. Choosing wisely to be influenced by those who have absorbed the thoughts of gratitude expressed in *Tehillim,* we will open our eyes and see many things for which to be grateful.

Even people who are generally very positive, grateful, and joyful, will find that, if they spend an extended amount of time around someone who consistently focuses on the negative and always finds something to complain about, something about which to complain they will be adversely affected to some degree.

Your thoughts are who you are. The difference between an elevated, refined, noble, and righteous person and an evil person, is in their thoughts. Our thoughts create our feelings, our words and our actions. Thinking the thoughts of great people, makes us greater. Consistently studying Torah, influences our thoughts and elevates the way we speak and what we do.

Throughout the day, a multitude of thoughts pass through our minds. By consciously choosing to read and hear elevating thoughts, we will be increasing the number of higher thoughts that spontaneously pass through our minds. Habit becomes second nature. This applies to our thoughts, our words, and our actions. And this is why verses one and two in chapter one, serve as an Introduction to Psalms. Let us resolve to keep away from negative influences and to think Torah thoughts. This will make our entire beings more elevated.

> *There were two great Torah scholars who lectured in a yeshiva in pre-war Europe. After the Second World War they became the heads of a yeshiva in the United States. A number of years later, one commented to the other, "We've*

been in America, but we haven't been influenced negatively by the materialism of the country." His colleague responded with a smile, "That is the power of negative influence. We are influenced so much that we don't even realize that we have been influenced."

א אַשְׁרֵי־הָאִישׁ אֲשֶׁר לֹא הָלַךְ בַּעֲצַת רְשָׁעִים ...

1 Praiseworthy is the person who walked not in the counsel of the evil...

The Midrash (*Yalkut Shimoni* to verse 1:1) makes note of the fact that King David praises those who keep away from the path of the evil. He could have worded this in the negative, "Cursed is the one who walks in the counsel of the evil," or, "Cursed is the one who doesn't walk in the counsel of the righteous," but King David carefully chose his words. He praises the person who acts properly and points out to us that this is the path that we should choose. This serves as a model of how we should word the statements we make.

King Solomon, the son of David, put it this way, "There is one who speaks [harshly] like piercings of a sword, but the tongue of the wise heals" (*Proverbs* 12:18).

As the Vilna Gaon explains, "There are two basic approaches that are possible to take, when you see someone doing something wrong. One is to speak harshly to the person and tell him that what he is doing is wrong. This approach however, does not tell people how they should behave and how they can correct what they did wrong. This is like stabbing someone with a sword; it is not a healing approach.

"The approach of the wise is to show people how they can correct what they did wrong. This is a healing approach and the only words that are said are those conducive to healing." (see *Consulting the Wise,* p. 28)

Every time we recite the first verse of *Tehillim* we once again have a reminder: "Remember to word your statements positively. Praise the positive path. Focus on the beauty and benefits of speaking and acting in positive ways."

This lesson is very important for parents when speaking to children, for teachers when speaking to students, and for each and every one of us, when we speak to others. It is even important for ourselves, when we give ourselves motivating soliloquies.

By speaking positively, we sanctify our mouth and power of speech. This elevates our ability to talk. Now that we have resolved to speak consistently with positive patterns, we are prepared to utilize our mouths to sing the praises of our Father, our King, Creator and Sustainer of the universe, and to ask Him for our needs.

A teacher who had had considerable influence on many students, shared the following with me: "When I first started teaching, I had the impression that if I kept reprimanding my students, telling them how they will be wasting and ruining their lives unless they spend their time wisely, they would heed what I said. I was used to this approach from the house in which I grew up, and from some of my teachers in elementary school. Students were fearful of my raising my voice and speaking sternly. I viewed their fear as an accomplishment. 'This will certainly keep them in line,' I said to myself.

"What gave me a change of heart were a number of wake-up calls that occurred over a short period of time. I used to smoke cigarettes. A doctor gave me a long, harsh lecture about how I was putting my health and the health of my family at risk. This frightened me. I was so stressed from this that I smoked a number of cigarettes to calm myself down. I realize now that this was a ridiculous response, but that is what happened. I drove over the speed limit and a policeman pulled me over. He aggressively told me that I'm a potential murderer. He had a relative who was killed by someone who drove too fast and he viewed speeders as ruthless killers. I agreed with him that I need to be more careful about how I drive, but I was indignant that he considered me a potential murderer. This put me into an awful state of mind, but I didn't feel strongly motivated to heed the speed limit.

"A couple of days later a father of one of my students asked to have a meeting with me. 'My son hates to go to school,' he candidly told me. "He says that you're mean and all the children dislike you. My son is sensitive. At home we speak to all our children in positive ways. We keep pointing out to them what we like about the way they speak and act. This is our main focus and they feel good about speaking and acting positively. May I please suggest that you experiment with this approach for a couple of weeks, and see what happens.'

"This hit home. I saw that I resented what the doctor and policeman had said to me, even though I am an adult and know that they are right. Now, I needed to see things from my students' point of view. I resolved to see everything I said to them, from inside their minds. I realized that focusing on praise of the positive, was the correct way to speak to them.

"A week later the father said to me, 'I admire and respect your willingness to follow through on what we spoke about, a week ago. I didn't mention to my son that I had spoken to you. On his own he told me that he is beginning to love school. Your approach is inspiring him and his friends.' I saw how much I personally appreciated this positive feedback. And from then on, I didn't need any more reminders."

א אַשְׁרֵי־הָאִישׁ אֲשֶׁר לֹא הָלַךְ בַּעֲצַת רְשָׁעִים ...

¹ Praiseworthy is the person who walked not in the counsel of the evil...

The Midrash (*Yalkut Shimoni* 611) comments on this verse that, when someone sits and refrains from doing something improper, he is rewarded as if he actually did a proactive good deed. Making a decision not to walk in the counsel of the wicked, is as if one has walked in the counsel of the righteous.

There are many situations throughout our lives when we are not "going places." We might be busy taking care of seemingly mundane tasks at home. We might be feeling unwell. Our initial tendency might be to feel a bit down, even slightly depressed. "I'm not accomplishing very much right now," we might be telling ourselves. We might feel envious of others who seem to be accomplishing so much more than we are.

But here we learn that not doing negative things is in itself a positive accomplishment. With every *mitzvah* (good deed) we do, we should feel joy for the eternal benefits of the good we are doing.

Whenever we avoid negative influences, we are protecting all the positive influences that we have already experienced. We are also protecting future positive influences and opportunities for inspiration.

> *"Some of my friends go places that I have decided not to go," a teenager told his rabbi. "It's not that they are actually forbidden, but I know it wouldn't be good for me spiritually. Sometimes I end up feeling deprived and sad that I am missing out."*
>
> *"How would it be, if you experienced more pleasure and joy from what you were doing instead?" the rabbi asked. "Would that make it easier for you?"*
>
> *"Yes," the fellow replied. "I think that would be a choice I would feel good about making."*
>
> *"When you focus on the long-term benefits of these types of choices you are making, you will eventually experience more joy in not going to those places than you would if you were to have gone. Visualize yourself experiencing tremendously positive feelings for keeping away from negative influences, and you will derive some of the future benefits, right now."*

Every time you recite *Tehillim,* not only are you gaining all the spiritual benefits of the elevated thoughts you are thinking and the prayers you are saying, you are actively not involved in anything negative. Add this to the sense of accomplishment of what you are doing.

⋅⟨ **2 / ב** ⟩⋅

יב **אַשְׁרֵי כָּל־חוֹסֵי בוֹ:**

¹² *Fortunate are all who trust in Him.*

Who would we consider fortunate in life? Someone who has abundance. Someone who is successful. Someone who is healthy. Someone who is intelligent. Someone who is popular. Someone who, in the vernacular, would be called lucky, that is; many good things occur in this person's life.

The essential factor behind those who would be considered fortunate is, that they have an inner sense of well-being. This well-being is a feeling of inner peace and security. This is a state of serenity, of being calm. When you have an inner sense of well-being, you are in a state of happiness.

It is not the abundance itself, that makes a person happy. It is the feeling of well-being that one experiences, when one considers oneself as having abundance. It is not success itself that makes a person happy. It is the feeling of well-being that one experiences, when one considers oneself as being successful. It is not the good things themselves that occur in a person's life that make one consistently happy. It is the feeling of well-being that one experiences, when good things consistently happen. Good health alone doesn't make one happy. Many people who are healthy, take it for granted and it doesn't affect their emotional quality of life. When one feels a sense of well-being because of one's good health, then one feels happy.

What one factor will consistently give a person feelings of well-being? The knowledge that Hashem, Creator and Sustainer of the universe, is behind each person. That Hashem wants what is good for a person. That Hashem might challenge a person, but He wants the person to grow and benefit from all challenges (*nisyonos*). Hav-ing this awareness, gives you a feeling of well-being. The stronger the awareness, the more consistent the feelings of well-being.

Some people experience well-being, once in a while. They need the external world to live up to their expectations, in order for them to be happy. They need other people to speak and act in ways that they wish. They need a multitude of factors to be in alignment with the way they want them to be. This, then, is why so many people on our planet, lack a consistent feeling of well-being. The conditions they demand are not always met. People whose feeling of well-being is at the mercy of external factors over which they have no control, are like puppets. Many other people and many other occurrences and many other circumstances, control their emotions, their moods, their state of mind.

The person who is truly fortunate in this world, is the one who has authentic trust in the Almighty. He is able to sustain a feeling of well-being when things go well as well as when things are challenging. He experiences a sense of well-being whether he has a lot or a little. He experiences this well-being whether people meet his expectations or whether they don't. His well-being is constant, because his trust in Hashem gives him the awareness and thoughts that his life has a plan that is specially designed for his welfare. The nature of that plan, becomes clearer all the time. The reality of what occurs in his life is what Hashem in His infinite wisdom knows, is ultimately best for his unique spiritual needs.

The benefits of abundance and success pale, in comparison with the benefits of trust in Hashem. Keep upgrading this trust and you will be elevating yourself spiritually as well as ensuring yourself a life of well-being.

I met an elderly person who viewed himself as one of the wealthiest people in the world. When people would ask him how things were, he would invariably say, "Things are fantastic for me. There is something I own that is making my life a life of joy. I am as comfortable as a human being could be."

Many people assumed that he owned real estate or stocks that brought him a steady income. Many people his age were living on social security and pension funds, in constant state of mild anxiety over their meager incomes. But he had an authentic sense of abundance and well-being.

At his funeral the picture became clearer. Someone who knew him well, eulogized him as one of the greatest Baalei

Bitachon (*one who has integrated trust in Hashem*) *of the generation.*

He had no more money than other elderly people, whose funds were limited. But he had a possession that made him wealthy. His wealth was an inner security in the knowledge that Hashem was taking care of him. Every thing he owned was precious: It was a gift from Hashem. About the future, he had not one worry. All would be exactly as Hashem felt was best for him. The "something" that made his life a life of joy, was his trust in Hashem. He was always as comfortable as a human being could be. His mental awareness made him one of the most fortunate people in the world.

This mental mindset is available to each and every one of us. This is a life-transforming awareness. To obtain this possession, you need to make the choice to view yourself and your world in this light. And you can do it now.

⊰ 3 / ג ⊱

ג רַבִּים אֹמְרִים לְנַפְשִׁי אֵין יְשׁוּעָתָה לּוֹ בֵאלֹהִים סֶלָה:
ד וְאַתָּה יהוה מָגֵן בַּעֲדִי כְּבוֹדִי וּמֵרִים רֹאשִׁי:
ה קוֹלִי אֶל־יהוה אֶקְרָא וַיַּעֲנֵנִי מֵהַר קָדְשׁוֹ סֶלָה:

³ **Many say of my soul, 'there is no salvation for him from** Hashem**'.**

⁴ **But you,** Hashem**, are a shield for me, for my soul, and the One who raises my head.**

⁵ **With my voice I call out to** Hashem**, and He answers me from His holy mountain Selah.**

King David had to flee from his son Abshalom. This was a most tragic situation. A son who should honor and revere his father, turned against him. But even in highly distressful situations, one's spirits can be lifted by friends and well-wishers who offer encouragement, reassurance, and hope. Being told that things will eventually turn out well, can strengthen one's hope for a brighter future.

However, King David faced a tremendous challenge which was compounded by the negative and pessimistic reactions of many. They said that, because he had sinned, he would not be worthy of Divine assistance. Without the Almighty's help, one is totally lost.

Nevertheless, King David's absolute belief in Hashem's goodness and compassion was so strong that, not only could it help carry him through the severe test he was facing, but it also helped him transcend the negativity of many people. Rashi's explanation details more fully the source of the negative remarks King David heard. On the word *rabim,* Rashi explains that this refers to people who were "great in Torah, great in wisdom, great in wealth, and great in stature." If there are many simple people who are negative, one can more readily assume that they are mistaken. However, when people who are great in many ways paint a negative picture, it's much easier to assume that their understanding of the situation is correct. The situation might truly be hopeless.

Even though he was faced with a mighty challenge compounded by those whose opinions could cause despair, King David's complete belief in Hashem's unlimited goodness and compassion was powerful. His knowledge of Hashem's benevolence was so *strong* that, not only did it help carry him through the severe test he was facing from his son's rebellion, but it also enabled him to transcend the negativity of many, regardless of how great they were.

People are fallible. Humans can project negativity. They can feel certain that they are not being pessimistic, but realistic. They can give many logical, rational reasons why they feel someone is doomed. But the will of the Almighty is stronger. Connecting to the kindness and compassion of Hashem, always gives hope.

There are many life situations and circumstances in which it is easy to be pessimistic. It might be easy to give up hope particularly when others make discouraging comments. Let us learn from King David. Let us always believe in the benevolence of our loving Father and powerful King. Let this belief be so strong that nothing anyone says, can cause us to lose hope.

> *I once asked someone who survived a concentration camp in the Second World War, "What was most difficult for you during the entire ordeal?"*

"The negativity of others," he replied. "In the home where I grew up, my parents had high levels of bitachon, total trust in the Al-mighty. I was frequently told, 'No matter how bad a situation might seem, Hashem can help you in a moment.' This was so deeply ingrained in my mind that, on my own, I never lost hope. But hearing people who were older than me telling me that I was a dreamer and I wasn't realistic, began to shake my hope. My mother was a "Tehillim-sayer." She constantly read Tehillim. She would repeat frequently, 'We must learn from the trust in Hashem of King David.' I remembered how King David called out to Hashem, even though others told him that it wouldn't help him. I drew upon the inner strength of King David, to increase my own inner strength. And this enabled me to give encouragement to many others."

⊰{ **4 / ד** }⊱

ט בְּשָׁלוֹם יַחְדָּו אֶשְׁכְּבָה וְאִישָׁן כִּי־אַתָּה
יהוה לְבָדָד לָבֶטַח תּוֹשִׁיבֵנִי:

⁹ **In peace, in harmony, I lie down and sleep, for You** HASHEM **will make me dwell solitary and secure.**

When things quiet down and we are ready to go to sleep, our inner sense of serenity, or lack of it, plays a major role.

A person who tends to worry will be hit by worrisome thoughts. A person who is anxiety-ridden will be too anxious to fall asleep, easily. A person who is full of anger and blame will recall the resentments of the day, of the week, of the month, and of a lifetime. A person full of self-doubts and insecurity will tend to obsess over these distressful thoughts and the feelings they create. Someone who is blocked by many fears will dwell on those fearful thoughts and feelings.

Uncomfortable thoughts and feelings prevent a person from

relaxing and getting proper rest. He might remain awake and obsess over these thoughts. Instead of clearing his mind and renewing his energy, he tosses and turns. After these disturbing mental sessions, he will probably have unpleasant dreams. When he wakes up in the morning, he is likely to be just as tired as he was when he tried to fall asleep.

Our verse describes the ideal for which to strive. Trusting in the compassion and kindness of Hashem gives us feelings of security and well-being. These thoughts are gently soothing. They create peaceful and serene feelings. This inner peace allows you to let go, and rest. You will find it much easier to fall asleep. In fact, you might even be able to fall asleep as soon as your head hits the pillow. Your spiritual connection with Hashem is emotionally healthful and healing. The next morning you will be energized and ready for a full day of serving Hashem with serenity and joy.

There were many instances in my childhood, when I found it difficult to fall asleep. I would call out to my mother, "Ma, I can't fall asleep. I'm afraid that I will be too tired tomorrow, to pay attention in school."

I remember my mother's soothing message: "It's all right. Just relax. When your head is on the pillow and you relax, it's almost as beneficial as if you were actually sleeping." This relaxed me to such a degree, that I quickly fell asleep.

When I was older, I found that repeating calming verses from Tehillim *had an even greater soothing effect, when I heard my mother's reassuring voice in my mind. They became associated in my mind and created a spiritual lullaby.*

I would like to close this section with a story from one of my young grandchildren. One night when she couldn't fall asleep, she cryingly said to her mother, "I'm afraid to fall asleep. Last night I had a scary dream, and I'm afraid that I might have another one tonight."

"I have a solution," her mother said. "Say a chapter of

Tehillim *before you go to sleep and it's very likely you will have pleasant dreams."*

Hearing this, her daughter burst into tears.

"What happened?" asked her mother. "I just suggested what you can do, to solve the issue."

"Yes, you did," answered the seven year old. "And that's why I'm crying. I'll say a chapter of Tehillim, *and then I won't have any more nightmares. Then when I'm a mother and my children have nightmares, I won't know how to help them."*

A short while later, she realized that, just as Tehillim *helped her, it would also help her children in the future.*

⋅⦅ **5 / ה** ⦆⋅

ב אֲמָרַי הַאֲזִינָה יהוה בִּינָה הֲגִיגִי:

ג הַקְשִׁיבָה לְקוֹל שַׁוְעִי מַלְכִּי וֵאלֹהָי כִּי־אֵלֶיךָ אֶתְפַּלָּל:

² **Hear my words, HASHEM, perceive my thoughts.**
³ **Hearken to the sound of my outcry, my King and my God, for to You do I pray.**

In verse 5:2, we express two ideas in our request for Hashem to listen to our prayers. The first part of the verse refers to our verbal expression of our wishes. When we say this half of the verse, we are asking Hashem to hear the words of prayer that we explicitly state. The second half of the verse, takes this much further. Here, as Rashi explains, we are asking Hashem to understand our inner thoughts, even when we are too exhausted to openly express them.

The Hebrew word *binah* in the second half of the verse means more than to simply hear words. *Binah* implies a deeper and more profound understanding.

When we make a request of someone, there is a basic level: he hears the words that we say. This requires a focus of attention which is the process by which we hear the words that are actually spoken. On a deeper level, a wise person is able to understand what we mean, even though the words themselves do not convey the full meaning. The Almighty takes this understanding to the fullest level possible. Our inner most wishes, are fully perceived and understood.

Being understood by a fellow mortal is a pleasure. Especially if a person has often been misunderstood, meeting someone who truly understands him, brings a feeling of relief. It is one of the greatest emotional pleasures, that one can experience. The greater the person who understands us, the deeper and stronger are the good feelings.

The ultimate in being understood, is being understood by Hashem, our Creator. When reciting the words of this verse, focus on how much it would mean to you if you knew, with total clarity, that Hashem presently understands how you feel.

In verse 3, we continue with our request for Hashem to hear our outcry. This refers to a strong feeling of distress. We mention in this verse that Hashem is our King, our God. Our acknowledgement of this, raises our consciousness and makes us more worthy of our prayers being accepted and answered. To strengthen this awareness we say explicitly, "for to You do I pray."

At times, we might ask someone to kindly do us a favor, and help us out. We need someone to assist us. In fact, there are many candidates who could possibly do what we need done for us.

At times, however, there aren't many who are able to do what we need done. When we encounter the unique individual who has the knowledge and expertise that we so desperately need, we make a plea from the bottom of our heart. "You are the only one who can help me. I can't ask anyone else, only you."

Being on the receiving end of this special request gives one a stronger sense of obligation and responsibility, to come to the rescue. This is what we are essentially saying when we recite this verse. "We pray to no one else, Hashem. We recognize that only You can help us and therefore our thoughts and words of prayer are directed exclusively towards You."

Someone who had been out of a job for a while was feeling intense pressure and stress. He had been looking for a job for quite some time, without success. He intensified his search, but nothing seemed to work. He went to one interview after another, and, although he consistently made a good impression, he was told again and again, "We see that you are a fine person and regret turning you down, but you just are not what we are looking for."

This fellow consulted an expert for advice on making a good impression at interviews, and improved his presentations. Still, he could not find a job. He lowered his expectations and was resigned to accepting the kind of job that previously he would not have considered. Still nothing worked for him.

He consulted a Torah scholar who told him, "From what I can tell, your approach to seeking a job is sensible and you are a qualified candidate. However, I feel that you are relying too much on your natural skills. I would strongly suggest that you deepen your awareness that Hashem is the ultimate source of the fulfillment of your wishes and the answer to your prayers. Speak from your heart and tell Hashem that you have gained a greater awareness of your need of His Divine assistance.

The fellow told me that, after hearing this, he prayed with a depth of feeling more profound than he had ever felt before. He added to his prayers, "I ask Your forgiveness, Hashem, for acting as if I were praying to humans and not just to You. The rejection after rejection that I have been experiencing has given me a greater awareness that, on some level, I have been rejecting You. I fully accept You as being the real source of my income."

A week later, an opportunity to make more money than he had expected came up. This was not in the form of a regular job, but an opportunity to be part of a creative team that would start a business. He could never have done this, on his own. Rather, through a fortuitous meeting with someone he didn't know very well, he was introduced to a couple of people who were the answer to his prayer.

As he expressed it to me, "As long as I considered my seeking a job the only thing that I could do, I was limited in my search. When I realized that I needed to pray to Hashem in a manner that was more intense than before, I realized that Hashem could answer my prayers in ways that were far beyond my limited thoughts. This opened up my eyes to unlimited possibilities. I immediately felt better. My confidence intensified. It didn't come from just my personal strengths, but from the knowledge that Hashem could help me in infinite ways. Before the solution arose, I would have considered what did eventually happen an actual miracle."

חוַאֲנִי בְּרֹב חַסְדְּךָ אָבוֹא בֵיתֶךָ אֶשְׁתַּחֲוֶה
אֶל־הֵיכַל קָדְשְׁךָ בְּיִרְאָתֶךָ:

8 And I, through Your abundant kindness, I will enter Your house, I will bow myself towards Your holy sanctuary in awe of You.

I n this verse we state our appreciation for Hashem's kindness for allowing us to enter His house. When someone is permitted entry to the home of a greatly respected, elevated person, he is grateful for the privilege. And this appreciation is increased, when the great person says, "Please make my home your home. You are welcome to visit here, as often as you wish, for as long as you wish."

The home of Hashem is the Holy Temple that was in Jerusalem. Places that will retain aspects of this sanctity are the synagogues and yeshivos where we pray to Hashem and study His Torah. Whenever you enter one, you are entering the home of Hashem, Creator and Sustainer of the universe. Imagine how increasing this awareness, will add a depth of appreciation for the merit you have of being there.

The *Metzudas David* explains that, in this verse we make the statement, "I will come to Your house, Hashem, to express my gratitude to You."

When Hashem causes good things to happen to you, add a deeper feeling of gratitude the very next time you enter a house of

Hashem. As you walk through the doors of a house of prayer and Torah study, let those thoughts and feelings of gratitude be at the forefront of your mind.

There is a custom to recite this verse when entering a house of prayer, in the morning. While saying this, one bows one's head towards the Holy Ark containing the Torah scroll. The verse states that this is done with a feeling of awe. The awe comes not from the physical structure of the building, but from the consciousness that here is a place where the spiritual energy, is on a higher plane. Here is a place where one comes for *Avodas Hashem*, to serve the Almighty. The sanctity of this place makes it more conducive for our praying to Hashem with a greater sense of devotion and connection.

We need to increase our sense of respect for Hashem, whenever we enter a house of prayer. We also need to sustain this, the entire time we are there. The question to challenge ourselves with, is, "Am I acting with the respect that is appropriate for the house of Hashem?" Put in the special effort necessary to consistently maintain high levels of respect.

I gained a much stronger appreciation for the kindness of Hashem's enabling me to enter His house, from an incident in which I was accidentally locked out of a house where I was a guest. It was a rainy day and I didn't know anyone who lived in the area. I had to wait a few hours until someone would be home. I was thinking about how grateful I would be if I were to meet a friendly person who would invite me to his home. Walking down the street, I passed a synagogue that was open. As I entered the synagogue, I felt an especially joyful feeling. Although I was someplace I had never been before, I was entering my Father's Home. This was familiar territory. I no longer felt like a stranger in a strange land. At that moment, all the synagogues I had ever been in, formed a mental network of "Homes for Hashem." Even those I had never yet been in, were part of that network. My affinity for all those who came there to pray, became stronger. We were all Hashem's children gathering at His home, to connect with Him.

יב וְיִשְׂמְחוּ כָל־חוֹסֵי בָךְ לְעוֹלָם יְרַנֵּנוּ
וְתָסֵךְ עָלֵימוֹ וְיַעְלְצוּ בְךְ אֹהֲבֵי שְׁמֶךְ:

¹²*And all who take refuge in You will rejoice,
they will sing joyously forever, You will shelter
them; and those who love Your name will exult
in You.*

There are times when one finds oneself in a highly challenging place where one might feel very lonely and when it is easy to think sad thoughts. This breeds distress and emotional suffering one wishes one were someplace else.

It is in times and places like these that we can dramatically transform the experience with one thought: We are always in the presence of Hashem. Hashem is there with us. We can take refuge in Hashem, with our prayers, with our Torah study and with the verses of *Tehillim* that we recite.

"All who take refuge in Hashem will rejoice." Even if previously we were not on the highest spiritual level, now — at this moment — we can take refuge in Hashem. "All" refers to everyone.

As soon as we take refuge in Hashem we can rejoice, even though, a moment ago, that feeling might have seemed almost impossible. Now we can sing joyously. We might not be able to sing out loud for others to hear but, inside our minds, we always have the freedom to speak and sing with joy to Hashem. When we do this, we will feel the relief of being sheltered by Hashem. We are connecting with Him.

"And those who love Your Name will exult in You." Every time we mention Hashem's name with love, we are connecting with eternity. We are not merely in the physical spot where we stand or sit. We are between two eternities: The eternity before this moment, and the eternity after this moment. We are connecting with the Infinite. Whenever we say Hashem's name, we should consciously bear in mind that, "He is the Master of all that exists. He always was, He always is, and He always will be" (*Shulchan Aruch* 5:1).

In 1856, Rabbi Avraham Yaakov Friedman of Sadugura was arrested and kept imprisoned due to a libel.

"I am permitted to serve the Almighty undisturbed," Rabbi Avraham Yaakov told his visitors. "What difference does it make whether I am here, or anywhere else?"

His father-in-law, Rabbi Aharon Perlow of Karlin, who was allowed to stay with him for a while in his cell, asked him, "How do you feel in this awful place?"

Rabbi Avraham Yaakov replied, "Does the place one is in, make a difference? The Almighty's glory fills the earth. He is everywhere — even here."

("Men of Distinction," vol.1, p. 15; cited in Gateway to Happiness, p. 247)

"I read this when I was hospitalized in a highly distressful place," someone told me. "I found that this thought made a major difference for me. I was no longer in the limited physical place that I had been in, a few moments ago. The space I occupied in the universe was the place where I could connect with our loving Creator. It was a place where I could grow and develop. I looked for opportunities to help others, less fortunate. This was the place where Hashem chose to give me an opportunity to continue on my path of spiritual growth."

⊰{ **6/1** }⊱

בְּ יהוה אַל־בְּאַפְּךָ תוֹכִיחֵנִי וְאַל־בַּחֲמָתְךָ תְיַסְּרֵנִי:

² HASHEM, do not rebuke me in Your anger, nor chastise me in Your wrath.

King David asks Hashem not to punish him, in anger, for any wrongs he had done. Even when someone needs to be rebuked, there is a major difference between being rebuked out of compassion and love, and being rebuked from a place of anger.

When a parent or teacher needs to correct a child, the goal is to do so, for the welfare of the child. When this is the sole motivation, what is said or done is weighed carefully. The pressure applied is only that which is necessary to accomplish the goal. The parent or teacher wants the child to understand that he did something wrong. He wants him to be careful not to repeat his mistake in the future.

When parents or teachers lose their temper, then the focus is on releasing their own frustration — their own emotional distress. What they say or do to the child reflects their own need for release. They want to feel better. Only after they punish with enough vengeance, do they release their own pent-up frustration.

Let's look at this from the child or student's perspective. When he sees the angry look on the teacher or parent's face, he feels frightened. (Depending on past history, he might even feel terror. If in the past he has been badly hurt, (emotionally or physically), the memories and feelings bind together to create profound emotional distress. Is this a positive and healthy learning experience for the child? Not at all. He might be more careful not to anger the parent or teacher, but it does not teach him the true importance of the value that the parent or teacher wants him to integrate.

This form of abuse can teach a child that, when someone gets angry, he lacks control of what he says or does. That is a highly counterproductive lesson for a child to learn and there is a strong possibility that the child will make this pattern his own. He too may overreact when he is angry and feel justified in doing so. His mentors do it, so it seems the right, or at least normal, thing to do. As a result this anger and its negative consequences, carry over from generation to generation.

When a child does something wrong, there is a need to correct him. The feelings of authentic care and concern for the child, need to be manifest in what the parent or teacher says and does. Our tone of voice communicates messages that can be louder and clearer, than the actual words that are said. The spirit of our message is conveyed, every time we speak. When a child or student receives a penalty or punishment that is clearly for his ultimate good, he will usually accept it, even though he might not like it. Looking back later, he will acknowledge that it was fair and deserved. He will receive the message that was meant to be sent.

When we recite this verse, we ask our powerful Father and King to refrain from rebuking and chastising us, with anger. To be worthy of our request, we need to make this our own model when situations arise where we need to rebuke someone else. As we repeat this verse, let us resolve to increase our own level of compassion. Let this compassion come through in our choice of words and in our tone of voice. Let it come through in the actions taken to discipline those in our charge. And let our own compassion and true caring, be a model for our children, students, and anyone who observes us.

> Someone who rebelled against the Torah teachings with which he was raised, met a kindly rabbi who befriended him. They arranged to study Torah at regular intervals and, little by little, the young man became aware of the beauty of the Torah. The rabbi invited the student to his home for Shabbos, and the student enjoyed the visit immensely. After eating at the rabbi's home a number of times, he shared the following with him:
>
> "My parents had low tolerance for frustration. Every time I misbehaved, even slightly, I was shouted at and often hit. I was told that if I keep acting badly, I would ruin my life. I was told that I would end up being a criminal, since I acted so badly. Even at a young age, I realized that they were exaggerating and, though they might have meant well, their frustration and anger toward me, were ruining my life. After a while, just thinking about my parents was a source of distress for me.
>
> "When you acted friendly towards me, I thought that perhaps you had ulterior motives for doing so. You might have just wanted to influence me and that was the only reason you were acting nicely to me. However, after visiting your home a number of times, I saw how consistently kind and gentle you were with your children. Your sincere love came through. What impressed me most, was the way you spoke to your children when they misbehaved. You never raised your voice. You didn't threaten them, and you didn't say anything that implied that you looked down at them. I saw how your children respected you, and how they accepted your discipline. I said to myself, 'This is how I want to

be when I get married and have children.' I am resolved to coming back to a life of Torah. Now that I have you as a role model, I have a clearer map of how I want to be."

יא יֵבֹשׁוּ וְיִבָּהֲלוּ מְאֹד כָּל־אֹיְבָי יָשֻׁבוּ יֵבֹשׁוּ רָגַע:

¹¹ **Let all my enemies be shamed and utterly confounded, let them regret and they will be shamed for an instant.**

Metzudas David explains: King David was grateful that Hashem answered his prayers. (See verses 9 and 10: "Hashem has heard the sound of my weeping. Hashem has heard my plea.") When his enemies see David's tremendous success they will realize that Hashem has made him successful and they will be utterly surprised and shocked at this. They will realize that they persecuted David wrongly and will feel embarrassed and ashamed at how they tried to harm him. But their shame will be for only an instant because, from then on King David will never mention their wrong again, in order not to cause them emotional distress.

This verse is recited daily in the *Tachanun* section of the morning and afternoon prayers and it contains a message that we need to repeat often, since it is a potentially challenging one to internalize.

This is a powerful lesson in forgiving people for the wrongs they have done. Once they have asked our forgiveness and we have forgiven them, we should allow feelings of resentment and bitterness to melt away. Some people tend to say, "I can forgive, but I cannot forget." Of course, we cannot consciously order ourselves to forget something. However, when we have sincerely forgiven someone, when we do think of them, we should always remember that, in the present, we have created a new relationship with them. View them with the post-forgiveness attitude. Do not say anything that will needlessly remind them of the past which they now regret.

When you forgive someone, you personally gain. Holding on to grudges is unhealthy, both spiritually and biologically. When a person keeps thoughts and feelings of resentment, bitterness, and anger, he eats himself up. These thoughts and feelings are like an acid that can cause great damage to the containers that hold them. Everyone wants to experience the positive emotional states such as happiness, serenity, and a general feeling of well-being. Your emotions are self-created with your thoughts. Choose those that are elevating and life-enhancing.

Have compassion on people who have previously wronged you, but presently are sorry about what they have said or done. It is even a higher level, to forgive someone even if he has not had the courage or awareness to apologize to you. Note that King David was not saying that he personally would do anything to cause them shame or embarrassment. Rather, they on their own would recognize their mistakes, and this awareness would arouse feelings of shame. He himself would not say or do anything to add to their distressful feelings.

Remember that the people you might be tempted to resent, are also children of Hashem. From Hashem's viewpoint, He wants what is spiritually and emotionally best for all of His children. Allow your love for Hashem to arouse your kindness and compassion for all of His children. Saying words of *Tehillim* connects you with Hashem; acting in elevating ways greatly strengthens that connection.

> *A young man who was involved in a quarrel with his brother told me, "My first reaction was always to forgive wrongs and to let go. I always wanted to follow in the footsteps of the great spiritual giants who had such love and compassion that, caring about the total welfare of others was a much higher priority than getting revenge. I tend to be joyful and experience enthusiasm for life and the development of my character. However, some friends of mine who felt that I was a bit naive, encouraged me to 'teach my brother a lesson,' as they put it, so I said and did things that added to a bitter quarrel; I became obsessed with the entire situation. I didn't realize, at the time, how much I lost out by devoting so much time and energy to a feud, that just kept getting worse. When I heard the lesson of this verse, I realized that my natural tendency to let the past go, and to allow love and compassion to fill my consciousness,*

was the correct way to be. I cannot take back the past, but I can resolve to live with this awareness, from now on."

This lesson is very important for parents and teachers. At times they will need to reprimand and censure their children and students, but let it be for just a moment. The goal is to correct the children and students, not to embarrass them. The goal is that they should be resolved to improve from now on. The goal is that they should have a self-image of knowing that, deep down, they want to do what is good and right. Choose what you say accordingly.

⹽ **8 / ח** ⹾

ה מָה־אֱנוֹשׁ כִּי־תִזְכְּרֶנּוּ וּבֶן־אָדָם כִּי תִפְקְדֶנּוּ:
ו וַתְּחַסְּרֵהוּ מְּעַט מֵאֱלֹהִים וְכָבוֹד וְהָדָר תְּעַטְּרֵהוּ:
ז תַּמְשִׁילֵהוּ בְּמַעֲשֵׂי יָדֶיךָ כֹּל שַׁתָּה תַחַת־רַגְלָיו:

⁵ **What is frail man that You should remember him, and the son of mortal man that You should be mindful of him?**
⁶ **Yet, You have made him but slightly less than the angels, and crowned him with soul and splendor.**
⁷ **You give him dominion over Your handiwork. You placed everything under his feet.**

I n this chapter of *Tehillim* we find a contrast in the value and importance of human beings. On one side, we can see the smallness of each human. Compared to the size of the universe, we are miniscule. We start off in life, as helpless infants. We know nothing and can do nothing. We can not talk nor walk nor do absolutely anything for ourselves. We are totally dependent on the good will of adults. (This is the connotation of *ben adam,* children of man.) Eventually we die and return to the earth and entire earthly material matter decomposes, and turns to dust. (This is the connotation of *enosh.*)

Together with this view of the limitations and weaknesses of humans and their frailties, there is an opposite perspective. Hashem has given us an immortal soul. Our soul, which is our real essence, is an aspect of the Divine. And we humans have ruling power over the rest of creation. We have been given intelligence, and with this intelligence we can benevolently conquer the entire world.

Without the value and power that our Creator has given us, we are nothing. We are dust and ashes. With the value and power that is the gift to each one of us by our loving Father and King, Creator and Sustainer of the universe, we are remarkable beings. The entire world was created for us.

This view of humanity can instill in us both humility and positive self-esteem. Our value is given to us by Hashem, no human being can take it away. We do not need any mortal's approval or appreciation, to claim our value. It is a given. There is no validity to boasting, since no matter what our accomplishments and positive attributes, we are still miniscule, limited, and only temporarily in this world. At the same time, we have no need to boast since our value is so immense that, whatever one would be tempted to boast about, pales in comparison to the greatness that our Creator has bestowed upon each and every one of us.

> *I spoke to someone who has counseled many people over the years. He told me that he considers one factor to be at the root of a wide variety of problems — low self-esteem. When people feel that they are essentially rather worthless, this affects their thoughts, words, and actions in all areas of life. They do not strive towards worthwhile goals, since they feel that they will not be able to reach them. In truth, they could accomplish a great deal. However, when one believes that one will not be able to accomplish something, that belief prevents the brain from thinking of ways to do it. If you feel that you cannot find solutions and creative answers, you block your brain from thinking of them. If you feel that you cannot approach people to ask for assistance and guidance, your brain will not give your feet the power to walk over to people who could help, and it will not give your mouth orders*

to say what needs to be said. Emotionally, a person with feelings of worthlessness will easily become sad, discouraged, and depressed. When it comes to developing positive character traits, a person with low self-esteem will not have the energy to think, speak, and/or act in an elevated manner. Low self-esteem blocks a person in countless ways.

The entire picture changes when you know that your value doesn't come from you, but from the Creator of the universe. The Creator has given you intrinsic greatness, "slightly less than the angels."

I recently spoke to someone who speaks and acts in ways that show he lacks self-respect. I spoke to him about the immenseness of his true worth, which is granted to him by his Creator.

"I hear what you are saying," he acknowledged. "But to me, this is only an abstract idea. I don't feel that I have inner greatness. And knowing that I **should** feel better about myself makes me feel even worse. Not only do I feel bad about myself, I feel guilty and stupid for not feeling better."

"Let's try the following," I suggested to him. "Tonight before you go to sleep, imagine that during the night when your soul is closer to Hashem, Hashem blesses your soul in a special way. When you recite the "Modeh ani" prayer tomorrow morning, you will feel that your soul has been especially blessed to realize its value. And live the entire day tomorrow, as if you actually felt this fantastic blessing. You are now modestly great. Think the way you would think, if you were modestly great. Speak the way you would speak, if you had thoroughly integrated the fact that you are modestly great. And act the way you would act, if you knew that you were crowned with splendor. See how this affects your prayers. See how this effects the way you interact with other people. See how this affects your actions throughout the day."

The look on his face expressed that now this was more than just a fleeting idea, but something that he was committed to actually work on.

Right now picture in your own mind, how the day will go tomorrow when you apply this practice. Right before you go to sleep tonight, picture it again. You can quickly imagine this again and again — the more repetitions, the more powerful the effects. This has helped many people. Let it help you.

◦⦃ **9 / ט** ⦄◦

ב **אוֹדֶה יְהֹוָה בְּכָל־לִבִּי אֲסַפְּרָה כָּל־נִפְלְאוֹתֶיךָ:**

[2] **I will thank HASHEM will all my heart. I will proclaim all Your wondrous deeds.**

Malbim comments on the first half of this verse: The classic work *Chovos Halevavos* states that, for most people it is difficult to truly thank Hashem for the good that He has done for them. Yes, they are grateful for the good things that they have already experienced, but there is the tendency to always hope that, in the future, Hashem will also bestow upon them, positive things. As such, their minds and hearts are not fully involved in the gratitude. Part of their consciousness is focused on the wish that the future should be good and positive and this takes away from the present feelings of gratitude. Therefore King David proclaims, "I will thank Hashem with all my heart." That is, my gratitude will be a total and complete gratitude.

"What have you done for me lately?" is Mr. Taker's mission statement. "No matter how much you have done for me already, the main thing is what you will do for me now."

Imagine someone who continually wants more assistance and favors from other people. He is a taker and, regardless of how much he has already taken from others, he is consistently occupied with wanting more from them. Such a person might express words of gratitude to others for what they have done for him but, understanding the inner workings of his mind, we can easily fathom that his appearance of being grateful, is really a strategy to get even more from others. This is not the picture any student of Tehillim *would want to have as a reflection of who they are.*

Being sincerely grateful means that, even if the grateful person knows that the one who is the source of his gratitude will never again do anything for him, he is still full of gratitude for the service already done for him. When you feel this way towards people, this will be reflected in your gratitude towards Hashem.

What would it be like to be a master of the attribute of gratitude? A truly grateful person is a joyful person. He is grateful for the past positive things Hashem has done for him, and he appreciates all the present things for which he can be grateful. This gratitude fills his heart and mind. His gratitude-consciousness is such an integral part of him, that it has nothing to do with what will occur in the future. The present gratitude is total and complete. King David is our role model. We too wish to be able to say, "I will thank Hashem with all my heart."

For the next two minutes, express your gratitude to Hashem with all your heart. Imagine that nothing else exists in the world except you and Hashem. Imagine that the only time that exists is the present. The past only exists as a source for your having experienced things, for which to be grateful. And if any thoughts of the future come to you right now, let that serve as a reminder to come back to the feelings of gratitude, in the present. Fill up your mind with mental pictures of those thing for which you are grateful. Let your words flow with gratitude to your Father, your King, Creator and Sustainer of the universe.

Two minutes is not very long. When you express total gratitude for two entire minutes, you will see that you will want to experience this many more times.

Let this verse frequent your lips: "I will thank Hashem with all my heart." As you keep repeating it, you will keep thinking of what you can be thankful for. The first things to come to your mind might be: "I am presently alive. My brain is working and I am able to repeat this verse. I am grateful that I know this concept."

⊰ **10 / י** ⊱

יז תַּאֲוַת עֲנָוִים שָׁמַעְתָּ, ד' תָּכִין לִבָּם, תַּקְשִׁיב אָזְנֶךָ:

¹⁷ **The desire of the humble You have heard,
HASHEM; guide their heart; let Your ear be
attentive.**

Ramban in his classic *mussar* letter cites this verse in
reference to having *kavanah*, paying complete attention to
what you are saying, when praying.

He tells those who read his letter that they should clear their
minds, before prayer. When your mind is clear, then you are able to
concentrate on the words you say, when you pray. Part of the
preparation for prayer is to be careful with every word that is said.
When you think before you speak about what you should say, you
will be saved from transgressing with your words. This elevates
your mind and your prayers. Then you will be worthy of having
Hashem answer your prayers and meet your requests.

Learning how to clear one's mind is one of the most important
skills we can master. Our mind is precious. The thoughts that we
think, create us. You are whatever your dominant thoughts of the
entire day, make you. When you practice clearing your mind, then
you can direct your thoughts in the direction that is consistent with
Hashem's will.

We need to pray to Hashem to help us, with this challenging task.
We ask Hashem to guide our hearts and our minds. Every time we
pray, we have another exercise in mastering the skill of clearing
our minds.

It is normal for minds to wander, so we frequently need to bring
our minds back to the words we are reading from our prayer books
or reciting by heart. Be calm about the entire process. If, or rather,
when, your mind wanders, gently and calmly return your attention
to the place where you were.

I spoke to a person who clearly had high levels of concentra-
tion, when he prayed. I asked him if it came easily to him or

whether he had to work on it.

"It does get easier over time," he shared with me. "In the beginning, this was highly challenging for me, but my desire to connect with Hashem through prayers, was strong and I was determined to master this. Someone once told me of an article he had read, about a person who wanted to win a professional sports championship. He said that the main difference among professionals is their ability to be totally focused and concentrated. Often, their skills are fairly similar, but the individuals who are able to clear their minds and focus their full attention on what they are doing, are able to practice and perform better. I said to myself, 'If these people are able to do this for their personal egos and financial benefits, I certainly need to be able to concentrate, at least as well as they do. This motivated me. I felt ashamed not to be able to master having total concentration and from then on, my prayers improved."

⋅≼ **15 / טו** ⍾⋅

א-ב מִזְמוֹר לְדָוִד יְהֹוָה מִי־יָגוּר בְּאָהֳלֶךָ מִי־יִשְׁכֹּן בְּהַר קָדְשֶׁךָ. . . .וְדֹבֵר אֱמֶת בִּלְבָבוֹ:

1-2 **A psalm by David. H**ASHEM**, who may sojourn in Your tent? who may dwell on Your holy mountain? ...And speaks the truth from his heart.**

Metzudas David explains that this chapter begins with a question: Who is worthy as it were of, dwelling in the *Bais Hamikdash*, Hashem's sacred house? A number of qualities are listed in this chapter. Right now let us focus on "Speaking the truth from one's heart."

This refers to a level that goes beyond, not speaking dishonestly. Even in the privacy of one's heart one must be honest.

The Talmud (*Makkos 24a*) states that the level being referred to is one exemplified by R' Safra. Rashi in his commentary, cites a source (*She'iltos,* 36) that elaborates on this. R' Safra had a certain item that he wanted to sell. Someone who had heard about it approached him and said that he wanted to buy it, and he named a price. R' Safra was in the middle of reciting *Krias Shema* and there-fore did not reply, though mentally agreeing to sell at the stated price. The potential buyer thought that R' Safra had not responded because he wanted more money, and therefore he stated that he was willing to pay a higher price. When R' Safra finished praying, he told the person that he would accept the original price. This is considered speaking the truth from one's heart.

There is no legal obligation, in such a situation, to accept the original price. R' Safra did not verbally commit himself to this person, but to someone like R' Safra, even one's thoughts are precious. Merely thinking a commitment, is considered a commitment. The other person would never know that R' Safra had made such a mental commitment, and even if he did know, the deal was never finalized. Yet, for R' Safra, truth was of such a high value that he was happy to take a financial loss in order to act on the mental agreement to sell at the first price.

"The seal of the Almighty is truth" (*Shabbos* 55a). There are many levels of what would be considered a lie and what would be considered truth. One who wants to attain the seal of approval of Hashem, needs to speak and act in accordance with the highest spiritual standards.

Imagine how careful we would all be with the truth, if we realized that "truth" is our passport to the Mountain of Hashem. When challenges arise and we have a question about whether something is truthful or not, we can ask ourselves, "If I knew that my right to be accepted into Hashem's home was dependent on my speaking the truth, how would I speak and act right now?"

I met someone who was consistently careful to speak the truth, even when it was difficult to do so. I asked him how he developed this attribute.

"I am grateful to my mother for my having this quality," he told me. "Many years ago, when my brothers and sisters were growing up, my mother showed us, in action, how

important she considered it for us to tell the truth. If one of us broke something and she asked whoever did it to acknowledge it, as soon as one of us admitted that he was the one who did it, she said, 'I respect the fact that you were honest. Please be more careful in the future.'

"Some parents might consider it a high priority to mete out a punishment, in such a situation. But my mother was wise. Her goals were clear to her — she wanted us to develop positive character traits. With her approach, we integrated the important of telling the truth, and we were so grateful not to be punished, that we made an effort to be as careful as we possibly could.

"As a child, I had some friends whose parents frequently punished them for the standard misdeeds that children do. I noticed that these children tended to make up stories and even lie outright. They were too afraid to admit that they did something wrong, so they grew up viewing lying as the only sensible thing to do. Why cause oneself problems when one could avoid it?

"If I did something wrong and admitted it, my mother would say to our father in front of me when he came home, 'I am glad that Reuven told the truth today, even though he knew that he would receive a lecture about what he did wrong.' Since I appreciated the positive words of praise and felt good about them, I was much more open to listening to the lectures about the importance of acting properly."

ה כַּסְפּוֹ לֹא־נָתַן בְּנֶשֶׁךְ:

5 Who lends not his money on interest.

This verse follows the first verse in this chapter that begins with the praise of those who act properly. People who do the following, will dwell close to the Almighty. One of the items on this list is, someone who lends his money and does not derive any tangible benefit from this act of kindness.

Rabbi Chaim Shmuelevitz, the late Rosh Yeshivah of Mir,

frequently mentioned that the laws of the prohibition against taking interest, are a lesson to us that applies to all aspects of doing kindness.

There is a natural tendency for human beings to keep their focus on "What's in it for me?" Every infant is focused on its own needs, and, as we grow up, this tendency remains. It is normal and natural, and it is incumbent upon us to elevate ourselves to go beyond this. That is what the Torah commandment prohibiting the taking of interest, teaches us. When we have money, we could gain by using that money for ourselves. We could buy and sell, become partners in a business, or find other ways to make more money.

Many people find themselves in situations where they need to borrow money from someone else. People who are deeply in debt have this need, and even the wealthiest might find themselves short of cash at times and need to borrow from another person. If you have the money that this person would like to borrow, you fulfill a Torah commandment of doing acts of kindness, by helping this person out and lending him the money. Many people would be happy to pay you, for your kindness. They need the money now and it would be worth it for them to pay you later on, for the help that you are giving them now.

But the Torah tells us: Do acts of kindness soley for the sake of helping another person. Realize that you are both children of the Creator, and the Creator wants His children to help each other. The Torah tells us to love other people as ourselves (*Levitcus* 19:18). When your right hand gives an item to your left hand, it does not ask for a reward. When your right hand puts food in your mouth, the right hand does not expect a favor in return. There is a unity and a oneness; this is the Torah concept that we learn from the ban against taking interest.

Even though we are permitted to take payment for other acts of kindness besides lending money, here we have an example of pure kindness and goodness. We might not always be able to maintain this high standard in other areas, but acting according to this elevated principle gives us a moment to reflect on the beauty of pure kindness. One good deed leads to another. This altruistic kindness will lead to other positive words and actions. Acting this way truly puts us on the path of dwelling close to Hashem, the very source of kindness.

> *Someone once told me about a relative of his. When guests would come to his town in Europe, he would greet them with warmth and friendliness.*
>
> *"Do you need a place to stay?" he would ask.*
>
> *"Yes," he was often told.*
>
> *"Good," he replied. "Then I will offer you a real bargain. We serve people just as the fanciest restaurants and hotels do, but you won't have to pay such a high price."*
>
> *The guests assumed that this person would charge them, and ate to their heart's delight. The food was special and they felt that they were getting a bargain, since the price would be cheaper.*
>
> *When the guests were ready to leave after a day, or two or after a week, they would ask for their bill.*
>
> *"There isn't any," the host told them.*
>
> *"But the quality of what you did for us gave us the impression that we would save money, but we would have to pay something," the surprised guests invariably said.*
>
> *"I just said that to you so you would feel comfortable, enjoying yourselves to the fullest extent. I had no intention of taking any money for this opportunity to do kindness."*

⋇ **16 / טז** ⋇

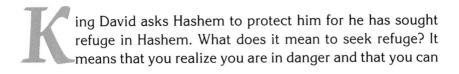

א מִכְתָּם לְדָוִד שָׁמְרֵנִי אֵל כִּי־חָסִיתִי בָךְ:

> ¹A [song of the] michtam [a musical instrument] by David. protect me, o, God, for I have sought refuge in You".

King David asks Hashem to protect him for he has sought refuge in Hashem. What does it mean to seek refuge? It means that you realize you are in danger and that you can find safety. The cities that were known as refuge cities (*arei miklat*) were specially designated areas to where someone who killed another person unintentionally, could flee. A potential avenger was forbidden to take revenge for the death of his relative, while the perpetrator was in the city. It is with a similar concept that King David asks Hashem to guard over him wherever he is, because he is relying on Hashem to protect him.

If someone has enemies who want to cause him physical harm, he is likely to experience anxiety. Those enemies are searching for him and he is in danger of injury and even death. If he hires bodyguards, he will become calmer. The bodyguards keep vigil and are using their strength and skill to protect him. But he is still in danger. The enemies might overpower the bodyguards. They might set a trap and outsmart the person they are pursuing. No human plan for protection, can be foolproof. The ability of human beings to protect someone, is always limited. Even mighty emperors and dictators have eventually met their ends through assassination or capture. The recent example of the capture of the cruel tyrant Saddam Hussein, dramatically sent a message throughout the world, showing the folly of someone who thought he could hide forever.

When we recite this verse, we ask the Almighty to watch over us. When Hashem guards us, we are safe. Why do we feel we have a right to ask Hashem to protect us? Because we have relied on His protection!

To get a stronger feeling for this, imagine how you would react if someone with less power, strength, knowledge, or skills would come over to you and say, "I respect your power and your abilities. I am helpless by myself. I desperately need your assistance. From the bottom of my heart I beg you to help me. I am relying on you. Please do not let me down."

If you actually did have the ability to help, and you sincerely care about the welfare of this person, would you not feel a much stronger sense of obligation and responsibility to help him? He is relying on you. So you will do all that you can to be there for him.

Get in touch with sincere feelings of relying on Hashem to help and protect you. Then, when you say these words, you will not merely be parroting them, but will experience the thoughts and feelings that enable you to merit Hashem's guardianship.

> *A number of years ago, I spoke to someone who was shot at by terrorists. I had spoken to a number of different people who had been in similar situations. Many described a feeling of panic and utter bewilderment. They realized that their lives were in danger. There was a strong possibility that they might be seriously injured, even killed.*
>
> *I asked Reuven how he dealt with the trauma. He acknowledged that being shot at was the scariest situation he had ever experienced in his life, but, in the midst of the drama, he felt an inner calm. He realized that he was completely in the hands of Hashem. In other challenging situations, he always felt that there were things that he could do to protect himself. Here. he realized that there was nothing he could do on his own. As he put it later, "I would not trade what happened to me for all the money in the world. The elevated spiritual feelings of relying totally on our compassionate Heavenly Father, was one of the most uplifting moments of my life. Nothing I have ever experienced before or after, could compare with this total sense of spiritual connection. Afterwards, I would remember those feelings when more minor challenges arose."*

יִרְבּוּ עַצְּבוֹתָם אַחֵר מָהָרוּ ד

⁴ Their sorrows will multiply, those who rush after.

The comprehensive work *Mei'am Loez* cites two explanations for this verse, neither of which is the simple meaning of the verse, but both give us important messages for life.

The first interpretation is: Through their rushing they caused themselves sadness. This is the essence of the wise saying, "The fruit of rushing is regret." Here the translation of the verse would be: *They multiply their sadness because they rush.*

We need the patience to think matters over carefully, before we act. Being impulsive causes many problems and difficulties. When one speaks or acts impulsively, he may certainly say and do things that he will regret. "An ounce of prevention is worth a pound of cure," goes the familiar saying. Does it not take time to think before you speak and act? Yes, it does. But this will be much less time than the time it will take to correct the errors and mistakes of impulsiveness.

Before speaking and acting, think! Think carefully. Try to see the big picture. What will be the consequences and ramifications of what you are about to say or do?

Focus on the great benefits of thinking before acting. And focus on the potential loss and harm of acting without thinking. By thinking carefully, the opposite of this verse will be true for you. "They will increase their happiness, those who think first."

Enjoy the process of thinking about what you are about to do. Each time you do so, you are making this habit more and more automatic and spontaneous. You will be enhancing your life now and in the future.

> *"I've been highly impulsive my entire life. I was told over and over again to think, before speaking and acting. But all the admonitions haven't made a major difference — I still tend to act impulsively. I made a decision that I would do whatever is necessary to change when I realized that I was making mistake after mistake. I spoke to a number of people and they were all helpful, but I still did not make a major change.*
>
> *"Finally, one person I spoke to, gave me some advice that transformed my life. He asked me, 'What do you keep repeating to yourself?'*
>
> *"'I keep saying, "Don't be impulsive!"' I told him.*
>
> *"'You deserve credit for trying,' he said to me. But you are going the wrong way. You need to repeat to yourself what you do want. Therefore, word your sentence, "I will think before I speak, and I will think before I act." When you mention the word "impulsive" over and over again, your brain makes pictures of you being impulsive. Even though you are saying you don't want to be this way, you are still reinforcing the pictures in your mind, of being impulsive.*
>
> *" 'In addition, along with repeating to yourself that you will*

think before you act, keep making mental pictures of your-self, thinking before you speak. Make those pictures over and over again. See yourself in various places and with various people and, each time, see yourself stopping for a few moments and thinking first. This does not have to take a long time in most situations, even 15 seconds is long enough. Since you are not used to this right now, it might seem like a long time. But the tremendous benefits of this pattern, will be clearly evident very soon.'

"He was right. This one habit has enhanced every area of my life."

Another explanation that we can find hinted at, in this verse is: "There are people who are sad, even though they have a sufficient amount for their needs of today. Even though they have enough for the present, they worry about tomorrow. *They increase their sadness.* Why? Because they *hurry to think about what will be later.*

Of course we need to plan for the future but appreciate first what you have now. Taking pleasure in what you presently have is the only way that you can live a happy, joyful life. A person who fails to appreciate what he has in the present, will live a very unhappy life. Even if he has enough for today, for this week, for this month, for this year, he can still be full of anxiety and nervousness. "But what about tomorrow, next week, next month, or next year?"

The Almighty gives you gifts for today. Enjoy them. Appreciate them. Be grateful. And with this sense of joy for what you have, you can calmly think about what you can do, for your future needs. The emotional state you will be in, will be conducive to clearer thinking.

By mastering gratitude for the present, you will always find things in the present for which to be grateful. Right now, ask yourself, "What am I grateful for — this moment?"

"I used to be a tremendous worrier," a very calm and serene person related. "I would consistently be nervous about what I might be missing later on. I spoke to a wise rabbi who taught me a lesson, that changed my life.

"You have frequently been worried for many years now," he asked me. "Is that correct?"

"I'm afraid it is," I answered.

"Please tell me the truth," he said to me. "What has caused you more suffering in life what you actually were missing, or your worry about what you might be missing in the future?"

"I hadn't thought about this, in that way," I acknowledged. " I have to admit that, there is no comparison between the two lists. I've always managed quite well, in the present. The greatest source of my suffering throughout my life has been worrying about a tomorrow that never turned out as bad as what I worried it might be. Looking back, I am embarrassed about how much needless pain I caused myself."

"So does it not make sense to be totally resolved to keep your major focus on gratitude for all the good in your life?" he said to me. Plan for the future? Yes! But do not waste time and energy worrying. What is worry? You focus your mind's attention on what might be missing later on, and right now you suffer the anxiety of missing — what you fear might be missing! One can do this one's entire life, even if one never actually misses anything that is really necessary for them. Keep moving your thoughts to gratitude and this will automatically free you from the negative. When you consistently think about gratitude, this will become a spontaneous habit."

"This made perfect sense to me. While I still needed to put in a lot of effort to gain greater mastery over my thoughts, this conversation was the beginning of a major breakthrough in my becoming a happier and calmer, more spiritual person."

ה **יהוה מְנָת־חֶלְקִי וְכוֹסִי אַתָּה תּוֹמִיךְ גּוֹרָלִי:**

5 HASHEM is my allotted portion and my share. You guide my destiny.

Rashi explains that Hashem guides our destiny as a father guides a child. Imagine that a child sitting at a festive meal, must make a choice. To his right is good food, and to the left is spoiled garbage. A young child might stick out his hand toward the spoiled garbage, but his father will gently direct his hand to choose the healthful food. Similarly Hashem tells us (see *Deuteronomy* 30:19) to choose life. He places before us life and death, blessing and curse, and He tells us to choose the words and actions that lead to life and blessing.

A key question for each of us in life is whom we shall choose as our guide. Suppose you had to make a dangerous trip through high mountains and deep valleys — through forests and jungles — through streams and rivers. There are many robbers and bandits along the way — wild animals and poisonous snakes — narrow paths and slippery terrain. Would you try to do this alone? Of course not. The most important thing for your journey would be a wise and knowledgeable guide who has made this trip many times before, and who has brought those who followed him, safely to their destination.

Whom will you choose to be your guide in your journey through life? There are various possibilities. For many, the guides are advertisers, who want people to spend as much money as they can to buy expensive items, even though they do not really need them. Even worse, there are people who make money from cigarettes and alcoholic beverages that are dangerous to one's physical health. Worse even, are the people who make money from things that are spiritually unhealthy. These are guides who bring harm and destruction.

Some people allow their own impulses, to guide their destiny. They like to do what feels good at the time and do not focus on the potential harmful effects of certain words and actions. Others who like to do what is easy and comfortable, let feelings of laziness and sluggishness, take over as their guide. It takes effort and it is difficult, their lazy feelings guide them to be passive and take it easy. Why exert yourself when you don't absolutely have to? These feelings prevent their owners from accomplishing and doing what needs to be done — not a very reliable guide.

Who is the ultimate guide for us? Our loving Father, and powerful King, Creator and Sustainer of the universe. He knows which path leads to harm. He knows which path is cursed. He loves us and wants us to choose life. He loves us and wants us to choose the pathway to blessing. He wants us to choose the thoughts, words, and actions that will give us an elevated and spiritually-oriented life. He wants us to get through this world in ways that are for our ultimate best interests.

In this verse, King David states that Hashem guides his destiny. He is open to selecting the choices that Hashem wants him to make. Let us choose his Guide as our Guide. And let us constantly hear Hashem telling us, "Choose life." When do we need to hear this? Every time we need to make a choice. And we are doing that every time we choose what thoughts to think, what words to say, and what actions to do. We are choosing every minute of our lives. Let us choose wisely.

> *Today more and more people hire personal coaches, to help them reach more of their potential. They want coaches to motivate them when they might not feel like doing all they could, to succeed. They want coaches to remind them of what they already know, but do not always do. They want coaches to hold them accountable for their time and energy. Did you do all you could, yesterday? Did you choose to use your time wisely? What more could you have done, yesterday? And what will you do today? What words and actions today, will make the greatest difference in your life?*
>
> *The greatest coaches, have their own coaches. They know that, even though they are objective when it comes to someone else, they personally might fall into habits that are not the best for themselves. Outsiders can see things about ourselves, that we might not notice.*
>
> *There are people that I coach, and there are people that I choose, to coach me. When I meet someone who has made a lot of progress in a relatively short time, I often ask, "What has helped you lately to do and be more?" I pick up a lot of helpful coaching tips for myself and which I can share with others.*
>
> *One person who recently transformed his life in amazing ways, shared with me the following. "I have an encounter every morning and evening with my Heavenly Father. I feel Him asking me, 'What are your plans for greatness for today? What will you do? What will you be very careful not to do?' And at the end of the day, I feel Him asking me, 'What were*

*the highlights of your day? What are you grateful to Me
about, today? And what will you plan to do tomorrow?'*

*"Throughout the day, I ask myself, 'What would the
Almighty Guide advise me to choose right now?'"*

ח שִׁוִּיתִי יהוה לְנֶגְדִּי תָמִיד:

8 I place HASHEM before me constantly.

Before we can focus on feeling Hashem's presence "constantly" we must first understand what it means to place
Hashem before us for even a few moments. This would
mean that we have a full sense of the reality of our Father, our King,
Creator and Sustainer of the universe. We would feel His presence,
right at this moment, in the exact place in which we are right now.

Let us take a look at what the Chazon Ish wrote about this
experience. I've cited this many times since, reflecting on what the
Chazon Ish wrote, is life-transforming.

The Chazon Ish (*Emunah U'bitachon* 1:9) described the effects of
awareness of the Almighty: "When a person merits becoming
aware of the reality of the Almighty's existence, he will experience
limitless joy. All the pleasures of the flesh immediately disappear.
His soul is enveloped in sanctity and it is as if it has left the body
and floats in the upper Heavens. When a person transcends to this
level, an entirely new world is open to him. It is possible for a
person to be, momentarily, like a celestial being in this world. All
of the pleasures of this world are as nothing compared to the
intense pleasure of a person cleaving to his Creator" (*My Father,
My King*, p.22, Artscroll).

Imagine the powerful effects this will have on you if you read it
daily, for at least a month. Copy it and put it in a place where you
will remember to see and read it.

It is most likely that we will not be able to experience these
profound feelings each time we place Hashem before us. But
knowing that this is possible for us, gives us a taste of it. And with
repetition we will integrate this more and more all the time.

Let us add to this a statement from the Chofetz Chaim, that

should be repeated a number of times each day: "Hashem loves each person more than each person loves himself" (*Shmiras Haloshon, Shaar 1, chapter 1*).

The Chofetz Chaim wrote this to motivate us not to speak negatively about other people. When you realize that Hashem loves the person against whom you are tempted to speak, you will find it easier to refrain from negative speech about him.

In reference to our verse: How will you feel when you realize that you are in the presence of Hashem? Right at this moment, you are in the presence of the Creator and Sustainer of the universe Who loves you personally, more than you love yourself. Let this expand your awareness. You are never alone. You are always in the presence of the Ultimate One Who has intense love, care and concern for your welfare.

The Baal Shem Tov's thoughts on this verse can have a major positive impact on our lives. The first word, *Shivisi*, which is usually translated as, "I place," can also be interpreted as, "I consider all things to be equal." This refers to the many situations and circumstances that arise in our lives. Some, we spontaneously consider good and positive and some, bad and negative. When things happen that we consider good and positive, we feel good. We feel a sense of well-being and inner calm. And if something happens to us that we consider bad and negative, it is easy for us to feel bad.

The awareness of this concept will enable us to sustain a feeling of well-being, even in potentially challenging situations. How? *Shivisi.* "I consider all the events in my life as equally positive and am always able to maintain my sense of well-being. And this is possible for me, because I am aware that Hashem is before me at all times." Therefore, we will be able to keep our sense of well-being whether someone praises us or insults us. True, we would prefer to be praised, rather than insulted, but since our mind and consciousness are engaged with the awareness of Hashem's loving presence, there is no room left for negative thoughts about this limited mortal's negativity.

This can be compared to someone who had just won a huge fortune in an international lottery, and is ecstatic. Then, someone who was jealous wanted to take away some of his good feeling, and tried to say something that would lessen his joy. "Oh, this reminds me of the time when you were planning a picnic and it rained that day." Even if that person felt bad on the day of the canceled picnic, right now, nothing can rain on his parade. His mind, consciousness, and thoughts are all consumed. They are permeated with joy.

Some people become irritated, upset, angry, disappointed, unhappy, or experience other distressful feelings, when minor and/ or trivial annoyances occur in their daily lives. They lose their sense of well-being quite easily. This thought of the Baal Shem Tov on our verse, can free their minds from the thoughts that create distressful feelings. By integrating and internalizing this powerful message, they can view those occurrences as irrelevant and inconsequential. They will notice those events, situations, and circumstances, but they will not be considered matters of importance. They will live the motto, "Don't sweat the small stuff, and it's all small stuff." Their minds will be taken up with the awareness of the greatness of their loving Father and powerful King.

Let us summarize this principle:

To the extent that our minds, consciousness, and thoughts are permeated with the awareness and realization that Hashem, Creator and Sustainer of the universe, loves us and is here right now, we are free of the types of thoughts that could possibly cause distress.

Spend time contemplating this. Meditate on it. Let this thought become part of you. Do this gently and patiently. You can't push or force this idea. Trying to do so, will not bring you the realization that you want. You simply need this understanding to exist in your mind.

Repeat this verse regularly. Keep it written in places where you will see it frequently. Your sincerity in wanting to actually feel this thought, will bear fruit and with Hashem's help you will succeed. The very act of trying, elevates you. Your mind will be actively engaged in the process of placing Hashem before you.

This verse is cited in the introduction of the classic *mussar* work "*Orchos Tzaddikim*" ("The Ways of the Righteous"). There the author elaborates on the importance of being constantly aware of our many character traits. The positive traits elevate a person and with positive traits you can live a high-quality life. The negative traits, on the other hand, are harmful. A wise person constantly makes wise choices of thoughts, words, and actions. Your positive traits lead you on a positive path. But there is always a potential challenge that the negative traits could lead one away from truth, kindness, and goodness. About this the verse states, "I place Hashem before me at all times."

This means that we constantly ask ourselves, "What are the positive ways that Hashem, in Whose presence I now am, wants me to speak and act?"

Keep in mind that Hashem loves you and wants you to succeed in life. The ultimate success is to constantly speak and act in ways that are considered walking in Hashem's ways. This is the source of our obligation to develop and refine positive character traits.

Every positive thought and every positive word and every positive action is part of the process of developing your character, in the presence of your loving Father and King, Creator and Sustainer of the universe. Allow yourself to feel joyful feelings for every moment of success, in this process. If your thoughts, words, or actions stray from the desired goals, gently bring them back to more positive ones. Do so calmly. Each time you bring your mind back to this, you gain greater mastery over the ability to do so.

> I suggested to a group of young men that they focus on being in Hashem's presence for an hour a day for a week. They could divide this up into 3 segments of 20 minutes each. Of course, if they wished they could do this for longer. They should focus on the fact that Hashem loves them and wants them to speak and act with positive character traits. And they should allow themselves to experience joy in the process.
>
> Here are some of the comments:
>
> - "I have an issue with getting angry easily. Little things that are not to my liking bother me. I've tried many times to overcome losing my temper, but I find it very difficult. When I was aware that I was in Hashem's presence, I felt that I just couldn't get angry. I realized that what used to bother me was petty, compared to being in the presence of the Creator and Sustainer of the universe. Knowing that Hashem loves me, I know He doesn't want me to

harm myself physically, emotionally, and spiritually with anger. I found it so much easier to be calm."

- *"I am a Torah teacher and I was going through a rough time. I was under a lot of stress because of financial pressures. I became easily irritated with pupils who weren't paying attention or who were acting like the young children they were. I was committed to teaching for a full day with the awareness that I was in the presence of Hashem. He loves me and wants me to succeed in the holy work that I am doing. He loves the children that I am teaching Torah. This gave me an elevated perspective, and I found my stress melting away. I was much calmer. If people whom I wanted to impress were to enter the classroom, I would try my very best to teach well. All the more so, this should be my attitude when I realize that Hashem is there. I was completely dedicated to teaching that day with joyful enthusiasm. I wanted to inspire the children — to bring out their best. It was the best day of teaching that I ever had."*

- *"In every synagogue there is a sign with the verse shivisi. I've seen it so many times that I usually take it for granted. When it was suggested to me to focus on the ramifications of this verse, I didn't realize how powerful it would be. The very next time I entered my synagogue, my eyes immediately focused on the words of the sign. It was as if this was the first time I really understood the tremendous significance of those words. I was entering the sanctuary where I would be speaking to my beloved Heavenly Father and powerful King. I would be talking to Him in prayer. He wasn't far away, but right before me. I prayed with great fervor and concentration. All parts of the prayers became much more meaningful to me."*

- *"I would do people favors, but quite often I would be doing them, because I found it difficult to say, 'No.' When I focused on being in Hashem's presence, I viewed the kindnesses that I could do, in an entirely new light.*

The people who were asking me for various favors, were children of the Almighty. I realized that Hashem was aware of my reactions. I realized that Hashem loves this person and wants me to help His children whenever I can, in whatever ways that I can. It's not as though you do someone a favor and you hope that his distinguished relative will eventually hear about what you did. Rather, I am in Hashem's presence. He wants me to emulate Him, by becoming a kinder person. I felt better about doing acts of kindness, than I had ever felt before."

● "I tend to be shy and easily intimidated by other people. This has held me back in my life in many ways. Even when I feel a need to ask other people questions or seek information, my lack of appropriate assertiveness, prevents me from speaking up. I became more aware of Hashem's presence and the empowerment this can give me. I began to realize that all I need to clarify for myself is, 'Is what I would like to say consistent with the will of Hashem? Is this something that Hashem would want me to say?' If I would have a few powerful friends present who are encouraging me to speak up, I would find it relatively easy. This thought made the entire process of being more assertive, especially when it came to areas of Torah study and asking people to help others, much easier than I had ever imagined."

⊰ **18 / יח** ⊱

א לַמְנַצֵּחַ לְעֶבֶד יהוה לְדָוִד אֲשֶׁר דִּבֶּר לַיהוה אֶת־דִּבְרֵי הַשִּׁירָה הַזֹּאת בְּיוֹם הִצִּיל־יהוה אוֹתוֹ מִכַּף כָּל־אֹיְבָיו וּמִיַּד שָׁאוּל:

[1] **For the conductor; by the servant of** HASHEM, **by David; who spoke the words of this song to** HASHEM, **on the day that** HASHEM **delivered him from the hand of all his enemies, and from the hand of Saul.**

The term *Lamenatzei'ach*, which is the first word of this chapter, is translated as "Conductor." The term "Conductor" is understood to mean that, when music was played, there was a conductor to lead the musicians and the singers. But the term can readily be understood to refer to the Ultimate Conductor of the Universe. Hashem is the Ultimate Power and Mind behind all that occurs in the world.

We constantly need to increase our understanding that, all that happens to us in life, was orchastrated by the One Who directs all events, situations, and circumstances. We are the actors who perform against the background that has been set up for us. However, unlike an actor in a major play where the entire script of what will be said and done has been written by someone else, in our lives we have total free will to choose what we will say and what we will do. It is our choices of words and actions that will make our lives a tremendous success or an utter failure. The criteria for success and failure has nothing to do with how eloquently we speak or how dramatically we carry out our actions. Rather, success is speaking and acting according to the will of Hashem. Failure is the opposite.

The background of events, situations, and circumstances is not always to our liking. Many things happen in the world in which we live, that we find challenging. That is however, exactly what makes a great actor — one who utilizes the difficult factors and performs magnificently, nevertheless.

Thus, with this in mind, when we are faced with a challenge, we should ask ourselves, "What are the wisest things for me to say and do now, that will ensure a great performance?" The Judge of our performance is Hashem, Creator and Sustainer of the universe. If He approves of what we say and do, then our life performance is an unqualified success. If He disapproves, then even if we have the approval of other mortals, we have not yet accomplished our life's mission.

Let us be resolved to living our lives in ways that are pleasing to our loving Creator. With this in mind, all that arises in our lives are more opportunities to serve Hashem in ways that will enhance us.

"By the servant of Hashem, by David." King David calls himself a servant of Hashem. This was the great praise that the Torah (*Deuteromony* 34:5) uses to praise Moshe Rabbeinu, our great teacher Moses, at the end of his life. What is a servant? There is a general principle: Whatever a servant has, belongs to his master. Thus, a servant is one who identifies fully with his master. All that he does, he does for his master. Even when he does things for his personal health and well-being, it is ultimately for his master that he is doing those things; so that he will have the energy and vitality to carry out his master's will. That is the great praise of Moshe Rabbeinu, and this is what King David considers himself. This is what each of us can use as a model, of how we wish to be.

I found myself feeling emotionally down, a good part of the time. I felt that I was never good enough. I made many mistakes. I wasn't as brilliant as some other people I knew. Spiritually I had many ups and downs. I was feeling discouraged and lowly.

An elderly Jew told me this, about an experience he had had many years ago.

" 'I consulted a great Rebbe," he told me. These words of that spiritual master, have been my guide over the years:

" 'If the servant of a great King walks around as if he is one of the saddest people in the world, he is not honoring the King. You are a servant of Hashem. Let the joy of knowing this, give you a constant sense of happiness. Your all-knowing Father in Heaven does not expect you to be perfect, but He does expect you to use your mind and your heart to serve him, with all that you have. If you make a mistake, that mistake is in the past. Express your regret to Hashem, and continue making wiser choices now in the present. Let the smile on your face be an announcement that you are happy to do the will of Hashem, our loving Father and powerful King.' "

That was enough to inspire me for the rest of my life. I know I am imperfect. And I know that I always want to be a servant of Hashem. I utilize my mistakes to become a better servant now — in the present.

בּ וַיֹּאמַר אֶרְחָמְךָ יהוה חִזְקִי:

גּ יְהֹוָה סַלְעִי וּמְצוּדָתִי וּמְפַלְטִי אֵלִי צוּרִי
אֶחֱסֶה־בּוֹ מָגִנִּי וְקֶרֶן יִשְׁעִי מִשְׂגַּבִּי:

² **He said, 'I love you, HASHEM, my Strength.**
³ **HASHEM is my Rock, my Fortress, and my
Rescuer; my God, my Rock in Whom I take
shelter, my Shield and the Horn of my Salvation,
my Stronghold.**

Here King David makes a statement that he loves Hashem.
Rashi explains that the Hebrew word *Erchamcha,* means
"I love you," and he cites the verse of "Love your neighbor
as yourself," where the Aramaic translation of the word for love is
the term that is used in our verse.

Rabbi Samson Raphael Hirsch comments that *Erchamcha* comes
from the word *rechem,* womb. This is the love that a child feels for a
parent, because the parent gave birth to the child. The child
realizes that its very life is because of the parent.

This is the love that is the essence of our love for Hashem, our
Creator and Sustainer. Our entire existence comes from Hashem.
All the good in our life comes from Hashem. The greater and
deeper this awareness, the more love we have.

Hashem is our strength. All our energy is from Hashem. Every
good in our lives comes from Him.

There is a constant *mitzvah* (commandment) to love Hashem.
This is a *mitzvah* that applies day and night, every moment of our
lives. The way to connect with this awareness of love for Hashem, is
to constantly be aware of our life being a gift from Hashem. From
the very moment we were born our life was a gift, and it is only
through His constantly giving us life that we are alive.

There are many dangers in life, and only because Hashem is our
shield and our fortress can we maintain our existence.

The oxygen that we breathe to keep us alive, is a gift from
Hashem and the food that keeps us alive is from Hashem. Our
immune system that wards off illness is a constant gift from
Hashem — everything that enhances our life is a gift from Hashem.

We receive gifts from Hashem each moment. When we are asleep we have these gifts but our conscious mind is sleeping and we lack this awareness, but as soon as we wake up in the morning we can once again focus on the kindness of Hashem. As soon as we wake up, we can choose to be aware of Hashem's loving-kindness to us, and immediately focus our attention on love of Hashem, the Giver of our lives and all our gifts.

When someone lives with the awareness of Hashem's love for us and our love for Hashem, is a life of spiritual elevation this will be a life of joy.

What does it take to live a life of love for Hashem? It takes a conscious choice of thought. At any given moment you can choose to focus your attention on the gift of life that Hashem gives you and all that it takes to keep you alive, and when you do so, you have what it takes to create positive feelings.

We have a built-in feedback machine that informs us when we are not thinking of appreciation for Hashem and His gifts. Whenever we are turning to thoughts of complaint and blame, we are not in touch with thoughts of love for Hashem. When our thinking is off balance, our feelings will be off balance. Therefore, this is a reminder for us: "Remember to allow thoughts of appreciation for Hashem and love for Him to enter your mind."

R' Akiva, who reached the highest level of love for Hashem even when he was tortured to death by the Romans, is the one who constantly taught, during his life, what it means to appreciate the goodness of Hashem. R' Akiva taught us the statement, "All that Hashem does is for our ultimate good." This thought is the mindset of one who realizes that Hashem loves us.

Do you want to enhance your life? Keep repeating throughout the day, "I love you, Hashem, my strength." As you repeat this a number of times each day, you will feel yourself being strengthened spiritually and emotionally. You will be able to remember that Hashem is your Rock, your Fortress, and your Rescuer. Hashem is the source of your strength. Recognizing this, gives you an inner strength that will sustain you on a high level each and every day.

"I used to view myself as weak. I had a tendency towards worry and fearfulness. My mindset was that I was greatly

limited, and I used to complain a lot. Things were never exactly the way that I wished they would be. I would blame others for what I was missing: what I was missing in material matters and what I was missing in my character. I always considered it the fault of others, that I lacked courage and inner strength.

"*Looking back I now realize that I could have lived my entire life with this limited and fearful mindset. Then one day I had a wakeup call. I had to have a medical test for a potentially serious illness. I was frightened. My entire future was now uncertain. The days before the test were full of apprehension and anxiety.*

"*Fortunately the tests showed that my worries were unfounded. Something was found, but it wasn't a serious problem. I felt tremendously relieved and it was then that I realized that this relief would only be short-lived, if I reverted to my habitual patterns of thought.*

"*I made a decision that I did not want to live a life full of anxiety and worry. I wanted to live a more spiritual life and a more joyful life. I was committed to increasing my love for Hashem and to filling my mind with thoughts of gratitude and appreciation for His goodness. I would trust in Him, and I would view Him as my source of inner strength. Of course, the world has so many potential dangers that as a simple mortal there is nothing I can do to protect my-self in every way that I would need, to be safe. I was, however, determined that I would increase my awareness of Hashem as the source of my life and that He constantly sustains my life. I wanted to feel, on a regular basis, the good feelings that I had when I was told that I was basically healthy.*

"*From that time on, my basic mindset is that I love Hashem, He is my source of strength, and He constantly protects me. This has been a source of many wonderful thoughts and feelings.*

"*Of course, I have my ups and downs. My thoughts have not always been on the level that I would have wanted them to be, but whenever I realized that my thoughts had strayed from what I had decided to focus upon, I would calmly bring them back, and I would say, 'Hashem, I love You. You are my strength and my shield. I am grateful to You for all the good in my life.' After repeating this a few times, my feelings are once again influenced by love for Hashem and the awareness that He is the source of my strength."*

⊰{ **22 / כב** }⊱

וְאָנֹכִי תוֹלַעַת וְלֹא־אִישׁ ז

⁷ I am a worm and not a man.

Commentators explain this verse to mean that King David is saying that, since he considers himself a worm and not a man, he doesn't rely on his own strength and intellect. He trusts completely in Hashem, because without Hashem, the ultimate in strength and intelligence, he knows he is nothing.

What King David is telling us here, is the foundation of the attribute of humility. Whatever strengths we have are really nothing. We are weaker than a worm, unless Hashem gives us strength. The fact that we can lift anything with our hands, is only because Hashem gives us the strength to do so. Any intelligence we have is a complete gift from Hashem, and without Hashem giving us this gift, we have the intelligence of a rock. Even a worm is more intelligent than this.

However, if a person considers himself a worm, doesn't that rob him of self-esteem? Isn't that a low self-image that will cause a person to limit himself in many ways?

Let's look at our role model for the idea that one is a worm. It is the mighty King David — the powerful king, the one who led the Jewish people in a key time in our nation's history. The one who wrote Psalms that we recite in the daily prayers and whose words are a constant source of inspiration for us. He didn't feel that viewing himself as a worm, in the context of relating to Hashem, was a form of belittling himself. Rather, he viewed this awareness as empowering. The ultimate empowerment comes from realizing that you are one-hundred-percent dependent on Hashem for every bit of intelligence that you have. You are totally dependent on Hashem for anything you are able to do.

There are many challenging situations in life when we feel helpless. We realize our weaknesses, we know that we lack the knowledge and resources to do what needs to be done. Some people feel lost and begin to despair, but this is exactly the type of situation that can teach us *bitachon*, trust in our powerful Father and King, Creator and Sustainer of the universe, whose abilities are limitless.

A young child might want to lift an object that is very heavy. He can't do it on his own he is too small and the weight of the object is too great. However, when he knows that he can call upon his father to help him, his ability to carry heavy objects has been greatly multiplied. Knowing that Hashem can help us, enables us to expand our sense of possibilities. What at first might seem impossible, is now feasible.

There are people who feel as if they must climb a towering mountain, when they are trying to marry off a child. Either the process of finding a suitable marriage partner appears extremely difficult, or else the financial aspects involved are intimidating. They don't know how they will manage. Trust in Hashem, lightens their burden.

There are people with health challenges, family problems, difficult decisions where all the options seem daunting, and many similar problematic and complex issues. We are like worms that are asked to do things, that seem utterly beyond us. This is where trust in Hashem is the answer. "This is another opportunity to strengthen my *bitachon*." Experience the hope that this will constantly give you.

> *I used to be a world-class worrier. I grew up believing that there weren't many things that I knew how to do. When I would think about facing new and unfamiliar situations, I was frightened. How will I manage? was the question that kept repeating itself in my mind, and every time I thought of this, my anxiety and nervousness kept increasing.*
>
> *"I spoke to a righteous Torah scholar and this is what he told me: Be grateful for this pattern. This is going to be the*

ladder that will lift you up spiritually. You can transform these thoughts from a source of distress to a source of spiritual elevation. Since you are talented in the skill of thinking of situations that you don't think you can handle on your own, utilize this as a tool to increase your level of trust in Hashem. Since you see that the power of your imagination is so strong that it can create painful feelings about imaginary occurrences, you can use that power in a positive, constructive way. See yourself having high levels of Trust in Hashem. Feel yourself being calm and serene. Even if you aren't yet on this level, you can still visualize yourself being this way, on the screen of your mind. See yourself becoming calmer and more serene. See yourself with a clearer mind. See yourself finding solutions that would never have occurred to you, before. See other people helping you out. As you practice this, you will be internalizing the attribute of bitachon.

This was life-transforming for me. I was now mentally prepared to face any challenges that would come my way. Each challenge I imagined, added to my spiritual connection with Hashem and gave me inner resources to cope with what I didn't previously think I could handle. "

❧ **23 / כג** ❧

א מִזְמוֹר לְדָוִד יהוה רֹעִי לֹא אֶחְסָר:

¹ Hashem **is my shepherd, I shall not lack.**

The Malbim comments that, in his youth, King David was a shepherd, and therefore he uses the metaphor of Hashem being a kind and compassionate shepherd.

"I shall not lack." This is a profound statement. In essence this is saying: I know that if I were to truly need something, Hashem would definitely supply me with that need. If I do not yet have something that my all-knowing and all-powerful, loving Father wants me to have, I will soon acquire it. Even if at present I do not have any idea how that will happen, I am certain that it will happen. In Hashem's world there is abundance, and therefore He will certainly supply me with all that I need to fulfill my personal life mission. If I am not able to get something, that certainly is because the One Who knows my needs, knows that I do not truly need this. I might want more things than I need, so I will not always get what I want or desire. But my true needs will always be met.

Some people go through life with a constant feeling of lack. When this sense of lack comes from a spiritual emptiness, no amount of physical and material attainments will be able to fill the black hole. For such people, illusory potential appears to shine brightly. "This will do it for me. That is what I need. When I have this specific thing, then I will really be happy. That accomplishment or attainment will give me a feeling of success." They chase dreams, but, in the end, they always come back to a feeling of emptiness and lack. They are trying to fill a real void with things that do not have true substance; this path is hopeless.

Connecting with Hashem is the only solution. "Hashem is my shepherd." He shows me where to go and what to do. Hashem is the source of true abundance. Hashem is the source of absolute meaning. Hashem is the source of life and eternity.

Looking in the wrong place, you will never find what you are looking for. Only by searching in the right place, will your search be successful. If you lost your keys or your wallet in one area of the city, and you keep looking in another area, you will not find them. If you feel a lack, start out by recognizing that Hashem, your Father and King, Creator and Sustainer of the universe, is your Shepherd. He is your Leader, your Advisor, Your ultimate Source for what you need. With this awareness, all that you do have and will attain, will be a source of fulfillment and lasting happiness. You will be full of appreciation and gratitude, and this total sense of trust in your Shepherd will give you inner peace and serenity.

" 'Keep your eyes open for people who have a sense of abundance and for people who have a sense of lack and scarcity, and notice the difference.' This is what my rabbi suggested to me and a few other students. I would like you to learn a valuable lesson for life, he told us.

"This exercise had a profound effect on me. I noticed that the difference between the people who experienced abundance or scarcity was not a material difference, but a spiritual one. There were people who were financially wealthy with an abundance-consciousness, and people who had the same amount of wealth — yet they had a scarcity-consciousness. The latter had a lot of money and possessions, but emotionally they were paupers. And there were people with a minimal amount of money, but they viewed themselves as wealthy — they were emotionally rich. They felt; I always have what I need — I'm not missing anything. On the other hand there were people with the same amount of money who kept complaining about the money they wished they had. They were resentful and envious of those with more.

"Those who internalized that the Almighty is always there for them, experienced an inner happiness. This was noticeable by the looks on their faces and the way that they spoke. I then realized that I had to make it a higher priority to experience Hashem as my provider, rather than to focus on just having more money. When I say, "I have all that I need," I want to sincerely experience this as my constant reality."

ד **גַּם כִּי־אֵלֵךְ בְּגֵיא צַלְמָוֶת לֹא־אִירָא רָע כִּי־אַתָּה עִמָּדִי**

⁴ Though I walk in the valley overshadowed by death, I will fear no evil, for You are with me.

"For You are with me." What is the difference between just repeating these words of Psalms, and actually experiencing them? It is the difference between living life with inner peace and tranquility, and living life with anxiety and despair. It is the difference between feeling a sense of togetherness and oneness with the Creator and Sustainer of the entire universe, and feeling alone and lonesome. It is the difference between constantly feeling a sense of meaning and purpose, and feeling a sense of emptiness and futility. Experiencing these words emotionally, makes a qualitative difference in one's life.

"For You are with me." What does this mean? It means that you are aware that Hashem, your loving Father and powerful King, is with you wherever you are. Hashem is with you in the most challenging times and the most deserted places. Hashem is with you when you celebrate and when you grieve. Hashem is with you when you are ill or hurt, as well as when you are healthy and vibrant. Hashem is with you in times of war and in times of peace. Hashem is with you when you need to ask someone for help, and when you receive a response — whether favorable or not. Hashem is with you when you pursue your goals and reach them, or when you see that this goal is not one you will accomplish. Hashem is with you now, when you are reading this, and you can experience this whenever you think about this verse.

Think back in your life about different times when you might have lacked the awareness that Hashem was with you. Now relive some of those situations with the greater awareness that Hashem was with you. How would you have felt differently if you had been aware of Hashem's presence? How would you have reacted differently? See yourself feeling the way you would have felt, had you been aware of Hashem's presence. See yourself acting the way you would have acted. From now on, this more elevated awareness will be part of your inner resources that you carry in your brain, wherever you go. This will make it easier for you to access this awareness in present and future situations, and the more frequently you are aware of this, the more likely it is for this to become your spontaneous way of thinking.

Imagine the benefits of having the words of this verse instantly come to you, whenever you begin to feel worried or anxious. You will find yourself becoming calmer and more serene. Your awareness of Hashem's loving and compassionate presence will melt away tension and stress. Right now you can build this into the library of your mind. Replay this happening to you, again and again. As you do so, your mind will automatically associate this verse and its tranquil effects, with the earliest stages of your needing its benefits. Be patient. Practice making this association, until it becomes automatic.

"I used to be a worrier and frequently had distressful night-mares. The negative effects of these unpleasant dreams, would last for a long time. They seemed so vivid and real, that I experienced them as if they actually were happening to me. I worried that, perhaps, they were giving me a disturbing message and, even if that were not so, the very thoughts created so much stress that I was worried about my health. A turning point for me was when I attended a Shalosh Seudos *(third meal on Shabbos), where they sang this entire psalm with an inspiring melody. While I had recited this psalm many times before, this time the melody caused me to relate to this verse, almost as if it were new to me. I reflected on how my life would be so much more serene if I truly felt Hashem's presence in my daily life. This would enable me to be calmer, when facing the mundane and standard chal-lenges of life, and would help me even more if I were faced with a life-threatening situation. I pictured the tranquil faces of those who recited this chapter of psalms throughout history, to help them cope with adversity. I strongly resolved to repeat this verse until I, too, would be able to say, 'I will fear no evil, for You are with me.'"*

ה **כּוֹסִי רְוָיָה:**

⁵ My cup runs over.

In the 23rd Psalm, customarily recited at the third meal on Shabbos, King David states that his cup runs over. This is a metaphor telling us that he is tremendously grateful to Hashem for all the good things that Hashem has given him.

Rabbi Avigdor Miller (*Shaarei Orah, vol. 1,* p.96) commented on this verse in a *mussar vaad* (a group of students working on character development): "A cup can only run over if it becomes full first. If there is a hole in the cup, it will never become full and will never run over. This is a lesson for us to constantly remember the good things that Hashem does for us. Never forget them. Then the good things will add up and your happiness will flow."

We humans, by nature, always keep our focus on what we want now. We consider what we already have to be grateful for as a given, taken for granted and therefore it is usually easier to feel a constant sense of lack. "I'm lacking now everything that I presently want to have or to happen." Those who are experts at this way of life, feel bad more often than they feel good. Even when they feel good, it does not last for very long. They immediately focus on the next thing they need or want.

The quality to master, is to constantly be grateful for all the good things in our lives. How do we do this? We need to answer the question: What are some of the good things that I have already experienced in my life? Now, in the present, think about being appreciative and grateful for those things. When you consistently do this, you will consistently feel happy and joyful. Your mind will be so thankful that there will not be room for the negative thoughts and negative feelings that come to a mind that is empty of gratitude.

If you had a cup in which you poured expensive wine and the wine leaked out from a hole at the bottom of the cup, how long would it take you to realize that it is important to fix the cup? Obviously you would take care of this, right away. Preventing the multitude of things for which to be grateful from leaking out of your mind, should be an even higher priority. Losing expensive wine is only a slight loss, compared to those who go though life consistently sad and miserable. The way to master happiness and joy is to master gratitude, thankfulness, and appreciation.

Be grateful to Hashem for all that you have as often as you can. As an exercise, compile a list of 200 things for which you could be grateful, that have happened to you at any time during your life. For those who feel that this is a lot, did you eat 200 meals in your life? The reality is, that we each have many thousands of things that should be acknowledged some major, some minor. The more you think about this, the more things you will notice. Even if you find it difficult to write up this list at one sitting, you have the rest of your life to reach the minimum of 200 items. One thing you can appreciate is, that you are reading this section in this book and you now have another reminder to be more sensitive to Hashem's gifts.

"*Growing up, I constantly heard from my parents, 'You are so ungrateful for all the many things that we do for you.' This did not make me into someone who is full of gratitude. Rather, I would always accept this, as my identity. 'Who am I? I am a person who lacks gratitude. That's just the way I am.'*

"This changed when I had a teacher who told me to list five good things that happened to me, that day. He shared with us that he had heard from someone who suffered a lot in his life that, even on the roughest days, there are always many good things that happen. Usually people label the day as good or bad and this colors their memories for that entire day. We need to go beyond this tendency. We need to increase our awareness of what is happening to us that is good, when it happens, and we need to increase our memories of the good things in our lives. This will upgrade our appreciation for Hashem; it is the way to live a happy life.

" 'Whatever you focus on, gets reinforced. When you make an effort to keep noticing something, that is what your brain's R.A.S. (Reticular activating system) will cause you to notice. Kvetchy people focus on what there is to kvetch about, and joyful people focus on what there is to be happy about.' This made sense to me and I saw how this would make a major difference in my life. I was highly motivated to put this into action. I developed the habit of always thinking of at least five positive things from each day, before I went to sleep.

"From time to time, I would ask myself the question, 'What good things happened to me throughout my life?' This has made it easier for me to focus on those good things again and again. I could easily observe that, as my thoughts increased, the amount of time they were thoughts of gratitude and appreciation, I became a generally happier person. Even though I would have appreciated it if my parents would have expressed their wishes for me to be more grateful in a mo positive way, I see clearly they were right. I now appreci their good intentions and all the many good things the for me.*"

﴾ 24 / כד ﴿

:אֱ [לְדָוִד מִזְמוֹר] לַיהוה הָאָרֶץ וּמְלוֹאָהּ [תֵּבֵל וְיֹשְׁבֵי בָהּ]

¹ The earth and its fullness is HASHEM's [the inhabited land and those who dwell in it].

Many people have the custom of writing this verse in Hebrew in their Torah books. Only then do they write their own names. This serves as a constant reminder that the earth and all its contents truly belong to the Creator. The Almighty allows us to use what we need to meet our mission in this world, but ultimately all belongs to Him.

This is why the Talmud (*Brachos* 35a) states that someone who derives pleasure from this world without making a blessing first, is considered as if he took property belonging to the Holy Temple and illegally used it. When you recite a blessing over food, you acknowledge your awareness that Hashem is the Creator of the world and the Creator of the specific food that you are about to eat. With your blessings, you connect with the Creator, and this gives you the right to partake of the Almighty's food.

The lens created by seeing the world from this perspective, is tremendously far-reaching and elevating. When you see mountains, you are seeing Hashem's mountains. When you see a waterfall, you are seeing Hashem's waterfall. When you see trees, flowers, and grass, you are seeing beautiful scenery that the Creator has provided for your enjoyment and benefit. The animals, fish, and birds, all add a special dimension to our world. Some animals serve as food to give us energy. Using this for spiritual enhancement elevates those animals which are contributing their part to sanctify the Creator, for every living creature you see, is part of the Creator's world.

With the awareness that everything on our planet belongs to Hashem, we can gain a deeper understanding of the prohibition against needlessly destroying fruit-bearing trees, and by extension-anything else that could be used constructively. Use wisely what you have a right to use, but destroying and wasting is damaging the

Almighty's property. Refraining from doing so, gives you the merit of maintaining the Creator's world.

> *It was suggested to me that, for an entire month I should frequently repeat the (above) verse, — The earth and its fullness is Hashem's."*
>
> *"How often should I repeat this?" I asked.*
>
> *"At least a hundred times a day," I was told. "Throughout the day, repeat this verse. Let its message seep in. Let this give you a new respect for the natural riches of the world. Let it give you a new view of all the many products that have been manufactured by humans. The Creator created the raw material that human ingenuity shaped and molded and put together to enhance our lives."*
>
> *"I wrote this verse on a card that I would see throughout the day. I repeated the verse over and over again. During the month that I had resolved to repeat the verse, it became 'my verse.'*
>
> *"I repeated it when I used a telephone. I now realized that the telephone I was using and the entire world-wide network of telephones, belonged to the Creator. This gave me an added incentive to speak positively about Hashem's children and avoid speaking and hearing negative remarks.*
>
> *"I repeated this verse when I used my refrigerator and freezer. This helped me appreciate Hashem's gifts, more than ever before. I was grateful for the appliances themselves and all the food in them.*
>
> *"I repeated the verse when I traveled in a car or bus. I felt a deeper sense of gratitude for all forms of transportation from which I benefited. I repeated it when I saw airplanes flying. and, when during that month, I flew overseas in one of Hashem's planes. It elevated that entire experience.*
>
> *"When I took a pen in my hand, I repeated the verse and realized that both the pen and the paper I wrote on, were items Hashem is letting me use. Did this have an effect on what I wrote? It certainly did!*
>
> *"The more often I repeated the verse, the stronger were its effects. I plan to tell others to experience this for themselves."*

‹{ **27 / כז** }›

יד קַוֵּה אֶל־יהוה חֲזַק וְיַאֲמֵץ לִבֶּךָ וְקַוֵּה אֶל־יהוה:

¹⁴ Hope to HASHEM. be strong! strengthen yourself and He will give you courage and hope to HASHEM.

This nine-word verse (in Hebrew) has three parts. The first three words tell us to hope to Hashem. And then this message is repeated in the last three words. The middle three words tell us to strengthen ourselves, and then, as the Ibn Ezra explains, after you strengthen yourself Hashem will give you courage.

Any human being can strengthen his will and resolve. This can be a conscious decision that we all can make, even if we do not have any rational reason for doing so. This is similar to the decision to strengthen our muscles or to let them go and become relaxed. But *Tehillim* tells us a reason for strengthening ourselves. "Hope to Hashem." Hashem is your loving Father. Hashem is all-powerful. When Hashem wills it, miracles happen. As *Metzudas David* writes, this trust in Hashem is a special merit that makes one worthy of Hashem's help and deliverance.

What is the root element of having hope in Hashem? You realize that He is the very essence of kindness and compassion. You realize that He loves you on the deepest level possible. You realize that He is all-powerful and has the ability to help you. So your having this hope, is making a powerful statement of your basic belief and trust in Hashem. Thinking the thoughts of hope to Hashem is spiritually and emotionally life-enhancing.

Rashi explains why the message of hope to Hashem is repeated a second time. Our first prayers might not be accepted and therefore, we need to resiliently hope to Hashem once again.

Malbim comments that hoping to Hashem is different from hoping that another human being will help us. With another mortal, the hope isn't a goal in itself. Rather, the hope is a means to an end. With hope to Hashem, however, that itself is our goal. The hoping itself connects us to Hashem and is spiritually elevating.

How persistent are you when it comes to hoping to Hashem? Is there an amount of time that would cause you to say, "That's it! There is no more hope!"? The goal to strive for, is to never give up prematurely. And as the saying goes, "It's not over until it's over." Before it's over, keep up your hope for Hashem.

What is the difference between having this hope and not having it? Lack of hope causes discouragement and depression. Pessimism creates a self-fulfilling prognosis. If you believe that you cannot succeed at something, it's highly likely that you will act in such a way that, you will be successful in creating the lack of success that you were predicting.

On the other hand, hope gives you positive energy. Hope creates optimism and resourceful emotions. Hope gives you the strength to keep trying, until you succeed. Your optimism breeds the kind of success that will give you further reason to be optimistic, again and again.

Help other people strengthen their hope. When you do so, do so in an encouraging, empowering manner. Some people tend to rebuke others. "Your problem is that you lack hope in Hashem. Your hope is deficient. You don't hope sufficiently — strongly enough." This is likely to weigh the person down with feelings of guilt, in addition to the feelings of hopelessness. The person's burden becomes even heavier and he is likely to become more pessimistic and weakened.

Inspire and encourage. Show people how much they will gain by increasing their hope to Hashem. Collect stories of how people's lives have been improved even after it seemed close to impossible for things to get better. Collect stories of people who faced near disasters, and at the very last moment were rescued.

This verse can serve as a powerful focus of meditation. Keep repeating it over and over again, slowly and repeatedly. You might want to chant it with your own spontaneous tune. As you repeat it, feel the hope-giving message becoming an integral part of the way you view life. A life of hope is a life full of light. Let this light brighten up your future.

"I made it through the darkest days of the Second World War because of the hopeful messages my father gave me, before

the war broke out," a holocaust survivor related. "He told me how his father had told him the importance of frequently repeating verses of **bitachon**, trust in the Almighty. And, when the war began and we knew that we would be facing unknown challenges, my father emphasized the importance of repeating verses of **bitachon**. The easier it would become to give into discouragement and despair, the stronger the need to resist. The early warning signals of pessimism served as a reminder to intensify hope and trust in the Almighty. Our people would not be around today if bleak situations would have caused us to give up. The stronger your hope, when hope does not come easily, the more you strengthen this attribute, my father told me.

"I call it, 'The power of **Kavei'** (the Hebrew word for hope). This verse (27:14) saved my life, during the war, and it gave me the strength to rebuild my life, after the war."

◆{ **28 / כח** }◆

ט הוֹשִׁיעָה אֶת־עַמֶּךָ וּבָרֵךְ אֶת־נַחֲלָתֶךָ
וּרְעֵם וְנַשְּׂאֵם עַד־הָעוֹלָם:

⁹ **Save Your Nation, and bless Your inheritance;
tend them and elevate them forever.**

This Hebrew verse contains exactly ten words. Because of this, it is frequently used as a tool for counting a *minyan* — ten people are needed to constitute a quorum for prayers. Only when ten are present are certain prayers, such as *kaddish* and *kedushah*, recited.

There is a custom not to count people directly. When only three or four people are present, it's immediately obvious that there are not ten present. But when eight or nine, ten, or eleven are present, not everyone can tell the exact number at a glance. This verse is used to count to ten. There is a sense of celebration when the entire verse is finished, one word for each person. Now the prayers can begin.

Those who use this verse to count, have an opportunity to make the most of the experience. They are blessing the people who are present right now, together with the entire Jewish nation. Add mindfulness to the words that you are saying. This is not a meaningless substitute for numbers; rather, it is an elevating blessing. You are asking Hashem to save, bless and watch over His nation as a shepherd watches his sheep, and to elevate them forever. Isn't this beautiful? As you reflect on the meaning of the blessing, you will gain a greater appreciation for what you are doing, right now. You are not merely blessing a single individual, or only the people who are present, when you are counting; you are blessing an entire nation.

Even if you are not able to complete the entire verse because a person or two is missing for the full count of ten, you have still expressed a powerful blessing. Let the joy of reciting it, outweigh the disappointment that you do not yet have ten people present. And when the tenth man joins the group, your joy is multiplied. Prayers can start and the blessing is complete.

Look for more opportunities to recite this verse's blessing. When setting a table for family or guests, you can count the places with this verse. When counting how many people arrived for a meeting, you can recite this verse. The same holds true for counting students or attendees of a lecture. Reciting the entire verse 3 or 4 times will show you when you reached the thirty or forty mark. You elevate yourself as you bless others and you are included in the blessing.

*Hearing about the importance of mindfulness when reciting the blessing of this verse, I became aware of how often I said these words without **kavanah** (concentration). I made a resolution that, before using this verse for counting, I would say to myself, "Right now I am about to bless the entire Jewish nation." This had a surprising effect on me. I realized that there were often people present who irritated me, and I did not have the most pleasant thoughts when I looked at them. Now I realized that I was blessing them — that the Almighty should take good care of them. This gave me an entirely different perspective towards the people whom I was* *counting. It upgraded my consciousness that I truly cared about the welfare of these people. These individuals were part of the entire nation that I was asking the Almighty to save, bless, and elevate."*

⊰{ **29 / כט** }⊱

יא [**יהוה** עֹז לְעַמּוֹ יִתֵּן] **יהוה** יְבָרֵךְ אֶת־עַמּוֹ בַשָּׁלוֹם:

¹¹ HASHEM **will bless His people with peace.**

The Talmud (*Megillah* 18a) states in reference to this verse, "The blessing of the Almighty is peace."

The ultimate blessing for our people is peace. War causes death, pain, destruction, grief, anguish, despair, depression, heartache, and any other term expressing the worst feelings human beings can have. Those who have been witness to the aftermath of terrorist attacks, can attest to their unspeakable horror and tragedy.

When people are involved in family quarrels, ugly arguments between two erstwhile friends, vicious disputes, and many forms of disagreements that have gotten out of hand, the scene may not be as gruesome as an actual battlefield, but the emotional pain can be just as deep and long-lasting.

"The blessing of the Almighty is peace." The question to ask ourselves is, "What can I personally do for the sake of peace?" The first step to creating peace, is in the way we talk to others. The contents of what we say and the tone of voice in which we say it, will be key factors in whether a disagreement or displeasure is expressed with mutual respect or the lack thereof.

When we become frustrated, upset, or angry, we might be likely to insult someone or put him down, in some way. Our tone of voice, an expression of our frustration and anger, creates negative energy. The recipient of that distressful energy, might easily create an emotional boomerang. Each exchange of negative energy adds fuel to the fire of negativity. There is an escalation in the detrimental way that each party speaks to the other and this results in mutually distressful arguments, quarrels, and fights.

"The blessing of the Almighty is peace." Realizing this, we will make peace a high priority. We will be fully committed to speaking in ways that are conducive to peace. When someone speaks to us with respect and positive regard, this is easy. When we are pleased with what someone says, this is easy. When someone goes out of his way to help us in a significant way, this is very easy. However, it is challenging when someone does something that we did not like. It is even more difficult when someone not only does something that we did not like, but also speaks to us in a negative, condescending, sarcastic tone of voice, insulting us.

"The value of the good we do is increased, when it is difficult." How can we prepare for a difficulty? Make a clear picture in your mind about how you can speak and act, in ways that are conducive to peace. Visualize yourself being respectful and dignified in the face of challenges. Just as professional actors practice their lines over and over again, we too might find ourselves in situations that we need to prepare for, with a similar amount of time and effort.

You can prepare for a challenging encounter with a tape recorder and a mirror. Use the mirror to receive feedback about the potential effects of your facial expressions, on the other person. Tape what you would like to say, then listen to it from the perspective of the person to whom you will be speaking. Ask yourself, "How do I think this person will respond, if I speak this way?" Keep upgrading your presentation, until you feel confident that what you will say and how you will say it, will be conducive to peace. Practice over and over again. Practice until speaking in a peaceful way, becomes your second nature.

Professional actors have professional coaches. In extremely difficult situations, you would be wise to consult and practice with an expert on positive, effective communication. Peace is worth it.

"The blessing of the Almighty is peace." Be sure not to carelessly say something that could cause or maintain a quarrel between two people.

"The blessing of the Almighty is peace." Whenever you realize that there is a quarrel between two people or two groups, think whether you could possibly say or do something that might lessen the tension and bring about peace. Be careful — some well-meaning people have been known to make things worse! However, if you can make peace, you will be following in the footsteps of Aharon, the first High Priest.

"The blessing of the Almighty is peace." Therefore, allow yourself to experience joy every time you go out of your way or make a sacrifice, for peace. The long-term benefits of peace are so numerous and all-encompassing that it is considered the blessing of the Almighty.

> *I had an opportunity to observe a rabbi who was an expert at making peace between people, in a situation that seemed almost impossible to resolve.*
>
> *"What is your secret?" I asked him.*
>
> *"I don't have any secrets," he replied. "But I do have an approach, that can be learned with practice.*
>
> *"There are many ways to look at each situation. When two people are involved in a quarrel — and a bitter one, at that — one thing is certain: they are viewing the situation differently. Each one sees what is going on, from his own perspective. Each one thinks that his position is correct and right. Each one thinks that the other's position is wrong. Each one feels justified for speaking the way he does, and each one feels that the other person is making a mistake. The other one is speaking rudely and disrespectfully. The other one is stubborn. The other one is the cause of the fight.*
>
> *"My goal is to teach both parties to see the situation from more than one perspective. Each one needs to enter the mind of the other person, for a while. He does not need to agree with the other one, but he does need to review what was said and done from that person's perspective. After that, he needs to see the situation from the perspective of an outside observer. Each outside observer might also look at it differently, so I have each one imagine an outside observer who would agree with the other person, and an outside observer who would agree with him.*
>
> *"Depending on with whom I'm talking, I make suggestions as to the identities and approaches of various role models. One favorite is looking at the situation from the perspective of Rabbi Levi Yitzchak of Berditchev, who was famous for his*

love of people, and his mastery of judging people favorably. How would he view this situation? What would he say to each person? What would he suggest I say and do?

"At times, I will tell the people involved to view the situation from the perspective of a professional humorist. What would he find funny, ironic, comical, and ludicrous about the way both people are speaking and acting? I am careful to be sensitive to the hurt feelings and dignity of each person involved, but when the participants themselves are open to this, they often acknowledge that the way they are handling this challenge is a bit silly.

"I often ask them to imagine that they would be given a gigantic fortune of money, if they would make peace. From this perspective, what would they be willing to say and do for peace?

"The ultimate point of view I ask them to integrate is to see the situation from Hashem's perspective. Hashem is their loving Father. How would He want them to speak and act? Hashem sees infinitely and eternally. How would they see what they were saying and doing from the entire scheme of the universe and their own purpose in life?

⊰{ **34 / לד** }⊱

א לְדָוִד בְּשַׁנּוֹתוֹ אֶת־טַעְמוֹ לִפְנֵי אֲבִימֶלֶךְ וַיְגָרְשֵׁהוּ וַיֵּלַךְ׃

¹ By David, when he disguised his sanity before Abimelech, who drove him out, and he left.

King Saul viewed David as a threat to him, and David had to escape. David lived among the Philistines and for a while, he was safe there. Then his life was endangered. David acted as if he were mentally imbalanced. and seeing this, King Abimelech assumed that he was crazy. Instead of harming him, he merely sent David away.

This was a narrow escape, and David expressed his depth of gratitude to Hashem. Previously, David had wondered about the purpose of insanity, but then he saw how he could imitate this pattern, in order to save his life.

"A wise person learns from everyone" (*Pirkei Avos* 4:1). Every person who comes your way may have something to teach you. You can never know how someone's pattern might be exactly what you will need to model at some time in the future. The entire world is a Divinely-sent institution of education for you. Each words and actions pattern you see may come in handy some day. You might find yourself in situations and circumstances that you would never have thought possible. What you have learned from another person, might even save your life.

When you actually use a pattern that you have once seen, express your gratitude to Hashem for His having sent it to you.

On the verse, "King Solomon became wiser than every other person," the *Midrash* states: even wiser than idiots. The question is obvious. To say that King Solomon was wiser than other wise people would be great praise, but what is the praise of being wiser than idiots?

R' Elchonon Wasserman explained: King Solomon became wise from learning from everyone — even from idiots. The verse is not telling us that he was wiser than idiots. Rather, it is telling us that every single person was a source of wisdom to him; even someone whom most people would view as being unable to teach him anything.

Whenever Hashem sends a pattern of human behavior that could be beneficial for you in some way, learn from it. (Of course, you need wisdom to know when to apply it and when not to.) Realize that as soon as you see it, it is stored in the magnificent brain that you carry with you wherever you go. Be grateful for your brain in general, and this specific pattern in particular.

Someone who was meticulously careful not to speak against others and not to listen to others speaking even slight lashon hara (derogatory speech) once told me that he used King David as a model of what to do in challenging situations. When he was a teenager, if he was around people who began to speak against others, he would make strange, even weird, faces. His friends would laugh at his crazy-looking antics.

The he would begin to speak about another subject. The would-be lashon hara *speaker was distracted, and the others would be saved from hearing the* lashon hara.

I once asked him about how he picked up this pattern.

"When I was a child, someone in my neighborhood involuntarily made these faces. I was fascinated by this and I tried to imitate it. I looked in a mirror and found it funny. I felt that one day I would be able to utilize this, positively and I did find a number of positive uses. When I see someone I know who gets angry over some triviality, I sometimes make these faces and he laughs and lets go of his anger."

ט טַעֲמוּ וּרְאוּ כִּי־טוֹב יהוה אַשְׁרֵי הַגֶּבֶר יֶחֱסֶה־בּוֹ:

⁹ **Contemplate and see that Hashem is good, praiseworthy is the man who takes refuge in Him.**

The first word in our verse is *taamu,* literally meaning "taste." This refers to thinking deeply. The sense of taste seems to us more real than merely seeing something. When we see something, the object is some distance away from us. It is external to us. The light reflecting from that object goes through our eyes to our brains. Our consciousness of that object then registers on our mind.

When we taste food, however, we take the object that started outside of us and place it inside. We chew it and swallow it. It goes to our digestive system and from there, the nutrients travel through our circulatory system to nurture all the cells in our body. The food that was outside is not only inside us, but actually becomes us. It is integrated into our very being.

This is a metaphor for understanding the goodness of Hashem. When we gain a deep understanding of the power and might of Hashem and how He has created us and our entire world, we experience the goodness of Hashem in a way that could be considered "tasting." It becomes an integral part of who we are.

This profound level of understanding enables us to see Hashem's good. That is the second word in our verse, *u'reu*, and see. This sight is how you will now view all the gifts that Hashem bestows upon you and the entire world.

As R' Moshe Chaim Luzzatto stated in *Derech Hashem* (Part 1; ch. 2): The purpose in Hashem's creating the world was His will to bestow from His good onto others.

Hashem is the ultimate good and the source of all good. We humans connect with Hashem and His goodness by emulating Him.

The good that we do in our lives is the highest form of greatness that a human being can reach. There are many people who enjoy watching professional sports events. Why? Because they hope to identify with the glory of the winners. The victories of an individual or a sports team for which they are rooting, gives them a feeling of self-esteem. "We won. Therefore I, too, am great." But sports are an artificial illusion, invented for entertainment. The power of this use of thought and imagination can be seen by the elation (in victory) and deflation (in defeat) of those who arbitrarily connect with this virtual reality.

Speaking and acting with kindness connects you to true and authentic greatness. You are connecting with the Creator, the source of all goodness.

This verse ends with the words *ashrei hagever yecheseh bo*. The standard translation is, "praiseworthy is the man who takes refuge in Him." With the thought expressed above, we can define *yechese* as being related to the word *yichus*. Having *yichus* means that one has illustrious ancestors of whom one is proud. Having *yichus* with Hashem means that we act in the kind and compassionate ways of Hashem's attributes, because we realize our deep connection with Him and His ways. Thinking, speaking, and acting this ways makes a person praiseworthy.

Imagine how the entire world would be, if every human being would live with this profound understanding of true greatness. We would all live in a most heavenly atmosphere, here on earth. Every encounter with another person would be a source of giving and receiving "good" — kindness in thought, word, and action. Just entering the presence of another person, would be a source of good feeling. The goodness radiated by everyone on the planet would elicit warm and comfortable feelings. There would be a sense of harmony. This utopia is for the future, but each and every day, we can do our own part in speaking and acting in ways that add to the total goodness on earth.

> " 'See the goodness of Hashem' ; this is what I was told by someone whom I consulted for help with the emotional suffering I was experiencing. I was overwhelmed with feelings of sadness and hopelessness. Nothing seemed to be going right for me. I had just lost my job. I had debts that needed to be paid. I felt lonely and lost. The stress I was experiencing would not let me fall asleep. My mind was in turmoil. The lack of sleep plus the worrying I was consumed with because of my problems, made my life one moment of torture after another.
>
> "I was shocked that someone could say this to me, the way I was feeling. The person to whom I was speaking, had listened carefully to what I had told him. I could see from his facial expressions that he had understood what I was saying. He knew how negatively I was seeing everything in my life. How could I possibly see the goodness of Hashem? This seemed unrealistic for me.
>
> "But even though the words he said didn't seem to be one bit relevant to me, I did feel much better by unloading what was on my mind. I felt understood while I was speaking. His sincere compassion seemed to lighten my heavy load. I noticed that I was breathing better now and the tension in my muscles relaxed a bit.
>
> " 'How could he say this to me now?' I thought to myself.
>
> "Almost as if he could read my mind, he said to me, 'I know that if I were feeling the way you were, what I have told you would seem totally off the mark. But please try out what I am telling you. I have seen this one thought, work miracles for people.'
>
> " 'No matter how awful we feel, we are always only one thought away from a feeling of well-being. That one thought is that Hashem is good. When you view life with this attitude, you see a totally different world. When you are feeling discouraged and hopeless, you focus only on thoughts that

reinforce these pessimistic feelings. As soon as you allow yourself to consider the thought that Hashem is good, you start to see all the good in your life. You don't need a lecture from me on this. All you need is to experience this yourself. Come back in a few days and we'll discuss how your experiment went.'

"I knew that he knew what he was talking about. So even though I was highly skeptical about how this would work for me, I resolved to keep repeating this thought to myself, – 'Hashem is good.'

"After a complete day of thinking this way, I was amazed. I felt better than I had in a very long time. I started noticing all the good in my life and all that there is to be grateful for, all around me. I began to smile to people and they smiled back. I had plenty of food and I had nice clothes to wear. I had taken all of this, for granted. I noticed every little kind thing that anyone said to me or did for me. Each time, I said, 'Do you know what, Hashem really is good to me.'

"I started doing trivial kind things for others. Most people smiled and thanked me. Each time I felt better and better. I noticed that enjoyable thoughts were on my mind, and I became more and more optimistic.

"When I went to sleep, I was exhausted from all the recent distress, but I was much calmer. My dreams were dreams of hope, before I fell asleep and while I was sleeping.

"I woke up the next morning with heartfelt gratitude for being alive. And throughout the day, I kept repeating, 'Hashem is good.' The day went so much better and I decided that I felt good enough to look for a job. I asked some people for suggestions and everyone I asked tried to be helpful. 'Hashem is good,' was the uppermost thought in my mind. It gave a positive color to everything else that I thought about that day.

"The next day I called up the person who had advised me to repeat these words. 'I can't thank you enough. You have transformed me.' I told him.

" 'You've made my day,' was his first comment. I could see how happy he was to hear how much happier I was. 'What can I do to remember to keep this up?' I asked him.

" 'Do the same that I did,' he told me. 'Whenever you can, suggest this to others, and this will keep the thought alive in your consciousness. When you get positive feedback from those who have remembered to keep this thought in their mind, it will be an added incentive to remember to keep it up.'"

"He couldn't see the great big smile on my face through the telephone, but I am certain it came through in my voice. Since I have heard this, I have passed it on to others and my life has taken on a completely new vitality and spirituality."

יג מִי־הָאִישׁ הֶחָפֵץ חַיִּים אֹהֵב יָמִים לִרְאוֹת טוֹב:
יד נְצֹר לְשׁוֹנְךָ מֵרָע וּשְׂפָתֶיךָ מִדַּבֵּר מִרְמָה:

¹³ **Who is the person who wants life, loves days to see the good.**
¹⁴ **Guard your tongue from evil and your lips from speaking deceit.**

---

ere King David gives us a formula for long life. What can we do spiritually that will fill our days with good? We need to be careful with what we say. Refrain from speaking *lashon hora*, speaking negatively against others. Refrain from speaking *ona'as devarim*, that is, words that cause pain to someone else.

The verse does not tell us only, not to speak against others or cause others suffering, with our words. Rather, the verse tells us, "Guard your tongue." Just as we watch and guard our money and possessions, we need to guard our mouths. The words we say can be precious, and can do much good, but, just as a person who owns a dangerous weapon needs to guard it to prevent accidental harm and damage, so too we need to watch what we say. Otherwise, one might carelessly cause others immeasurable pain and suffering.

What does it mean to guard what we say? It means to think first. As someone new to this concept once asked me incredulously, "Does this mean that we are supposed to think before we speak?" Yes, that's exactly what this means. If a person knows that each word he says in a given encounter will affect his entire life, he will think before he speaks, he will think while he speaks, and he will think after he speaks — to see if he needs to correct anything.

Doesn't this become a burden? Not when we fulfill this *mitzvah* with joy. Be grateful for the understanding and realization that, what you say is valuable and important and makes a difference. Be grateful that each time you speak, you have an opportunity to fulfill Hashem's commandments. And be grateful for the elevation of your character and your soul.

These are the verses that the saintly Chofetz Chaim would frequently quote and elaborate on. R' Yisroel Meir Hacohen of Radin wrote the classic work on the Torah laws relating to proper speech. He wrote his first book anonymously. And the title was taken from this verse. *"Chofetz Chaim"* means who wants life. Once it became known that he was the author of this book, everyone called Rav Yisroel Meir "the Chofetz Chaim." His life was a living example of someone who is careful with what he says — and he lived until the age of 94! By observing verse 14, he merited the blessing of verse 13. May we all follow in his footsteps. This is a non-competitive goal toward which everyone can strive.

I heard many times from R' Chaim Shmuelevitz, the late Rosh Yeshiva of Mir in Jerusalem, "The commandment to refrain from speaking negatively against others, does not start with what we say when we speak. Rather, it starts with what we think about, when we think about another person."

The Torah obligation starts with our thoughts. When your main focus is on the wrongs that people do, on their faults and limitations, on their weaknesses and failures, you will end up saying negative things about them. When, however, you master the ability to see what is good about other people, their virtues and positive attributes, their strengths and accomplishments, then you will speak positively about them. And knowing that they have many positive qualities and have done much good, you will find it easier to refrain from violating the Torah prohibition against *lashon hora*, evil speech.

The classic *mussar* work, *Chovos Halevavos* (Duties of the Heart), tells the story of a teacher who was walking with his students when they passed a dead dog. One of the students commented, "*Oy,* what an awful smell." The teacher gently pointed out, "Look at the beautiful white teeth."

There isn't any violation of Torah law to speak against a dead dog, but he wanted to teach his students a lesson. Even when passing a dead dog, train your mind to look for something positive. When you master this habit, your entire life will be better. Your inner mind will apply this principle of seeing the good in all areas. Of course, we need balance. We need to protect ourselves and others. We need to differentiate between what is positive and what is negative. At the same time, however, we need to make seeing the good and the positive, our initial reaction.

There is a question that some people ask, when they think about guarding one's tongue: "If one doesn't speak *lashon hora,* what else will one talk about?" Even a little thought will provide an answer. We live in such an amazing and fascinating world. Speak about the greatness of the Creator and how we can live a joyful elevated life. Speak about Torah and *mitzvos.* Speak about acts of kindness and the skills that will help you help more people. This will always give you positive things to talk about. When you develop this habitual way of thinking and speaking, the challenge of guarding your tongue will become much easier. This will shed much light on your entire life.

*Over the years I've spoken to many people who made resolutions to be careful about not speaking **lashon hora.** I've often asked people, "How has this affected your life?" Here are some of the responses:*

- *"I always considered myself a kind and caring person. I wouldn't want to cause anyone harm or damage. When I started studying the laws of careful speech, I was shocked. I didn't realize how often I would repeat 'innocent' pieces of negative gossip. I saw that it was true that I didn't want to hurt anyone. But I was very sociable. It seemed to me that part of being sociable was sharing the bits and pieces of gossip, that others told me. I had to make a strong effort to refrain from this habit. Once I stopped, I was even more aware that I had caused harm and embarrassment to people. At first, I felt devastated. My positive self-image was shaken, and I understood* that the painful feelings I felt about my self-esteem being lowered, was exactly what I had caused to others. I was strongly committed to being consisten with the self-image I had wanted of being kind and caring."

- "Even before studying the laws of **lashon hora,** I usually didn't speak negatively against others. However, whenever I was upset or irritated with someone, I would tell everyone I knew about how badly this person had acted. Though there wasn't any practical benefit, it was just my way of getting even. I would say to myself, 'I have to teach them a lesson.' To be honest, I wasn't teaching anyone a lesson — I was just taking revenge. Now I have learned to speak directly to the person with whom I am upset, and I try to work things out in a way that is mutually respectful."

- "For me the challenge was not refraining from speaking against others — I did not find that very difficult. However, I was naturally curious and I always wanted to be "in the know." This led to my hearing a lot of negative things about others. Eventually, I made it a higher priority to avoid listening to **lashon hora,** than to find out about everything that aroused my curiosity. The pleasure of self-mastery made me feel far better than the pleasure of hearing the negative about others."

- "What motivated me to be careful about speaking **lashon hora** was a new person that I had met, only a couple of months before. I respected him right away and enjoyed talking to him. He was highly intelligent and insightful, and I always gained a lot from our conversations. After a while, I noticed that he was avoiding me. At first, I was not certain if he did this on purpose, but as time went on, I felt sure that it was. I asked him about this. 'Did I do anything to offend you?' I asked him. 'Yes,' he answered straightforwardly. 'I'm new in this area and I appreciated our conversations, but you spoke against other people. I noticed that, when I met those people, I felt much more positive about them than the negative way you spoke about them. Your negativity was like a *thought virus that I had to overcome. In addition, I figured that if you speak against others to me, it is just a matter of time before you will be speaking against me to others. That's not the pattern I want in a friend.'*

"I thought it over and a few days later I approached him and thanked him. 'What you told me was painful, but true. I do not want to lose your friendship and respect. I make a resolution that I will study the laws of guarding one's speech, and follow through on what I learn.'"

• *"After I studied the Chofetz Chaim's books on watching what one says, I wanted to apply what I learned. I was concerned, however, that if I would tell others who tried to tell me* lashon hora *that I didn't want to hear it, they would make fun of me. I am not so perfect and I felt that they would point out my faults, if they felt that I was acting on a higher spiritual level than I was actually on. Nevertheless, I told myself that I would be careful with what I said and heard, even if I have to face ridicule. To my pleasant surprise, nobody reacted as strongly as I was worried they might. A few people told me that they respect my commitment, and someone later came over to me and told me that he is grateful to me. He had also felt that he should be more careful, but he didn't want to be the only one to do so. My being a pioneer among our friends made it easier for him to follow my example."*

טו **סוּר מֵרָע וַעֲשֵׂה־טוֹב**

15 **Turn from bad , and do good.**

These four Hebrew words, *"Sur meira, va'asei tov,"* contain an all-inclusive formula for living life. In English, this can be summarized in five words, "Don't do bad; do good." The benefit of a short formula is that it can be easily repeated over and over again, and thus serves as a comprehensive guide.

The previous verse (14) tells us to guard our tongue from evil, and this verse adds to it. Not only should we not speak evil against others, but we should do good. The first step is, to refrain from speaking against others and to refrain from causing them pain with our words. The next step is, to utilize our power of speech, for good. We should use our words for kindness and compassion: to help others in as many ways as we can, to encourage, to alleviate distress, to comfort and console, to give beneficial suggestions and advice, and to share helpful knowledge and information.

The major choices that we constantly select are in three areas: our thoughts, our words, and our actions. Our thoughts lead to our words and our actions. Our thoughts either elevate us or lower us. Our thoughts might be on what is wrong with people and with situations, or our thoughts can be on what we can do to improve ourselves, others, and situations. If you find yourself automatically thinking thoughts that are counterproductive or negative, let the words of this verse pop up in your mind; "Turn from bad; do good"

When you are upset, irritated, frustrated, or angry, you might be tempted to say things that will be detrimental to yourself or distressful to others. Hear the verse, "Turn from bad, do good."

You might be tempted to take some actions that are clearly wrong. At times, the actions that you impulsively would like to do might not be absolutely wrong, but they certainly are not right. Hear the verse, "Turn from bad; do good." Don't just refrain from doing things that are wrong; put all your efforts into doing good.

Think of a specific area of your life that is a challenge for you. What do you need to refrain from, in that area? And what positive things can you do, instead? As you think about that area right now, repeat the verse, "Turn from bad; do good," over and over again. When you do this a sufficient amount of times, your brain will automatically remind you of this verse in connection with that area, and then think about the good you can do. Follow through as soon as possible.

> *I recently paid a shiva call at the house of someone from my neighborhood, whose father had just passed away at the age of 80. The son, a man in his mid-fifties related that his father used to live in Lodz, Poland, before the second World War, and was sent to a concentration camp right after the Nazis captured Poland in the beginning of the war. He survived 12 concentration camps in five years, though he almost died a*

number of times. Once, in Auschwitz, he was so emaciated and so weak, that his heart stopped. A Nazi thought that he had died, and brutally picked up his body to throw him onto a wagon to be taken to the crematorium — but this Nazi unwittingly saved his life. The force that this brutal beast used to throw him down, was so strong, that his heart started working again.

I asked the son, "Did your father tell you what gave him the inner strength, to endure such a long ordeal?"

"About six months before the war broke out, my father went to the Gerrer Rebbe, R' Avraham Mordechai Alter, and asked for a blessing. 'Always be a Jew,' the Rebbe, to whom he was related, told him. He wondered about this blessing, but, later on, this became clearer.

"When my father was marching with fellow concentration camp inmates in the cold of the winter, tired from lack of sleep and the exhaustion of hard labor, and starving from lack of food and drink, he would think to himself, 'Let me compare myself with my captors. They are wealthy, they have captured the wealth of other countries, and yet, are as evil as a human being could possibly become. They are cruel and lack even a minimum of kindness. We, on the other hand, do not do anything wrong. We not only do not harm anyone, but the whole day we keep looking for opportunities to help everyone we can. We speak words of encouragement to each other, and help one another in whatever way we can, even with our limited resources'. The thoughts of keeping away from doing wrong, and doing as much good as possible, were so powerful that they sustained him for five years, in the worst conditions possible."

טו בַּקֵּשׁ שָׁלוֹם וְרָדְפֵהוּ:

15 Seek peace and pursue it

Peace is one of the most beautiful words that there is. A person with inner peace has inner harmony. When our entire being is in harmony, we speak and act in ways that enable us to achieve. On the other hand, inner conflict creates stress and tension. We try to make and reach goals, but we may not be consistent. We might start and stop, not follow through and then become easily distracted while claiming to want to reach our goals. Inner peace, however, is a prerequisite for reaching our optimal level.

The same applies to peace with others. When we interact peacefully, we bring out the best in ourselves and the best in the other person. Quarrels cause much pain and suffering to all those involved. During an angry quarrel, two, otherwise sensible and kind individuals, can say and do things that contrast totally with their usual character.

People can have diverse opinions. They can have different personalities. They can have different goals and objectives. Even so, they can choose to interact in peaceful ways, and discuss their differences with mutual respect. At times they will work out solutions to their mutal satisfaction, and at times they will not. Nevertheless, they can be calm, and think clearly about the wisest course to take.

People who tend to quarrel, can get involved in loud and aggressive fights over trivial matters. Nothing is too small and anything may be taken as a personal affront. Everything is a matter of principle that one needs to shout, scream, and yell about, to show that the matter is important to them. They create problems for themselves and for those with whom they interact.

Tehillim tells us to constantly seek peace. As Hillel states in *Pirkei Avos* (1:12), "Love peace and pursue peace." Make peace a high priority. When peace becomes an important goal for you, many things which previously would cause quarrels, become much less important.

Why is peace so important? You are a child of Hashem and so are the people with whom you might quarrel. Every parent wants their children to get along with one another. From this perspective, you will find it easier to speak in ways that are conducive to peace. The person with whom you might quarrel might not, at this moment, seem like someone you respect. However, when you focus on the fact that He is precious to your Father and King, you have a much more expansive view of who he is.

Expressing views that differ, is acceptable. Throughout Torah literature Sages disagree with each other, commentators have different interpretations, but a deep sense of mutual respect is present at all times.

Peaceful communication creates peaceful relationships. This means that your tone of voice, as well as the choice of words, sound peaceful. Messages that linguistically appear only slightly different, could be worlds apart. One is said in an angry tone of voice with words that are sarcastic, attacking, and condescending, while the other is said in a pleasant tone of voice with objective words that convey ideas, without eliciting negative responses.

Pursuing peace means that, at times, we will have to go out of our way for peace. We might need to apologize. Some people tend to view apologies as a sign of weakness. While, in truth, an apology is a manifestation of inner strength.

Pursuing peace means that we might have to strive for peace over and over again. How many times is sufficient? Until we achieve the goal of peace; real peace is worth it.

> Someone who used to argue a lot with his wife, told me that they went to an expert on **Shalom Bayis** (domestic harmony). He reported that he has a first-hand appreciation of the difference between peace in the home and the opposite.
>
> "My wife and I were ready to tell him, in great detail, about the many fights and quarrels that we experienced. Each one wanted to blame the other. If the other would be more 'normal,' we wouldn't be arguing so much."
>
> "The Rabbi listened carefully, to get a picture of what the present situation was like. Then he told us that, when a professional wants to see a sample of blood, it is not necesary to take a large amount. Even a tiny drop is sufficient, to see what is right and what is wrong. He told us that, if we felt a need to relive all our arguments, it could take many days, even weeks, of counterproductive arguments. There would be arguments about the arguments. More provocative statements would be made, and the strife level would rise.
>
> " 'What is your real goal?" he asked us. "Is it to win arguments, or to have a harmonious, joyful marriage?'
>
> "We both responded that, of course, our real goal was to have harmony in our home and to experience an inner happiness.

" 'Arguments will cause disharmony and can even make your home dysfunctional. Everyone loses out.'

"We had to agree with this. It was definitely true in our case.

" 'When two marriage partners speak with mutual respect in a calm, pleasant tone of voice, you can speak about your disagreements, and you don't have to be disagreeable. You won't lose anything. The other way, you both suffered. On a scale of 1 to 10, with 10 being a high level of importance, how important is it, to have a serene atmosphere in your home?'

"We both agreed that this was a 10 for us.

" 'And think about some of the specific quarrels you have gotten into lately — how important in your lives were they on a scale of 1 to 10? I am certain that, once you got into the habit of quarreling, you argued vehemently about matters that were only 1, 2, or 3 on the scale of making a major difference in your lives. Keep thinking about this. Always remember that interpersonal peace is a 10, and then you will be able to discuss your differences much more calmly.'

This worked 10 on a scale of 10.

⁕{ 35 / לה }⁕

כח וּלְשׁוֹנִי תֶּהְגֶּה צִדְקֶךָ כָּל־הַיּוֹם תְּהִלָּתֶךָ׃

²⁸ **And my tongue will express Your charity. Your praise all day long.**

Metzudas David explains that the charity that King David was referring to, was the kindness and charity that Hashem bestowed on him. Out of gratitude and appreciation for this, King David would praise Hashem all day long.

Let us emulate King David. Imagine what your life would be like, if you were to gain an immense appreciation for the personal kindnesses that Hashem constantly does for you. Imagine what a day would be like, if it were full of praise of Hashem.

Fulfillment of this one verse, would guarantee a person a life of happiness and gratitude — an elevated and spiritual life.

Some people might be afraid to try to follow through on this: "How can I keep this up?" they are likely to say to themselves. "What if I get tired of telling Hashem how appreciative I am? What if it gets too difficult for me to do this, all the time?"

Taking on too much at one time, can be overwhelming, and when we feel overwhelmed, we find it too difficult to do even a relatively small amount. There is an old riddle, "How does one eat an entire cow?" (Some people ask the question about an elephant. But even in a riddle, let's choose a kosher animal.) And the answer is: one bite at a time. And this is how we go on any long journey: one step at a time.

To jump in and immediately accept upon oneself to reflect on Hashem's kindnesses to us, and therefore praise Him the entire day, each and every day, might be taking too large a bite for someone not used to doing this. So let's start with a day at a time, praising Hashem in our own way, one minute each hour. This is not quite the entire day, but it is an important start.

People who tend to be negative thinkers and negative speakers, keep their focus on what is wrong. They find it easy to go through an entire day, enumerating a lengthy list of complaints. And someone who is an expert at this, will be willing to repeat the same complaints many times in a day. They will repeat the same and/or similar complaints the next day and the day after that. Let us learn from them how to praise Hashem for His kindnesses. Let the negativity of others be a springboard for you to remember how to praise Hashem for what you appreciate.

If you personally find yourself complaining about things that you cannot take action to correct, let this serve as a reminder to recall the good things in your life for which you can be grateful.

> *"I grew up being a complainer. I would find it easy to whine on and on about what I did not like. I used to feel sad and depressed. I could remember more miserable days than joyful ones. I spoke to many people about what I could do to become happier but, looking back, I realize that my goal was not really to change my pattern, but to justify my lack of happiness.*
>
> *"I spoke to a rabbi who suggested that I try, for an entire day, to praise Hashem for all the good that He has done for*

me. 'You can't be serious,' I complained to him. 'There are so
many things in my life that have already gone wrong, that
are going wrong right now, and are likely to go wrong in the
future.' He did not dispute these facts but he did raise a
challenge.

" 'What has your emotional quality of life been, with the
pattern you have already mastered?' he asked me. I had
to acknowledge that I was usually quite sad and miserable.
'I realize that what I am asking you to do, will be difficult,
but I am positive that if you make an effort for an entire
day, you will be able to do this exercise. Imagine if someone paid you a fortune of money to do this for one day —
you would somehow find the inner strength and ability to do
this. Throughout the day you will find yourself greatly
challenged, so do not aim for perfection. However, do direct
your thoughts and your words to focus on praises of
Hashem.'

"That day was a changing point in my life. It was harder
than I thought it would be, but the difference in the emotional and spiritual quality of that day will forever remain
with me. From that day on, my life was never the same. I
realized, on an experiential level, that the sadness that was an
integral part of me, came not from the external situations, but
from my own thoughts and words. I am still far from perfect
and I need to keep working on myself, but thoughts and
words of praise to Hashem have given me a happy, spiritual
life."

⊰{ **41 / מא** }⊱

בְּ אַשְׁרֵי מַשְׂכִּיל אֶל־דָּל בְּיוֹם רָעָה יְמַלְּטֵהוּ יְהֹוָה:

**² Praiseworthy is the one who contemplates the
needy, on the day of evil Hashem will deliver him.**

Metzudas David explains that this verse refers to someone
who gives charity to a poor person, in a clever way. The
needy person might feel embarrassed to take charity,

and therefore it is praiseworthy to give the money in a way that the recipient feels comfortable about taking it.

This explanation is based on the Talmud Yerushalmi's (*Yerushalmi Peah 8:8)* interpretation of our verse. The Talmud praises R' Yonah for using subterfuge when giving money to someone from a dignified family who, due to a setback, had lost all his money. He would approach the person and say to him, "I heard that there is an inheritance that is coming to you. I have some extra money now. Please take it and when you happen to get money in the future, you can pay me back."

He took the initiative to approach the other person, and he was willing to make up a story, in order to save that person from feelings of embarrassment. In such an instance, it was not considered wrong to say something that wasn't true. Rather, it was for this person's benefit. We see here a situation where two Torah values seem to conflict: the value of being truthful, versus the value of helping another person and at the same time making certain not to cause distress, in the process. The value of doing an act of kindness while distorting the facts to protect someone from shame, takes precedence.

Some people say things that cause embarrassment to another person, and when confronted about it, they are likely to say, "But it's the truth, and therefore I had a right to say it!" The severity of causing another person the emotional pain of embarrassment is so strong that, even when your action is for his benefit, you need to be sensitive to prevent his humiliation. All the more so, we need to be careful not to embarrass someone, just because we are angry or impatient.

Having you ever witnessed someone helping another person in a sensitive way, that was especially designed to protect his feelings? Can you recall an instance when this happened to you, and you were grateful for both the help and the sensitivity?

Right now, think of a way that you can put this beautiful concept into practice. Think of what you can do, to help a person who might be reluctant to accept your help. It might be a matter of financial help, or perhaps someone who is highly self-sufficient, but now overwhelmed and exhausted, could use a hand. Their first reaction — when someone offers to help — is, "Thank you, but I don't need any help." Spend time thinking about what you can say, that would let the person be happy to agree to accept your help. For example, you might want to go shopping for someone who isn't feeling well, but that person would refuse to allow you to do so. You might be able to think of something that you yourself want to buy in that store. Then you can tell that person, "I am going to that store to get something for myself. Would you like something from there? I feel better about carrying more things than just an item or two, since it makes my trip seem more worthwhile." What we see from the Talmud Yerushalmi is that, even if you do not actually buy something for yourself, you have a right to claim that you will, if that is the best way to offer your assistance.

Rashi defines the Hebrew word *dal* as "someone who is ill." This is based on the Talmud (*Nedarim 40a*) that states, "Whoever visits someone who is ill will be saved from the judgment of *Gehinnom* in the afterlife."

When you visit someone who is ill, you could be doing that person a great service — maybe even save that person's life. You can give hope and encouragement or help with practical matters, that they could not do on their own. You might be able to find out that this person needs the type of medical attention that he would not be able to receive on his own, or he might not have realized that he needed to do more than he is doing.

I always remember meeting R' Shimon Schwab at a Torah Umesorah Convention a number of years after my father, of blessed memory, was no longer alive. He told me that, for a long time, he had wanted to share with me his gratitude toward my father. When they were both students in the Mirrer Yeshiva in the city of Mir, he was ill on Yom Kippur. My father went out of his way to visit him on that day, and he would never forget how much that meant to him.

It takes good judgment to visit the sick properly. One needs to know exactly how long to stay, how often to visit, and what to say and not to say. This takes contemplation. Each individual is unique. Some people appreciate many visitors. They like to talk, and it is a release and pleasure for them to be able to speak about their illness with others. Others prefer short visits by a few close friends — they do not want to speak about illness at all, not theirs and not the illnesses of others. Some people appreciate speaking about light topics, while others would prefer speaking about the important issues of life. Some people appreciate humor; others might find attempts to make them laugh, annoying.

One way to find out what a specific person would prefer, is to ask. Do not assume that you can always figure out by yourself what someone would really want, but ask in a way that the other person will feel comfortable enough to be honest with you. Some people who are ill, might not want to hurt your feelings by telling you that they would prefer not to have visitors. At times, you might find out what would be best for this person by consulting a member of his family.

Go out of your way to find people who are ill, who would greatly appreciate your visit. If you cannot visit someone in person, call him up and wish him well, or write and let him know that you are thinking about him and care about his welfare.

> *"Everyone is needy in one way or another," one of the kindest people I've ever met, said to me. He would cite this verse from Tehillim and say that, each day we should think about ways we can help someone. He would help people with encouraging words and with loans. He would help people with advice and by sharing his knowledge. He would help people with his smile and with his actions.*
>
> *Someone once asked him, "Don't you feel that you are being unfair to yourself? You are always thinking about others and constantly doing things to help them. Don't you sometimes resent that you do not have enough time for yourself?"*
>
> *With a big smile, he replied, "I'm always doing things for myself. My biggest pleasure in life is to help others, and since everyone I ever meet is always needy in some way, I consider myself one of the most fortunate people in the world. There is always something I can say or do that is a major source of meaning and pleasure in life."*

⋅≪ 44 / מד ≫⋅

יח כָּל־זֹאת בָּאַתְנוּ וְלֹא שְׁכַחֲנוּךָ וְלֹא־שִׁקַּרְנוּ בִּבְרִיתֶךָ:

¹⁸ All of this [misfortunes] came upon us, yet we have not forgotten You, and we have not been false to Your covenant.

Metzudas David explains, "We have not forgotten to thank You." In this chapter King David describes misfortunes that the Jewish people suffered. Even though they experienced adversity, they didn't forget to be grateful to the Almighty for the positive factors in their lives.

When everything in one's life is proceeding according to one's wishes, it is relatively easy to be grateful to Hashem for the good. When experiencing adversity, however, one's mind tends to focus on the distressful and the positive factors tend to be overlooked. The ideal approach is to train one's mind to constantly focus on gratitude to Hashem. This takes a conscious decision — the spiritual and emotional benefits make the efforts worthwhile.

Did you ever meet someone who was a master at finding things to complain about? Even when he was engaged in a celebration, his mind focused on minor details that were not to his liking — this trivial matter or that tiny facet was not the way he would have wished. Such people complain and they blame.

We can all learn from one aspect of their skill. They can ignore the larger part of the entire picture, and they focus on a smaller portion. The way they do it causes them and others suffering, but this pattern can be wisely applied in reverse: Always keep your major focus on those things for which you can be grateful.

At any given moment, we can only focus on a limited amount of data and at times we forget to focus on the other things. Keeping "everything" in mind at one moment is humanly impossible. The question is always: Right now what do I remember to remember and what do I forget to remember?

The thoughts you have at any given moment, create your reality at that moment. The thoughts you forget to think, do not. Never forget to think of Hashem. Never forget to think of being grateful for all of His kindness to you.

This takes us to the second half of the verse. By being grateful to Hashem at all times, even in times of adversity, we are therefore steadfast in the observance of Torah. We remember that we have an everlasting covenant with Hashem and we staunchly and consistently act, in accordance with that covenant.

> When people who survived the Holocaust came to the late Satmar Rebbe, R' Yoel Teitelbaum, for a blessing, he would say to them, "Having suffered the tortures of our enemies and nevertheless remaining steadfast in Torah observance, elevates you to such a degree that I need to ask you for a blessing."
>
> Once at a shiva call in my neighborhood, someone related that, when he was a few days old, his father approached the Satmar Rebbe and asked him to be the sandek at his newborn's bris milah (circumcision). The Satmar Rebbe was visiting Jerusalem and had a very busy schedule. The man who approached the Satmar Rebbe wasn't chassidic, and not at all a follower of the Satmar Rebbe. His mode of dress showed that he was a simple laborer. To the surprise of everyone, the Rebbe immediately accepted the request. The VIP password was, "I'm a Holocaust survivor and I am Torah-observant."

כג כִּי־עָלֶיךָ הֹרַגְנוּ כָל־הַיּוֹם

23 Because for Your sake we are killed all the time.

The Talmud (Gitin 57b) states that this verse refers to Jews who were willing to give up their lives due to their total dedication to Hashem and His Torah. The Talmud relates the story of a mother, Chanah, and her seven sons. The Emperor commanded them to bow down to an idol, or they would be killed. One by one, each son cited a different verse from the Torah and refused to bow down. After the first six sons were killed, the Emperor told the youngest son that he did not have to actually bow down to the idol to save his life, but rather, the Emperor would throw down his royal signet ring, and the young boy could just bend down to pick it up. He really was only retrieving the ring, but to others it would look like an act of worship. The young boy responded to the Emperor, "You are wasting your time, Emperor; you are wasting your time, Emperor." For emphasis he repeated this statement twice. "You are so concerned about your own honor. How much more so, must we be concerned about the honor of the Holy One, may He be blessed."

After the Emperor ordered him to be killed, and the soldiers were taking him out to follow the evil orders, the young boy's mother said to them, "Let me approach my son and kiss him before you kill him."

The mother approached her son during the last moments of his life, and said to him, "Go to your forefather Abraham, and say to him, 'You were ready to give one son as a sacrifice on the altar, and I have given seven sons as sacrifices on the altar.'"

I heard a number of times from the late Mirrer Rosh Hayeshiva, R' Chaim Shmuelevitz, that this is what she meant: "How could a simple woman like myself reach the level of willingness to sacrifice her seven children, rather than give in to forced idol worship? It is only because of your example. You, our father Abraham, were willing to make the tremendous sacrifice of slaughtering your cherished and beloved son. This planted within the hearts of your descendants such a love for Hashem, that even I, a simple person, had the heroic inner strength to make the ultimate sacrifice that I have just now."

In the Stone edition of the Artscroll *Tanach* there is an explanation of this verse: "When one performs the *mitzvos* in the face of jeers and humiliation that cause one's face to blanch, it is as if one is sacrificing his life for God's commandments" (*R' Yehudah HaChassid*).

Usually there are two fundamental principles that we can assume about people. It is very important for them to be accepted by others, and it is very important for them not to be rejected by others. People are willing to do many difficult things over a long period of time, in order to win the acceptance of others. Moreover, the suffering of rejection can be excruciating. To be considered an outcast is one of the worst fears for many.

A person with a lofty level of love for Hashem considers it highly important to be accepted by Hashem. When he performs a *mitzvah*, he feels such a confidence in the rightness of what he is doing that, no matter how many humans might react unfavorably to what he is doing, he will not be deterred.

This can be compared to an intelligent, educated person who lives among primitive people who have no sense of hygiene or health. They lack an understanding of why he eats what he eats and does what he does, and why he doesn't act the same way they do. They think he is foolish for acting the way he does, and they make fun of him. They constantly point to him with hand motions that convey the message that they consider him abnormal. Will he be impressed by their ignorance? Will he risk his health and his life just because they lack an understanding of the vital importance of his actions? He knows that his entire future depends on his being careful with his health.

Similarly, imagine that a brilliant inventor has just created an amazing new invention. He has spoken to a few experts who do not follow the general crowd of professionals, but are all true geniuses who are known to be consistently objective about weighing the possibilities that something will or will not work. The consensus is that this invention will succeed. The inventor has to invest a lot of time, effort, and money into his invention. In the media he is mocked, and those who think they are funny try to make jokes at his expense. He knows without a doubt that his invention will work. He has conducted test after test and it has worked every time. Will he be dissuaded by the laughter of people who lack his knowledge, wisdom, and experience? As the saying goes, he knows that eventually, he will be laughing all the way to the bank.

When we realize with great clarity the importance of doing *mitzvos* and grasp its eternal value and benefits, we won't allow anyone's negativity to stop us.

More in line with the literal translation of the words of our verse, there is a practice that we see in the Talmud (*Brachos* 61b) that R' Akiva made into a habit. That is, to imagine that one is literally giving up one's life out of love for Hashem, to imagine that someone is threatening to kill us if we do not forsake Torah observance, and instead of giving in out of fear, we strengthen our level of courage and willingly give up our life. Our love for Hashem is greater than the love we have for living. Rabbi Akiva mentally practiced this, throughout his life. This became such an integral part of who he was that, when he was actually tested by the Romans, even though they tortured him to death, during his last minutes he serenely recited the verse *Shema Yisroel*. When his students asked him how he could stay so calm at a moment like this, he replied that his entire life he had prepared himself for this moment.

This is a mental practice, that is highly elevating. When you know that you are willing to give up your life for Hashem and His Torah, you are completly committed to dedicating your life to *living* according to Hashem's will.

> *A number of years ago, there was a young man who had a love of excitement and adventure, and felt that studying in yeshivah was boring. He dropped out of yeshivah, and engaged in activities that were not only inappropriate for a yeshivah student, but could cause him serious legal problems.*
>
> *His parents had been told that pressuring him would only backfire; they had already tried it and had seen that it did not work. They tried to be as patient and gentle as possible, but the situation was deteriorating rapidly and they knew they had to do something drastic, in order to save their son.*
>
> *Someone suggested to them that they should have their son speak to a certain Holocaust survivor, who was known to have repeatedly put his life in danger during the Second World War, in a ghetto and a concentration camp, in order to observe as many mitzvos as he could. He would put on tefillin every day, obtained matzos on Pesach, a lulav and esrog on Succos, and observed Shabbos in ways that caused him to be brutally beaten by sadistic Nazis.*
>
> *The man was modest and never boasted about his experiences, but when he was approached about speaking to this boy, he said that he appreciated the opportunity to have a positive influence on the entire future of someone, through his relating stories of his suffering and courage in order to show his love of Hashem and His Torah.*
>
> *The discussion with this boy went on for over three hours. The boy was visibly shaken from what he heard. He made a*

commitment to his parents that, from then on, he would be strictly mitzvah-observant, even though he didn't have the patience to study the entire day. He would study Torah every day and would regularly attend prayers in the synagogue.

When asked about what the Holocaust survivor had told him, he said that the man shared with him how terrifying it was to defy the Nazis. If they saw someone fulfilling a mitzvah, they would not simply shoot him on the spot. First they would derive pleasure from torturing those who kept the mitzvos. What enabled him to withstand the beatings was that he visualized in his mind that — in the future — if he survived, he would use his experiences to motivate other Jews to renew their commitment to keeping the Torah.

"Don't let the Nazis win, years after they were defeated!" the courageous survivor pleaded with him. "Every **mitzvah** you do from now on, is a victory over the Nazis. If you want excitement in life, now you can have it. Please do me a personal favor and, retroactively, make my suffering meaningful. The more difficult it is for you personally to do a **mitzvah,** the greater the value of the **mitzvah.** I had to overcome fear of death and torture — you need to overcome your dislike of being bored. I realize that your challenge is truly a heavy one, but I know that Hashem gave me the strength to withstand my test. With the merit of my suffering, I bless you that Hashem should give you the strength to overcome the test of boredom."

"How could his sincere words not have a motivating effect on me?" the boy concluded.

◄ **מה / 45** ►

רָחַשׁ לִבִּי דָּבָר טוֹב ₃

² My heart is astir with a good theme.

The Midrash (*Midrash Tehillim*, no.45) states that this refers to people who were not able to explicitly express words of repentance with their mouths, but only thought thoughts of repentance in their hearts — and Hashem accepted their repentance. Whenever a person speaks, (even before he actually says the words out loud), as the words are forming inside his mind, Hashem understands what he is about to say.

R' Nosson Tzvi Finkel, the late Rosh Yeshivah of Slobodka, commented on this that, even if someone has done much evil, when he thinks thoughts of repentance, he becomes a new person due to his power of free will. We each have a constant choice of what we will think, say, and do. Regardless of any wrongs that a person might have already done, at this very moment he has the ability to choose to think elevated thoughts. He can think about what the Creator wants from him right now. By means of making an intense decision to regret the wrongs that he has already done, he totally transforms who he is. With his present awareness of what the Almighty wants from him, and his sincere wish to act in all ways according to his present realization, he changes the essence of who he is. (See *Ohr Hatzafun,* vol.1, p.17).

There is tremendous power in our thoughts. Those who use the biofeedback machine called Emg (electro-myograph) find that the muscle tension of one's muscles changes, even before one says something. Just thinking about saying something, immediately changes the tension of the muscles. Your muscles constantly emit electrical energy that is measured in micro-volts (a millionth of a volt), and when you think of saying something that causes you tension, your muscles become tense and they give off more electricity. When you think of saying something that is calming and relaxing, your muscles immediately become more relaxed and give off less electricity. Anyone who uses such a machine, can see the power of thoughts in action.

Some people tend to experience strong feelings of guilt when they do something wrong. This shows a deep sensitivity and concern for doing the right thing, but an excessive amount of guilt can be counterproductive. As *Rambam* tells us about all traits, the goal is to maintain a sensible balance. If you or someone you know experiences excessive guilt, it is a high priority to realize the great power in thoughts of repentance. Realize that Hashem is a loving Father, Who wants what is best for us, spiritually and emotionally. As R' Nosson Tzvi Finkel said many years ago, "Even a weak repentance in time of great duress, is still infinitely valuable. Angels cannot transgress — humans can. Therefore, when a human repents for any wrongs that he has done, he is elevating himself above angels."

I once met a rabbi who told me that his life's mission is to encourage people who are discouraged as a result of the wrongs that they have done. This is what he shared with me: "Some people don't take their wrongdoings very seriously, and it is people with this tendency whom many speakers address, when they speak sharply. They build up a picture of the severity of doing wrong. They point out how a person lowers himself, by transgressing. They contrast the loss of doing wrong with the great benefits of speaking and acting properly. However, there are serious-minded people who need an opposite approach. They easily experience guilt and their problems are a result of feeling overwhelmed with guilt. It is people with this tendency whom I try to address. I know what it feels like because, when I was growing up, I used to feel greatly depressed for even minor wrongs that I had done. A great teacher of mine pointed out to me that it was wrong for me to go around looking so depressed, but that I should spend more time focusing on Ahavas Hashem, love of our Heavenly Father. I felt that this approach was life-saving for me. Seeing the difference that this made in my life, I am dedicated to teaching this to others who need it."

ⷈ **49 / מט** ⷈ

יז אַל־תִּירָא כִּי־יַעֲשִׁר אִישׁ כִּי־יִרְבֶּה כְּבוֹד בֵּיתוֹ:
יח כִּי לֹא בְמוֹתוֹ יִקַּח הַכֹּל לֹא־יֵרֵד אַחֲרָיו כְּבוֹדוֹ:

¹⁷ Don't cause yourself distress when another man becomes wealthy, when the honor of his house increases.

¹⁸ For when he dies, he won't take anything, his glory will not descend after him.

The literal translation of the first two words of verse 17, *al tirah,* is "do not fear." *Metzudas David* explains that this means, "Do not worry out of envy." Therefore, to convey the meaning of this verse, we have translated it as, "Do not be distressed." Fear is a distressful emotion. Worry is a distressful emotion. Envy is a distressful emotion.

When we see or hear that someone is highly successful, we have a choice as to what our attitude will be. Those who focus on the joy and pleasure of the gifts that the Almighty has given them, will be free of envy. Their minds are so full of gratitude and appreciation, that they gain all the benefits of what anyone else has. True, someone else might have more than they do, but the benefit of what the other has, is that it gives that person joy. This joy can be yours when your mind is joyful with what you have. It is not how much anyone has, that makes the true difference in one's life. It is the emotional quality of one's life — lived with what one has. This is created in your brain with the thoughts that you think. Allowing the messages from *Tehillim* to permeate your thinking will enhance your emotions regardless of what anyone else has, does, or is.

Our verse addresses a person who has not yet mastered this attitude. He focuses on the amount that someone else has and says to himself, "*Oy gevalt.* How awful! This person has a lot — I have only a little. His life is so much better than mine. He has made it in this world — I have not. I will now choose to feel highly distressed whenever I compare what I have, with what he has."

Here King David is telling him, "Wait a moment. Your distress comes from a major error in your thinking. You think that this person's wealth makes him fortunate? That is an error."

What is the error? His wealth does not make him live, "happily ever after." Rather, his wealth is only temporary. All his wealth and superficial honor and glory, do not follow him to the grave. When his physical body stops functioning, he is penniless. As the saying goes, "You don't take it with you in the end."

What is truly valuable? Spiritual wealth. When you nourish your soul in this world, your soul is truly wealthy, for all eternity.

The good deeds that one does, are eternal. A person with financial wealth can transform this into spiritual wealth by doing many acts of kindness with his money. He can help worthy institutions and causes. He can help individuals in financial need. He can support Torah and those who study it.

So is there not a danger that a person might be consumed with distress that someone else has amassed considerable spiritual accomplishments with his money, and has a potential for even more? One might, but when it comes to spiritual accomplishments, one does not need a large amount of money to carry out many acts of kindness. A person who has only a small amount of money to give to a needy person, can still carry out a multitude of kind verbal acts. With your words, you can visit the sick and help others in myriad possible ways. Then you, too, will have spiritual wealth.

You can nourish your eternal soul with words of prayer and praise to the Almighty. You can study Torah and teach it — all this creates spiritual wealth, and anyone can accomplish this, without the prerequisite of having vast financial means.

Envy is a foolish waste of one's precious time and mental energy. Imagine someone standing at a seashore with a large group of people. All of a sudden, an ancient buried treasure of gold coins is brought in, with the tide. Everyone gets into action to gather as many coins as he can. One man has gathered more coins than some people, but much less than certain others. He then stops gathering more coins and starts whining: "Woe is me! I have less than these people. Isn't it terrible that they have so much more than I do? I feel deprived. My self-image is diminished when I see that they have more than I do."

Someone who cares about this person will tell him, "My dear friend, stop whining and continue collecting. The more you collect, the better off you'll be. Be joyful with what you have. When you experience joy for what you have, you have the main benefit of what they have."

This will be helpful for anyone who integrates this sensible and rational way of responding.

Now imagine a wise person who realizes something that the others do not yet realize. He tries to enlighten the whiner, "The coins are an illusion — they are not real. They are not buried treasure of pure gold, but instead, are toy coins that someone made for his young children to play with. They are only cheap metal plated gold. The paint will eventually rub off and there is no value in the metal itself. Children can play with it for a while, but it has no real market value."

The listener might be skeptical at first, but the wise person rubs off the gold and points out to him, "Open your eyes and observe what I'm showing you."

And now the whining stops — true awareness has changed the entire situation.

King David's wisdom enables us to see this world with greater clarity. Someone once coined the term "un-sanity" for basically normal people who create a false map of the world. Sanity is seeing reality as it actually is. Sanity and intelligence mean internalizing the awareness that long term spiritual meaning is the goal for which we should strive. This is what we would be wise to consider our top priority in life.

יט כִּי־נַפְשׁוֹ בְּחַיָּיו יְבָרֵךְ וְיוֹדֻךָ כִּי־תֵיטִיב לָךְ:

19 Though he may bless himself in his lifetime, others will praise you if you improve yourself.

Rashi explains that this verse is comparing two different paths that people take. The first path is the path of an evil person. Regardless of the amount of wrongs that he commits, he considers himself to be perfect. He blesses himself and says, "All will be well with me." Even though he blesses himself, others will not react towards him the same way. They clearly see his faults and his negative behavior.

However, if a person is willing to correct himself, others will praise him because they will see his positive words and actions.

There are two patterns that are diametrically opposed. One is the path of a person whose main goal is to consider himself a good person, regardless of what he says and does. "I'm perfect the way I am," he expresses either explicitly or implicitly.

Others can easily see how he speaks to others and how he treats them. They see how he wastes his time, and his negative patterns — but he has blinders on. He sees only what he wants to see. He sees the few good acts he does, and totally overlooks the wrong, the negative, the bad.

If anyone tries to correct such a person, he denies the validity of what they say to him. He might defensively attack them, and say that they have faults themselves; how can they than tell him anything?

His situation is similar to someone who keeps claiming that he is in perfect health, while anyone who looks at him can readily see that he is obviously ill. "I've never been sick a day in my life," he claims. He conveniently forgets all of his many colds, flus, and viruses. His fear of being seriously ill is so strong, that he prefers not to be checked by a physician.

People who are sincerely concerned with his welfare try to point out to him that it would be wise to consult a doctor, but the more they try to pressure him, the angrier he becomes.

"Leave me alone already. Why are you trying to make my life so miserable?" In reality, they aren't. His passivity towards improving his health is leading him on a path of destruction and disaster, while if he were to listen to their beneficial suggestions, he would be able to improve his health and live a much better life.

The second pattern that King David describes is that of someone who is willing to acknowledge his wrongs and mistakes. It is initially distressful to do so, but this leads to true improvement and personal growth. Such a person begins to make wiser choices of thoughts, words, and actions. When he improves himself, they recognize it and they praise him. The emphasis is not on the praise, but on the actual positive changes that he has made. Their praise is merely feedback — it serves as an objective indicator that he has become a better person.

> *Someone shared with me: "I used to have a terrible temper, but I kept denying it. Looking back, I now recognize that I was a terror to deal with. I would verbally lash out at my spouse and my children, frequently getting into quarrels with anyone who disagreed with me. Whenever someone tried to tell me that I was verbally abusive, I would shout at them, 'I'm just raising my voice a little bit. I'm righteous not to tell*

everybody what I really think of them.'

"*A couple of my few remaining friends tried to point out to me that I was destroying my life, spiritually, emotionally, and physically — but I denied it.*

"*'I'm not claiming that I'm absolutely perfect,' I humbly consented. 'But no one I know is better. If you would focus on all the good I do, my minor faults would be totally inconsequential.*

"*What woke me up was reading an article that stated, 'The worst criminals are the first to say that they do only good and don't have any serious faults. The more elevated and enlightened someone is, the more they recognize even relatively minor faults and lapses.'*

"*The person who showed me the article did not know me very well and did not have any agenda. He just said to me with a smile, 'Do you personally focus more on how good you already are, or on what you can do to improve? It takes courage to be an objective observer of oneself. Not everyone has this courage. Do you?'*

"*The way he said this to me, hit home. I had to admit to myself that focusing on finding and improving faults was not my strongest virtue, and I felt challenged. I responded, 'Of course, I have a lot of courage — I am not afraid to say anything to anyone.'*

"*'Yes. There is an aspect of courage in that,' he commented, 'but it takes more courage to be honest with yourself about your true self. Do you have the courage to ask the people who know you well for their totally honest thoughts and feedback? Try asking them, "In what ways do you think that I need to improve?"'*

"*At first, I found this tremendously difficult. In fact, it was one of the most difficult projects I've ever attempted, but then it became easier.*

"*I realized I was succeeding at becoming a better person when three different people commented to me, 'It's impressive the way that you've improved your character.'*

"*It took an awareness that I am not perfect, for me to truly become better.*"

⊰{ **50 / נ** }⊱

יד זְבַח לֵאלֹהִים תּוֹדָה וְשַׁלֵּם לְעֶלְיוֹן נְדָרֶיךָ:

14 Offer HASHEM confession, then redeem your vows to the Most High.

This verse refers to a time when the *Bais Hamikdash*, the Holy Temple in Jerusalem, was in existence. People would make vows to bring offerings to the Temple. We are told here to purify and elevate ourself before bringing our offering. How? By repenting for the wrongs that we have done. An integral part of repentance is to verbally state the nature of the wrong we have committed. This is called *viduy*, confession to Hashem. After we clear our souls, then we are on the spiritual level of bringing a sacrifice.

In our times, when we do not have the Holy Temple, we have prayer. This fulfills part of the role that we served by offerings in the Temple. The purpose of the offerings was to raise our consciousness and to become closer to Hashem, Creator and Sustainer of the universe. That, then, is the purpose of prayer.

What exactly is prayer? Is it simply reciting words from a prayer book by rote? Or having the words memorized, and just rattling them off?

The words we say and read are symbols for the ideas and objects to which they refer. For example, we pray for health. Health is just a word. It refers to us — human beings — being in a state of health and not in one of illness. When we pray for health, we gain a certain awareness — the realization that our health comes from Hashem. Every time we say this prayer we, once again, focus on the acknowledgement that our physical well-being depends on Hashem. If someone we know is ill, or when we are not in a fully healthy state, we make a request for healing. With repetition, this awareness becomes stronger and stronger.

Every day in the *Shemoneh Esrei* prayer, we ask for intelligence. We ask for *daas*, understanding and wisdom. This is an important need. As King Solomon so wisely understood, wisdom is the ultimate factor that one needs, to live a high-quality life. When we recite the prayer *Atah chonein l'adam daas,* we state that Hashem, to Whom we are now speaking, is the One Who gives us wise intelligence. This consciousness becomes more and more a part of our integrated understanding, every time we repeat the prayer.

For our prayers to be on an elevated level, we need to purify and cleanse our souls. That is the purpose of *teshuvah,* repentance, and confession. In the *Shemoneh Esrei* prayer, we explicitly ask for Hashem's help to enable us to sincerely and completely repent. We can do this in our own words, before each prayer. This is an appropriate time to do so.

If a person would have an audience before a powerful King and needs to make requests, he wants to make certain that he has the best possible chance of his requests being accepted and fulfilled. If someone knew that the King has a complaint against him for defying his wishes, it is obvious that he needs to ask forgiveness for his wrongs, before he makes his request. Failure to do so, lessens the chances of the King's granting his wishes.

Moreover, he would feel embarrassed to stand in the King's presence if he were to know that the King is looking at him with a critical eye, because of his wrongdoings. He must clear up things between himself and the King in order to feel a sense of calm well-being in the presence of the King.

So before prayer, clear things between you and Hashem, by asking Him for forgiveness for the wrongs you have done. Then, your mind and soul will be ready for all the benefits of prayer to body and soul. In prayer you have an encounter with Hashem — clear your mind and allow yourself to savor the experience.

Someone told me that, for years, he had a difficult time praying. It is not because he did not appreciate the power of prayer, but just the opposite. It was due to of his tremendous sense of anxiety and apprehension when it came to prayer. He had a strong awareness of Hashem, and it was exactly this strong awareness that caused him to dread praying. He always felt that he was imperfect. He had made so many mistakes in religious matters. His character traits needed a great deal of repair. He tended to be lazy and did not perform good deeds in the way they should be performed. So, when it came to praying, he would always hear an inner voice, "Who are you to pray with fervor in the presence of Hashem? You know you have so many faults. The Omniscient One is even more aware. Whom are you trying to fool?"

He spoke about this problem with a rabbi who was sensitive to these issues. The rabbi understood what was bothering him and said, "Throughout the ages there have been many great people who have felt the way you have felt. Usually it is the people who aspire to reach high spiritual levels, who feel this way. Coarse people and truly evil people are often blinded to the extent of the negativity of their words and actions. The way that this has been dealt with by many, is the following: They say to themselves. 'It is true that I have many faults. It is true that I might not be on the proper level, later on. But now that I am about to pray to Hashem, my very apprehension about praying to Him, makes me worthy of prayer. Right now I ask forgiveness for any wrongs I have done. I regret not having done sufficient good in my life. I humbly ask forgiveness.' After saying this out loud or in their minds, they feel a lightness and hope that enables them to stop thinking about themselves. With a clearer mind, they have been able to focus on the present and fill their mind with the elevated thoughts of prayer."

Following through on this, he was able to pray with an inner peace that he had never experienced before. Later on, he did have his ups and downs, but, realizing that these apprehensive thoughts were a catalyst to elevating himself through repentance, he appreciated them and that greatly decreased his feelings of distress. Now he actually looked forward to the prayers, which gave him thoughts and feelings that were far beyond those he had imagined he would be able to experience.

כג וְשָׂם דֶּרֶךְ אַרְאֶנּוּ בְּיֵשַׁע אֱלֹהִים:

23 And one who orders [his] way, I will show him the salvation of HASHEM.

The classic work on character development, *Orchos Tzaddikim,* cites this verse in reference to taking action to refine our traits. "Ordering one's ways" means to give thought to where we are now in a given trait and to make a plan to improve our traits.

The first trait that is discussed in this great book is the attribute of arrogance. This is what is stated: "Someone who wants to uproot the trait of arrogance completely cannot do so by merely by changing one's thoughts. Rather, one must go to the opposite extreme, in action." He goes on to give details of what this would mean, in practice. If a person has the fault of arrogance and dresses in an arrogant way, he needs to dress — for a while — in the opposite manner. If he said and did things in order to get honor and glory from others, for a while he needs to, not only stop doing those things, but he should do actions that are the diametric opposite. He should maintain this until he feels that he has totally uprooted this trait from his being.

Similarly, it is written in *Orchos Tzaddikim* that, if someone sees that he has a bad temper and angers easily, he should go — for a while — to the opposite extreme. While going to the opposite extreme, he should ignore all slights and insults. He should keep acting this way until the anger is totally uprooted. Then a person should select the "middle path," and act this way for the rest of his life.

This is the model we need to follow with all negative traits. First we need to go to the opposite extreme and, after acting this way for a time, we should act in a balanced way. This is the way to repair all negative traits.

"All who want to serve Hashem with all of their character traits should place this path before him and before his friends. In reference to this our verse states 'The one who orders [his] way, I shall show him the salvation of Hashem.' "

In order to do this properly, make a list of positive traits that you want to improve, and make a list of negative traits that you want to overcome. Then, consistently speak and act in ways that fit the positive patterns. With those negative traits that are the most challenging for you, act according to the opposite positive traits for a time.

When we think of different traits as being positive or negative, we need to keep in mind that every trait has its positive times and places, and every trait could be used negatively. When we refer to a trait as being positive or negative, we mean that it is usually positive or negative.

Awareness of our level in reference to various traits is the starting point of knowing what we need to focus on, to grow and improve. The *mitzvah* to develop our character traits is the command of "Walking in Hashem's ways" (Rambam, *Hilchos Daios*, ch.1).

Here is a list of traits to consider when working on self-development. Each trait has a pattern of thoughts and feelings, words and actions. This is just a partial list and you might think of other characteristics that are important for you to overcome and to refine.

POSITIVE TRAITS:

Alacritous (*Zrizus,*) / Ambitious / Appreciative / Awed by the wonders of Creation / Balanced / Brave / Calm / Careful not to cause pain with words / Caring about others / Cautious / Charitable / Cheerful / Compassionate / Concentrates well / Confident / Considerate / Consistent / Cooperative / Courageous / Dependable / Dignified / Diligent / Dutiful / Effective / Efficient / Empathetic / Encourages others / Enthusiastic / Forgiving / Friendly / Generous / Giving / Goal oriented / Grateful / Happy / Honest / Honors others / Hospitable / Humble / Joyful / Keeps one's word / Kind / Meets obligations / Merciful / Organized / Patient / Peace-loving / Peace of mind / Persistent / Positive-thinking / Punctual / Reliable / Resilient/ Respectful / Responsible / Self-controled and Self-disciplined / Self-respecting / Serene / Spiritual / Tactful / Time management / Trustworthy / Truthful / Will-power

NEGATIVE TRAITS:

Aggressive / Aimless / Angry / Argumentative / Arrogant / Attention-seeking / Bitter / Blaming / Blocked / Chutzpahdik /

Complaining / Conceited / Contemptous / Critical (excessively) / Cruel / Deceitful / Despairing / Dishonest / Disrespectful / Envious / Fearful / Flattereing / Frustrated easily / Gossiping / Greedy / Hasty / Hostile / Impatient / Impulsive / Inconsiderate / Inconsistent / Insecure / Insensitive / Irresponsible / Irritable / Jealous / Jumps to conclusions / Lazy / Liar / Mean / Merciless / Nosy / Passive / Quarrelsome / Quitter / Reckless / Resentful / Rigid / Rude / Ruthless / Sad / Self-centered / Selfish / Sloppy / Stingy / Stubborn / Unforgiving / Unfriendly / Unhappy / Worrier

> *A student once asked his rabbi, "What should a person do if he can't find any traits to work on?"*
>
> *"Then one knows for certain that he must work on over-coming arrogance and conceit," was the reply.*

⋇ **51 / נא** ⋇

יב לֵב טָהוֹר בְּרָא־לִי אֱלֹהִים וְרוּחַ נָכוֹן חַדֵּשׁ בְּקִרְבִּי:

¹² **Create a pure heart for me, o God, and a steadfast spirit renew within me.**

This is a very moving verse that many great people would repeat over and over again. It is both a prayer and an affirmation. When you repeat it over and over again, the message of this verse becomes integrated and internalized. You are expressing your fervent desire to have a pure heart. You are asking for a renewal of your spirit.

The Talmud states that when one sincerely wants to purify himself, the Almighty will purify him. Just reading this verse once halfheartedly, is not sufficient. Certainly making the statement even once points one in the right direction, but the stronger your wishes and desires to be purified, the more powerful it is. The Chofetz Chaim cites this principle in the laws of Yom Kippur (*Mishnah Berurah* 623:3). He is referring to the *Neilah* prayer at the end of Yom Kippur. He writes that, even though one might feel exhausted because of the fast, one should strengthen oneself, and he adds, "When one sincerely wants to purify himself, the Almighty will purify him." We can apply this concept to our verse. Even when you feel that you are far from having a pure heart, strengthen yourself and ask Hashem, your loving Father and powerful King, to create a pure heart for you. "Please, Hashem, create for me a pure heart."

"Create" implies it does not exist and must be created. So, even if you feel that you lack a pure heart, the all-powerful Creator, Who created the entire universe, can create a pure heart. Your heart already exists; it does not need to be created. And the Creator of your heart can purify it. But you must start. And asking for a pure heart in prayer is the way to begin the process.

What specifically would "a pure heart" mean to you? In what ways could you refine yourself? Purity means 100%, as in the statement "pure gold." Think of a specific way that you could use a purer heart. Ask Hashem for His assistance in this area.

One basic way to grow would be, to channel your motivations to be more sincerely *l'sheim Shamayim,* for the sake of Heaven. When you feel that your motivation is not as pure as it should be, that is a perfect time to repeat this verse.

> *A student told me that his main challenge is anger. He realized that for him, a purer heart would mean that he would see the good in Hashem's children, and he would interact with calm respect. He was motivated to overcome his negative pattern of feeling an excessive level of anger as well the quarrels he got into, because of the way he spoke when angry.*
>
> *He had worked on his anger for a while, and even though he did see some progress, he realized that he still had a long way to go. I suggested that he ask Hashem to help him. His intentions were good, and with his sincere efforts, he was sure to receive the help of Hashem. Our verse is a fitting one for this form of prayer.*
>
> *"You need patience," I told him. "With many repetitions, you will eventually succeed."*
>
> *"How many repetitions is sufficient?" he asked.*
>
> *"That's easy to answer. As many as it takes for your heart to become so pure, that you stay calm. When you are consistently calm in situations that used to be a challenge for you, then you know that you have repeated this verse enough times. The message is now strongly entrenched in your*

brain's neurons. You have this verse with you wherever you go. Imagine challenging situations, those that you've already experienced and those that might arise in the future, and repeat this verse. Then the purity of your heart will be associated with these situations. This will be manifest in your way of speaking and acting."

I can see the big smile on his face when he reported to me that he had repeated the verse enough times. He knew it was enough because of the positive feedback from his family members who appreciated his consistent calmness and pleasantness.

טו אֲלַמְּדָה פֹשְׁעִים דְּרָכֶיךָ וְחַטָּאִים אֵלֶיךָ יָשׁוּבוּ:

15 I will teach transgressors Your ways, and sinners will return to You.

If we see someone transgressing, there are many ways we can react and respond, While some people are critical and even condemnatory. They just think negatively about this person and might even make a comment to themselves or to someone who is standing near them, "Isn't it awful!"

Others react passively. Some are apathetic. "This is none of my business." Others say to themselves, "I wish I knew what to say." They do not approach the person to try to educate him.

Then there are those zealous individuals who feel that they need to protest. They speak in a harsh, angry, or aggressive tone of voice, and they tell the wrongdoer that he needs to be admonished and censured. The transgressor hears that he has done wrong and is evil, but this cannot truly be called teaching. It rarely influences the wrongdoer to return to his loving Father in Heaven.

Here King David tells us the ideal. "I will teach transgressors Your ways," and the approach he will use is an approach that will accomplish the goal of "and sinners will return to you."

It is not that he is personally offended by this person's improper action, but rather, his goal is to motivate wrongdoers to return to their Heavenly Father.

As the Vilna Gaon writes: "When you sincerely love someone, you care about his spiritual welfare and are motivated to help him improve" (*Proverbs* 3:12).

The first step in successfully influencing someone to stop doing wrong and to begin to do good is, to sincerely care about this person's welfare. When you have profound concern for another person then, regardless of exactly what you say, that person will experience your sincere caring. However you think and feel, that is the way you will talk. When you are motivated by sincere concern, what you say will be more conducive to effective results.

Believe strongly in this person's ability to make positive changes. Believe strongly in the essential goodness of this person's soul. Believe strongly in your own ability to reach and educate people.

Learn from effective communicators. Learn from people who excel at reaching people. Be yourself and speak in your own style, but modify your approach with the knowledge you gain from expert communicators. The more motivated you are to help people spiritually, the more you will keep learning about the wisest things to say and not to say, to do and not to do. Learn from each and every experience. It is easy to develop the habit of using just one approach and then applying it all the time, whether or not it is actually effective. However, when your goal is clearly to motivate and influence, you become aware of when you need to modify or even totally change what you say and how you say it.

Look at the situation from Hashem's perspective. Look at the situation from the perspective of the person you want to influence. Then, look at the situation from the perspective of someone who honestly and truly cares about the eternal well-being of the present transgressor, who will one day be on the path Hashem wants him to live.

> *Someone who was considered very rebellious as a teenager shared with me the following: "Now that I'm in my thirties and have a family, I appear to any outsider as a regular Torah-observant head of a household, but when I was nineteen I was wild and irresponsible. People who knew me kept telling me how poorly I was acting. They would try to make me feel guilty for being the way I was. I didn't enjoy their lectures, but they still did not motivate me to act any*

better. I felt that they had their own agenda for trying to get me to conform to their standards. Some people did not say anything to me. I could see that they looked at me with a critical eye: they gave up on me. I do not blame them, but their negative opinion about the unlikelihood of my improving the way I was, only added to my own feelings of discouragement about ever becoming a better person.

"Deep down, I wanted to improve, but I felt that this was too hard for me. I tried to give the impression to others that I was cool, and I knew what I was doing. I felt so badly about myself that I did not have the inner strength to acknowledge that I needed to make major changes.

"The turning point in my life was when someone I hardly knew came over to me and said, with the kindest look on his face and in the tone of his voice, 'Can we have a talk?' My immediate response was, 'Of course.' I had rebuffed many other efforts by people who tried to get me to change, but this was different. He did not act like he thought he was superior to me in any way, even though he was much older and more accomplished.

"It took a while until I actually did transform myself into the way that I had secretly wished' that I could be. I don't remember the exact words this person said, but he conveyed to me the feeling that I was important to him and to Hashem. He let me know that I had much greater potential than I thought I did. He gave me a sense, a vision, of myself that I felt I wanted to live up to. And now, my most intense wish is to be able to do for others what this person did for me."

יז אֲדֹנָי שְׂפָתַי תִּפְתָּח וּפִי יַגִּיד תְּהִלָּתֶךָ:

[17] **Hashem, open my lips, and my mouth will declare Your praise.**

W e repeat this verse as an introducion each time we recite the *Shemoneh Esrei* prayer. Before we begin praying, we ask Hashem to give us the strength and energy to be able to pray. This is a statement of awareness that our very ability to speak at this moment, is a gift from the One we will now address in prayer. In essence, we are praying to be able to pray.

Contemplating how amazing it is to be able to speak, helps us be grateful to the Creator for this ability. How do we decide to move our lips and make sounds? It is thanks to a miraculous mind-body connection. With our minds, we will our physical mouths to move. We don't need to consciously move the muscles that control our lips, our tongues, our cheeks, and our jaws. In fact, we don't have any notion at all of what we must do to project the sounds that make up our words. These all function spontaneously when we decide to say something. The wish of our inner will puts the complex machinery into motion. Our brains send the commands, our lips open, and from our mouth flow the words we choose to say.

Three times every day we have an opportunity to build up our appreciation for the gift of being able to speak. And the most magnificent use of our power of speech is to utilize it to connect with our Creator.

Many have noted that this is a strong lesson in how careful we must be, with what we say throughout the day. We ask Hashem for the ability to speak in prayer before Him, but what about speaking in ways that are against His will? If we ask for the right to recite what we know He wants us to say, this should be a message to us to be careful not to speak negatively against others, not to insult people; in short, not to cause any form of verbal harm to the Almighty's children.

Rashi comments that King David was asking for forgiveness for his transgressions so he would be worthy of the right to declare the praises of the Almighty. Each time we recite this, we also are asking that Hashem forgive us for the wrongs that we have done and then we, too, will be worthy of pronouncing Hashem's praise. Thinking thoughts of repentance elevates us and lays the ground-work for our improving our actions.

> *There was a rabbi who was consulted by people who found it difficult to be careful not to speak* lashon hora *(derogatory speech). He would advise them to repeat this verse at least ten times a day, and then express their gratitude to the*

Creator for the magnificent world that He created. Many found that, for a while after saying this, they were much more careful with what they said.

Try this for a week. Ten times a day recite the verse, "Hashem, open my lips, and my mouth will declare Your praise." Then say, "I am grateful to You, my Father, my King, Creator and Sustainer of the universe, for the magnificent world that You created."

יט זִבְחֵי אֱלֹהִים רוּחַ נִשְׁבָּרָה לֵב־נִשְׁבָּר וְנִדְכֶּה אֱלֹהִים לֹא תִבְזֶה:

19 The sacrifices God desires are a broken spirit; a heart broken and humbled, o God, You will not despise.

This verse seems to be the basis for the well-known aphorism of the Kotzker Rebbe: "There is nothing as whole as a broken heart."

We always have thoughts and feelings about our thoughts and feelings. This is known as being in a meta-state; meta means "about or above." For example, some people feel very sad and upset with themselves about feeling depressed and broken. This makes them feel even worse. And then they feel even worse about feeling worse. And this, too, makes them feel even worse than before. This negative chain can keep perpetuating itself. Eventually — hopefully — something good will happen and the person will likely feel better.

But there is a faster and better way to create a more positive feeling, than to simply wait until the feelings change through happenstance. There are a few basic choices with a multitude of variations. You can take positive actions. Perform a *mitzvah* and experience joy for the good deed you are doing. Also, you can remember the good in your life and the positive things that have happened to you in the past. If need be, you can find a positive lens through which to see your present distress.

This latter option is an important message that we can learn from this verse. Realize that when you are feeling broken in spirit, your feelings can help you approach Hashem with humility. You are feeling low. You are more thinking about how tiny — even microscopic — you are, when you compare yourself to the Creator and His magnificent universe. Those feelings of humility can be compared to offering a sacrifice in the Holy Temple. When someone offered a sacrifice, he would vicariously experience a total giving of himself. When someone is brokenhearted, his ego is diminished, and his sense of self is lessened. This can serve as a stimulus to remember the Creator and His infinite wisdom and power. The broken feelings now have elevating meaning — they are no longer simply distress and suffering. They are a catalyst to coming closer to Hashem, and you are raised from the depths of despair to great spiritual heights. You yourself are elevated. You are now a being who has given his total self to God. Nothing can be higher.

Thus, the very same feelings can be a source of great suffering to one person and, to a person who utilizes them properly, a source of greatness — the greatness of becoming close to Hashem.

I have a friend whose highest priority is to help lift people who feel depressed and discouraged. He considers it his mission in life to give hope to those who have given up hope. He is a person who overflows with love for Hashem and love for other people. He points out to them that precisely because they are feeling so bad, every good word they say, and every positive act they do, is worth much more than if it were easy for them.

"I consider myself to be like a Kohen (priest) in the Holy Temple," he said to me. "By showing people how their brokenheartedness is a tremendous asset, I give them a ray of light, when they feel that all is dark. They begin to feel an inner strength they did not realize they had. I point out to them that they can use their present emotional suffering as a starting point of great spiritual and emotional growth. I plant the idea in their minds that, as they grow from their present challenge, they will be able to utilize the lessons that they learn to be a source of inspiration and strength to many other people. They can start visualizing this now and these mental pictures will help them cope better immediately."

A few days after speaking to him, I had a few setbacks and was feeling down. Suddenly I remembered how my friend had shared his approach with me. I said to Hashem, "Please accept my broken feelings as a sacrifice in the Beis Hamikdash, *and let me be able to use my experience to do acts of kindness."*

This helped me immensely. I shared this with my friend and he thanked me profusely for the feedback, "Your giving me feedback adds to my awareness of how important it is to lift up those who are feeling down."

⋅᯽{ **52 / נב** }᯽⋅

‏ֿחֶסֶד אֵל כָּל־הַיּוֹם:

³ The kindness of HASHEM is all day long.

Whatever day it is right now as you are reading this, the kindness of Hashem has been there for you from the beginning of the day, until this moment, and the kindness of Hashem will be with you for the rest of the day until the new day starts. Tomorrow again you will be a beneficiary of the kindness of Hashem, and this will continue each and every day for your entire life. This has been going on from your very first day of life and each and every day after that until this moment.

Imagine how you will feel when you experience an entire day with this consciousness. From the moment you open your eyes in the morning until you go to sleep at night, every moment will have awareness of Hashem's kindness towards you.

Allow yourself to be aware of being the recipient of constant kindness for an entire day. Every movement you make is an aspect of Hashem's kindness. Everything you own is an aspect of Hashem's kindness. Every interaction with other people has aspects of this kindness. Every bit of food you eat and every drop of water you drink, is an aspect of this constant kindness.

And what about the things that you usually overlook? On the day that you decide to become more aware of the kindnesses you experience, you will notice more and more things. You will see what you might not have seen before, and you will hear what you might not have heard before. You will feel feelings of gratitude and joy that you otherwise might not have felt.

You will find yourself being more aware of Hashem's presence, and you will allow your mind to be filled with thoughts of appreciation for Hashem's kindness to you. You will be more present-oriented, and you will focus less on anything you are dissatisfied with about the past. You will be free from stressful thoughts about the future — you will be focused on the present kindnesses.

When you do this, if your mind needlessly wanders to some thoughts that are not conducive to appreciation of kindness, you will gently and lightly re-direct your consciousness to the present kindness that you are experiencing. Just knowing that your mind has the ability to direct your thoughts, is a wonderful kindness of Hashem. Just how does your mind direct your thoughts to thoughts of kindness? We have no way to explain this with our present limited knowledge, but the knowledge we do have of what we are able to do, is something for which to be grateful.

What would your entire life be like from now on if you would take this verse as a concept to focus on frequently? There is only one way to really answer this question accurately, and that is to make this a verse that will frequently be on your lips. For when you repeat it out loud and to yourself, your inner mind will focus on the kindnesses that you are experiencing right now, on this very day.

> *A joyful middle-aged man was asked, "What was a major breakthrough in your life?" He related, "I used to be what one would consider a negative person*
>
> *"Until about ten years ago I would frequently complain and kvetch, I usually focusing on what I did not like. Each and every day a number of things were not going exactly as I wanted them to. This would make me unhappy. I considered myself a constant victim of circumstances. I would have been much happier if other people, and my life in general, would be more the way I wanted. In addition, I never had enough money, and I was terrified that in the future I would be short of the money I needed. I was filled with insecurity and anxiety.*

"Then a rabbi told me that he could tell me four words that would totally change my entire emotional life. I was skeptical.

" 'Four words?' I challenged him. 'Do you really believe that after three years of therapy that helped a bit but did not make me a happy person, you can just tell me four words and those four words will transform my entire life?'

" 'I'm not claiming that these four words are magic, and that just by my saying them or your repeating them, you will become a happy person. What I am saying to you is that these four words contain a mind-set that can totally transform your life when you give thought to what they mean, and you frequently think about this during the day. I'll only agree to share them with you if you give me your word that you will make a serious effort to apply them for just one day.'

" 'One day is a long time,' I argued. 'What about for just one hour?'

" 'Nothing doing!' the rabbi said firmly but kindly. 'If you are not committed to think about this for an entire day, I don't think that you are serious when you say that you would like to know how to improve your emotional condition. If you do not care about your own well-being, my just wishing you well will not really help you. For this to work, you need a real commitment. After a day of applying what I am suggesting, if you feel that you prefer to be grumpy, negative and depressed, that will be your choice. However, I must know that you really mean what you say, when you say that you truly want to become a happier person.'

"I saw that the rabbi was going to be stubborn, or as he would say, 'steadfast,' about not telling me his formula unless I committed to giving it a try for an entire day, so I reluctantly said I would do it.

"He then told me the verse that has been my motto and blueprint for life, ever since that moment. The four Hebrew words are **Chessed Keil Kol Hayom,** the Kindness of Hashem is all day long. Since I said it in Hebrew it was just four words.

"He told me that I should start the next day from the moment I woke up until the end of the day. It was amazing! That day *was one of the best days of my life. I kept projecting how wonderful my life would be if I kept this up each and every day. At times I would feel badly that I had wasted so much time in the past feeling needlessly miserable, but that too would be a lack of focusing on the kindnesses of Hashem. I realized that it would be much wiser to view my past unhappiness as a way to gain greater appreciation for the present happiness in my life."*

⊰{ **נה / 55** }⊱

כג הַשְׁלֵךְ עַל־יהוה יְהָבְךָ וְהוּא יְכַלְכְּלֶךָ.

²³ Cast your burden upon HASHEM, and He will sustain you.

E veryone in the world has burdens. Some are heavier than others — some are lighter. Some people have greater inner strength to carry their burdens. Some people have learned the skill of how to carry their burdens in order to make them lighter. Some people have others who help them carry their burdens, but the common denominator is that everyone has a burden, and usually it is not only one burden, but many. You cannot always tell how heavy someone else's burden is; you only have the subjective experience of your own. But know, with clarity, that just as you have burdens, so does everyone else.

Here we have the ultimate advice on how to handle your burdens: Do not do it alone. You never have to do it all yourself. As a matter of fact, it's impossible to do it all yourself. You can call upon the Almighty, your Father, your King, Creator and Sustainer of the universe, to help you, and our verse tells us that, you can give over your entire load of baggage to Hashem and He will sustain you.

Imagine that you have a very difficult job to do. You are feeling completely overwhelmed, and you have no idea how you will be able to do the job. It is too hard for you. You lack the knowledge, you lack the energy and you feel lost and full of stress. Then you are approached by someone who is intelligent, physically strong, creative, has high levels of energy which he can sustain for a long time, and is absolutely motivated to do all he can to help you.

To your amazement, he says to you, "I see that you have a heavy burden. Relax. Be calm. It is no longer your burden. I will take care of it for you."

You begin to feel better already. You feel lighter and much more comfortable than before.

Then he adds, "Not only will I help you myself, but I have an entire network of friends and acquaintances who will join me. They will use their knowledge, strengths, and resources to help you carry your burden. You can consider it done."

You are now facing a totally different situation. Previously, you had a heavy load to carry — and now that load is gone, it will be taken care of for you. See how the stress and tension you were experiencing, melts away. If you were looking at yourself in a mirror, you would see the stress that was written all over your face, disappear. Instead, you would see a big smile radiating back to you.

When you hand over your burden to Hashem, that is the relief you will experience.

But what if it is difficult for you to actually feel this way? Mentally rehearse this feeling. One way to do this is, to imagine that you are carrying an extremely heavy package, containing expensive glassware, or a delicate electronic device. It weighs much more than you can handle, and you are about to drop it. You are nervous, because, if you drop it, it will mean a great loss. Now, you can put it down. Breathe the way you would breathe, when you exhale in a deep sigh of relief. This form of breathing together with your imagining that you are putting down the heavy package, sends a calming and relaxing message to your brain. Now imagine this again, and heave a sigh of relief, once again. Do this at least ten times. Each time feel a great sense of relief flowing from your head to your toes.

After you practice this, feel yourself handing over your heaviest emotional burdens to Hashem. Breathe a great sigh of relief. Feel yourself being full of gratitude to Hashem for relieving you of your burden. Keep repeating this verse, and let its message become a part of your daily thinking. The calm and serene feelings that will become your second nature, will help you spiritually, emotionally, and in all areas of health. Your loving Heavenly Father wants your welfare and wants you to throw your burdens to Him. He asks you to let Him carry them for you. Don't refuse!

I met someone who was constantly worried and over-whelmed. "I have so much to do," he told me. "So many things can go wrong. Before I take care of everything I need to take care of, more things pile up for me to do. I feel tremendous stress. I don't know how long I can keep on going."

"You seem like you are carrying the entire weight of the world on your shoulders," I said. "Wouldn't it be wonderful if you could release some of your stress?"

"There's nothing I can do about it," he argued. "I objectively have an enormous 'to do' list. I never finish everything that is on my list. And each day more new things are added than are taken care of, from the previous list."

After he told me about all the things he had to do, I heartily agreed with him that he did have a lot to do. "But even though you do have a heavy burden, you can make it much lighter. You are familiar with the verse in Tehillim *that advises us to cast our burden on Hashem."*

"Yes, I know that," he said. "But it's easier said than done. I still feel a lot of stress."

I didn't make much progress in trying to decrease his stress. He said that he really wanted to make his burden lighter, but he claimed that he wasn't able to do it. His father and mother were both highly stressed people, and feeling stressed was in his genes. This was just the way he was, and the truth is that, if someone believes that he cannot do anything about his stress, he will hold on to it. The first step is believing that you can decrease your stress and the second step is to be motivated enough that this becomes a high priority.

I did not see him for a while. The next time we met, he looked much calmer and more relaxed than before. "You look so much better now," I said to him. "How did you do it?"

"I didn't do it, Hashem did," he told me. " I was experiencing such high levels of stress over a long time, that I suffered a mild heart attack. The doctor told me that I was fortunate

that the damage to my heart was relatively light. He told me to watch my diet and to get more rest, but the most important thing was for me to decrease my stress — to a minimum. If I did not do this, he felt my life was in danger."

"So how did you succeed in becoming a calmer person?" I asked him.

"I had heard from many people before, including you, that I need to cast my burdens on Hashem. But I guess I was not motivated enough. After my heart attack and my talk with the doctor, I knew that this just had to be my highest priority. I felt I had no choice. It was either that I would let Hashem carry the burden, or I would not be alive to carry any burdens at all.

"When I was in the hospital and recuperating at home, I realized that so many things I felt were absolute necessities for me to do, were not all that important. I started to weigh my priorities. I analyzed all of my activities and figured out what I really needed to keep doing, and what I could let go or delegate to others. Both these factors together, my increased relying on Hashem to help me and my cutting down on non-essential tasks, have made a major difference in my life. I find that I am praying better than ever before and I have found more time to study Torah and to be with my family. I feel like a new person. I am constantly grateful to Hashem for showing me a wiser path."

﴾ **59 / נט** ﴿

עֻזִּי אֵלֶיךָ אֲזַמֵּרָה כִּי־אֱלֹהִים מִשְׂגַּבִּי אֱלֹהֵי חַסְדִּי: ‏יח

18 My power, to You shall I sing, for HASHEM is my stronghold, the God of my kindness.

The only way we can take any action, even a very slight one, is because we have the energy to do so. Our energy system, that flows from our brain down to our muscles, is amazing. We need to eat and drink to have the fuel for our energy. We are all aware of how we feel and function when we have recently eaten energizing food, and how we feel and function when we are hungry and thirsty. Even when we have eaten properly, each day our energy wears out and we need to sleep to recharge the energy "batteries" in our brain. We are all aware of the difference in how we feel and function when we are alert and wide awake, and when we are tired and worn out. Even with tremendous fatigue, we still have some energy left. Every moment of our lives there is energy flowing, and Zero energy means that someone is no longer alive.

The power source of our energy is Hashem, Creator and Sustainer of the universe. Energy is the power we have. It takes energy to lift up even a tiny object, more energy to lift up heavier items, and it takes a great deal of energy to feel and function well throughout a day. The power we have to do anything, is based on the energy we have. Here King David is telling us that Hashem is the source of his power. Everyone needs energy to be empowered, whether a mighty king or a young child.

Recognizing that Hashem is the constant source of our energy and power, we gain an increased awareness of His moment-by-moment influence on our lives. Being grateful to Him for the energy and strength that He gives us, will lead us to sing His praises out of profound gratitude. "To You shall I sing," will be our inner feeling. Song is more than simply words expressing thoughts. Song that comes from within, is an emotional component that is added to the words that we say. It means that we feel those words and they permeate our entire being.

"The God of my kindness" reflects the awareness that we experience the kindness of Hashem, constantly. This kindness is manifest in myriad ways, all the time. Both the spiritual and emotional quality of our lives are raised immensely, when we focus on the moment-to-moment kindnesses that Hashem bestows upon us.

The inner song that we will be singing throughout each day, will be the background music that accompanies us wherever we are and whatever the circumstances. Some people have frequent negative inner chatter. They talk to themselves in ways that cause negative feelings, regardless of all the good in their lives. By changing their self-talk to messages of realization of the kindnesses that Hashem is granting them, they will transform their lives. We notice what we think about regularly. Thinking about the kindnesses that Hashem bestows upon us, will strengthen our pattern of noticing them. As we master this, our hearts will be full of song to our loving Father and powerful King, the source of all of our energy and of all the good in our lives.

"What do you consider the biggest problems in people's lives?" I asked someone, who is highly successful in helping people overcome distress and enabling them to live happier lives.

I thought he would list some of the major difficulties and challenges that people face. Instead he said, "There is one essential problem, that is at the root of much of the suffering in the world. Do you know what it is?

"It's the pattern of our thinking," he informed me gently.

"Those who consistently think about what is wrong and what is not to their liking, suffer a lot from even minor irritants, frustrations, and setbacks. They cause themselves much unnecessary pain. Even when things are going basically well, they do not enjoy life. Their minds dwell on thoughts of what is not to their liking, and these thoughts create negative feelings.

"The solution to this is to realize that Hashem constantly gives us good, in our lives. It is up to us to focus on it. It is as if a person has a gigantic screen in front of him, and he has the free will to select what will be on the screen. He can choose pictures and scenes that are depressing, that arouse discomfort, that elicit anger and resentment, or even breed discouragement. The music and words that accompany the pictures in these categories, match the emotional climate of those pictures. Running these frequently, guarantees a life of misery.

"On the other hand, he can choose to run pictures and scenes that are conducive to happiness, joy, celebration, gratitude, appreciation, serenity, inner peace and calm. The music and words match the feelings created by the pictures. The benefits are numerous. One can think clearly and be more in touch with one's inner wisdom. One makes better and wiser choices and decisions.

"A person who chooses the distress-causing pictures, scripts, and music, might blame the distress on the specifics of what appears on the screen. But the reality is that, his own choice is the root cause.

"We each choose the thoughts and images that appear on our mind's screen. Even when a person has challenges to face, with the right selection of thoughts and images, he will find the strength to handle those challenges wisely. He will be able to appreciate that each challenge is sent to him from his loving Father and powerful King to help him grow spiritually. They will help him develop his character traits. They will make him deeper and wiser."

◄§ **61 / סא** §►

> זָמִים עַל־יְמֵי־מֶלֶךְ תּוֹסִיף שְׁנוֹתָיו כְּמוֹ־דֹר וָדֹר:

> **7 May you add days onto the days of the king, may his years be like all generations.**

The Midrash (*Yalkut Shimoni* 843) explains that this verse refers to the seventy years that Adam, the first human in the world, gave as a gift to King David. Originally Adam was to live forever. Then his life was shortened after transgressing in the Garden of Eden. He would now live only one thousand years. Having been endowed with the special ability to see all future kings and the history of their reigns, he realized that, in order for King David to be king, he needed to receive years of life as a gift, and these were "the years that were added onto the days of the king."

R' Nosson Tzvi Finkel, the late Rosh Yeshivah of Slobodka, noted that all the many accomplishments of King David were only possible, because of the years of life that Adam donated to him. This established the dynasty of King David's house, which included King Solomon who built the Holy Temple in Jerusalem, and eventually the Messiah, who will come from this family and bring the final redemption to the world. All this was after Adam's transgression. What we see is that after the biggest destruction and disaster there was the seed of building the greatest phenomena (*Ohr Hatzafun,* vol. # 2, p.73).

After disasters, it is easy to become discouraged and to feel like giving up. "What will happen?" people ask. "Will we ever be able to rebuild?" It might seem that all is lost and nothing can be salvaged. But the reality is, that we humans were given free will, as R' Nosson Tzvi points out in the above-cited essay. Even after the biggest fall and greatest mistake, we can choose to start building. We can begin again, at that very moment.

When you make a serious mistake, and you see that the consequences of that mistake are truly terrible, you still have a choice. As long as you are alive you can decide — at this very moment to make wiser and more elevated choices.

"How can I build right now?" is the question you need to ask yourself. Spending an excessive amount of time on feeling devastated by the mistake, could prevent you from devoting all of your energy to building right now. True, you do need to be aware of the weight of the mistake — realizing the severity of the wrong that you did — and repent for the transgression. However, you need to strengthen yourself, and keep your major focus on the present. The good that you can do now will not get done, unless you make the correct choices now.

We also see here that Adam realized that, enabling someone else to accomplish, was considered an accomplishment for himself as well. He might have felt that he would like to have these seventy years himself to utilize for himself but, knowing that King David's accomplishments would be so great, he felt that taking into account the comprehensive picture, it would be preferable to sacrifice what he himself would have been able to do during those seventy years.

The practical application of this is, that teaching and influencing others, takes time away from one's own accomplishments during that time. However, the positive words and actions of others that you made possible, are credited to you. Not only are you not losing out but, rather, you have greater merit than you would otherwise have had.

I shared the above-cited Midrash with a number of students. I suggested that they realize that whenever they recite Psalms, whether as part of the morning prayers or any other time, they were benefiting from Adam's sacrifice. "What can you learn from this for yourselves?" I asked them. "Think it over and see what you come up with."

- *"I was attending the wedding of a friend," one student related. "It was an extremely lively wedding. My friend was very outgoing and kind — he was well liked by many. Those in attendance felt a special desire to make his wedding a joyful occasion, and, as such the general atmosphere in the wedding hall was that of a great cele-bration. Later, during the dancing and singing, an illustri-ous Torah scholar entered the wedding hall and the band immediately started playing the tune for,* "May You add days onto the days of the king." *The entire scene was electrifying, the joy was palpable — those dancing at the wedding increased their fervor. That was one of the most intense weddings that I ever attended. What made it extra-special for me, were the thoughts that went through my mind about the Midrash that I had just recently heard. Adam sacrificed seventy years of his life, to make King David's existence possible. This great scholar sacrificed much of his own time and energy for others. People would constantly contact him, in person and through writing. He gave an unbelievable amount of himself. I am motivated to use him as a role model for myself."*

- *"After you mentioned the idea of sacrificing for others," another student said, "I realized how far away I was from this ideal. I get annoyed when people take my time, even when they really need me to help them out with answers to questions they have, or to explain passages in texts that they find difficult I often feel that spending my time on them is taking me away from my accom-plishing everything, that I would like to. Reflecting on the Midrash to this verse, I realized that I should consider their gain an integral part of my own accomplishments. I felt the difference the next time someone approached me to help him out with something, that would take at least fifteen minutes of my time. I actually felt happy that I was able to help him. I no longer viewed this as* taking away from my own accomplishments, but rather, this added to what I was achieving in this world."

- "I have to confess that when I heard the Midrash I was a bit cynical," another student revealed. "That's all fine and well for Adam, to think this way. He was donating the years of his life to King David. First of all, King David was a direct descendant of Adam — many grandparents are happy to make sacrifices for their grandchildren. In addition look at all that King David accomplished — He was a great King, he wrote Psalms and the Messiah will be his descendant. However, the people who make demands of my time are so far from being this way, my first reaction was, that I cannot apply this to the individuals with whom I would be interacting. Then I thought about this a bit more. It hit me that I, too, am a descendant of Adam. It was my great great great etc. grandfather who had the greatness to do this. This was no longer the story of someone who had no connection with me, who did something great. In addition, not only am I a descendant of Adam, but so, too, are all the people whom I would be spending time helping. This thought made it much easier for me to think about what I could do to emulate this magnanimous act with historic repercussions."

- Another student focused on the first insight. "I tend to become greatly discouraged when I see that I am trying and trying to make positive choices of thoughts, words, and actions, and then, boom, the evil inclination gets me and I fall. 'Why should I keep trying?' I ask myself. Whom am I fooling if I think to myself that, when I try again I won't fall this time? Contemplating this Midrash and the lessons to be learned, I realize — that even when I fall, the downside is not as destructive as the downfall of Adam. He raised himself, and that is what I need to do. Every time I hear this song in the future, I'll view it as a message to be more resilient. Knowing that I can bounce back and still accomplish in positive ways, gives me the strength to continue to do much more in the present."

﴾ **62 / סב** ﴿

וֹ אַךְ לֵאלֹהִים דּוֹמִּי נַפְשִׁי כִּי־מִמֶּנּוּ תִּקְוָתִי:
זֹ אַךְ־הוּא צוּרִי וִישׁוּעָתִי מִשְׂגַּבִּי לֹא אֶמּוֹט:
חֹ עַל־אֱלֹהִים יִשְׁעִי וּכְבוֹדִי צוּר־עֻזִּי מַחְסִי בֵּאלֹהִים:

⁶ For HASHEM *alone, wait silently my soul,
because my hope is from Him.*
⁷ He *alone is my Rock and my Salvation; my
Stronghold, I shall not falter.*
⁸ Upon HASHEM *rests my salvation and my glory,
the Rock of my strength, my Refuge, is in
HASHEM.*

King David speaks to his soul (verse 6) and tells it to wait silently. Why? Because his hope rests on his awareness of Hashem being his salvation and glory. He knows that Hashem is his rock of strength and his refuge.

When we are agitated, worried about the future, and full of anxiety, our inner soul is calling out in turmoil. We are afraid of the unknown. We are worried that we might suffer. We are in a state of despair.

Just as a loving parent soothingly tells a young child that all will be well in order to calm the child, so too King David speaks to his inner soul and tells it that it can feel at peace.

When we feel a sense of well-being, we are calm inside. Our mind is clear. We think at our best. We are more creative. Our muscles throughout our body, are relaxed. We feel good. When we know we are safe, we automatically feel this way.

However, as soon as we feel there is danger, our entire muscular system tightens up. It is a warning signal to our minds that we must do what we can to protect ourselves. We might have to be ready to flee to safety. We might need to hide or fight. We need all our protective inner resources to be on the alert.

Some people feel this way all the time. Even when they seem safe, inside they are always fearful and anxious. Some danger might be lurking somewhere or someone might say or do something to cause them harm. Over time, the stress they experience from being in this mode constantly, takes its toll on their emotional and physical health. This can cause a great deal of suffering.

When facing potential danger, if we know for certain that we will be fine, we will be able to maintain a sense of calm. On our planet there are numerous possible dangers that may occur at any time. How can we overcome this stress? We can emulate King David. We can soothe our souls and internalize the awareness that Hashem is our rock and our salvation. This will enable us to become serene, and maintain this serenity.

> "I grew up in a nervous family. There was a lot of love and caring, but worrisome statements were common. 'Oy, what if this happens?' 'The latest news cannot help but cause stress.' 'No one has a guaranteed solution to the dangers we face.' There is a strong possibility that we might face a catastrophe.' 'If you do not worry, it's a sign that you are not living in reality.'
>
> "I thought that stress and nervousness was the sign of an intelligent person, someone who is aware of reality and does not want to hide his head in the sand, like an ostrich. The main role models in my life tended to be fearful and frequently anxious — it seemed normal to me.
>
> "Then, 'there was a turning point in my life when I met a childhood friend whom I had not seen in a long time. He seemed so calm and relaxed. I remembered him being rather timid and fearful when we were growing up and I asked him how he kept calm. You probably try to hide yourself from hearing the latest news, I said to him. If you read the papers and listen to people talk about what is going on in the world, it would be impossible to maintain this calm manner — unless you are really more nervous on the inside, than is noticeable on the outside.'"
>
> " 'I do feel calm on the inside, he told me, and I do keep up with the latest current events, I do happen to hear negative predictions, and my initial reaction is often one of great concern. I have not yet mastered the ability to be fearless no matter what, but I am careful not to take needless risks to my health and safety.'

" 'So what is your secret?' I asked him.

" 'I talk to my soul with words of bitachon *(trust in Hashem),'* he replied. *'I gently and calmly tell myself, "My trust in Hashem is getting stronger and stronger. The more trust I experience, the calmer I feel. Every time I begin to feel anxious, I will increase my feeling of inner trust. I am becoming more and more calm and relaxed all the time."*

"I have repeated these encouraging words of hope so many times, that they are on my mind as soon as I need them. They have freed me from much of the distress that many people suffer.

"I have realized on a much deeper and more profound level that the thoughts that I have, create my emotional reality. Any time my muscles become needlessly tense, I tell myself, 'Thank you, Hashem, for giving me a reminder that I need to increase my trust in You.' I am becoming more proficient at this all the time. My goal is, that this should become an automatic part of my thinking, and it will seem the most natural thing in the world for me to remain calm and serene — regardless of the circumstances."

ט בִּטְחוּ בוֹ בְכָל־עֵת עָם שִׁפְכוּ לְפָנָיו לְבַבְכֶם אֱלֹהִים מַחֲסֶה־לָּנוּ סֶלָה:

⁹ **Trust in Him at every moment, o people! pour out your hearts before Him, God is a refuge for us, forever.**

The first part of this verse tells us to trust in Hashem at every moment. There are moments when we might feel worried and discouraged, and there are times when we feel a complete lack of hope. *Tehillim* tells us to have *bitachon*, trust in Hashem, at all times. No matter how bleak a situation seems to be, keep up your sense of hope that Hashem will save you. He has been a source of refuge in the past and will be so in the future as well.

Two people can seem to be experiencing the exact same external situation, both facing severe challenges, but one has hope and the other does not. Thus, in reality, they are not both in the same circumstances. One is experiencing a hopeless situation, while the other is experiencing a difficult situation, but knows that the picture can change at any moment.

This can be compared to two people who were facing execution by a firing squad. One feels absolutely doomed. Since no one is appealing for a stay of execution and no one has filed a motion to push off his imminent death. He knows that this is the end. The other person, however, knows that he has friends in high places in the government. In fact, his closest friend is doing all he can to obtain a presidential pardon. On the day that he is supposed to be executed, his friend sends him a message, "Don't give up! There is a good chance that I will be successful at saving you. Have hope."

A person who knows that Hashem is his source of refuge, realizes that he has the ultimate Highest Power on his side. He has an awareness that, even at the very last moment, the message can come through that he will be a free man. His main focus, then, is not on his being killed in a few minutes, but rather, on the hope and prayer that the pardon will come through on time. He has no guarantee and, therefore, he is far from being relaxed, but the sense of hope gives him inner strength. The look on his face will be very different from the look of the other person, who is totally without hope.

"Pour out your hearts before Him." When you are in emotional turmoil and emotional distress, verbalizing your thoughts and feelings, lets off steam. Talking to someone who cares about you and understands you, melts away stress, tension and emotional pain. Pouring your heart out to your loving Father and powerful King, Creator and Sustainer of the universe, is a wonderful way to release the negative energy that you are feeling. After pouring out your heart, your heart becomes lighter.

One might think that, after someone meets the requirements of the first half of the verse, one does not need the second half. Having constant trust in Hashem should take away anxiety and emotional distress, and for some people it will. However, for others, there is still a strong need to express themselves verbally, and if you have this need, do not just keep your weighty feelings inside. Express yourself. Pouring out your heart means that you are not just coldly and objectively stating how you are thinking and feeling. Rather, your deep emotions are strongly felt and the way that you express this, dramatizes what is going on inside you. This is not always appropriate or possible with other people, but it is always appropriate and possible with our loving Father in Heaven.

"I was a private person and did not like to let others know my inner thoughts and feelings. It is nobody else's business. I grew up in a family where people never spoke about their feelings. When I was a child, I was told to keep it to myself, if I was upset. 'You're not supposed to be upset about trivial things and everything is trivial,' I was often told.

"In my forties, I was living a successful life and felt that everything was just fine, but I began feeling chest pains and tiring easily. I spoke to my doctor about it. He was highly insightful and had a great understanding of his patients.

" 'How do you handle being under a lot of stress?' he asked me.

" 'I don't think that I am under more stress than anyone else, who is in a similar profession and has a life situation that compares to mine.' I told him.

" 'I think that you are in denial,' he said. 'And this is not good for your health. You bury your distress. This does not eliminate the stress, but it prevents you from doing anything about it. I would advise you to find a professional counselor to whom you can speak.'

"I realized that many people do gain from finding someone who will listen to them, and share their burdens, but that was not for me. I did not like the idea of having to tell anyone else about the details of my life, since I was always independent and wanted to do things by myself. However, the doctor had a point. I was under more stress than I had realized, and for the sake of my health, I had to find a way to release it.

"The next morning during prayers, I realized that I was praying out of obligation and habit. My heart was not in

what I was saying. I envied people who prayed with fervor. When prayers were officially over, I said to myself, 'Let me express myself to the Almighty in my own words.' I waited until I was in my car, so no one would overhear me, and I began to verbalize the heaviness that I was feeling. I began to put all my worries into words, as I expressed to the Almighty my frustrations and disappointments. This was the first time I had ever poured out what was on my heart, in this manner. Fifteen minutes of this brought me an inner calm that I had not felt in a long, long time. I resolved to keep this up as a daily practice.

"On my next visit to my doctor, he said to me, 'I do not know with whom you are talking but, whoever it is, has created a miracle for you. You have improved greatly, in a short while.'"

⦅ **63 / סג** ⦆

א מִזְמוֹר לְדָוִד בִּהְיוֹתוֹ בְּמִדְבַּר יְהוּדָה:
ב אֱלֹהִים אֵלִי אַתָּה אֲשַׁחֲרֶךָּ צָמְאָה לְךָ נַפְשִׁי
כָּמַהּ לְךָ בְשָׂרִי בְּאֶרֶץ־צִיָּה וְעָיֵף בְּלִי־מָיִם:

¹ **A Psalm by David, when he was in the wilderness of Judah.**
² **O God, you are my God, I seek you. my soul thirsts for You, my flesh longs for You; in a parched and thirsty land with no water.**

King David is in the Judean desert. There is no water, the basic element that we all need to keep alive. Especially in a hot climate, one becomes dehydrated easily. But what does he long for? What does he seek? He seeks Hashem. Water is necessary to keep our bodies alive. Water is needed for our inner systems to work properly, but Hashem is the source of our lives. Our everlasting souls need a connection with our loving Father and powerful King. This thirst for Hashem is the thirst felt by our spiritual souls.

This verse is cited in the classic work (Duties of the Hearts) *Chovos Halevavos* (*Shaar Ahavas Hashem,* chapter 3) to demonstrate the feelings of one who has reached a high level of love for Hashem. There will be a deep longing for Hashem — one will feel joyful when one connects with Hashem. These thoughts come to us after we free ourselves from the mundane pleasures of this world, and allow our minds to be filled with the wonders of Hashem and His creation. We realize the greatness of Hashem and our own tiny place in the entire universe, and we realize the extent of the kindnesses of Hashem that are always with us. We feel grateful and feel love for the source of all the good in our lives.

It is highly recommended that one study the entire section in *Chovos Halevavos* dealing with love for Hashem. In this 10th *Shaar* (Gate), the author elaborates on various aspects of this lofty level. He explains how love for Hashem is the highest level of serving Hashem. He answers questions such as: How do we define love for Hashem? In what ways can we love Hashem? How do we reach the level of loving Hashem? Can a human being really reach this level? What things prevent a person from reaching love for Hashem? How can we recognize if a person truly loves Hashem? What are the actions and patterns of someone who loves Hashem?

Rabbi Noah Weinberg (of Yeshiva Aish Hatorah) has taught many newcomers to their Jewish heritage that, the greatest pleasure in life is love for Hashem, and that many people settle for much less in life than they could achieve, by lacking this understanding.

> *Someone who wished to connect with Hashem on a regular basis, asked his rabbi for a tool that he could use as a reminder to remember to love Hashem.*
>
> *"We say the verses of* Krias Shema *daily, which state explicitly that we are to love Hashem with all our heart, with all our soul, and with all that we have. You have reminders all the time," the rabbi replied.*
>
> *"True, this should really be sufficient for me to remember to love Hashem, but having regularly recited* Shema *for so long, I would appreciate a special reminder to assist me to*

advance beyond my habitual saying of this verse. A new tool could add a fresh dimension for me."

The rabbi suggested to the student, "Whenever you are thirsty and drink water to quench your thirst, you can recite this verse from Psalms. 'My soul thirsts for You, Hashem.' This will serve as a daily reminder that, just as you need water to stay alive and healthy, you need Hashem even more. This inner association of water quenching your thirst will gave you a greater realization that, quenching your thirst for Hashem, does even more for you."

The rabbi himself had not done this before, and a few weeks later he went over to the student and said, "I have to thank you intensely. I had just thought of that exercise when you asked me for one. I found that this gave me a greater personal experience of what lacking Hashem in one's life is like, and how life-giving increasing love for Hashem truly is."

⊰{ **64 / סד** }⊱

ג תַּסְתִּירֵנִי מִסּוֹד מְרֵעִים מֵרִגְשַׁת פֹּעֲלֵי אָוֶן:
ד אֲשֶׁר שָׁנְנוּ כַחֶרֶב לְשׁוֹנָם דָּרְכוּ חִצָּם דָּבָר מָר:
ה לִירוֹת בַּמִּסְתָּרִים תָּם פִּתְאֹם יֹרֻהוּ וְלֹא יִירָאוּ:

³ **Hide me from the counsel of the wicked, from the assembly of evildoers,** ⁴ **Who have sharpened their tongue like the sword, and drawn their arrow — a bitter word —** ⁵ **To shoot in conceal-ment at the innocent, suddenly they shoot him and they are unafraid.**

Here King David is talking about evildoers who spitefully and wickedly use their power of speech, to cause harm to others. Words are capable of serving as weapons of destruction; words can kill. Words can be like a sharp sword to destroy someone's confidence and to lower his self-esteem. Words can be like arrows to knock someone down. Though a person might be innocent, a false story told cunningly to strike down an adversary or a competitor, or for revenge, can cause a lifetime of anguish and damage. David asks Hashem for His help to hide him from the negative effect of harmful words.

The vast majority of people who will be reading a book on insights into Psalms, would not spitefully and maliciously try to harm another person. But it could happen — people can respond out of character when they are very angry. They can say and do things that they would never think of saying or doing, when they are calm. We need to internalize the importance of watching what we say when our minds are clear. We need to think about this often and then, as this value will become an integral part of our identity, we will even be careful with what we say when we are angry. For this reason the Sages say that we reveal our character when we are angry. Having self-discipline, even when we are angry, shows that the Torah values of guarding our tongues are strong and deep.

People tend to rationalize when they are upset. They can argue about why someone with whom they are quarreling, needs to be critisized. If someone had a bow and arrow and feels that his life is threatened by someone, even though he might not actually be in any danger, his erroneous thinking could possibly lead to an attack on an innocent person. A similar situation exists with words. In a quarrel, there is a strong tendency to see oneself as totally right and the other party as totally wrong. The words and actions of the other person might appear to be threatening, and a person might feel that his own sharp words are simply self-defense. But in reality they are wrong — and an innocent person pays a heavy price.

This verse also even addresses a kind-hearted, well-meaning person: Be careful with your words. You might have positive intentions. You might think that if you reprimand someone who needs to make positive changes, your words will be beneficial, but if your words are like a sword or an arrow, they could cause much grief.

We all realize that a loaded gun is dangerous. One needs proper training to use it; it is not a toy. Someone who is only fooling around with a gun, can seriously maim or kill. Not long ago I read about a five-year-old boy who accidentally killed his sister and a friend while playing with his father's gun. The father had a license to use the gun, but he was careless, and the outcome was tragic. Words should be viewed with similar responsibility.

"Just joking" is not a valid excuse for saying things we should not say. "I assumed he would not mind," is not always a valid assumption. It's preferable to assume that people will mind, unless they tell you otherwise. "I repeated his secret because I felt that the person I related it to, would not pass it on further." You passed it on; why should you assume that someone else would be more careful!

No one would want to be considered part of the "counsel of the wicked." That's commendable. So be careful with what you say and you will prevent yourself from unintentionally becoming part of that group.

I heard a speaker elaborate on the topic of not believing negative comments and statements about others. Just as it is forbidden to speak lashon hara *against people, so too it is forbidden to believe a negative report, as the complete truth. When the information is necessary to know for practical and constructive purposes, you are allowed to exhibit caution to protect yourself, but you are not allowed to accept it as the absolute truth.*

Someone in the audience asked him, "How do you do this? Even though you say that you do not believe him, don't you have inner doubts that maybe what he is saying is true?"

"If you happened to speak to someone who was guilty of shooting many innocent people and he told you something negative about another person, would he have any credibility in your eyes? You would wonder why he is saying this to you; what is his hidden agenda? Even if he does tell you something that he thinks is valid and true, because of his crimes and lack of kindness and responsibility, you will always entertain the possibility that he is making a mistake. He does not seem like the type of person who is careful with the truth, since the crimes that he has committed are much worse than distortion of the truth. That is the attitude we

should have towards someone who maliciously talks against others. His own offense is often much worse than the offense that he blames on others."

יא יִשְׂמַח צַדִּיק בַּיהוָה וְחָסָה בוֹ וְיִתְהַלְלוּ כָּל־יִשְׁרֵי־לֵב:

---

¹¹ **The righteous one will rejoice in HASHEM and take refuge in Him; and all who are upright in heart will be glorified.**

This verse is cited in the classic work *Chovos Halevavos* as a description of the rejoicing that those who love Hashem will experience, through their connection with Hashem. They will cleave to this love for Hashem, as they have total trust in His compassion and mercy. This love will fill their consciousness, and they will not fear anything else besides Hashem. Thoughts about Hashem will constantly be on their mind and never leave them. If they are ever alone, Hashem's presence will be there to keep them company. Even in a wilderness, Hashem will be with them. A busy marketplace with throngs of people will be the same as an empty place without anyone else present, and a place that is empty of other people will be like a place that is full. They will never be bored — even without any human companionship. They will be in a constant state of joyfulness with their consciousness of Hashem and their personal relationship with Him. They will constantly seek out His will, and their inner longing to meet with Hashem (as we see in this verse), will give them joy (*Shaar Ahavas Hashem*, ch.#3).

Reading and re-reading these thoughts from *Duties of the Heart* will help us integrate this elevating way of thinking. As with mastering other lofty levels, this takes time and effort. Be patient. When we truly want something, it can be challenging to be patient, but — without patience — we will never reach the goal for which we are striving.

Regardless of our actual physical location or who else is present, we are, in fact, in the place on which our inner thoughts are focused. If a person is a worrier and tends to think about what might go wrong in his life, it is easy to worry, whether he is alone or with others. It is easy to worry whether attending a wedding or a funeral. It is easy to worry whether traveling or staying home.

The opposite is true as well. If someone recently experienced a great thing in his life: he just got the job of his dreams, he won a great award, he had his first child or grandchild, the person whom he or she was hoping to marry said yes, the house that he considered ideal just became available at a price he could afford, then one's thoughts will be totally focused on this good thing. Regardless of where a person is, the outside circumstances are not where his mind is. His mind is full of joyful celebration, whether he is by himself or with others.

Such is the mind of the righteous. They are always thinking of Hashem. They are thinking thoughts of studying Hashem's Torah, of praying to Hashem and reciting blessings for all the good in their lives, and thoughts of kindness, which is emulating the ways of Hashem by being kind to His children. Thinking of Hashem gives them joy, and they are always thinking of Hashem. This is an amazing goal toward which to strive.

> *Someone approached Rabbi Gavriel Ginsburg,* mashgiach *in Telshe Yeshivah in Wickliffe, Ohio (later Rosh Yeshivah of Ner Israel of Toronto) and complained, "Rebbe, from the bottom of my heart I want to reach high spiritual levels, but I find my quest very disappointing. I'm not able to maintain the levels that I yearn to reach."*
>
> *"Let go of your distress," he said, "It is not going to help you reach the levels you want. However, wanting to reach high levels and feeling this aspiration is a positive level to be on. When you reach for the stars you might not catch any, but at least you will not get your hands in the mud."*
>
> *That student related that this last sentence has been a motto with which he has lived. Many people refrain from making positive goals for themselves because they are afraid that they will not reach them. Knowing that striving for the heights helps you reach higher than you would have other-wise, is inspiring and motivating.*

❧ **68 / סח** ❧

ד וְצַדִּיקִים יִשְׂמְחוּ יַעַלְצוּ לִפְנֵי אֱלֹהִים וְיָשִׂישׂוּ בְשִׂמְחָה:

⁴ And the righteous will be joyful, they will exult before HASHEM; they will rejoice with joyfulness.

Human beings want to feel good, and they do not want to feel bad. Therefore, human beings seek pleasure and they look forward to experiences that give them joy. Pleasure and joy are different, but they both are aspects of feeling good.

If one thinks about it, there are certain similarities between a righteous person and an evil person. They both are doing things that they think will give them positive feelings and, even though a righteous person has more self-discipline and self-mastery, he realizes that he will have more pleasure and joy in the long run by having that self-discipline and self-mastery.

There are many facets to this but, in the context of this verse, let us gain a greater realization that the path of the righteous person is much wiser than that of the evil person, or even that of the simple person. The pleasure and joy in their lives will be much more long-lasting than the pleasures of a so-called pleasure seeker.

Commentaries (cited in *Mikdash Me'at*) note that, when we look at the standard pleasures of a pleasure-seeker, we will realize that his actual experiences of pleasure are temporary and short-lived.

When a person who is focused on the physical pleasure of eating and drinking anticipates a good meal, he feels excited. He is about to partake in something he enjoys, and while he is eating and drinking he experiences the taste of the food and drink and enjoys it. However, the moment he is through eating, the pleasure is immediately gone, and if he ate too much or drank too much, as is quite common, he will even feel upset. When thinking about the weight he has gained, he will regret that he indulged himself, and if he is conscious about the health issues involved, he will wish that he had been more careful with what he ate. Even if he did not indulge himself, the moment the experience is over, the pleasure dissipates.

On the other hand, when a righteous person does a good deed, he feels joy when he looks forward to doing the good deed, he feels joy while he is doing the good deed, and he feels joy when he looks back at the good deed that he has performed. He too will eat and drink, but he eats and drinks to be healthy. He eats and drinks to have energy so he can think, speak, and act according to Hashem's wishes. He eats and drinks to honor Shabbos and holidays. This eating and drinking is a *mitzvah,* and therefore he feels joy before, during, and after. He is full of joy in connecting with his beloved Father, and powerful King, Creator and Sustainer of the universe. He is full of joy when his thoughts are focused on the eternal benefits of what he has done.

If people who only seek worldly pleasures would be more aware of what they would gain in terms of living a joyful life by gaining a *mitzvah-* orientation to life, they would upgrade their entire way of thinking and acting. They want pleasure and joy, and they would realize that the way to long-lasting pleasure and joy is rejoicing in Torah and *mitzvos.*

> *"I try to be a good person. I study Torah each day, I pray in the synagogue, and I give money to charity, but I lack happiness in my life," I complained to a wise rabbi to whom I had traveled some distance. "I do have happy moments in my life, but my general feeling is not happy. I probably have many more moments of distress than I do of joy but I am not what anyone would consider clinically depressed. My quality of life is just as good as the professional psychologists and social workers that I have met. I even went to a few therapists for counseling, but each time I was told that I do not really have any problems that they can help me solve. I was told to relax more, exercise more and eat healthier food, but I know that there must be a way to live a happier life than I am living."*
>
> *" 'If you will experience joy every moment of your life, you will always be happy,' the rabbi told me with a warm, fatherly smile. And he gave me a blessing that I should have much joy in my life. 'Think carefully about what I have told you.*

"That was one of the most surprising statements that I'd ever heard. It was like being told, 'To be happy you just have to be happy.' Or, 'To be calm and serene you just have to be calm and serene.' It was a tautology. It was true, but it did not seem very helpful to me.

"Later that day I attended a lecture that this rabbi gave to a number of his students. He mentioned how we are always in the present, and in the present we should constantly be aware that Hashem is our loving Father and that it is our greatest privilege to study His Torah and fulfill His commandments.

"Hearing this gave me the insight I needed. I was used to constantly thinking about what is going to happen in the future: I need to feel more joy later on. I need to feel calmer and more serene later on. I realized however, that all I ever really needed to do was, to be joyful in the present. Since I was always in the presence of my loving Father, and I always had ways to serve Him with my thoughts, words, and actions, I always had cause to rejoice. That is all I and every-one else needs to do — to be joyful right at this moment.

"We live our lives, moment by moment. We are always in the present — the past is always over, and the future is never here yet. I did not need to focus on <u>always</u> *being joyful, because then I might be overly concerned about how I will be joyful later on, and that will cause anxiety and stress. I mentally pictured myself applying this, and I felt joy that very moment.*

"I see that I know how to do this. I know that, just as I can talk and write in the present moment, so I can always talk and write. So too, I now know that just as I can be joyful in the present moment, so too I can always be joyful. It's my choice to think these thoughts — I felt a tremendous break-through. This did not come from just hearing these ideas or knowing that I could repeat them — it came from making them my everyday reality."

The way to a joyful life seems so simple once you hear it: Rejoice with joyfulness right at this very moment. Every moment you rejoice with joyfulness you will experience joyful feelings. Calmly and patiently practice this and it will become your instinctive attitude. If you ever get off track, which almost inevitably will happen, calmly bring yourself back to being joyful in joyfulness. Every time you do this, it is stored in your brain's mental library and it becomes easier and easier to do, again and again. You only need to do this, in the present. The future is only a concept — the present is your only reality. Think about this thought, reflect on it, and allow its awareness to elevate your life.

כ בָּרוּךְ אֲדֹנָי יוֹם יוֹם יַעֲמָס־לָנוּ הָאֵל יְשׁוּעָתֵנוּ סֶלָה:

20 Blessed is HASHEM *day by day He supplies us, the Almighty of our salvation. Selah.*

This verse tells us that we should bless Hashem each day for that with which He supplies us. Each and every day, we should trust in Him that He will help us with what we need for that day.

The vast majority of people have what they need for today. Today, they know they can manage. What they are worried about is tomorrow, and the next day, and the day after that. Some people have enough for this month and some people have enough for this year. But they might worry about what they will have next month or next year.

People who keep worrying about "later on" will always experience the distress of worry because, regardless of what they have today, they will worry about having enough for tomorrow. And regardless of how good things are going for them today, they will worry about how things will be in the future.

Since today one can never know exactly how things will be in the future, if one lacks trust in Hashem, one can always worry about how things will be, after today. Even if one has abundance for today, how can he be certain that he will still have abundance tomorrow? This mindset will guarantee constant anxiety; regardless of how successful one is right now, how can he have a one-hundred-percent certainty about how life will unfold for him after today?

This verse teaches us the lesson we need in order to master the emotional states of serenity, appreciation, and gratitude. Be grateful to Hashem for what Hashem has given you for today.

You have a choice. You can focus on what you do not yet have for the unknown tomorrow, or you can focus on what you do know you have today. The wise choice is the decision, "I will be grateful to Hashem each and every day for all the good of today. I will bless Him for this, and I will trust that He will save me whenever I need salvation."

Right now, allow yourself to experience appreciation for that which Hashem has given you for today. Feel this. Keep your focus on this present moment and this present day. Be completely here right now and feel any anxiety and worry about any time in the future, melt away.

Keep reciting this verse: "I bless Hashem day by day." Then you will always find something for which to be grateful, on each and every day.

> *A businessman told me, "I grew up in a home where financial security was a very high priority. Although we always had enough so that we did not have to worry about today, as well as many days to come, nevertheless, we were often told, 'We need to plan ahead for a rainy day. No matter how much you have, you never know how much you will need later on. Save and keep saving.'*
>
> *"On one level, this was a sensible attitude; financial planning makes sense. However, my father was always a nervous wreck about money. He would lash out at anyone in our household who was not careful not to waste money. He would often yell at my mother that she should have been more careful not to waste money. If I or my brother and sister ever spent more money than necessary, we would hear a long speech — about how money does not grow on trees — about how we would end up in the poorhouse if we spent too much — about how we would suffer in the future if we spent too much money now. My father would work the entire day, from early morning until late at night, never taking vacations regardless of how tired and worn out he was.*
>
> *"Frequently, he would tell us, 'True, I have enough money for this year — but next year things might be rough and we*

need to make certain not to waste a single penny'. While we were considered wealthy by most people's standards, according to my father, we were far from wealthy. His constant stress and nervousness, gave us the feeling that we were among the poorest people in town. My friends had a much easier time asking their fathers for money than we did, even though, as I found out later, we had much more money in the bank than their families did.

"I inherited my father's attitude towards money. Money was a constant source of tension for me, also. What changed this for me was a class in Chovos Halevavos (Duties of the Heart) that I attended. The Rabbi taught us the section about having trust in Hashem. He painted a picture of what it was like to lack trust in Hashem and how much emotional suffering this would cause. This could be a source of great conflict in families, and being in a constant state of worry and stress could cause heath problems.

"The rabbi cited the Talmudic statement that, since we never know whether we will still be in this world tomorrow, we should never worry about the next day. We definitely can and should plan for tomorrow; the goal is to be calm and serene about tomorrow. A mind that is free from worry is free to think more elevated thoughts. 'If you do not appreciate what you have today — right now — then you are likely never to appreciate what you have because, on any given day, there is always another day that you can worry about. When you master the ability to be grateful for what you have each and every day, you will be able to experience happiness and joy, each day of your life.'

"This made sense to me. I could immediately see how much I would gain from making this my own way of thinking. As soon as I made a resolution to make this attitude my own, I felt calmer than I had felt for longer than I can remember. I have made this my goal. While I will go back to my old familiar pattern of worrying about the future every once in a while, it has become relatively easy for me to return to thoughts of appreciation for the present gifts that Hashem gives me."

ה יָשִׂישׂוּ וְיִשְׂמְחוּ בְּךָ כָּל־מְבַקְשֶׁיךָ

⁵ *Let all who seek You [HASHEM] rejoice and be glad in You.*

Seeking Hashem is a source of happiness. Reaching the goal gives us a great sense of joy. Even the path of seeking the goal is a path of joy and gladness.

Usually when people seek something, they feel a degree of anxiety, to some extent. The more important the thing they seek is to them, the easier it is to feel anxious. "What if I do not find what I seek?" they say to themselves, and the way you speak to yourself is the way you will feel.

When you seek Hashem, you can feel inner joy in knowing that you are on a life-mission that is of the highest caliber. It takes time and effort to elevate oneself, and that is the way that it is meant to be. When it comes to spirituality, there is not a lottery ticket that you can buy. With a lottery ticket, a person pays money for the ticket, and that is all that he must do. Having the winning number is not based on effort and study. A person sits back passively and hopes that the number he has chosen, or that has been chosen for him, will be the winning number.

When it comes to developing our connection with Hashem, however, we must make an effort. There are challenges and obstacles that we must overcome. It is easy to have ups and downs.

When seeking Hashem, we need to keep focusing on our goal. We need to elevate our thoughts, our words, and our actions; this is an ongoing life process. There is never a moment that we can say, "Here I am. I've reached the top of Mount Everest and I am totally successful." Rather, at every given moment, we need to strengthen our connection with Hashem.

Those who view seeking Hashem as a heavy burden, can easily become tired. The effort needed is so great that it is possible to feel, "I cannot keep this up, this wears me out. I am so exhausted that I am feeling overwhelmed."

We have the blessings of King David. "Let all who seek [Hashem]" Yes, "all" — every one of us. Every person in King David's generation, and every person in every generation thereafter. That includes our generation right now, and all future ones. King David has asked our loving Father and powerful King to give us rejoicing and gladness when we seek Him.

Allow yourself to accept this blessing. Imagine that you personally had an audience with the great King David and you are standing in front of him while he is seated on his throne. You know the power of his words and his prayers — he is the appointed one from Hashem — and he gives you this blessing: "You will have the greatest of joys possible in this world by seeking Hashem." Imagine the inspiration that you would feel. You would walk out of the palace with such an elevated feeling that nothing else could compare to it. You have been guaranteed success in the most important endeavor possible in this world.

This blessing will give you joy in all that you do on that day and the next day and as long as you allow yourself to feel it. Your prayers will be on a higher plane. Your Torah study will be filled with the great joy of seeking and connecting with Hashem. You are studying His will, and you are committed to putting it into practice. Every act of kindness that you do will give you great joy. "Right now I am actively being kind to another child of Hashem. I emulate Hashem with the words that I say and the actions that I do."

Rejoice right now and rejoice each day. You, too, are a recipient of King David's powerful, life-transforming blessing.

> *A sincere young fellow spoke to his rabbi about a general feeling of sadness. "For a long time now, I feel an inner emptiness," he said. "I experience this throughout the day. Even when I pray and study Torah, there is very little emotion involved. If my mind were focused and I were growing intellectually, I would feel a sense of satisfaction and accomplishments, but I keep telling myself that I am far from the spiritual level that I crave for. I have to force myself out of bed in the morning since I am not motivated and, while I keep trying to be better than I am, I do not see real progress. What can I do?"*
>
> *The rabbi recognized the good intentions of his student, and he knew that if the young man tried too hard, he would*

experience a great deal of tension and anxiety. The stress would simply prevent him from accomplishing even a fraction of what he could. The Rabbi said to him, "Don't force yourself to feel joy serving Hashem. Rather, act the way a joyful person would act, and speak the way a joyful person would speak. Little by little you will find yourself thinking the way a joyful person thinks. Eventually you will actually become a joyful person."

"I don't like to act," the fellow said. "I want to be truthful. I want to be real and authentic."

"That's definitely the goal," the rabbi said. "Rambam in Hilchos Dei'os tells us that the way to become a kind and giving person is to do many acts of kindness. Eventually you will actually be a kind person. This will be a trait that is part of your very being. In the beginning, however, you need to start off by acting the way you wish to be. For most people, doing acts of kindness out of a sense that this is the way that you eventually want to truly be, is easier than acting the way a joyful person acts. However, this will work when you consistently act this way. It is about percisely this that R' Moshe Chaim Luzzatto wrote (Mesilas Yesharim, ch.#7), "Your external movements influence your inner self." Make a mental picture of how a person who experiences joy serving Hashem, will speak and act. Now, follow through and speak and act this way, as an exercise in making this your reality. What you tell yourself about this, is a key to making it work. Make your self-talk encouraging and motivating. Keep telling yourself, 'Keep speaking and acting the way a joyful person does. Each word I speak and each action I take with joy, makes me a more joyful person.'

"Enjoy the process. Every step of the way you are engaged in thoughts, words, and actions that connect you with Hashem. You are seeking Him, and that itself is reason to rejoice and be glad."

A month later the young man contacted the rabbi to thank him. "This has been the greatest month of my life," he reported. "I now see what you mean; the longer I keep this up, the more natural it becomes."

﴾ **73 / עג** ﴿

כח וַאֲנִי קִרֲבַת אֱלֹהִים לִי־טוֹב

[28] *As for me, HASHEM's nearness is my good.*

R' Moshe Chaim Luzzatto comments on this verse, "The only thing that one can truly call good in this world is, closeness to Hashem."

The value of anything is based on comparison. When you browse in a jewelry store, you can determine whether or not an item is truly valuable, according to its price. There is often a large gap between the price of the most expensive item in the store and the least expensive one. Therefore, the value of any single piece in this store can be determined by how close it is to either end of the spectrum.

People often say about a service or product, "That's expensive." And the best response is, "Compared to what?"

Suppose someone offers outstanding service in an area that will greatly enhance one's entire life. On the other hand, another person offers a small service that takes just a short amount of time to do, the benefits last just a short time, and it will not make much of a difference in one's life. It is not a valid question to ask a person offering the first service, "Why do you charge more than those people do for their service?" Of course this costs more. It is worth so much more. The other person's price is irrelevant.

When we think about what is of the greatest value and importance in this world, closeness to Hashem is far beyond anything else. It is infinite and eternal — nothing can compare.

The price one must pay for this closeness is not measurable in money. Acquiring this closeness takes time and energy. It takes thought and effort — it is not easy. "But why should I have to make a payment of time, energy, and effort when other things are much easier and simpler?" some might ask. And here, too, the answer is obvious. The benefits you gain are so great that all the work you put into it is only a minimal payment for the tremendous reward in the end.

R' Simcha Zissel of Kelm (*Chochmah U'Mussar*, vol. 2, pp. 33-4) cites this verse and explains that closeness to Hashem means that we emulate Him. We elevate our essence, our conduct, our character to the level where they could be considered walking in Hashem's ways.

The more you appreciate someone's greatness, the more you would like to emulate that person. R' Simcha Zissel wrote that he personally had tremendous respect and appreciation for his great teacher, R' Yisroel Salanter. He appreciated his wisdom and depth of understanding. He appreciated his kindness and compassion and his greatness of character in all ways.

The more we recognize the greatness of our loving Father and powerful King, writes R' Simcha Zissel, the stronger will be our intense will to emulate His kind and loving ways.

Every time we pray, we have an opportunity to become closer to Hashem. Every time we study Torah, we have an opportunity to become closer to Hashem. Every time we do an act of kindness, we have an opportunity to become closer to Hashem. And every time we work on developing our character, we have an opportunity to become closer to Hashem. This is the greatest good. So let us strengthen one another in our journey of elevation.

I knew someone who was a wonderful person, but he had one major fault; he was far from reaching his actual potential. True, you could say that this is true of almost everyone. We all have so much more potential than we actually utilize, but this person was extreme in this way. He thought of many plans, learned great ideas, started many books that he did not finish, and wanted to do so many wonderful things, that he would start one project and, before he got very far, he would stop doing that and begin to do something else.

There was an approach that was helpful for him and I think that this will be helpful for others. Think about your most important goals and rate the most important a 10. There are many potential distractions that will arise. Some of them will be minor things to do; whether or not you do them will not affect your life very much. Rate the ones that are the least important a 1, while other distractions might be a 4 or 5 or a

6 in importance. Keep your major focus on those activities that you would rate 9's and 10's. Thinking in these terms, you still will need to take care of items that have a low rating but, since you will be consciously aware of how much or little importance they are to you, you will not spend more time than necessary, on those things. This will help you eliminate your major time-wasters.

When it comes to activities that enable you to become closer to Hashem, thinking in terms of a scale from 1 to 10 will be very helpful. When questions come up for you about how you can and should utilize your time, ask yourself, "How would I rate what I am considering doing on my 1 to 10 scale?" As you keep thinking in these terms, you will find yourself making wiser choices.

≈{ **81 / פא** }≈

ב הַרְנִינוּ לֵאלֹהִים עוּזֵּנוּ הָרִיעוּ לֵאלֹהֵי יַעֲקֹב:
ג שְׂאוּ־זִמְרָה וּתְנוּ־תֹף כִּנּוֹר נָעִים עִם־נָבֶל:

²Sing joyously to the God of our strength, call out to the God of Jacob.
³Raise up a song and sound the drum, the sweet harp with the lyre.

In these verses we hear a call to sing joyously to Hashem; not just to sing with words, but also to play musical instruments, to sound drums and to use sweet harps and lyres, which play beautiful music.

What was the purpose of these instruments? Different sound vibrations create different feelings in us as human beings. When drums are played rhythmically, the sounds arouse various feelings and thoughts. The sound of the harp and lyre put people into elevated states of consciousness. Together with the spiritual words that were said, they brought out an awareness that enabled those who heard them, to connect with Hashem in loftier ways.

All noise is made up of vibrations. The waves that are caused are picked up by our ears and reach our brains. Some sounds are annoying, and/or distressing while certain prolonged sounds can even cause headaches and other symptoms of stress and tension. We feel a strong need to escape these sounds; if at all possible, we try to block out these distressful sounds.

Singers whose vocal cords are able to vibrate in ways that create sounds which others enjoy, are highly appreciated. People pay money to listen to them in person, and to buy their recorded singing.

Mentally, compare the sound of a professional orchestra or a band that you enjoy, with sounds that elicit negative feelings in you. What sound do you personally enjoy the most and what noises do you find the most unpleasant? Compare the effects that both have on you.

The awareness of the power of sound to influence our feelings and emotions is vitally important, when it comes to our speaking voice. This does not refer to public speaking, but the way you sound when you speak to family, friends and strangers; the way a parent sounds when talking to a child, and the tone of voice of a child speaking to a parent, the way an employer sounds when talking to an employee and the way a clerk sounds when talking to someone making a request.

Every time you speak — to anyone — your tone of voice is either going to be similar to pleasant music, or to distressful noise. When a person is frustrated or angry or overwhelmed, the tone of voice emits very different music than when a person is calm and serene, happy and joyful, kind and compassionate.

The Torah forbids us to cause pain with our words; this is called *ona'as devarim.* Not only must we be careful with the content of what we say, but also with the way we say it. Particularly when you are upset, tired, or angry, consciously make an effort to speak in ways that will not be distressful to the ears of the listeners.

If someone would have to sing at his best professionally, regardless of how he felt a few minutes earlier, he knows that he has to put himself into the state of singing well. The more important the reason for singing well, the more motivated he would feel to do the best job he possibly could. That should be our attitude when speaking to another child of Hashem. We are speaking in the presence of Hashem, to one of His children. Speak with a tone of voice that is conducive to harmony with others.

In challenging situations, ask yourself, "How would I sing now if my life depended on it?" And then, "Since my spiritual well-being will be affected by the way I speak to other people, who are created in Hashem's image, how would I speak if I were utterly resolved to speak at my best?"

> *I spoke to someone who does family counseling and asked him, "If you could think of one factor that makes a major difference in the way that family members interact with each other, what factor would it be?"*
>
> *This is what he said: "In the years that I've being doing counseling, I have found that, tone of voice is the key factor. When husbands and wives raise their voices, or sound angry or condescending, whatever they disagree about, will turn into a fight. It could be over a trivial matter, but the negative tone of voice will bring out the worst in them. When they decide, that regardless of the issue, they will speak with a tone of voice that reflects mutual re-spect, issues get resolved. Even if an issue is not resolved right away, the respect in their voices brings out the best in them.*
>
> *"The same applies to parents with their children, children with their parents, and children with each other. Teachers should impress upon their students that their tone of voice makes a difference. Just as someone who wants to sing well will practice, so too we all need to practice our tone of voice. Professional public speakers who want to excel, will ask others for feedback about their tone of voice when speaking. They know that their livelihood depends on it and that, if they want to have a positive impact on others, they need to upgrade the way their voice sounds. We all need this. Knowing how important it is will make it a high priority for anyone who does not live in a cave all by himself."*

﴾ 84 / פד ﴿

ה אַשְׁרֵי יוֹשְׁבֵי בֵיתֶךָ עוֹד יְהַלְלוּךָ סֶּלָה:

⁵ *Praiseworthy are those who dwell in Your house, continually they will praise You.*

This verse is the beginning of the famous *Ashrei* prayer. The main part of the *Ashrei* prayer is chapter 145, but this verse is recited as an introduction.

The Hebrew word *Ashrei* is often translated as "praiseworthy," but the word also means "fortunate" or "happy." The word *osher* spelled with the letter *ayin* means "wealth," and the word *osher* with the letter *aleph* means "fortunate" or "happy." Though one frequently hears the comment that being happy is more important than being wealthy, there is a commonly given blessing which wishes that someone have *osher*, both with an *ayin* and an *aleph*."

In his commentary on the first word of Psalms, *Radak* notes that the word *ashrei* is always in the plural. The reason for this, he states, is that a person is not fortunate when only one good thing happens to him or he experiences only one success. Rather, a person needs to have many good things happening to him to be considered a fortunate person.

In this verse who is considered fortunate? The one who dwells in the Almighty's house. *Metzudas David* explains that this refers to the ultimate house of Hashem, which is the Holy Temple that was built in Jerusalem on the Temple Mount. Fortunate are the ones who would be there when it would be built, says King David.

This house of Hashem also refers to the houses of prayer and Torah study. These are places where one experiences the spirituality of connecting with the Creator. We can pray wherever we are, and can study Torah wherever we are, but there is a unique sanctity in a place that is totally dedicated to connecting with our Father, our King, Creator and Sustainer of the universe.

A plurality of much good fortune applies to those who are frequently in the houses of Hashem. Every time one visits one of these houses, one is in a very special place. Visiting the White House to speak to the President of the United States is a special experience. Being invited to such an event is a great honor; protocol requires that one never refuse such an offer. Being invited to the palace of a King for a special meeting with the King is also considered a great honor by his loyal subjects. A simple peasant who will be honored by the King for his loyalty, considers this to be the highlight of his life. That is a fraction of the honor and glory of being invited to the house of the Creator and Sustainer of the universe.

Does every person feel this tremendous honor and privilege each time he visits a house of prayer or a yeshiva devoted to Torah study? Familiarity often makes us take things for granted. The goal to strive for, is to increase our appreciation for the privilege of connecting to the Almighty in a place of worship. Remember, a synagogue or study hall is called *Mikdash Me'at* — a miniature *Bais HaMikdash.*

I was studying in Telshe Yeshiva in Wickliffe, Ohio, in 1967. I remember our exhilration during the Six Day War when it was publicized that the Western Wall was in our hands. We can once again pray there. This is only an outer wall to the Holy Temple — not the Holy Temple itself — yet it is considered a tremendous privilege to think about the possibility of going there to speak to Hashem and to pray to Him. Some of this same excitement and joy should be ours when we contemplate the great privilege of being able to praise Hashem and pray to Him in one of His palaces. Even if the place in which you pray is far from looking like a palace, it is still the dwelling place of the Almighty. Cherish each moment. You are fortunate every time you enter.

> *"When I heard about appreciating each time we pray in a synagogue, I felt a bit guilty. At times I consider this a burden and not a privilege. Even when I am more positive about praying, I take entering into a synagogue for granted. I decided that I needed to build up my appreciation for what I was doing each day.*
>
> *One morning I woke up twenty minutes earlier than usual, to reflect on the immense spiritual possibilities that are available during prayer in shul. I visualized what it would have been like to be among the first people who prayed in the*

first Holy Temple after King Solomon completed building it. Then I visualized what it would be like to be among the first people to enter the Third Holy Temple when it will be rebuilt. This visualization became very real to me and it felt very special. Right after this, when I entered the shul where I pray, I felt a sense of specialness that I had not felt before. Even though I knew that I probably would not be able to have these feelings each time I entered a shul, this experience still gave me a more elevated feeling for quite some time. I am committed to repeating this visualization from time to time to renew these feelings."

אַשְׁרֵי אָדָם עוֹז לוֹ־בָךְ מְסִלּוֹת בִּלְבָבָם: ו

⁶ **Praiseworthy is the person whose strength is in You, those whose hearts focus on upward paths.**

There are various ways that people try to create and access inner strength. Some are positive, and some can be negative and counterproductive. This verse tells us that the best and most praiseworthy way is, to derive inner strength from Hashem, the ultimate source of all strength.

One of the most problematic methods attempted to achieve a feeling of inner strength is, to use various forms of alcohol and similar substances. Alcohol temporarily lifts one's state, but the potential for addiction and for distortion of one's ability to think and analyze objectively, makes this dangerous. Even in the best circumstances such a "solution" is not based on one's clarity of thought. Rather, far from coming from the depth of one's own inner being, the feeling is a result of a purely artificial chemical reaction in one's brain and blood system. Since it is not based on a sense of perspective and it is certainly is not spiritual, it is nothing more than a temporary superficial sense of empowerment.

When you create your inner strength from an awareness of Hashem, the Creator and Sustainer of the universe, it has a powerful foundation. You are connecting your own inner energy with Hashem, the Creator of all the energy that exists, thereby gaining the greatest mental, physical, emotional, and spiritual strength.

How much energy is there in the created universe? There is so much that we have no way to fathom its magnitude. The well-known formula $E=MC^2$ means that in every bit of mass (M), that is, every single object that exists, the amount of energy (E) hidden within is equivalent to the speed of light multiplied by itself (C squared). The speed of light is 186,000 miles per second. When you multiply this by another 186,000 you get quite a large number. The power of this is the power of a nuclear bomb, which causes an explosion of the energy inside a relatively small amount of uranium.

All the power and energy in all the matter of the entire universe is still nothing, compared to the unlimited power of Hashem. When your own inner strength is empowered by the energy of Hashem, you yourself can accomplish amazing things.

The verse gives us an idea of how to create this inner strength: "Those whose hearts focus on upward paths." *Rashi* explains that this refers to people who examine themselves; they think about their patterns of speech and actions to make certain that they are on the right path.

Some people simply live life without self-examination. They do not reflect on their words and behavior — they just live life. They might think about improving themselves from time to time, but they do so in a haphazard way.

Those who are serious about their wish to become closer to Hashem, however, will contemplate and reflect on where they are in the present. They will evaluate their thinking and they will try to clarify if their motivations are on the level they would like them to be. They will think about the ways that they speak and the ideal Torah ways to use one's power of words — they will think about their actions and see what they can improve.

Some people are concerned that self-reflection can lead to sadness, guilt, and discouragement. However, when one's goal is to become closer to Hashem, this gives inner strength. As our verse states, *"Oz lo boch."* There is strength from Hashem when this is carried out in a healthy and spiritually uplifting way.

"I view myself as a weak person," someone shared with me. "I don't have as much inner strength as the people I admire. The inner weariness that I often feel, has a negative effect on all that I do. I feel tired when I pray. I am so used to rattling off the words of the prayers that I do not find them inspiring. I become exhausted as soon as I start trying to learn Torah. I feel too tired to go out of my way to help other people. I have been to a few doctors, and they have not found anything wrong with me. I was told to eat better, get more rest, and to exercise, but I am not motivated to keep this up even though I try it once in a while."

"Did you ever use rechargeable batteries?" I asked him.

"Often," he replied. "But what does this have to do with my problem of having low energy?"

"When you recharge batteries you look for a source of energy and let that energy fill up the batteries. Correct?"

"That is right, but I cannot just put my fingers into an electric outlet and give myself positive energy. That would be foolish."

"Exactly. You need to know what the proper source of energy would be for you. Hashem, the Creator and Sustainer of the universe, is the best source of energy for us as humans. Go to a quiet place, sit or stand, and close your eyes, and contemplate the vastness of the created universe. Then, visualize a tremendous amount of Divine energy coming down to planet Earth, to the exact spot where you are. This energy is a gift to you, from the Creator. Feel it entering the top of your head and going round and round in your energy system. Realize that Hashem is giving you the gift of this energy so you will have the power to elevate yourself and accomplish in this world.

"Did you ever read about a mother who was able to lift up a heavy car to save the life of her child who was trapped underneath the car? This has happened many times. These mothers were not professional strong men who train for years to do these types of feats — they were simply loving mothers. Their depth of love for their children enabled them to tap the tremendous amount of potential energy that we all

have. The life-and-death challenge of the situation gave them access to strength that they did not realize they had.

"You, too, have tremendous energy inside. Remember that you are a child of Hashem. Be grateful to Him for the energy you do have. Do not complain that you do not have enough — you do have plenty available even now, although you are not doing all that you could do. Repeat this verse over and over again and feel your energy increasing, as you recognize that Hashem can give you unlimited energy."

The gentleman I told this to, took the ideas seriously and he later reported that others had commented on his increased energy. "You, too, can connect with the source of my energy," he tells them with a smile. "The Creator has an endless supply for everybody."

יְהוה צְבָאוֹת אַשְׁרֵי אָדָם בֹּטֵחַ בָּךְ: ,,

13 HASHEM, Master of Legions, fortunate is the person who trusts in You.

Talmud Yerushalmi (*Berachos* 5:1) states, "Let this verse never cease from your lips: 'Hashem, Master of Legions, fortunate is the person who trusts in You.' "

Furthermore, the Talmud adds that, after we say this verse, we should recite this prayer: "May it be Your will, Hashem, our God and the God of our Forefathers, that You should save us from times of insolence, times of difficulty and times of bad that come into the world."

Our verse is recited each week at the end of Shabbos as part of the Introduction to the *Havdalah,* the prayer that officially ends the Sabbath, and is a very appropriate time to mention this verse. During Shabbos we have complete rest, calm, serenity, and peace of mind. When Shabbos begins, we are to view all the work that we have been involved with, in the past week, as already completed. We are to feel totally in the present, experiencing the sanctity of Shabbos. We are free from stress and anxiety.

When Shabbos is over, the new week begins. We begin to think of all the things that need our attention now, and it is so easy to feel a sense of uneasiness. We go from being fully at rest with a clear mind, to a mind that might be flooded with thoughts of all the many things that we must do. We may have financial concerns. We might need to go several places this week to accomplish many things, etc. Our "to do" list is once again activated.

What can enable us to plan properly and do what we must, and still remain calm, with peace of mind? Total trust in our loving Father and powerful King, Creator and Sustainer of the universe! He will be there to help us, since he has all the resources that we could ever need, to accomplish whatever we must do. How fortunate we are when we internalize these feelings of trust in Him and how praiseworthy is the person who has this trust — he is blessed with inner peace and happiness.

If you are experiencing difficult life challenges, after repeating this verse a number of times, add the special prayer cited above from the Talmud. May your prayers be answered.

Do not let this verse be only part of *Havdalah*. Repeat it often, and be aware of it everyday. If you ever begin to feel anxious, let this verse automatically come to mind. The more you repeat it, the stronger its message will become. The inner peace and serenity of trust in Hashem, will strengthen you spiritually and emotionally.

> *A gentleman I know was going through some especially difficult times, financially. He had some major debts that had to be paid immediately. Unable to pay his rent, he was pressured to come up with the money or else find another apartment. The salary money he earned from his job would not begin to cover the amount of the debts, and his creditors were becoming impatient. He had counted on a few possibilities to acquire the money, but they did not work out as he had hoped. Some of the people he was relying on, had their own financial difficulties while others had different priorities. Though they had money to give to a number of organizations, this person's request was too low on their ever-growing list of requests.*
>
> *The person in this situation worked on the attribute of trust in Hashem, but the situation was challenging, not only because of how it affected him, but because it affected other*

members of his family, as well. The strain and pressure prevented him from thinking clearly about a course of action that was likely to succeed.

I suggested to this person that he repeat this verse over and over again. This would awaken within him a level of the trust greater than he was experiencing. Moreover, when you repeat this verse over and over again, you are giving Hashem a message, that you are building your trust in Him. At the time of this writing, the person is still facing financial challenges, but the repetition of this verse has had a calming effect. Hopefully, by the time this book is published, the person's challenging situation will be resolved.

⊰{ **89 / פט** }⊱

עוֹלָם חֶסֶד יִבָּנֶה ₃

³ Kindness builds the world.

Without kindness we would not be here. When we were infants, we were totally dependent on acts of kindness from our parents and others to keep us alive, and we remain with this need for the kindness of others, throughout our lives. In one's old age, one often needs as much kindness as was needed as a young child. Many people who think that they are highly independent, need others to enhance their lives much more than they realize.

Whenever you engage in an act of kindness, you are building the world. Your kind words might appear relatively insignificant, but you are in the process of building a person's life. The same is true when you give someone change for a larger bill, tell someone directions to get someplace, offer someone food or drink, and myriad other small acts of kindness. You are participating in the building of another human being's life, and each human being is part of the world. In essence, therefore every bit of kindness is an act of building the world.

When one puts together a jigsaw puzzle, every piece is part of the entire picture and the picture remains incomplete if one piece is missing even small pieces are part of the large scene. This is particularly noticeable if someone is putting together a puzzle with a picture of the entire world (or at least of the planet Earth). Every time you add a piece of the picture, the world is being built.

This is only a fraction of what happens when you do an act of kindness. The jigsaw puzzle is an illusion; building people is a reality. Imagine how you will feel about every act of kindness, when you realize the lofty significance of your words and actions. You are involved in the process of building the world.

Do you feel that this is an exaggeration? Do you minimize the impact of words and acts of kindness? Think of a time when you felt an intense need for something that depended on the kindness of another person. It might not have been difficult for the other person to meet your needs. It might not have cost him much time or take a large amount of energy but, for you, it was a lifesaver. It alleviated your state of desperation, emergency, and crisis. This person's caring, compassion, or simple consideration and goodwill, made a difference to you — your world was being built.

We might say that major acts of kindness are the exception rather than the rule. Not every act of kindness saves a life, totally changes the direction of someone's life. Not every act of kindness is especially meaningful.

True. But every act of kindness is an act of emulating the Creator. Every act of kindness is part of the *mitzvah* to love other people as yourself. Every act of kindness helps a being who is created in the Creator's image. Every act of kindness does have an impact on at least two lives — the life of the benefactors and the life of the recipient of the kindness. The entire world is now a kinder place because you are a kinder person and your kindness has a ripple effect.

When you do an act of kindness and someone observes it, he is now more likely to act kindly, he is more likely to do something similar. Then, someone else might observe his act of kindness and do the same, and ten people later, someone might write about this, in one form or another. Now many more people will speak and act with more kindness, and this, too, will have an effect on more people's lives. Thus, a tiny act of kindness can set off a powerful chain reaction. The world has been built in ways that the first person had not imagined, even after the original doer of the kindness is no longer alive. His kindness lasts forever.

Help build the world. Look for opportunities that you might not have been aware of, had you not been seeking them.

> *A short while after writing the above section, I met a couple who shared with me that they had just returned from a trip to visit elderly parents. They themselves were highly self-sufficient and usually did not need to ask others for help. However, being away from home and having to be available for an elderly parent who needed constant assistance, taught them a powerful lesson about the importance of kindness. They could not have managed on their own; they needed a place to stay — they needed rides — they needed advice. They were used to helping and, now that the tables were turned, they saw what it was like to be in a difficult position. The giving attitude of those who helped them, gave them the feeling that they were doing a bigger favor for their benefactors, than their benefactors did for them. This made it much easier for them to be the recipients of kindness. You could tell from the way they related this, that many people would benefit in the future from their increased understanding of the value and importance of kindness.*

What can we do to increase our appreciation for kindness? Become more aware of how much you gain from the kindness of others. Remember past kindnesses that have helped you in life. Over the years the amount of kindnesses that you have experienced could probably fill many volumes.

Be aware of instances when you would have appreciated a kind and encouraging word, that you did not receive. Be aware of when you could have greatly benefited from the assistance of someone, but it was not offered. Let each instance serve as an intensification of your appreciation for the significance and magnitude of kindness. Let it increase your resolve to be available for as many people as possible, as often as possible. Keep participating in the building of the world. Think, speak, and act with kindness.

﴾ 90 / צ ﴿

תָּשֵׁב אֱנוֹשׁ עַד־דַּכָּא וַתֹּאמֶר שׁוּבוּ בְנֵי־אָדָם: ג

³ *You reduce humans to pulp. And You say, "repent!".*

his verse shows us the meaning and purpose of adversity
and suffering in this world. There is a message in suffering;
Hashem wants us to return to Him. He wants us to improve.
He wants us to become better. He wants us to stop doing whatever
we are doing wrong, and to start or increase the good.

All forms of suffering, whether major or minor, are statements to
us from our loving Father in Heaven. He wants to help us. Everything that happens in our lives is for our ultimate benefit, that
which we perceive as good, as well as that which we might not.

Even when we find meaning in suffering, it is still distressful and
difficult, but we can cope with it so much better than if we did not
realize that it is meaningful.

The meaning of all suffering is that it is a reminder to return to
Hashem. The Hebrew word *Shuvu,* which refers to t*shuvah*, is
usually translated as "repentance", but this has very different
connotations than the word "return." When we "return" to our
home, it is a time for celebration. The longer we were away, the
more we appreciate the return. A person who was a prisoner of
war in the hands of a brutal enemy, dreams constantly about
returning home. *Shuvu* means to "return." Connecting with
Hashem is the greatest good, but when we transgress and sin, we
are distant from Hashem. *Teshuvah* is the process of renewing
and revitalizing our connection with the Creator and Sustainer of
the universe.

We human beings always need reminders. We tend to get used to
a situation that has remained contant for a some time. People who
are responsible and organized use various methods to remember
to take care of what they must do. Some things we need to do have
a time element, and this helps us automatically remember. Most
people do not need to write down a reminder to eat breakfast.

Since this is an activity that one does each morning, one easily remembers to eat even if one is not hungry. At other times, hunger serves as a reminder to eat for energy and health, and thirst serves as a reminder to drink water.

Yom Kippur, is a day that is totally dedicated to *Teshuvah*. Throughout the prayers on this Holy Day, we repeat that we deeply regret the wrongs that we have done. Fine, but what about the rest of the year? How do we remember then, that we need to improve?

Adversity and suffering serve as reminders during the rest of the year, and it is very important that we keep in mind that this is the purpose of those reminders. Let us say that someone set an alarm clock to ring at a certain hour. He did this in order to remember to do something important for his health and when he hears the ringing of the clock, the brain's miraculous mechanism tells him, "I hear the ringing. I know that this is to remind me to (take my medicine, call the doctor, do my exercises, or something similar)."

What if a person hears the ringing and does not realize that it is a reminder to take care of something important? It will not get done. Someone who has memory problems, or is highly absent-minded, might be puzzled. "What in the world is this supposed to mean? I assume it's a message. But what is the message?" And the medicine will not be taken or the doctor will not be called. In fact, someone who does not remember that this was meant as a message, might become annoyed with the noise of the clock. "That is such an awful sound. What a nuisance! I wish it would stop already and let me continue in a state of peace as before."

Physical pain is a message from our body that something is wrong and needs to be corrected. A toothache is a wake-up call to visit a dentist and solve the problem. Pains in one's chest might be a wake-up call to take care of one's heart. Aches and pains might be a minor message or it might be a sign that something is seriously wrong, but, in any event, we need to pay attention for our health and our survival. From this verse we see that all suffering is a spiritual reminder. Hashem is telling us, "I care about you and your eternal soul. Wake up! Pay attention! Make the necessary corrections."

"I had been in a very serious car crash and I was grateful that I was still alive — but I hurt all over. My first reaction was that this was tragic. I would miss a lot of time from work — I might be handicapped in certain ways for life — my life would be much more limited. Many of my friends and relatives prayed for me, by reciting Psalms, and when I was told about this, I appreciated their efforts on my behalf. It made me feel good that they cared about me and wanted me to get well and I felt that the power of their prayers was helping my recovery. Since others were saying Tehillim for me, I figured that I should say some also.

"I came across this verse saying that "being broken" was Hashem's way of telling us that we need to do Teshuvah. This hit home. While I was in the hospital, I had a lot of time to think. My body was not the way it used to be, though my mind was clear, and I began to think about the real purpose of my life. I personally did not have what is called a 'near-death experience,' but I had read about others who did. They had felt that their soul was leaving them, and they had experienced a great light. Then they felt that, it was not yet time for them to die, and their soul returned to their body. Every person who had had such an experience, developed a much more spiritual perspective about life, afterwards. They realized that they were in this world for a mission. It is easy to get sidetracked and distracted but, after their experiences, they knew that they needed to stay focused on what is really important.

"I firmly resolved to grow from my own life-changing experience. It was not as dramatic as some others, but it turned my life upside-down. I thought about the different areas of my life, and in each area I made goals that I was determined to follow. This related to my Torah learning, my prayers, my interactions with other people, and the gamut of important character traits. Instead of just complaining and whining about my aches and pains, I elevated the painful reminders, to keep me on track. Two years later, when I looked back at that car accident, I saw how it was exactly what I had needed. I grew in those two years far beyond what I would have, had I not had that wake-up call."

⚜ 93 / צג ⚜

א יהוה מָלָךְ גֵּאוּת לָבֵשׁ לָבֵשׁ יְהֹוָה עֹז הִתְאַזָּר...

*1 HASHEM has reigned, He has donned grandeur;
HASHEM has donned strength and girded Himself*

Ramban in his classic *mussar* (ethical) letter cites this verse when he elaborates on the negativity of a human being having the traits of arrogance and conceit. He writes that someone who is arrogant and conceited is rebelling against the Creator and Sustainer of the universe. Grandeur, is the royal garment of the Almighty, the ultimate King of the world.

Ramban asks the rhetorical question, "About what can a human being be arrogant?" Can he be arrogant about wealth, fame, glory, or wisdom? All of this is nothing compared to the infinite wealth, glory, and wisdom of the Owner of the universe, Who has created everything that exists with the ultimate wisdom.

A young child who has just learned the Hebrew alphabet, might consider himself a great scholar. He now knows all the letters. But what is that compared to the greatest scholars of the present generation, all the more so of previous generations? He doesn't even know what he does not know.

A young child might know how to count to ten and be very proud of it, but he knows nothing about mathematics, especially when compared to Einstein, Newton, and other brilliant mathematicians and physicists. He does not even know what he does not know.

A young child might have received a few dollars from a grand-parent and he now considers himself wealthy. However, what is that, compared to the present wealth of someone like Bill Gates with his billions of dollars? He does not have any idea about what the world calls wealth.

These comparisons are nothing, compared to the absolute great-ness and wisdom of the Creator of all that exists. We do not even know what we do not know.

This arrogance and conceit are signs of foolishness and limited awareness. Even when a human being has more riches than anyone else on our planet, he has nothing, compared to the vastness of all the galaxies that exist in the universe. Even when a human being has tremendous genius and brilliance, he knows nothing compared to the ultimate knowledge and wisdom of the Creator of it all.

Riches can easily be lost in a short time and, regardless of anyone's intelligence, an illness that affects a person's memory and ability to think rationally, can cause him to lose all that he knows. All mortals are fragile. Every human being is a mortal and therefore, every human being is fragile. Someone whose possessions and intelligence are fragile, should not be arrogant or conceited, all the more so, when compared to the One Who is unlimited and infinite. Nothing can compare to that unlimitedness.

Humility is an automatic response of one who has even a small glimpse of the power and omniscience of the Creator. Therefore Moshe, who had the greatest knowledge and understanding of Hashem, was also the most humble person who ever lived. The more one knows about Hashem, the more one knows that one does not know very much and truly does not have any lasting power and strengths.

"Lower yourself and the Almighty will raise you," wrote *Ramban*. That is, you are automatically higher and more elevated, the more you realize that Hashem is all-powerful and all-knowing — and that you are very far from this.

These verses refer to the time of *Mashiach*, the Messiah, when the entire world will recognize Hashem's mightiness. May we soon merit to experience the great glory of our loving Father and powerful King and may we bask in the glory that He is our Father and King.

> *"I attended a lecture where the speaker emphasized the importance of having a positive self-image. One of those attending asked a basic question: Is it not conceited and arrogant to consider oneself great? Is not the quality of humility highly praised and the trait of arrogance harshly condemned?*
>
> *"The lecturer — who was clearly someone with humility balanced together with a positive enough self-image that he could speak in front of a large crowd quite comfortably —*

smiled and replied, When I was a student in the yeshivah I attended, my elderly Rosh Yeshivah once called me over and told me that I was walking round-shouldered, and I should stand up straight. "Don't try to act like someone humble," he admonished me. "At your age that is not what you should be working on. You need to appreciate the fact that you are someone who studies Torah, and that should give you a sense of importance. You are created in the Almighty's image and you are one of His children. Appreciate who you are. Of course, you should not be conceited when it comes to comparing yourself with anyone else but, in your own heart, remember that you are valuable and important. Be grateful for all the gifts that Hashem has given you. The more you realize that all you have is a gift, the easier it will be for you to have authentic humility. You do not have to act as if you are humble — you will have an inner modesty that is sincere.'"

" 'His words and more than that, his very personality has served as a role model that I have tried to emulate.' "

⟨ **96 / צו** ⟩

א שִׁירוּ לַיהוה שִׁיר חָדָשׁ שִׁירוּ לַיהוה כָּל־הָאָרֶץ:
ב שִׁירוּ לַיהוה בָּרְכוּ שְׁמוֹ בַּשְּׂרוּ מִיּוֹם־לְיוֹם יְשׁוּעָתוֹ:
ג סַפְּרוּ בַגּוֹיִם כְּבוֹדוֹ בְּכָל־הָעַמִּים נִפְלְאוֹתָיו:

¹ "Sing to HASHEM a new song; sing to HASHEM, everyone on earth.
² Sing to HASHEM, bless His Name; announce His salvation day to day.
³ Relate His glory among the nations; among all peoples, His wonders."

Meiri explains that, in the future at the time of the final redemption, the awesome miracles will be so great that all the poetic songs that were already written will not be sufficient. Therefore new poetic songs will have to be composed to fully express the depth of the remarkable and awe-inspiring events.

On the words "day to day," *Radak* comments, "Each and every day people will talk to each other about the great redemption. Even though they already know this information, it will be so treasured and cherished to them that, each and every day, it will be like something new. Usually when good things happen, at first, people are excited, and this is reflected in the amount of time they speak about it and in the excitement in their voices, but then the thrill and excitement begins to fade. However, with the final redemption the incredible feelings that one will feel initially, will last and last."

Think about times that you were initially excited about some good fortune that you experienced. It is safe to assume that, if time has passed since then, you do not feel the original thrill right now.

Each time you remember something special that happened to you and for which you do not now feel the same enthusiasm and excitement, let it serve as a reminder for the intense and ever-lasting joy of the great redemption our people will one day experience.

> *Once Rabbi Yosef Kahaneman, head of Ponevezh Yeshivah in the city of Ponevezh and later in Bnei Brak, went on a fund-raising trip for his yeshivah to South Africa, and afterward, paid a visit to the Chofetz Chaim in Radin. Someone present at the visit, was curious about the Chofetz Chaim's unusual interest in the primitive tribes. The Chofetz Chaim explained, "Not long from now, everyone in the world will sing songs of praise to our Father, our King. So I wanted to know more about the different groups that will extol Hashem's praises."*

> *I met a person who would react with a big smile, whenever he heard someone mention the size of the world's population. He would say, "Imagine a six-billion member choir. Each individual will sing new songs of praise to Hashem, and they will do this daily. It gives me joy right now, just thinking about this."*

⋅{ 97 / צז }⋅

יא אוֹר זָרֻעַ לַצַּדִּיק וּלְיִשְׁרֵי־לֵב שִׂמְחָה:

11 Light is planted for the righteous, and for the straight of heart, joy.

When we have light, we see clearly and the opposite is to be in the dark. Imagine trying to read something with very little light. You have to strain greatly, and it is very easy to make mistakes. The more light, the clearer and the further we can see.

When a *tzaddik* speaks and acts, he plants light. When you plant a small seed, giant trees can grow. From one seed you can have a fruit, and in each tree and fruit there are even more seeds that can create large forests and orchards. In the same manner, the light created by good words and deeds is eternal — even tiny words and deeds can create great eternal light.

Some people read this verse and say to themselves, "But I am not a *tzaddik*. I am far from being righteous." At any given moment, we can all ask ourselves, "What would a *tzaddik* say now? What would a *tzaddik* do now?" This question can give us light, it can show us direction.

No one is born a *tzaddik*. We all start off life as infants, without knowing how to speak or act, and we make choices. Those who consistently make righteous choices, are righteous. We, at any given moment, can make a righteous choice.

Imagine what your life would be like if, after every righteous choice of words and deeds, you were to see a bit of light being planted. As with compound interest, small investments can add up to very large amounts, and so too, investments in righteous words and actions, add up to a great eternal light. This vision will make it easier for you to make the proper choices.

Now let us look at the second half of this verse. Those who are "upright of heart" will have joy. In the book of *Koheles* we read, "The Almighty created humans straightforward, but they sought many calculations." R' Samson Raphael Hirsch commented that "these many calculations are the enemies of our happiness."

When you think "straight," you speak and act "straight." When you think straight, you appreciate the gifts of Hashem. When you think straight, you don't digress to the path of focusing on who has more than you and how you do not have all that you desire. Thinking straight means, knowing you have things to appreciate and, such, your thoughts are full of appreciation.

The natural state of a human being is, joy. Joy is a healthy state — is healthy for us spiritually, emotionally, and physically. Lack of joy comes from thinking in ways that block your joy. Different people have different obstacles to their joy. It is easy to blame other people, circumstances, or situations for one's lack of joy, but the only reason that other people, circumstances, and situations might cause a lack of joy is because of the way that one views those factors. The one who views everything in his life as an integral part of his service to the Almighty, will experience joy in dealing with whatever arises. " This, too, is part of my mission in this world." The one who is "straight of heart" finds meaning in everything that occurs. Life is full of joy.

Keep asking yourself, "What is the straight way to look at this?" This then will make it easier for you to ask yourself, "What is the straight thing to say now?" and, "What is the straight thing to do now?" By doing so you will live a more joyful life.

There is a well-known tune that is frequently sung to this verse. I have often heard this at weddings when a renowned righteous Torah scholar enters the hall. When reading stories about great, righteous people, we can repeat this verse a few times, and so this verse will become associated in our own mental library with the people we would like to emulate. Then, when we recite or sing this verse, we will be reminded of their elevated thoughts, words, and deeds.

≈{ **100 / ק** }≈

ב עִבְדוּ אֶת־יהוה בְּשִׂמְחָה בֹּאוּ לְפָנָיו בִּרְנָנָה:

² **Serve** HASHEM **with joy, come before Him with joyful song.**

*E*verybody seeks happiness, but for many people this is an elusive goal. They would like to be happy, but they make many conditions. Since they say, either explicitly or implicitly, "I will be happy when ..." There are an unlimited amount of ways that people finish this sentence. "I will be happy when I reach my next goal." "I will be happy when I am wealthy." "I will be happy when I'm married." I will be happy when I have children." "I will be happy when my children are married." "I will be happy when the weather is better." "I will be happy when the political situation is improved." "I will be happy when everything in my life goes exactly the way I want it to go." (This latter sentence is not often expressed clearly, but it is frequently in the person's subconscious mind.)

The Almighty created us to be happy. Only when we are happy, do we function at our full capacity. Only when we are happy do our mind and body work at their optimal levels. Many formulas for happiness have been suggested — it would be wonderful if we could have a guarantee.

This verse does give us an approach for happiness that will guarantee those who follow it, a lifetime of happiness. Those who apply this verse are the most fortunate people in the world. Their happiness is not dependent on any other person or any external circumstance. Rather, they create their own state of happiness by their choices of thoughts, words, and actions.

Every moment in our lives we can serve the Almighty. We can serve Him with our thoughts and with our actions. We can serve Him with our words and with our silence. We can serve Him when things are going the way we wish, and when they are not. We can serve Him when we are in the presence of other people and when we are by ourselves and — since we can always serve Him, we can always be joyful.

What if we do not spontaneously feel this joy when we serve Hashem? We can use the great power of our imagination. What great miracle would create joy for you? Visualize it in detail. As you feel this joy, imagine feeling even greater joy, for doing a single good deed.

In addition, we can use the power of acting with external expressions of joy. As the often-quoted statement of R' Moshe Chaim Luzzatto (*Mesilas Yesharim*, Ch. 7) puts it, "External movements of joy elicit inner feelings of joy." How do you speak and act, when you experience spontaneous expressions of joy? When you consciously speak and act that particular way while speaking and acting in ways that serve Hashem, this will become your internalized reality.

Why should one feel this great joy? When you do a good deed, you are connecting with the all-powerful Creator and Sustainer of the universe, Who loves you and cares about you. As the Chofetz Chaim wrote in *Shmiras Halashon*, "Hashem loves each person more than the person loves himself." The reward you will receive for each and every good deed, is immeasurable; it is eternal. If someone were to find a great treasure, he would rejoice — each good deed is an even greater treasure.

Feel some of this joy each time you repeat this verse — and repeat this verse over and over again. Let the words and the thoughts behind the words permeate your entire being. If you do not experience the joy contained in this verse right away, act as if you did. Realize that you have a formula for constant joy. Cherish this precious gift.

> Someone recently told me about a relative of his who is trying to remember a code, that he forgot. This person is an heir to a fortune in a secret Swiss bank account. He was told the code of the account and the password. He was also told, a number of times, that the money in that account would be his after the original owner passed away. He had written this down and had repeated it a number of times. Now he remembers the password but, even though he is trying as hard as he can, he cannot recall the number of the account. He knows that it is buried deep in his subconscious mind, but he cannot recall it.
>
> This story sounds like a rare, frustrating situation, but in truth, most of humanity is in the same position. The code to a life of joy is stored within our minds. With the code you can unlock a great treasury, but without it, one can live one's life in a more limited way, one where the person does not realize that, all he needs to do is focus on the tremendous joy available to those who serve Hashem with joy.

⁌ **קב / 102** ⁍

ח שָׁקַדְתִּי וָאֶהְיֶה כְּצִפּוֹר בּוֹדֵד עַל־גָּג:

⁸ *I have given thought, and I am like a lonely bird on a roof.*

King David states that he has given thought to his situation and after this contemplation, he realizes that he is like a lonely bird all alone on a roof (*Rashi*). What is it like being a lonely bird in a strange place? One is totally vulnerable — there are predators everywhere.

There is strength in numbers. When a bird flies with a large flock, they can all travel long distances together. They fly over mountains and forests, lakes and waterfalls, cities and farms. Regardless of what is down below, up in the sky they all have the reassurance that they are on the right track. The sight and sounds of the other birds flying together gives each individual bird a sense of belonging, a sense of being part of a large whole. In addition, when a bird lands in a field, meadow, or garden, there is food available. The presence of other birds also gives each one a feeling of safety, so that if danger approaches, there are always other birds around who will sense it and give the signal that they all must fly away.

A single bird, however, must be much more vigilant all of the time. His entire well-being is up to him alone, since he has no one to help him. Even having only one other bird present makes a difference. Each bird can communicate with the other which, in itself, is of great benefit. A lonely bird on a roof is sad, and there is no one there to help alleviate those feelings.

When a human being suffers some misfortune or has to deal with constant adversity, one finds consolation being with others who have experienced similar adversity and misfortune. They share their thoughts and feelings, and you share your thoughts and feelings. This sharing lightens the burden, and some of the distress is mitigated. Instead of your mind being completely taken over by the repetitive thoughts of how difficult your situation is and how miserable you feel, you are engaged in talking to people who understand you — and you can listen to what they have to say.

Even if you are not among people with similar experiences, if someone is wise he will know what to say and what not to say and he might be able to offer some thoughts that will give you a different perspective on your situation. He can tell you words of encouragement and inspiration, and he can offer you hope.

Likewise, even if someone has no idea what the right thing is to say, if he is a good listener, he will let you express yourself. He will not lecture you that you should not be feeling the way you are feeling. He will not blame you for being in the situation you are in, and he will not tell you what you should or should not have done, now that it is all over. Right now, you are in emotional pain. Right now, you need an understanding heart and a good listener knows this. He will listen in such a way that you know you are in the presence of a caring soul — an individual who listens non-judgmentally, and is able to quiet his own inner voice of unhelpful comments. He listens to understand you, as a unique individual.

It is tremendously beneficial to have someone with whom to share your thoughts and feelings, when you go through difficult times. King David tells us that feeling like a lonely bird on top of a roof, which is not the bird's natural place, is a highly distressful feeling. Let us do all we can to help others, when they are experiencing challenges. We might not have immediate answers, but we can always show this person that we care and are open to listening, with understanding and compassion.

> *An older gentelman, who was still single when most of his peers were married with families, shared the following with me:*
>
> *"It's rough being single when all your old classmates are married and have children. The loneliness I feel is deep, deep pain. It's amazing how off-track many people are when they speak to me. Instead of saying things that are helpful — and I realize that it is difficult for most people to know what to say — they criticize, judge, give useless advice, and — in many ways — say things that make me feel even worse. I realize that, on some level, they mean to be helpful, but if they would think more about how I probably feel and how I will probably react to what they say, they would be more careful to avoid hurting me so much.*
>
> *"People who are married and have children naturally talk a*

lot about their families. They talk about their children — and this is understandable. I can deal with this and I try to be happy for the good fortune of others. I try to enter their world and understand how they feel. I truly wish them well, and when I bless them, it comes from my heart. However, many fail to do the same for me. They tell me things like, 'You shouldn't be so picky.' (Do they suggest that I marry someone with whom I do not fell I will get along?)

'You might have missed your bashert.' (Great! What can I do about this now? And can't Hashem, the ultimate Matchmaker, arrange for me to meet someone appropriate for me, even though this person might think that Hashem is limited in what He can do?)

"What do I want from people? To enter my world for a few moments and to understand how difficult it is for me, emotionally. When people do this properly, I feel a little less alone and I know that someone understands. Then, when they offer heartfelt blessings and prayers for me with an authentic sense of caring, I appreciate it immensely.

"Most of all, I would ask that people not give up on me. Do not assume that I will always be alone, but keep making suggestions that might be appropriate. Every time someone does this, I know that there is hope for me — I see that people are trying to help me."

◈{ 103 / קג }◈

יג כְּרַחֵם אָב עַל־בָּנִים רִחַם יהוה עַל־יְרֵאָיו:

13 As a father is merciful towards his children, so has HASHEM shown mercy to those who fear Him.

On the words "As a father is merciful," the Midrash asks, "As which father?" And the Midrash elaborates, "As the most compassionate of the Forefathers. This refers to Abraham. When Hashem told Abraham that He was planning to destroy Sodom and Gemorrah, Abraham prayed that they should be saved." (*Yalkut Shimoni*, section 859)

The late Rosh Yeshivah of Slobodka, R' Nosson Tzvi Finkel, pointed out that Abraham was the essence of kindness. His entire life was devoted to kindness. In thoughts, words, and actions, kindness was his very essence. One might think that, if there were people who were cruel and evil — the antithesis of kindness, he would consider them his mortal enemies. In fact, Abraham reacted towards the people of Sodom, with deep compassion. He prayed to the Almighty that — in the merit of the righteous individuals in Sodom — the rest of the people should be saved. He first asked for compassion if there were fifty righteous people, and then kept bargaining with God, asking that even for a smaller number, they should be saved (see *Genesis*, chapter 18). Abraham did all that he could to save the people of Sodom (*Ohr Hatzafun,* vol. 1, p. 259).

Living with high ideals and values is our ultimate goal in life, but there is a danger. High ideals and values can cause us to be judgmental. It's easy to condemn and be callous towards the plight of those who lack those ideals and values, but true greatness of compassion means being compassionate towards those people. Compassion does not mean that we condone wrongs. It does not mean that we say to ourselves, "It's not my business if someone does not act properly." Abraham spent his entire life spreading an awareness of the Creator. Abraham was deeply aware of the kindness of the Infinite and Eternal One, and his own behavior served as a role model for others to emulate.

When we see someone who is homeless and starving, the attribute of compassion drives us to help them out in some way; give them some financial help, say a kind word, notify an organization that can help them, etc. So, too, seeing someone who does not live up to the ideals and values to which they should aspire, should arouse our compassion. What can I say and do to have a positive influence on the spiritual level of this person?

There are many possible roots of the motivations that drive some people to grow spiritually, upgrading words and behaviors. There are those who might come from a feeling of duty and obligation. Some might come from their own feelings of insecurity, while others — reversely — from arrogance and conceit, a general feeling of being better then other people. However, the ideal motivation is to act out of compassion. "I care so much about this person that I want what is best for him in all areas of his life."

When someone is in need, he wishes fervently that someone who has the power to help him, will act compassionately towards him. In this verse we express our recognition that our Heavenly Father is as compassionate as a loving father, to his child. Abraham was a child of the Creator and emulated Him. From Abraham's compassion we have a glimpse of what it means to be compassionate. The ultimate source of all compassion is the Creator. Let us make ourselves worthy of His compassion.

At this very moment you have an opportunity to emulate Abraham's compassion. Take two minutes to say a personal prayer to our loving Father and powerful King, Creator and Sustainer of the universe. In your own words, ask Hashem to have compassion on all the people in the world.

> *One person who said this prayer shared with me that, for him, this experience opened his eyes to the fact that he felt negatively towards more people than he had realized. These were not people who necessarily were truly evil. Various people just annoyed him. He did not like people who seemed to be arrogant and conceited — he looked down on people who were show-offs. In addition, there were people who had hurt his feelings in minor and trivial ways in the past. By praying for Hashem's compassion for all the people on our planet, he realized that the individuals he found challenging, were included. As he prayed daily for the welfare of others, he found that he began to view those very same people in a more positive light. Now he saw them as the people, for whose welfare he was praying.*

⊰ 104 / קד ⊱

כד מָה־רַבּוּ מַעֲשֶׂיךָ יהוה כֻּלָּם בְּחָכְמָה עָשִׂיתָ
מָלְאָה הָאָרֶץ קִנְיָנֶךָ:

24 How abundant are Your works, Hashem; with wisdom You made them All. the earth is full of Your possessions.

This verse contains the foundation of the secrets of the world. There are so many complex phenomena in the universe. Even the smallest living creature is so complex that, despite all the technology that is available today, no one has any idea how to build it on his own. Every cell in our body is complex, all the more so the trillions of cells that make up each human being, working together in magnificent harmony. There is tremendous complexity in the entire spectrum which we call nature: The universe with all of its galaxies and suns and planets. The oceans and seas and all of the fascinating creatures that call them their home. The world of birds and other flying creatures. The world of physics, the world of chemistry, the world of geology, the world of mathematics, the world of biology, are all manifestations of Hashem's infinite wisdom.

Understanding even a small part of the world, creates within us a tremendous sense of fascination and awe. Some people feel this with more intensity and others with less, but anyone who spends time thinking about this, will have a greater sense of appreciation for the wisdom of the Creator. We do not live in a mundane world.

Everything that we see on Earth was created by Hashem and ultimately belongs to Him. Why are there so many animals on the ground, in the air, and under water? Why are there so many trees and plants and flowers and fruit and vegetables? They are there so that we will see the wonders of our Creator, wherever we are. Each dog and each cat is a reminder of the wonders of the Creator. Each bird we see flying and each fish we see swimming, is a reminder of the wonders of the Creator. Each tree and each fruit, along with each colorful flower, is a reminder of the wonders of the Creator.

Since the most important thing we can do in this world is to connect with the Creator, we need to have as many reminders as possible, and we have them. All we need to do is open our eyes and we will see them, constantly.

I was visiting my grandparents and I was getting bored. I was only ten years old and would rather have spent the time playing with my friends. My grandfather was a sensitive man and he understood what I was feeling. He gently asked me, "You're bored now, aren't you?"

I nodded my head. I did not want to make him feel bad, but the truth is the truth. What he then told me made a lasting impression.

"I remember when visiting my grandparents as a child I, too, was bored. My grandfather knew what I was feeling and said to me, 'Hashem created a magnificent and awesome world. Each person decides how he will look at this world. We can learn to take things for granted and can pass by the most fascinating treasures and not see anything special. The wonders of Hashem are everywhere. Seeing a caterpillar crawling is an amazing thing. And one day this will be a beautiful butterfly. Looking at the sun we see tremendous light that was created by Hashem; it helps us see all that we see. And the eyes with whom we see and all the things in Hashem's world that we see, are amazing. The good smells that we smell are sensed by our noses, that are also amazing. Whenever you see a tree, think about it for a few moments. See the leaves and what grows on the trees. And let this give you a feeling of excitement.'

"Later on, I realized that my grandfather always had positive energy, and after what he told me that day, I could understand why. He lived in the same world as everyone else on our planet, but in an important way, his world was much greater and more impressive. He saw the work of the Creator every-where, and I decided that I wanted to do the same. It has given me a very fulfilling life, and I want to pass this on to you."

⋖{ **96 / קו** }⋗

‫ג אַשְׁרֵי שֹׁמְרֵי מִשְׁפָּט עֹשֵׂה צְדָקָה בְכָל־עֵת:‬

3 Praiseworthy are those who maintain justice, who perform charity at all times

---

The Talmud (*Kesubos* 50a) raises the question, "How is it literally possible to perform acts of charity at all times?" There are many other things that a person will be doing in life, so how can a person perform acts of charity at all times?

The Talmud explains that this refers to someone who raises his own children and supplies them with their food and other basic needs. He is constantly involved in this, and therefore is praise-worthy for being engaged in constant charity and kindness.

It is easy to view the kindnesses that we do for strangers as acts of kindness. The Talmud does go on to say that this verse also refers to people who raise orphans in their homes and then marry them off. We can all understand that taking someone into your home, who is not your biological child, is an ongoing act of kindness. Whoever does this, deserves the highest praises.

However, we might not view raising our own children, as an act of charity. We feel that this is the most natural thing to do. People all over the world do this, even those who are not viewed as particularly kind people will raise their own children.

Based on this verse, the Sages teach us that, everything one does for one's children is an act of kindness. *Rambam* writes in *Hilchos Dei'os*, the section of his classic work on Torah law, that the way to master a positive trait is to do many acts that are consistent with that trait. As we repeat those actions over and over again, those traits become an integral part of us. How is it, then, that not every-one who raises his children, fully intergrates the trait of kindness?

The answer is that it depends on the thoughts that they have, when they do what they do. If people act merely out of habit, even though they are doing positive actions, their lack of mindfulness limits the effects of what they are doing. True, they are doing many act of kindness each and every day for their children, but they do not view it that way.

Tremendous elevation is possible when raising one's children. Every bit of food you give to your children, is an act of kindness. Getting your children clothing and helping them get dressed, is an act of kindness. Teaching your children, is an act of kindness. Helping your children go to school, is an act of kindness. Taking care of your children if they are ill, is an act of kindness. In addition, the money you earn from the work you do, is an integral part of the constant kindness in which you are involved. You are expending time and energy to obtain the money you will need, to spend on your children. So, each and every day when you do the things that you need to do to acquire the financial ability to supply your children with the home, food, and the schooling that they need, you are involved in constant charity.

This elevates the value of what you are doing. Having this in mind will increase the joy you will feel while fulfilling the *mitzvah* of kindness. What others might consider mundane and trivial tasks, are really acts that help you emulate the kindness of Hashem. Appreciate all that you do. You are praiseworthy for doing so.

> *A father of a large family shared with me, "I used to be very frustrated when I had to do things for my children. I wanted to accomplish great things. I viewed everything I did for my children as time spent on something minor, when I really wanted to be involved in major projects. My attitude about this caused me a lot of frustration. I was constantly tense and stressed, since I considered what I did at home as something close to wasting my time. Because of the way I was feeling, it was easy for me to lose my temper, and when my children did not listen to me right away or do things as fast as I felt they should, I would get angry. This caused me to speak to them in a tone of voice that was an expression of my frustra-tion and anger. My children developed nervous habits that, I was told, was a product of the constant tension in our home.*
>
> *"I had a close friend who had a larger family than I and he actually seemed to enjoy being with his children. He was usually calm and a pleasure to be around. He accomplished a lot in life. So one day I asked him, 'Don't you feel frustrated when you spend a lot of time with your children? Don't you feel that you are missing out on doing more things, that would be greater accomplishments?'*
>
> *" 'Not in the least,' he told me. 'When I was growing up, my father had a joyful attitude about doing everything he could, to give us what we needed. He would teach us frequently and told us interesting stories. When we were with our father, we always felt as if he had all the time in the world. I can recall a number of times that my friends told me, that they envied the way that my father interacted with us.*
>
> *" 'I was always committed to treat my children, the same way that I was treated. My father viewed what he did for us*

as the highest level of kindness that he could do. In my mind I realize that all that I do for my children is part of my Avodas Hashem, *serving the Almighty. I am emulating Him, when I do acts of kindness for my children. What I am doing is a major accomplishment.'*

"*I appreciated hearing this from my friend and I decided to develop the same attitude myself. It has given my entire life a deeper sense of meaning.*"

≼ 109 / קט ≽

ד תַּחַת־אַהֲבָתִי יִשְׂטְנוּנִי וַאֲנִי תְפִלָּה:

4 In return for my love for them, they hate me. and I pray.

Metzudas David explains: King David states that, even though he loves others, his enemies hate him. Nevertheless, he constantly prays for their welfare.

Our natural tendency is to like people who like us and to be kind to people who are kind to us. Conversely, there is a strong tendency not to like people who do not like us, and not to be kind to people who are not kind to us.

Praying for someone's welfare is an act of kindness — when you pray for someone, you are asking Hashem to help him. King David says that he prays even for those who hate him. This is difficult to do, and yet, it is elevating. A person who can transcend a natural tendency and speak and act in higher ways, raises himself up.

The words *Va'ani tefillah,* which mean, "And I pray," can also be understood as, "I am prayer." This is to say that praying is such an essential part of his life that he himself can be considered "I am prayer." This is his identity. Being a person who exemplifies praying, means that, "I know that all is from Hashem. I know that Hashem is the ultimate decider of everything that has happened to me, is happening to me now, and will happen to me. Therefore I pray at all times."

This attitude towards prayers means more than simply praying when one is obligated to, at specific times. Rather, it includes one's personal prayers throughout the day. Whenever one needs something, whether large or small, one prays to Hashem in one's own words. When one needs knowledge and wisdom and understanding, one prays. When one needs material matters for oneself or for one's family, one prays. When one wants assistance in spiritual matters, one prays. When one hears that another person is in distress in any way, one prays.

Both ideas are connected. When we have the attitude that all aspects of our lives are from Hashem, and we express this by frequent prayers, we then find it easier to pray for the welfare of even those who do not reciprocate our positive feelings. Our main focus is on Hashem. We do not give other humans, power over us. We do not allow these people to decide how we will relate to others. Rather, we wish people well. We pray that Hashem will enable us to find favor in the eyes of others, even our adversaries, but, even if they still hold on to their negative feelings about us, we dissociate from their negativity and connect with Hashem. From this viewpoint, we wish them well, and when they will grow spiritually, they will surely upgrade their attitude towards us.

> "I could tell that there were a number of people who did not like me very much," said the young man. "My first reaction was to feel strong resentment. 'If they do not like me, I will not like them either,' I said to myself. Even though this sounded childish to me, I still did not have the emotional strength to feel positive about them. They, in turn, seemed to pick up my negative feelings and this increased their own negative feelings towards me. One time, I spoke to an elderly man who was known as someone who was kind and compassionate towards everyone.
>
> " 'If you had the choice of how to relate to those people, what would you choose to feel?' he asked me.
>
> " 'I would like to say that I would like to feel unconditional love towards them, but I do not know if that is really what I want to choose,' I told him honestly, although it was difficult.
>
> " 'The very fact that you are speaking to me about this and that you have an inner feeling that you wish you would want to feel positively toward them, is a good start,' he said to me.

'Each day, pray for the welfare of each of those people, and pray to Hashem that they should feel more positively about you, and that you should feel more positively about them. Make a mental picture of how you will feel when your prayers are answered.'

"His kind words, said with sincere gentleness, had a positive effect on me. I could see that he would do the same, as he advised. I kept praying for their welfare and for them to feel more kindly towards me. I made mental pictures of this becoming reality. When I saw any of those individuals, I was able to greet them in a friendlier way than I ever had before. They began to greet me in a way that showed that my efforts were bearing fruit. My praying for them came easier. With two of them I am now quite friendly in ways that I would not have ever believed possible."

⋇{ **111 / קיא** }⋇

רֵאשִׁית חָכְמָה יִרְאַת יהוה ׳

¹⁰ The beginning of wisdom is fear of HASHEM

The classic *mussar* work on character traits, *Orchos Tzaddikim* (The Paths of the Righteous), cites this verse in the first chapter of his Introduction. In the second paragraph, he elaborates on the tremendous value of human beings, and the uniqueness of a truly righteous person. He goes on to describe an essential distinction between a great person and one who is at the opposite end of the scale. Even though all human beings have much in common, the one who is elevated is the person whose wisdom rules his desires. In contrast, the person whose desires rule over his wisdom, lives a life of spiritual darkness. This, in essence, is the difference between having fear of Hashem or lacking it.

In the third paragraph of the Introduction, the author writes that we receive all the input from the outside, with one of our five senses; we see, we hear, we touch things, we eat, and we smell. From this input we think thoughts and then take action. The patterns created by our thoughts and actions, are our character traits. The rest of this classic work is a detailed description of the traits we should make an effort to master and the traits that we must overcome and transcend.

Fear of Hashem is an awareness of the greatness and power of the Creator. This awareness is the most fundamental wisdom that we mortals need to gain in this world. In the physical arena, the most important knowledge we need to gain is the knowledge necessary for our survival. After survival, we look for the knowledge that will improve the quality of our lives. However, without survival, there is no need nor use for anything else that we might have wanted. So, too, in the spiritual realm, the first knowledge we need is the knowledge that will give us a spiritual life. It is the knowledge we need to sustain our souls for all eternity.

The knowledge and wisdom we need in order to develop our entire character is, fear of Hashem. This attribute is the basis for how we will answer the question of how we should live in this world. The first thing that we need to ask in order to succeed spiritually is: "What does Hashem, my Father, my King, Creator and Sustainer of the universe, want me to say and do? And what does He want me to refrain from saying and doing?"

For physical survival we ask ourselves, "Will eating this, help me survive — or is it poisonous and dangerous?" "Will taking this action keep me safe, or will it cause me a potentially fatal injury or illness?" If we are facing a person who has the will and power to take our life, before we say anything, the most important question to answer is, "What can I say that will save my life? Will the words that I want to say now, help save my life or will it do the opposite?"

All the other knowledge in the world is worthless, at this moment. If you know mathematics, world history, the sciences, literature, and can speak 20 languages, it's irrelevant. The only information that counts is, "Is there anything that I know, that I can say now, that will convince this person to let me stay alive?" Knowing how to communicate to this individual, is the only knowledge that is relevant. If you have this knowledge, you are fortunate. It is worth more to you than any other knowledge you could possibly have learned.

Fear of Hashem is the spiritual equivalent of the knowledge you need, for physical survival. It is the wisdom that will affect everything you say and do. Your entire character and way of life will be affected, by your having this wisdom.

How can you internalize this most valuable wisdom? Constantly repeat to yourself, "If I had fear of Hashem, what would I say now?" "If I had fear of Hashem, what would I do now?"

A Torah scholar shared with me, "When I was younger, I thought that to have **Yiras Hashem** *(fear of God) one would have to be so serious, that one would not find any enjoyment in life. I felt that I would not be able to be myself. I knew some people who were very pious and it seemed to me that they rarely smiled. This was not a model that I wanted to emulate.*

"Then I met a great Torah scholar who was an elevated person. He was a master at thanking Hashem for all the good in His life. He was meticulously careful with following Torah law and he often spoke about having fear of Hashem.

"I asked him about my concerns. This is what he told me: 'I don't see how anyone could be happy in life without an awareness of Hashem. Missing this awareness, a person lives in an utterly meaningless world. Even if he has pleasure, it is all temporary and will not last. He will have to be afraid of illness and injury, always wanting more than he has, and there is nothing he can do, that will have true everlasting purpose.

"Awareness of Hashem and a strong wish to do His will gives deep, eternal meaning to all that one does in this world. Fear of Hashem elevates all that one does. This leads to constant gratitude for the good in our lives and for the good that we can do. Keep your focus on the joy of doing Hashem's will and — together with fear of Hashem — you will have a depth of appreciation for all the positive things you can do and all the negative things that you avoid.'

"I saw that he lived with this awareness, and so could I. No longer was I obsessively worried. Rather, what he told me, changed my entire outlook on life."

⊰§ 112 / קיב §⊱

גּ הוֹן־וָעֹשֶׁר בְּבֵיתוֹ וְצִדְקָתוֹ עֹמֶדֶת לָעַד:

³Wealth and riches are in his house, and his righteousness endures forever.

The Talmud (*kesubos* 51a) cites an opinion that this verse refers to someone who has Torah books and lends them to others. He still has "Wealth and riches in his house," since he still owns the Torah books, yet his "righteousness endures forever" because he is helping other people study Torah by lending them the books from which to study.

There are people who build up a Torah book collection for themselves, with the intention of running a library. Some set aside special hours when people can come to their homes to borrow their books, while others — with a smaller clientele or more time available — let others call them up at any time throughout the day, to come take books. In addition, there are those who have Torah tape libraries. They collect a large number of Torah tapes on many different subjects by many lecturers, and people are able to listen to inspiring and informative Torah classes, that they otherwise would not have heard. The merit of this Torah study, is eternal.

Even if someone is not able to run an official Torah library, everyone who has Torah books and tapes has an opportunity to lend them to others who, for various reasons, would not otherwise have acquired them. There are many books that have already been read, that now lie untouched on shelves. Think of individuals you know who would especially benefit from those books, and offer to lend them to those people. You have the eternal merit of spreading Torah.

A woman who ran a Torah library from her home was becoming overwhelmed from all the work involved in running it. Her health had deteriorated and she was finding it too difficult and she contemplated closing the library. She told a few of her regular "customers" that she might not continue for very long. They were disappointed to hear this, since this was the only Torah library in their area. One friend of hers, however, said, "I have admired you for quite a while now. I see how much time and effort you put into your Torah library, and I have always wished that I could have a share in your great mitzvah. Financially I'm not able to build up my own library; and also, since you had this mitzvah, I did not want to go into competition with you. Could I please be your volunteer librarian? I will come over to your house three times a week at certain hours. You will be doing me a bigger favor than I am doing for you, by allowing me to do this."

Everyone gained. The owner of the Torah books still had the merit of others utilizing her possessions, for Torah growth. The one who volunteered to run the library was able to be part of spreading Torah even though she did not have her own books to lend. Everyone who was able to borrow the books gained, and many more people were encouraged to borrow Torah books, since the new librarian was motivated to spread the word far and wide that a large selection was available. Every once in a while advertisements aimed at attracting an audience of potential readers who were not familiar with Torah literature, were placed in different shops around the area and this had a great impact on those who followed up on those advertisements. Even the local Torah bookstore gained, because people who borrowed the books wanted to own some of them for themselves, and they bought more of the books they found valuable, as presents for others.

ט פִּזַּר נָתַן לָאֶבְיוֹנִים צִדְקָתוֹ עֹמֶדֶת לָעַד
קַרְנוֹ תָּרוּם בְּכָבוֹד:

⁹ "He distributed widely to the poor, his right-eousness endures forever; his pride will be exalted with glory."

Chasam Sofer commented on this verse: Some people might give a poor person food to eat. This is an act of charity and is praiseworthy. However, the next day the poor person once again needs to eat and the yesterday's act, can no longer be discerned today. Therefore a truly thoughtful donor gives the needy person not only sufficient money so he can buy food for himself, but gives him so much that the poor man himself can now distribute some of what he received to others. This is a "right-eousness which endures forever." He is careful not to give to the poor person in a way that might be belittling. His distribution to the poor person is such that, now the person has an abundance-consciousness. He, too, is able to give to others. This raises the sense of self-worth of the recipient. It is such a kindness that lasts forever.

This comment of *Chasam Sofer* should be our guide, whenever we try to help other people, in any way. Some people give others advice, but they do so in a way that makes the recipient feel demeaned. Some people answer questions of others, but the way they answer, implies that they think the asker is deficient. Some people help others gain skills, but the student is made to feel belittled. The principle that we see here applies to all of these and similar situations.

Whenever you give someone advice, make certain that you do so in a way that enhances the recipient's self-esteem. Whenever you answer someone's questions, do so in a way that the person goes away feeling intelligent and has now increased his knowledge. When you help another person gain a skill, what you say and the way you say it, should give the student the feeling that you believe in his competence.

By enabling a person to raise his self-esteem, you are not only helping him at this moment, but in the future, he will also accomplish much more. Belief in one's ability to make and reach goals, is one of the most important steps to creating a life of accomplishment. Often people who reach greater goals than others, are not necessarily people with much greater levels of intelligence or education, but they do have positive belief in themselves. Just as giving someone who needs money more than he requires so that he can become a philanthropist, even in a small way, will upgrade this person's vision of who he is and what he is capable of, so too, in all areas of a person's life, say and do what you can to help them upgrade their self-image.

A teacher in a school of higher education shared with me that when he was a student he often was made to feel humiliated when he needed to ask a question to clarify something that he did not understand. Whether explicitly or implicitly, the message given was, "How can you be so stupid not to know or understand this?"

For many years he has been considered a master teacher. He always answers questions in a way that makes the student feel cherished. He will frequently say things like, "That's a good question. I'm glad you asked it." "That question makes me think. Thank you for pointing it out to me." "Yes, I do not think that I explained that clearly enough the first time. It's a good thing that you asked me for a further explanation. Now everyone else will benefit as I make myself clearer."

He told me that his own sensitivity to slights and putdowns, made him more aware of teachers' and lecturers' approaches to answering questions. Whenever he saw a pattern that he admired, he added it to his own repertoire. When he felt that a question was handled in a negative way, he made a special effort to avoid using that pattern.

⊰ **118 / קיח** ⊱

כא **אוֹדְךָ כִּי עֲנִיתָנִי וַתְּהִי־לִי לִישׁוּעָה:**

²¹ **I thank You [HASHEM] for You have answered me and become my salvation.**

Many commentaries translate the word *anisani* as "You have answered me", while *Malbim* translates it as "having caused me suffering." In this verse we see the concept of being grateful for adversity. Adversity itself is of great benefit, since suffering atones for our transgressions. "It's a *kaparah* — a process by which we are purified from our sins." When a precious metal is in a hot furnace, the base metal melts away. The precious gold and silver is left to shine, and has great value. Our souls are pure, but we might say and do things that darken our souls. Suffering washes away the darkness. Realizing the eternal benefits of suffering, we thank Hashem for enabling us to clear our slates. The suffering itself, is something from which we gain.

Isn't this difficult? Isn't it hard to truly be grateful for suffering of any type? Don't we all prefer to be free from suffering? The answer to all three questions — "Yes."

This positive attitude becomes easier when we repeat this verse over and over, with the intention of internalizing it. Imagine what it would be like if you were to already have made this a part of your actual belief system — not that you are only *trying* to think this way, but you actually do.

This is similar to thanking a doctor for performing a distressful procedure, that saves your life. You thank him wholeheartedly. "Thank you, doctor. I am intensely grateful to you." It is not too difficult to imagine being able to say this.

Now imagine thanking Hashem for something that you previously have not been grateful for.

In the future if you feel distressed about something not working out the way you wanted, develop the habit of saying this verse.

Think about situations in your own life when some form of suffering, ultimately led to something positive.

Relatives of my family were saved by being captured by the Russians during the Second World War and sent to Siberia. When this happened, they felt tremendous sorrow and distress and only afterwards did they realize that this had saved their lives — they were not killed by the Nazis. After the war, they raised a beautiful family, and, as the time passed, they realized even more that this apparent tragedy was the greatest salvation they could have had. In retrospect, they felt grateful. This was a guiding light for me. Whenever something did not go as I would have wished, I say, "Thank you, Hashem. Please show me how this will be the seed of a great benefit."

כג מֵאֵת יהוה הָיְתָה זֹּאת הִיא נִפְלָאת בְּעֵינֵינוּ:

23 This was from HASHEM. it is concealed from our eyes.

When good things happen to us, this verse applies: "This was from Hashem. It is concealed from our eyes," and when challenging things happen, the same verse applies: "This was from Hashem. It is concealed from our eyes."

When events occur in our lives, which they do daily, hourly, and minute by minute, they do not come with a written message telling us how to view them. Imagine what it would be like to view everything that happens to you, on a screen. You see every person you encounter, on that screen. You see every situation, on that screen. You see every occurrence, on that screen — those things that you like and those that are challenges. Displayed on the bottom of that screen is a vivid caption, with the message, "This is from Hashem. It is concealed from our eyes." What changes would this cause in how you reacted to those situations and events?

Realizing that the positive events and occurrences are from Hashem gives you a much deeper appreciation for them — they will fill you with more gratitude. It is not merely a positive happenstance — it was a planned event from Hashem for your benefit.

When a challenging event occurs, "This was from Hashem" is also meaningful and purposeful. The exact reason for it "is concealed from our eyes." You do not know specifically "Why?", but just knowing that it is meaningful, changes your perspective. You look at it differently. It is not an accident of fate. It is not random. It is purposely constructed for your ultimate benefit, by Hashem.

A young toddler with loving parents will not understand exactly why his father and mother do all that they do. Some of the things he will like, others he will not. They will take away his toys even when he wants to play longer and then he might cry and wail. The meanings of their actions are hidden from him. He does not understand that now he needs to eat to have energy and to be healthy, and at a different time he needs to go to sleep. And yet, another time, they are attending a wedding or a funeral and they need to take him to the home of someone who will watch him. They might need to take him to a doctor to prevent a minor problem from becoming a major one. He reacts according to his limited understanding of what is happening, but an intelligent observer knows that whatever they do for him, is motivated by love and concern. They are his parents and they have his welfare in mind even though their reasoning is concealed from his eyes.

This is how we should understand the events and occurrences in our lives. Our loving and powerful Father is behind them. The reasons may be concealed, but, deep inside, we know that what happens is out of love for us. Our limited understanding prevents us from total comprehension, but the underlying theme is: This is exactly what you need right now for your life-long character development and life-mission.

> I had a friend of many years who would remain calm and controlled regardless of what anyone ever said to him. He thought clearly, and he would serenely deliberate about the wisest thing to say or do. He was well liked by all who knew him. It was clear that he was consistently in positive emotional states, even when having to interact with people whom others found difficult.
>
> "How do you stay so calm when talking to such annoying and problematic people?" I once asked him.
>
> "I do not," he said.
>
> "But I have seen it a number of times;" I asked him.
>
> "What I mean is that I do not interact with annoying and problematic people," he clarified. "Every person I interact with, is sent by Hashem for me to grow from. I might be able to help someone in some way. I can learn from each person I encounter. I can develop more compassion or more gratitude or more patience, as each encounter is really from Hashem. I might not know the exact reason, but since I know it is always from Hashem, I find it relatively easy to remain calm."
>
> I gained tremendously from his perspective. I had a living example of how much I could benefit just learning from him. He, too, was sent to me by Hashem so I could learn a better way to react.

כד זֶה־הַיּוֹם עָשָׂה יְהֹוָה נָגִילָה וְנִשְׂמְחָה בוֹ:

24 This is the day that HASHEM has made. we will rejoice and be happy in it.

his verse is recited during the *Hallel* prayer on the festivals. Every holiday commemorates special events in our history, each having its unique messages and lessons. We experience special joy and happiness on these spiritually uplifting days.

This verse however, has an even wider application. Every single day in our lives has been created by our Creator. Every day of our life we have an opportunity to connect with our loving Father and powerful King in a way that is unique to that day. Every day we can be full of gratitude for the gifts of that day and every day we can learn more Torah and do more good deeds. Every day we have unique challenges designed to refine our character and bring out our best, so every day we can rejoice and be happy.

Apply this verse to all three time zones: past, present, and future. First, to the present: on this day when you are reading this. Right now you are reflecting on this verse. So, regardless of what has happened already today and regardless of what might happen later, this very moment of this day — you can rejoice. You are utilizing this moment of this day, to reflect on how Hashem created this day. So, rejoice. Let the joy spread from head to toe. Let this joy become an essential part of who you are. Let this joy make you a more joyful person.

Secondly, mentally visualize yourself having this joy in the days that you will experience from now on. See your future as being a procession of one joyful day after another. Some days will be easier and some days will be more difficult, but on all days you can think your way to joy. On all days you can connect with Hashem. On all days you can elevate yourself spiritually.

And thirdly, you can now look back at your past days. Rewrite those days with the knowledge and awareness that you presently have. See the hand of Hashem in your life. See how you can presently grow, and become a wiser and better person from what you have experienced. Learn from your mistakes. Gain an even greater appreciation for the happier days of your life. With your present lens, see how Hashem made each day to challenge you to become greater than the day before. And now, as you review previous days, you can learn things that you had not learned previously. Rejoice today for how you have grown, since the earlier days of your life.

> *I told someone who tended to be pessimistic, worried, and sad that he could gain greatly by internalizing the message of this verse. He laughed bitterly and — in an annoyed tone of voice — countered, "Who are you kidding? That is not me — I have a pessimistic personality. You have to have a certain type of personality to be happy even when things are going wrong."*
>
> *"It's not one's personality that is the key factor," I replied. "It's the thoughts that you think that make the difference. Don't take my word for it — test it out yourself. Repeat this verse again and again each day for a week. Start off with the assumption that, every day you will find things about which to rejoice. As a tool, keep asking yourself, 'If I were able to be joyful, what could I be joyful about, right now?'"*
>
> *The fellow was hesitant about trying. "Why are you reluctant to try?" I asked him. "You have nothing to lose and a lot to gain."*
>
> *"But it seems like such a lot of work and I do not really think that this will help me feel better," he said.*
>
> *"If someone who strongly cared about your happiness would offer you a large amount of money to try this for two weeks, would you give it a try?"*
>
> *"It would all depend on how much money he was offering," the fellow said.*
>
> *"What amount would move you, from being unmotivated to being motivated?" I asked him.*
>
> *"I do not know. I have not thought about it yet," he said.*
>
> *"But you agree that, if you were offered enough money, you would be willing to repeat this verse a great many times to test it out. So do it for the sake of creating a more joyful life. If you are afraid of being disappointed if you find that you do not feel any happier, give yourself credit for having the courage to try. View it as a courageous stretching of your*

capabilities. This will give you the inner strength to overcome fear of disappointment."

The fellow agreed to write this verse down on a card that he would carry with him, in his wallet. Whenever he needed to use his wallet, he repeated the verse. He immediately felt greater appreciation for the money he had in order to buy what he needed. When he gave money to charity, he gained a greater sense of joy for the service he could do for others with the money Hashem gave him.

He also wrote the verse down near his telephone and, whenever he went to use the telephone, he repeated this verse. This put him in a much better state of mind, every time he spoke to anyone on the phone.

I saw him a month later, and he had a big smile on his face, that loudly broadcasted his improvement. "I would not have believed that this one verse could make such a difference," he reported. "Nevertheless, seeing is believing. The feedback I get from others, keeps reinforcing the power of this verse for me."

כה אָנָּא יהוה הוֹשִׁיעָה נָּא אָנָּא יהוה הַצְלִיחָה נָּא:

²⁵ **Please, HASHEM, save now! please, HASHEM, bring success now!.**

T he two halves of this verse are separated in the *Hallel* prayer on the festivals, and are usually said with great fervor.

Let these two phrases be on your lips whenever you need Hashem's help. When you are faced with a difficulty of any kind, call upon Hashem to save you. Even when you need fellow human beings to come to your rescue, ask Hashem to send the right help at the right time. A fire engine or ambulance needs to arrive at the correct destination safely, to be of help. If you ever need their services, say this short prayer. If you need to ask someone for financial assistance, say this short prayer. If you are in a highly challenging situation, remember to ask Hashem for help. You might have an emergency that needs immediate attention. The first four words of this verse take only a brief moment to say. Call upon the Omniscient and Omnipotent One to save you.

When you repeat the second half of this verse, you are asking Hashem to make your efforts successful. We can say what we think needs to be said, for success. We can take the actions we think need to be taken, for success. We can make great plans and have ambitious goals. We can mentally visualize ourselves being successful. We can use affirmations and auto-suggestion. We can learn from the most successful role models that there are. We can hire a personal coach. We can network and gain rapport with all the right people. We can read the best-selling books on success, and listen to the latest audio programs. We can attend success seminars.

Ultimately, however, whether or not we will be successful will depend on the Almighty's will. If He wishes, we can be successful even if we do not do everything, that success experts advise us to do, and if Hashem does not want us to succeed, we will not even if we make all the proper efforts.

We need to do our part, and we should take the advice of experts and learn from those who have been successful, but uppermost in our minds should be our connection with our Father, our King, Creator and Sustainer of the universe. Repeat this verse whenever you need success: "Please, Hashem, bring success now." Together with whatever else you are doing, you are adding the most important ingredient for success.

Throughout your life you will strive for major goals. Your entire future may seem to depend on whether or not you will be successful. Ask Hashem for success.

In addition, there are relatively minor goals where you will want to be successful. Even a relatively mundane thing like going to the store to buy groceries, needs success. The same applies to many things that we often take for granted: Making a routine telephone call. Asking someone for directions to get somewhere. Buying or selling any item. Requesting a small loan. Arriving on time for an appointment — even getting the appointment in the first place. The impact of many of these things might not be great, but your success in your endeavors will enhance your life, while not being successful could cause distress. When you realize that your success is absolutely dependent on the will of Hashem and you connect with Him by asking for His blessing of success, the spiritual impact of what you are doing increases the value of your success. You are already successful, regardless of how the specific details ultimately unfold.

I was talking with someone who tended to panic easily. When faced with difficulties, he generally lost all sense of perspective. He viewed molehills as mountains, and as soon as anything would go wrong, he immediately pictured the worst possible outcome. His extreme anxiety prevented him from thinking clearly. When he was calm, he was able to come up with highly creative solutions. But his intense stress created such static, that his thinking process shut down. Anxiety blocked his ability to use his common sense, and he certainly could not think creatively — even obvious solutions were overlooked.

I suggested that he pray to Hashem for Divine assistance. Simply knowing that he had "dialed the number for emergency help" was likely to help him become calmer. Then he would be able to think more clearly. Even if he himself couldn't think of what to do, Hashem has many ways to assist him.

"But when I am in my panic state, I cannot pray," he said.

I recommended that he recite this verse, as his prayer. I told him he should practice saying it, when he is calm, and then, he could visualize himself being in his panic state. As soon as he was aware that he was experiencing panic, he should repeat this verse a number of times, and then he should see himself becoming calm.

"Keep imagining this, many times. Every time you visualize this, you are making these pictures stronger and stronger in your brain's neurons. Be patient. With enough practice, eventually — without any conscious effort on your part — you will automatically start asking Hashem to save you and make you successful. With your calmer state and with the power of prayer, you will find solutions faster than ever before. This has worked for many, and it is very likely that it will work for you."

Whether or not he persisted until this worked for him, you, the reader, can choose to put this into practice. All those who have done so — since the first time these words were written in *Tehillim* — have benefited spiritually, emotionally, and practically.

כו בָּרוּךְ הַבָּא בְּשֵׁם יְהֹוָה בֵּרַכְנוּכֶם מִבֵּית יְהֹוָה:

²⁶ **Blessed is he who comes in the Name of** HASHEM. **may you be blessed from the House of** HASHEM.

---

*R*ashi comments that the blessing mentioned in this verse was said to those who brought their first fruits to the *Beis HaMikdash*, the Holy Temple in Jerusalem, and also to everyone who came to the Holy Temple during the three major holidays, Pesach, Shavuos, and Succos.

During the period of the *Beis HaMikdash*, those who went up to Jerusalem, were already in a highly festive spiritual state. Those who brought their first fruits of the year's crop were joyful that, they could express their profound gratitude to the Creator. The fruit of that year would then be theirs to eat and to sell to others for income.

Those who celebrated the festivals in Jerusalem joined together with a massive throng of people, to serve Hashem. They would meet friends and relatives that they might not have seen, otherwise while even total strangers would instantly develop a rapport. They realized that they had a common bond — they were all there to experience the Divine Presence in the holiest possible place.

Even though those who gathered at the *Beis HaMikdash* experienced an amazingly lofty spiritual state, there are always higher levels that one can reach. The Almighty is infinite and so are the levels of connecting with Him. The blessing of *Baruch haba* — Blessed are those who come in the name of Hashem — gave them an increased awareness. Their motivation was to serve Hashem. They are being blessed from the house of Hashem. That is an incredible thing. Even those who had just arrived at the *Beis HaMikdash,* would bless those who came after them.

Every time you enter a house of prayer or a place of Torah study, you are entering a house of Hashem; you are joining together with other like-minded people. You deserve to be greeted with the blessing of this verse. You can picture in your mind the many times this verse was said when the first and second Holy Temples were alive with spiritual activity, and you can picture in your mind the future visits to the third *Beis HaMikdash*. Let the words of this verse, with the power of the future, greet you every time you enter a house of Prayer or Torah study.

Greet people with a blessing and a smile when they have arrived to fulfill Hashem's commandments, since your blessing is an expression of your appreciation for others' service of Hashem. This shows that your main focus is on sanctification of Hashem's Name. A person who has only concern for himself, will not feel anything special when seeing someone else do a *mitzvah,* while those who are God-oriented, feel joy when witnessing other people serving Hashem. Repeating this verse to others reinforces this way of thinking for you and for the recipient of the blessing, and for everyone else who observes this.

> *Interacting with people who are new to mitzvah observance has given me many opportunities to see how greetings and the lack of greetings affect newcomers.*
>
> *This is what one person told me:*
>
> *"I went to a synagogue before I was* mitzvah-observant. *I felt uncomfortable. This was new to me and I felt out of place. I was thinking that I would like to live a more spiritual life and I wanted to see what it was like to pray to God with others, in an organized way. Unfortunately, my experience was distasteful. I felt like a stranger in a strange land, no one greeted me, and I felt judgmental stares. In general, disapproval and criticism were distressful for me, and here, not only did I not feel any holiness, but I considered the way I was treated the opposite of what I expected in a house of God.*
>
> *"A few years later, I met someone who agreed to study Torah with me, once a week. After a while, he invited me to attend prayers with him. Based on my past experiences, I was reluctant to go with him, and I shared my fears with him.*
>
> *" 'Don't let one bad experience prevent you from trying again,' he said to me. 'The place where I pray might be*

different.' He was persistent and I agreed to try it out. It made sense to me that just because my last experience was negative did not prove that I could not have a positive experience in the future.

"He was right. The regular attendees of the synagogue could tell, that I was new to it all, and they went out of their way to greet me and make me feel comfortable.

"One greeting especially stayed with me. 'Welcome to our house of prayer. Our Heavenly Father appreciates when His children unite, to pray to him. I look forward to seeing you again. If there is anything at all that I can do to help you in any way, please feel free to contact me. Here is my telephone number. If you need assistance becoming familiar with what is going on, you can sit near me.'

"I felt that I was coming home and was eager to follow up on his invitation."

כח **אֵלִי אַתָּה וְאוֹדֶךָּ אֱלֹהַי אֲרוֹמְמֶךָּ:**

²⁸ You are my God and I will thank You, my God, and I will exalt You

---

The phrase "You are my God" personalizes your connection with Hashem every time you repeat this verse. *Metzudas David* explains the first two Hebrew words in this verse as, "You are my strength," King David's intention being that, "You have always been the source of my strength. And for this I thank You and I will exalt You."

Repeat the words "You are my strength." As you say this verse, of speaking directly to Hashem, realize that you are addressing the Creator and Sustainer of the entire universe and are expressing your gratitude to Him and are praising Him, for being your personal source of strength. Increase your awareness that Hashem hears you as you say this and intensify an ever-deepening sense of gratitude for the strength Hashem gives you. Let this strengthening become greater and greater, and let this increase your appreciation and gratitude for whatever Hashem does for you.

I was on an overseas flight from Jerusalem to Monsey, New York, to visit my elderly mother. While I was flying over the Atlantic Ocean, I came across this verse and decided to repeat it over and over again. I wanted to feel the connection with Hashem when I was in **"the heavens above the earth."**

The flight still had three-and-a-half hours left, before we would reach our destination. I overheard some people complaining that the flight seemed very long, and they could not wait until the plane would finally land in Kennedy Airport. When I kept repeating this verse in Hebrew, I remembered a very moving tune that often accompanies it. The thought came to me, "When I am aware of Hashem Who is my source of strength, and I express deep feelings of gratitude, it makes no difference where I am. Wherever I am, I am in the Creator's universe. Wherever I am, I can feel and express gratitude for His kindness."

I recommend to others to repeat this verse slowly and mindfully — over and over — when in the middle of a journey. You have left one place and have not yet reached your destination, and you might feel a bit impatient. You cannot wait to arrive home or to get to where you are going. That is a perfect time to connect with Hashem and to increase your awareness that you are never alone.

﷽ **119 / קיט** ﷽

ה אֲחַלֵי יִכֹּנוּ דְרָכָי לִשְׁמֹר חֻקֶּיךָ:

⁵ My request is, may my ways be firmly guided to keep Your statutes.

The classic *mussar* work *Chovos Halevavos* (Duties of the Heart) cites this verse in his Introduction. There he discusses the vital importance of, not only the actions that the Torah commands us to do, but also of our thoughts and feelings. Here *Tehillim* tells us to constantly yearn to fulfill *mitzvos*. This yearning, together with other basic *mitzvos* of the heart, such as love for Hashem and trust in Him, are *mitzvos* that apply "constantly, at all times, and in all places, as long as we are alive and our minds are working."

We yearn for those things that are highly important to us. A young child will yearn for the presents he will receive for his birthday. As we get older, what we yearn for, will change, but the factor that makes us yearn is, that something is a high priority for us. The higher the priority, the stronger and more intense the yearning.

When we realize the eternal value of Torah and *mitzvos*, we greatly appreciate every opportunity we have to engage in Torah and to perform the good deeds that we can. This increases their level of priority in our minds.

When someone makes a goal but it is not accorded a high priority, then even minor things can be distracting. This is one of the main reasons why many people do not reach the goals to which they allegedly aspire. They state verbally that this goal is important to them, but their inner feelings and desires seek something other than the efforts needed to expend, to reach those goals. Those other things get in the way, and they can lead a person to actions and behavior that are inconsistent with reaching the stated goal.

For example, people say that they would like to eat healthy food and watch their weight. However, when they see food they like, the desire to eat the food is stronger — at that moment — than their stated goal of eating healthy food with an appropriate amount of calories. When being healthy and at the right weight are the highest priorities at all times, then a person has the inner strength to make the healthiest choices.

Some people make Torah study goals and do not reach them. If they would utilize their time wisely and focus on learning what they say they want to learn, they would reach their goals. However, when other things come up that are more interesting to them or easier to do, they are distracted. On the other hand, when they make their Torah learning their highest priority, they are able to stay focused and fulfill what they set out to accomplish.

This is the lesson of our verse. Pray to Hashem that His Torah and *mitzvos* should be your highest priority; make them your dominant thoughts. People who yearn for other things might or might not actually acquire what they seek, and even if they do, they might be disappointed with the reality. When you yearn for Torah observance, however, you will definitely find fulfillment and meaning when you achieve your goal.

> "I wanted to do more good in life than I was doing. 'What stops me from following through on my good intentions?' I asked myself. But I could not figure out an answer that was helpful.
>
> "I remembered hearing that the best way to learn a new skill is, to find a few people who have mastered that skill. Interview them and ask for specific details on how they do it. Do not only ask for the obvious, but ask about their thoughts, what they say to themselves. Ask about the pictures they make in their minds, and about any other factors that they consider the keys to mastering that skill.
>
> "I thought of some people who excelled at making lofty goals and reaching them. The first few people I interviewed were not helpful to me — they did not have a clear plan or program that they could share with me. They both said that they grew up as children hearing the message, 'If you start something, finish it' but they were not aware of doing anything special to keep themselves motivated. The next person I spoke to told me that he used to find it difficult to reach the goals that he made for himself, because he was constantly finding other things that distracted him.
>
> "I was excited to hear this. I figured that someone who had to overcome the tendency not to follow through, might be more likely to have some ideas that could work for me, also.
>
> "He told me that what he did, took some effort, but he has gained tremendously from the practice that has helped him spiritually and in all areas of his life. When he made a goal, each day for an entire week he would repeat out loud — at least one hundred times twice a day — a positively worded short statement. For example, he would say, 'Each day I will joyfully do three acts of kindness.' Or he would say one hundred times, 'I will pray Shemoneh Esrei with total concentration.' Or, 'I will read this Torah book until I finish it.' Repeating the resolution one hundred times im-

planted the thought into his mental library. The large number of repetitions showed his brain that, this was a high priority to him.

"At first, the thought of repeating my resolutions one hundred times a day, seemed overwhelming. However, when I thought about how much I would gain, I realized that the investment of time and energy would be a bargain. I was told to do this with enthusiasm and to increase that enthusiasm as I got closer to the 100 mark. I marked off a straight line on a sheet of paper for each repetition. I could feel the messages I was repeating becoming integrated in my mind and the actual results of this relatively easy exercise were better than I thought. After a week of repeating this twice a day, I found myself doing the positive things that I wanted to do smoothly. This was much easier than pure will-power."

זֹאת נֶחָמָתִי בְעָנְיִי כִּי אִמְרָתְךָ חִיָּתְנִי:

50 This is my comfort in my affliction, for Your word preserved me.

King David suffered in many ways throughout his life. Regardless of the afflictions that befell him, he was still able to experience an inner comfort, by attaching himself to Hashem's words.

When we experience difficulties in life, our emotional experience will be based on the thoughts that we have. Two people can be in the exact same situation: nevertheless, what goes through their minds can be completely different. Take, for example, two people who are traveling in the same vehicle in the dark. Suppose there are no conversations taking place. One person is thinking about different things that might go wrong in his life and he will suffer from this worry. The anxiety that is created by his thoughts will be highly distressful.

The other person is thinking about all the things for which he is grateful. His mind is full of appreciation for the positive things in his life. Both of these individuals are in diametrically opposite worlds and places, even though the external circumstances are the same.

King David's mind was devoted to Torah thoughts. Even when he went through hardships, his mind did not focus on how difficult it was. Rather, his focus was on Torah. Words of Torah have the power to elevate and sanctify, give us knowledge and wisdom. Torah is light. Filling one's mind with this light creates a positive inner state.

When we are facing challenges, it can be more difficult to concentrate, when we try to study Torah. Focus instead on the spiritual connection that you are creating, by engrossing yourself in Hashem's words and let this give you feelings of inner comfort. Since your inner mind is focusing on the eternal benefits of the words of Torah that you are studying, you will transcend the present difficulties.

"I once had a conversation with a Holocaust survivor who shared with me that, reciting verses from Torah and Psalms by heart, had given him the inner strength and comfort to withstand the physical and mental agony. He did not have an particularly good memory, but he did know a number of verses by heart. He would mentally repeat them over and over again. He did this when he was marched to forced labor, when he was in freezing cold weather without warm clothing, and even, when he felt ill. The verses that he kept repeating, comforted him.

"He felt an inner victory over the Nazis. They could control his living conditions, they could control the amount and quality of food that he would eat, they could control the actions that he had to take — but they were powerless to control his inner mind, and his inner mind was focused on words of Torah. He felt a tremendous personal victory in being able to recite these verses. He would sing them to himself with his own private melody. He attributed his having survived, to the comfort the Torah verses gave him. I have found that in much easier-to-handle difficulties, repeating Torah verses has given me the strength that I needed, to cope."

ס חַשְׁתִּי וְלֹא הִתְמַהְמָהְתִּי לִשְׁמֹר מִצְוֹתֶיךָ:

⁶⁰ I hastened and I did not delay to fulfill Your commandments.

Procrastination is the enemy of accomplishment. On the other hand, taking action is the only way we can accomplish. Someone might have wonderful goals, be full of idealism, have ambitious plans, but failure to take action will leave the goals, ideals, and plans on the drawing board. The good intentions will remain intentions. The good that might have been, will not become reality.

Laziness comes from a desire for comfort. It is much easier to push off what we would like to do, than to actually do it. However, when we realize that we will gain greatly from doing something, we will apply the necessary effort to do it. The greater the benefit, the easier it is to do what needs to be done.

Imagine someone who is extremely lazy, always procrastinating. If something can be pushed off, he will push it off. He is never on time. He is late for appointments, late in paying his bills late for just about everything. One day, he checks out the winning number of a major lottery, and discovered that his ticket has won an international lottery. However, he was late in finding out the number. He was so certain that he would not win, that he did not exert himself to find out the number that won the lottery. Today, he decided that — since it is the final day — he might as well see if he won. He did! He's excited. He's thrilled. And he knows he has only today to present his ticket at the lottery headquarters. He'll rush, like he never rushed before. He still has six more hours to go. What is the rush? He could still wait five and a half more hours, but there's no way he'll delay this. He will go at top speed to present his ticket, because he now knows its value. It was always worth a fortune, but he did not realize it, so he dallied. With his present awareness, he will act with the speed of a rocket.

That is the message of our verse. Realize the eternal, immeasurable value of each good deed. We all have a deadline, but we have no idea when it is. Do all the good you can do in this world, and do it right away. Time is running out. Even if we have a long time to go, the more good we do, the greater our spiritual fortune.

Let this verse be your motto, "I hastened and I did not delay to fulfill your commandments." Since this verse is stated in the first person, "I hastened," and "I did not delay," every time you repeat it, you are reinforcing the positive self-image that you are a person who takes action right away. Even when you take action that is easy for you to do, repeat the verse, since this strengthens the idea that you are a doer of good deeds who does them as soon as possible.

> A friend of mine attended a seminar on how to achieve financial success. About a year later I met him and asked, "What lessons did you learn at the seminar?"
>
> "I learned something that I feel will change my life, even though I've known this already for many years.
>
> "Growing up I heard over and over again, 'Your biggest problem is that you procrastinate.' But knowing this, did not help me. As a matter of fact, it made things worse. It kept reinforcing my self-image of being lazy and, unfortunately, this was who I was, and I did not think I could change.
>
> "At the financial seminar the speaker asked us, 'What do you consider the main factor as to why you are not yet as successful as you wish to be?'
>
> "Different reasons were given, but the speaker told us that once one has the necessary knowledge to succeed, fear that breeds procrastination is usually the key element. When you feel highly motivated, you take action, and taking action is what you need to reach your goals. By definition, the moment you take action, you are no longer procrastinating. Visualize yourself feeling fully empowered to keep taking action, until you complete the deed that you set as your goal. Picture this over and over again. This stores those pictures in your brain cells and lead to your taking action.
>
> "When I heard this, I realized my mistake. I kept picturing myself, being lazy. I kept thinking, how hard it is to take action. When it came to studying Torah and fulfilling mitzvos, I needed to use the power of visualization, to see myself taking action. I repeated a mental picture of myself having tremendous pleasure and joy every time I took action, right away. I ran this picture on the screen of my mind again and again. The great

feelings I had when I actually followed through, made it easier for me to take action, in more and more situations. This changed my self-image. I now look at myself as someone who loves to do positive actions right away."

סג חָבֵר אָנִי לְכָל־אֲשֶׁר יְרֵאוּךָ וּלְשֹׁמְרֵי פִּקּוּדֶיךָ:

63 I am a friend to all who fear You, and to those who observe Your commandments.

R' Samson Raphael Hirsch commented on this verse: "King David is saying that, when he wants to elevate himself spiritually and to strengthen what is true and good, he does this by associating with people who fear Hashem and are true to their spiritual obligations."

As mentioned earlier, *Rambam* (*Hilchos Dei'os* 6:1) writes that the very nature of human beings is to be influenced by the attitudes and actions of the people with whom they associate. Therefore we should associate with righteous and with wise people in order to learn from their positive behavior.

Please note that the verse does not say only to *be near* those who fear Hashem and guard *His* commandments. "Rather, "I am a friend to all who fear You, and to those who observe Hashem's commandments." Whom do we choose for friends? People with whom we share a common interest.

A person whose main interest in life is business will want to associate with other business people. Even if he does not plan to do business with them right now, he feels comfortable in their presence, and they will want to discuss similar topics. A person who is interested in the latest news, likes to associate with others with a similar interest, and a person who has particular intellectual interests seeks people with whom he can discuss those subjects. People who are sports fans feel friendly towards those who root for the same team, or those who are at least interested in the same sport.

The loftiest level to be interested in, is Godly topics. When this is one's main interest in life, one will automatically consider another person with similar aspirations, a friend.

There is an expression that people often use when they meet someone with whom they share a mutual acquaintance: "Any friend of _____ is a friend of mine." That is a goal toward which to strive: If someone is connected to our Father, our King, we automatically feel closely connected to him.

> *I shared the above idea with someone who was very shy and frequently felt lonely. He did not relate easily to other people, and he often felt like an outsider when he was in a group. This is what he reported:*
>
> *"Now that I keep in mind that I view anyone who studies Torah, prays to Hashem, and fulfills* mitzvos *— as a friend, I feel entirely different in many situations. Not only do I feel much more comfortable in the synagogue where I usually pray, but even when I pray in another synagogue, I feel a sense of friendship with all those who have gathered to pray. I feel that I belong, just as much as anyone else. I remember a class reunion that I attended; it gave me a great feeling to be among childhood friends.*
>
> *I am now feeling similar feelings more often. When I am in a store and see that someone is careful about buying kosher products, I look at him as a friend. I went to a store that sold* sefarim *and I viewed everyone who was buying a Torah book, as a friend. I attended a Torah lecture and did not know many of the people who attended, but I said to myself, 'Everyone here is my friend.' I have found it much easier to greet people in a friendly manner. I find it amazing how this one idea, can make such an impact."*

צז מָה־אָהַבְתִּי תוֹרָתֶךָ כָּל־הַיּוֹם הִיא שִׂיחָתִי:

97 O how I love Your Torah! all day long it is my conversation.

T here are two ways to study Torah. One way is to intellectually know that it is highly important to gain Torah knowledge and to spend time studying it; done out of a feeling of obligation and responsibility. It is the right thing to do, so one does it. One knows that he "should" do this, so he does what he "should" do — but his heart is not really in it.

On the other hand, there is the ideal way to study Torah. One loves the Giver of the Torah. One loves studying Torah. When one studies Torah, one connects with our loving Father and powerful King. One appreciates each idea and concept, has an awareness of the eternal rewards for Torah study, and finds great pleasure in doing so. The ultimate level is to experience such an intense love for studying Torah that there is absolutely nothing else in the world that one would rather do. This love for Torah is manifest in one's making this the central topic of conversation by discussing Torah thoughts throughout the entire day.

Before my eyes is a picture of my Rebbe, R' Mordechai Gifter, the late Rosh Yeshivah of Telz. This was his *passuk;* that is, the verse he would say after finishing the *amidah* prayer, and this was his mindset throughout his life. He had an intense love for Torah study; his mind was fully concentrated on the Torah he was studying, and nothing else existed when he was engaged in Torah study. In his public Torah lectures and in private talks, we could feel the intense spiritual energy that radiated from him when conveying Torah thoughts.

Giving over this love for Torah, is the highest priority for those who teach Torah to children. Even more important than children gaining the knowledge of what they are studying, and remembering it, they need to gain a love for learning Torah. If a child does not enjoy studying Torah, he will study for the sake of getting good grades or because he does not want to feel embarrassed if he is asked a question and does not know the answer. However, a child who loves to learn Torah will find it easier to concentrate when he studies, and he will automatically remember it better. He will be able to study for longer periods of time, and the Torah that he studies will become an integral part of who he is.

In the morning prayers there is a blessing for studying Torah, that is said once every day. Part of the basic blessing is a prayer asking that Hashem should make the Torah that we study, sweet for us. At any time that we study Torah we can ask Hashem in our own words to implant within us a love for His Torah. May our prayers be answered.

A person who taught Torah told me that he had a problem with what is called "burnout." He was teaching the same material year after year for many years, and it was getting a bit stale for him. He realized that just as he was not enjoying teaching, his students were not enjoying his classes. He had considered quitting and seeking a job in an entirely different field.

As he was weighing the pros and cons of leaving Torah teaching, he realized that, when he had started teaching Torah, he had considered it the best possible activity in the entire world. He was enthusiastic about teaching. Remembering how he felt when he began teaching, he realized that this was his problem. He used to be enthusiastic about teaching Torah and now he was not. In addition, he realized that his enthusiasm for his own Torah study was waning. As he was thinking about this, a sentence passed through his mind. "Talk and act enthusiastically and you will feel enthusiastic."

He said to himself, "Before I take any action about finding another job, let me build up my own enthusiasm for studying Torah, and let me see what happens with my teaching."

He began to study Torah, talking and acting with the utmost enthusiasm that he could create. At first he was not concerned with actually feeling this, but only acting in the way the most enthusiastic person in the world would. He realized that he was exaggerating, but that was his plan. He went to a quiet room with no one else around and began reading the Torah text with intense excitement. He kept telling himself, "Even more enthusiasm! Even more enthusiasm!"

It took time, but it worked. It worked wonders for him. He began to get excited about what he was reading, and he felt this energy growing and growing. He realized that, just as he was doing this for himself, he should do this for his students. The first few moments of teaching Torah with this level of enthusiasm, felt strange to him, and he was a bit self-conscious about how his students would react. It did take them a little while to get used to this, but it happened much faster than he thought it would.

Ever since then, he is a changed person. His love for Torah has grown, he loves teaching Torah, and his students enjoy his classes and remember what they have studied better than ever before.

צט מִכָּל־מְלַמְּדַי הִשְׂכַּלְתִּי

99 **From all my teachers, I grew wise.**

This verse is cited in the fourth chapter of *Pirkei Avos* (Chapters of the Fathers, mishnah 4:1). There we find definitions of four key terms. The one relevant to our verse is: "Who is a wise person?" The mishnah replies: "The one who learns from everyone." And the source of this is, "From all my teachers, I grew wise."

R' Simcha Zissel Ziv, the head of the yeshivah in Kelm, commented on this that, as a rule, people notice only the specific areas that are of interest to them. A tailor will notice the clothing that a person is wearing, a shoemaker will notice the shoes that people wear, and a hat salesman will notice hats.

A person will notice the area related to whatever business in which he is involved. He will be aware of any words or actions that will have an effect on his business.

Even when it comes to spiritual matters, people will notice the specific areas that interest them. Only those who are truly interested in kindness, will notice every word and act of kindness that occurs in their presence. To learn from every person means that every possible area of learning and personal growth is important to this individual, and that is why such a person is considered a wise person (see *Chochmah U'mussar*, vol. 2, pp.92-3).

R' Shlomo Wolbe elaborates on the importance of learning from everyone. Each day we meet many people. Learn at least three things from others each day. Be open to learn something positive from people who work in a grocery store, a post office, or drive buses. Learn from janitors and young children. Each person — without exception — will have something from which you can learn. It might be a small action or a positive word. In the beginning this might be a bit difficult, but with practice you will find a new world (see *Alei Shur*, pp.193-6).

Realizing that you can learn something from everyone, will give you a much more positive view of other people. The question that you will constantly ask yourself will be, "What can I learn from this person?" When you keep asking this question, you will be surprised to find many things that you probably would not have noticed, had you not developed this habit.

I met someone who was an expert at learning positive things from others. "How are you able to notice so many things that most people miss?" I asked him.

"As I was growing up, my father would frequently quote the statement from Pirkei Avos *that a wise person is one who learns from everyone," he replied. "He would point out to me seemingly minor positive actions of others. He would notice the patterns of storekeepers that showed a sensitivity to the needs of their customers, and would point out positive character traits that he observed in total strangers. He was open to the original Torah thoughts of anyone who expressed a creative idea. My father's pattern came so natural to me that I wasn't fully aware that not everyone does this."*

Hearing this, I was more open to learning from the wisdom of this person's father, to developing this habit myself and teaching it to my young grandchildren.

קה נֵר־לְרַגְלִי דְבָרֶךָ וְאוֹר לִנְתִיבָתִי:

105 **Your words are a candle to my feet. and light to my path.**

A candle does not give off very much light, but with the light of a candle you can see what is directly in front of you. This will prevent you from tripping over obstacles and banging into walls. You can walk with an inner feeling of calm — you are safe.

In daylight you can see far into the distance. You have a broader perspective, since you can see the entire terrain. Now you have a more comprehensive picure of where you are going. You can see the path you need to travel on, to reach your ultimate destination.

The most important path we need to travel on, is the path of life. What is your life mission? What are your main goals in life? What do you plan to do with your time on this world?

Knowing your path gives you criteria from which to choose. What will your priorities be? You are constantly making choices of thoughts, words, and actions. Without a clear view of what is truly important in your life, you might waste much time on trivialities or, even worse, on actions that detract you from your true life mission. Not having a clear picture of where you want to go and not knowing the path, means that you are virtually traveling in darkness. We all need a guide or at least a map that shows us the path.

King David says to Hashem: "Your words, Hashem, as manifest in Torah, are a candle and a light." Your words prevent me from stumbling and falling and, what is even more, Your words are a great light in that they give me a path on which to travel. I know what is important for me, to reach my ultimate destination.

When you see candles, you have a reminder of this verse. As you see a candle, hear the words, "Your words are a candle for my feet", and this will remind you of the second half of the verse, "And a light for my path."

When an airplane travels overseas, a large part of the flight is off course. There are many zig-zags that a plane will make because of the blowing winds, but nevertheless, the airplane has a clear program of its destination. The computer that guides the plane has the information and the pilot knows it clearly — city "x" or "y" is my goal. Adjustments are constantly made so that the destination is reached safely.

This analogy is one we should keep in mind. Clarify your ultimate life goals, so that you can see clearly when you are on course and when you are off. Let the light of Torah shine in your life so your path will be a path of light.

> *"There were many things going wrong with my life and I was totally confused and overwhelmed. I was inconsistent. Some days I felt I utilized my time wisely, but there were many others when I felt that I was wasting much time and accomplishing little. I spoke to my rabbi about my distraught feelings.*
> *" 'What you need is a guide,' he said to me.*

Of course I do,' I told him, "and that is why I am consulting you."

"If you were to have a choice between the ultimate guide and a limited guide, which would you choose?" he asked me.

"Obviously, the ultimate guide," I said, a bit puzzled.

"Yes, obviously," he said in a friendly tone of voice. "And that is why you should choose the devar Hashem *(the word of Hashem) as your guide. Whenever you have a question about the right path for you to take, ask yourself, 'Which path would my loving Father and powerful King want me to take?' With this question as your criterion, the best choice will often be obvious. Sometimes, however, you will see that both choices will be equally satisfactory. While, at other times, you might want to consult a Torah authority. Even though the details will need to be worked out, the general direction will always be clear. Keep this in mind for an entire week and then let's discuss how this helped you."*

I agreed to apply this question, and the week was one of the best weeks of my life. I realized that I was on the right path.

קכו עֵת לַעֲשׂוֹת לַיהוה הֵפֵרוּ תּוֹרָתֶךָ:

[126] It is a time to do for HASHEM, they have violated Your Torah.

This verse teaches us that when we see that there are people who have violated and forsaken Hashem's Torah, we need to make a special effort to do all we can, to observe it. This is a time for action. When we see that others are forsaking Torah observance, we must make a supreme effort to do even more than we would otherwise.

When we think about *Ahavas Hashem,* love for Hashem, our Father, our King, Creator and Sustainer of the universe, we will feel a strong desire to do His will ourselves and will want others to as well.

When we observe others behaving improperly, it is often easy to merely complain about it, and to keep repeating, "Isn't it awful the way people are acting nowadays!" It is easy to keep thinking about how upset we are about the level of the generation, to simply criticize and condemn, but "talk is cheap." It's the lazy person's haven. "If I talk about how much I do not like the way things are, at least I feel that I am doing something!"

Action is what gets things accomplished. Doing even a little, accomplishes more than just talking about what needs to be done that "someone" should really do. When we see that something needs to be done for *Kavod Shamayim*, for the sake of Heaven, we must have the emotional energy that propels us to say, "I am going to do something constructive."

When there is a lack of Torah learning in the world, we should think about ways that we can upgrade our own Torah learning. How can we spend more time studying Torah?

When we see that there is a lack of *mitzvah* observance in the world, we should think about ways that we can increase the amount of *mitzvos* we ourselves do. And we should also think about ways that we can upgrade our own level of intent, when we do perform *mitzvos*.

When we see that there is a lack of prayer or quality of prayer in the world, we should think about ways we can upgrade our own level of prayer.

Not only should we upgrade our own level of Torah study and *mitzvah* performance, but we should also think about ways that we can motivate and influence others to observe Hashem's Torah.

The question that we need to ask ourselves is, "What can I do to promote and spread Torah learning?"

Some people are able to teach the Torah they know, even if they are not professional teachers. Others can organize Torah classes. While others can help financially support programs that spread Torah.

We should also ask ourselves the question, "What can I do to promote and influence greater *mitzvah* observance?"

When is the time referred to in this verse? The time is now. Each and every day, think about ways that you can do something for Hashem's honor.

This verse was often quoted by the saintly Chofetz Chaim and was a principle that motivated him greatly to spread Torah and mitzvah *observance. A disciple of the Chofetz Chaim once told a group of students that they should spend an entire month, thinking about this verse. "What can each one of you do to spread Torah awareness and observance?"*

Each member of the group was asked to think of some mitzvah *or aspect of a* mitzvah *that not everyone was as careful about, as they should be, and they should read source material about it. Then, for an entire month, they should make a special effort to talk to as many people as possible — in an enthusiastic way — about the importance of observing that* mitzvah. *They need not do this in a formal way, but informally — when they had a chance to share what they knew about the importance of this* mitzvah, *they should put their heart into discussing it with others. "Words that come from the heart enter the heart." We should never under-estimate the potential for being a positive influence on others, even when we do this on a small scale.*

So the challenge to you now is: "What can I personally do to apply this?"

קכז עַל־כֵּן אָהַבְתִּי מִצְוֹתֶיךָ מִזָּהָב וּמִפָּז:

[127] Therefore I have loved Your commandments more than gold, even more than fine gold.

What will people do for gold? The question should be, what won't people do for gold? When gold was found in distant lands, people would travel far from home. They were willing to live in the harshest circumstances, willing to risk all they had, even their very lives. Why? Because they had visions of how finding gold would transform their lives. Imagining this, they were highly motivated to do everything in their power, to attain riches.

A person realizing the eternal value of observing Hashem's commandments knows that, all the gold in the world cannot equal the spiritual benefits of doing the will of the Creator. Gold can help one enjoy life with its purchasing power. With gold one can make beautiful jewelry and ornaments, which can enhance one's life. However, gold is material and highly limited in what it can do for someone. Regardless of the amount of gold and other forms of money that one gathers, it can be lost. Obeying the will of the Creator, however, is spiritual. It is nourishment for our soul, and the key to eternal reward.

Besides what gold can buy, those who have wealth often feel better about themselves. Those who amass a fortune often feel a sense of importance and many people respect them more. "He is a wealthy person. Make sure to treat him in a way that is appropriate for someone of his stature." Some people with wealth truly do act in ways that are deserving of great respect, as they utilize their own abundance to help many others in a multitude of ways. They develop their character and do not allow their wealth to make them arrogant and conceited.

Those who understand the much greater value of *mitzvos* feel a stronger sense of elevation when they do the Almighty's will. With humility, their self-image soars. "How fortunate I am that I have merited to be engaged in the most important work that a mortal can do." Each good deed that they do, adds to their true net worth.

One of the secrets of financial wealth is to love the work that you do. Two individuals can be involved in the same profession. One loves what he does — he enjoys the entire process of what he is involved in — while the other dislikes the same job. The one who loves what he does, works with all his mind and all his heart; he is passionate about his profession. The one who dislikes what he does will not reach the same level of expertise and success in the field. He will not spend the same amount of time, and his mind is likely to wander as he wishes he were elsewhere.

Loving *mitzvos* makes you passionate about them. You do them with all your inner resources. When you see someone who is enthusiastic about making money, let that serve as a reminder to be even more enthusiastic, about doing the will of Hashem.

> *A friend of mine once told me: "A relative once invited me to a large convention of salesmen who worked for a giant company. The heads of the company did everything they*

could to create an atmosphere of excitement. Adults shouted
and screamed with the fervor of a five-year-old at an amuse-
ment park. The speakers elaborated — in glowing — terms
about the great joy that would be theirs when they would
successfully sell even more. It seemed to me to be highly
exaggerated but, looking at the faces of those attending, I
saw that they were seriously motivated to earn as much as
they could.

"I did not become caught up in their frenzied reaction, but I
did go away with a powerful lesson in how far away I was
from appreciating Torah and mitzvos to the same degree as
their excitement about money. This reminded me of role
models I had met, who did reach high levels of enthusiasm
for what is truly important in life. Afterwards I became more
aware of individuals who prayed with great fervor, of
individuals who were excited about Torah study, and individuals who loved to do acts of kindness and other mitzvos."

⦑ **121 / כא** ⦒

ה יהוה שֹׁמְרֶךָ יהוה צִלְּךָ עַל־יַד יְמִינֶךָ:

⁵ **HASHEM is your Guardian, HASHEM is your
protective Shadow, at your right hand.**

Walking through a dangerous neighborhood can be
frightening. Even if you do not see actual dangers at a
given moment, you are likely to be nervous — danger
might be lurking somewhere. Every minute seems like an hour. As
your eyes scan right and left, up and down, your entire nervous
system registers that you must be ready to fight or flee in an
instant's notice. Even for a short while, this is highly distressful and
all the more so, if one finds oneself in such a situation over a long
period of time.

Regardless of how dangerous a neighborhood might be, there is
a way that you could stroll through it with absolute calm — you can
serenely walk step by step and even enjoy the scenery. Why?
Because you have a powerful bodyguard, a bodyguard that no one

would dare antagonize. He is not only powerful himself, but is the head of the most powerful network of bodyguards. Anyone who would start up in even the slightest way, would have to answer to the roughest, toughest group of powerful warriors that have ever been assembled. As you walk through this neighborhood, you might even have a smile on your face. You are safe. You are protected. Potentially dangerous characters nod their heads with respect as you walk past – or, to be more accurate — as you and your bodyguard walk by.

This verse gives us a most reassuring message. Hashem is your Guardian. He is the ultimate bodyguard, as it were. As you walk through life, this will give you an inner feeling of calmness and serenity and a profound sense of well-being. You are completely at ease. Your mind is clear. You will have a smile on your face wherever you are. You are safe. You are protected.

Not only is Hashem your Guardian, but He is your Shadow, states the verse. Hashem is always to your right. In case you begin to feel a bit insecure, or start to feel anxiety and stress, simply turn to your right — the Almighty is there.

While we should not be foolhardy and put ourselves in unnecessary physical danger, when it comes to emotional well-being, having the awareness of this verse frees you from the fear of what other humans will think and say. This awareness is powerful — it makes a significant difference in all aspects of your life. You feel emotionally safe and protected wherever you are.

How can we keep this in mind? Every blessing that you make with Hashem's Name, is another reminder that Hashem is right here. Every time you thank Hashem for His constant kindness throughout each day and throughout your entire life, you have another reminder that Hashem is right there, with you. He is like your shadow. Nothing you can do will cause your shadow to disappear. Under certain circumstances it might be hidden, but it is always there.

Every so often, when you notice your shadow, remember this verse. "Just as my shadow is with me wherever I go and wherever I am, so too Hashem is always at my side." Let this strengthen you emotionally whenever challenging situations arise. With Hashem's help, you will be able to handle them gracefully and easily.

There is another well-known interpretation of this verse, often quoted in the name of R' Yisrael *Baal Shem Tov:* just as your shadow makes the exact same movements as you do, so too Hashem treats you measure for measure, the way you treat others.

If someone treats others harshly, that is the way he himself will be treated. If someone lacks compassion for other people in distress, he too will not be treated with compassion when he needs it, and everyone finds themselves in situations where they need the compassion of others.

On the positive side, when you treat others compassionately, thoughtfully, kindheartedly, that is the way that you will be treated.

> *I spoke to a father whose adult children were extremely kind and generous to others. They were compassionate with people whom most others found irritating. "What was your secret?" I asked him. "How did you raise your children to be so exceedingly kind and understanding to others?"*
>
> *He replied, "When my children were young, I would fre- quently repeat to them, 'Every time you need to make a choice about how to interact with another person, remember that Hashem will deal with you, measure for measure. The most selfish thing a person can do in life, is to be unselfish. Always be kind. Always judge favorably. Always be com- passionate. I love you and want others to be kind towards you. I want others to judge you favorably, and I want others to be compassionate towards you. The way to make this happen is for you to be kind and compassionate to others.*
>
> *You will be making me happy when you do this, for this is the way that I know you will constantly find happiness in your own lives, and you will be creating a lot of happiness for many people throughout your lives. The people who need your caring and compassion the most, will be the ones who act in ways that make it less likely that others will act this way towards them. Go out of your way and make a supreme effort, not to allow anyone's negativity to stop you from being positive towards them."*
>
> *This person's family was one of the happiest families I've ever seen, so I can testify that this approach works wonders.*

﴾ **127 / קכז** ﴿

א שִׁיר הַמַּעֲלוֹת לִשְׁלֹמֹה אִם־יהוה לֹא־יִבְנֶה בַיִת שָׁוְא
עָמְלוּ בוֹנָיו בּוֹ אִם־יהוה לֹא־יִשְׁמָר־עִיר שָׁוְא שָׁקַד
שׁוֹמֵר:

¹ *A song of ascents for Solomon. if* HASHEM *will
not build the house, in vain do the builders labor
on it, if* HASHEM *will not guard the city, in vain
is the watchman vigilant.*

Meiri explains that this verse was said by King David on
behalf of his son, Solomon, who was destined to be his
successor as king of Israel. King David wanted to build
the Holy Temple in Jerusalem, but he was told by the prophet
Nathan that he would not be the one to build it. Rather, it would be
built by his son Solomon.

For this reason King David is offering us spiritual advice: We
must know that whenever we undertake to accomplish any task or
project, it is ultimately Hashem Who decides whether it will
succeed. Even though the efforts we make to take action are
appropriate and are precisely what we should be doing, nevertheless the outcome of what we attempt to do is completely
dependent on the will of Hashem. As the Torah tells us (*Deuteronomy* 8:17,18), we should not say in our hearts that it was our own
power and the might of our hands that brought victory. Rather, the
energy and power that we have is as absolute gift from Hashem.

That is what this verse tells us. Even if someone does all that is
humanly possible, only with the will of Hashem will he be able to
build a house. During a war, even if the guards keep looking in all
directions, only with Hashem's help will they be successful in
protecting the inhabitants of the city.

The next verse (verse 2) tells us that even when someone gets up
very early to work and stays at the job until late at night, Hashem
can give someone else their livelihood — even someone who
sleeps more at night and gets more rest. This, writes *Meiri,* is not
telling us, not to make the effort to do what needs to be done.

Rather, the verse is telling us to constantly keep in mind that the essential ingredient for success in any endeavor, is the will of Hashem.

Being aware that the success of any venture is always in the hands of the Almighty will give us a deeper appreciation for the Almighty's kindness. Our prayers before and during our efforts will be more heartfelt, when we are conscious of this. Moreover, this will give us a sense of humility when we are tremendously successful. It is not our own efforts that were the decisive factor in succeeding. Rather, it is our Father, our King, Creator and Sustainer of the universe, Whose will creates success and failure.

Some people who tend to be lazy, might try to cite this verse and the next one as proof that working hard does not always give one more success than someone who works much less. Laziness however, is not trust in the Almighty. The person who trusts in Hashem is willing to exert as much energy as needed on a project. When it comes to spiritual matters, such as Torah study, prayer, and doing acts of kindness, he spends large amounts of time and energy. He puts his heart and soul into the projects that he works on. However, at all times, he recognizes that the basic factor behind his accomplishing whatever he wants to, is Hashem's will.

> Someone once shared with me that there was an acquaintance of his, who used to annoy him. This person would frequently boast about how smart and successful he was. "It is my intelligence that ensures that I will always be successful. I don't leave anything to chance."
>
> For quite a while this person's tremendous success, made him snobbish and arrogant — he looked down at others who hadn't prospered as he had. Unfortunately, a number of factors beyond his control took him close to bankruptcy and, as a result, he became very depressed and broken. It was not only the loss of money that caused him such tremendous distress, but his entire worldview had been shaken to the core. He had felt that he was invincible and now he saw that even if he did not make any mistakes, he could lose the fortune that had taken him so long to acquire.
>
> He told his acquaintance, "What I went through in the last six months was torturous for me, but it taught me a spiritual

lesson that I'll never forget. I see how vulnerable I am. With all my intelligence and with the lifetime of knowledge that I have gained, I see that there is a force in the world that is totally beyond me. My belief in God became much stronger. It took a near collapse of all that I have accomplished until now, to wake me up and make me realize that the Almighty runs the world. Even if I am able to make a complete comeback and once again become wealthy, I will have the humility to realize that all that I have, is a gift from Hashem. If I would have understood this earlier, the entire situation would have been much easier for me to accept."

ד **כְּחִצִּים בְּיַד־גִּבּוֹר כֵּן בְּנֵי הַנְּעוּרִים:**

4 Like arrows in the hand of a warrior, so are the children of youth.

One explanation of this verse is that it refers to the importance of a goal. When one shoots an arrow, the only way to succeed, is to be aware of one's target. An arrow will go far, but the way one aims that arrow, is the key factor determining where it will land. A *gibor* refers to a strong hero. Such a person knows clearly where he wants the arrow to go. He focuses on his target, and then, with expertise that comes from experience, the arrow reaches the intended destination.

So, too, when it comes to having a positive influence on youth. A parent or teacher must have the outcome in mind; the goal must be clear only then can one say to the child or student what must be said in that given situation, in order to reach the intended goal.

If someone aims too high or too low when shooting an arrow, the arrow will miss the target. Similarly, if the aim is too far to the right or left, the arrow might miss not only the bull's-eye, but even the entire target. You need to focus on the particular target you want to reach, and then aim.

Depending on the unique nature and personality of the child or student, the messages you give must be measured accordingly. A given statement could be perfect for one child, but for another it could be too difficult — he is not yet ready for this lesson. For another child, the message could be insufficient — this child could handle much more. A message that is too weak for him will cause needless limitation — he could accomplish more and go further.

You owe it to your children and students to aim just right. Give them the right amount. How can you tell if you aimed correctly? When it comes to shooting at a target, it's quite clear if your arrow hit the target or missed it. With children and students, the feedback might not be as obvious. Be open to learning from those with a lot of experience in teaching and reaching a wide range of children.

This verse can also be understood as speaking directly to the young person. An archer needs to clarify his target before he shoots. Similarly, the earlier one sets clear goals, the more one is likely to accomplish in life. Many young people feel that they are not yet ready to decide on clear goals. They know that they would like to accomplish much good in life, but the goals they want to reach are not yet clearly delineated. They should act like a master archer: Even if he doesn't yet know the exact target he will need to hit later on, he knows that, the more he practices, the better he will be — when his skills become necessary. A young person should keep upgrading his basic skills. Then, when the specific goals become clear, he will have the tools necessary to reach them.

> I once spoke to a Torah scholar who had a great influence on the lives of many yeshiva students.
>
> "What do you consider to be a key factor in the level of success that students will reach?" I asked him.
>
> "Making goals," he responded immediately.
>
> "Why do you consider this to be so important?"
>
> "In all areas of endeavor there is a major difference between those who make goals and those who do not. Take, for example, two people who want to start a business. One does not make goals. He might work hard, but since he is not focused on reaching specific goals, he usually will not accomplish as much as the person who strives towards reaching a particular aim. In financial matters, when a person makes clear goals, he will keeps his eyes open for opportunities that those who do not have goals, would never have seen. Though the goal-focused person might not work harder or more

hours, with the same effort and the same amount of time, he will act more intelligently. He will use his time more wisely.

"The same applies to Torah study, prayer, doing acts of kindness, and developing one's character. Setting goals for oneself creates a focus that those without clear goals, will lack.

"I consider goal-setting to be one of the most important skills and habits that one can teach. The practice of regularly making goals will transform a person's life. A question I commonly ask my students is, 'What goals do you have for yourself?'

"If someone is unable to answer this question satisfactorily, I set out to influence him to make at least a minor goal, and then to take — at least — some small action to accomplish that goal. Acting consistently this way will eventually lead to making major goals and to taking major actions to reach those goals.

"Reaching goals, even minor ones, is guaranteed to have a positive impact. When I was a young student myself, I observed the older students. I consistently saw that those who were most successful were the ones who made goals for themselves. I resolved to make goals myself and in a short time, I made more progress than I had ever made before. Goal-setting has become a valuable pattern for me and it has been a high priority for me to influence others to do the same. I consider my success in this area to be rooted in my having made this a goal for myself."

⌇{ **136 / קלו** }⌇

א הוֹדוּ לַיהוה כִּי־טוֹב כִּי לְעוֹלָם חַסְדּוֹ:

[1] **"Give thanks to HASHEM for He is good, for His kindness is forever."**

In all 26 verses of this Psalm, the phrase, "for His kindness is forever" is repeated. The number 26 has special significance; it is the numerical value (*gematria*) of one of the Almighty's

names. The Almighty created the world through the attribute of
kindness, and He constantly creates miracles both large and small,
open and hidden. He has already done many kindnesses for you,
He is presently doing many kindnesses for you, and He will
continue to bestow many kindnesses upon you.

Awareness of the Almighty's constant kindness to us, transforms
our lives. We easily notice the good things that happen to us that
are out of the ordinary, but we also easily take many good things
for granted. This is unfortunate. For a person who is able to
appreciate the constant kindness of the Almighty, King Solomon
says "The person with a good heart will experience life as constant
parties" (*Proverbs* 15:15).

Imagine what a day would be like if you were the guest of an
extremely generous, fabulously wealthy person who would bestow
upon you gift after gift — for a full day. Suppose he appreciated
you tremendously and wanted to do for you all that he could. Every
few minutes he would give you yet another gift. You would have
valid reason to thank him again and again. This reminds you of the
best presents you have ever received. This day would be a day to
remember, the rest of your life. The joy you would constantly
experience, would make this day one of the happiest days of your
life.

Awareness of the constant flow of gifts from the Almighty each
day, has the potential to guarantee us a joyful life. No human being
can give us, what the Almighty gives us each day; the ability to see,
to hear, to talk, to read, to study, to remember, to walk, to sing, and
the list goes on and on. The question we must answer is: How can
we maintain these joyful feelings? It's so easy to take what we have
for granted!

There is an exercise that we can habitually use to upgrade our
awareness of the Almighty's kindnesses to us. When you first
experience this exercise, allow yourself to become calm. Breathe a
few times the way you would breathe, if you were becoming calmer
and more relaxed. Allow your muscles to relax. Then calmly and
softly repeat the words, "His kindness is forever." Some people
find it preferable to say this in Hebrew: "*Ki l'olam chasdo.*"

As you gently and calmly repeat these words, think of some of
the things for which you are grateful. After each item, occurrence,

or situation that you think of, repeat the words, "His kindness is forever" (or *"Ki l'olam chasdo"*).

After thinking of things for which you are already aware that you are grateful, allow your mind to think of things, at random. As you visually or verbally remember specific people or items and situations, repeat the verse, "His kindness is forever." You are now building up a spiritual and gratitude association with more and more things.

You can become more grateful for relatives and friends. You can become more grateful for skills and talents that you have. You can become grateful for things that you own and things that you can use, even though you do not own them.

There are events in your life for which you are especially grateful. But ultimately we can develop our character and grow from many more events and situations that initially we did not realize were beneficial to us. Now that we are becoming more aware of the kindness of Hashem, we can perceive more and more manifestations of Hashem's kindness.

There might be people you find challenging. The way you view those people will be the way that those people affect you emotionally. Every person we encounter has the potential to build up our character, and now that you are associating those people with "His kindness is forever," you might find it easier to see how you can grow and upgrade your thoughts about those people.

Before going to sleep at night we might find that, a few minutes of contemplating "His kindness is forever", will help us remember more of the kindnesses that we experienced that day. Some kindnesses might be experienced frequently, and for that reason those kindnesses do not automatically register, unless we consciously remember to be grateful for them.

If you have to wait a few minutes for another person and are beginning to become impatient, spend those minutes repeating the words, "His kindness is forever." Instead of complaining about a traffic jam, it's a perfect time to calmly repeat, "His kindness is forever." When you are standing in a line that is going slower than you would prefer, view it as a Divinely sent opportunity to connect with your loving Father and powerful King by being grateful for His many gifts to you.

﴾ 137 / קלז ﴿

ה אִם־אֶשְׁכָּחֵךְ יְרוּשָׁלָ͏ִם תִּשְׁכַּח יְמִינִי:
ו תִּדְבַּק־לְשׁוֹנִי לְחִכִּי אִם־לֹא אֶזְכְּרֵכִי אִם־לֹא
אַעֲלֶה אֶת־יְרוּשָׁלַ͏ִם עַל רֹאשׁ שִׂמְחָתִי:

*5 If I forget you o Jerusalem, may my right hand
be forgotten. 6 Let my tongue adhere to my
palate, if I fail to recall you. If I fail to elevate
Jerusalem at the head of my joy.*

These two verses are an essential part of keeping the
remembrance of the Jewish homeland, and particularly
Jerusalem, at the forefront of our consciousness. Regardless of where we have been sent in our long Exile, we keep our
pledge never to forget Jerusalem. Just as we constantly recall our
right hand, we constantly remember Jerusalem. Moreover, our
very right to speak, is connected to our remembering the Divine
presence that was in Jerusalem.

This verse is declared publicly at the wedding ceremony, at the
height of the joy of the new couple's marriage! A glass is broken to
serve as a reminder that, as long as Jerusalem is still missing its
former glory, there is an aspect of sadness at even the most joyful
moments.

One of the great miracles of Jewish history is our people's
maintaining our Jewish identity, no matter where we have been.
We have been outnumbered and others have tried to influence us
to forget our roots as a people. Today there are many who want us
to give up this longing for Jerusalem. We are faced with powerful
hatred; there are people who view it as their greatest duty to make
us forget about our connection to Jerusalem. With unprecedented
wickedness, there are those who are willing to blow themselves up,
in an attempt to destroy us, but our people have made a longlasting pledge never to give up. Regardless of how often and how
bitterly we have been persecuted because of that for which we
stand, we maintain our love for Jerusalem and for Hashem Who
has chosen it to be the most special place in the world.

Each and every year on Tishah B'av, we cry that we are still in exile. Jerusalem is still lacking the most important, and valuable part of its very essence. The *Beis HaMikdash* (Holy Temple) has been destroyed and it is still missing. Jerusalem is still lacking its crown jewel. People come from all over the world to pray at the remaining Western Wall — people from all backgrounds feel its holiness — but this is just a spark of the spiritual potential of Jerusalem.

We remember Jerusalem each year on the days leading up to Tishah B'av, and on Tishah B'av itself. We remember Jerusalem at weddings. We remember Jerusalem in our daily prayers and when we thank Hashem for the meals that we have eaten. We constantly keep the memory of Jerusalem alive.

May the sacred city of Jerusalem return to its former glory with the rebuilding of the Holy Temple once again, and the days of mourning for its destruction and loss will be transformed into a day of celebration.

Over the years I have met many people who have been distressed for not feeling bad enough about the loss of the Holy Temple in Jerusalem. They fast on the days commemorating the Destruction, but they don't authentically feel sorrow. I share with them what I once heard from an elderly Torah scholar. "If you cannot truly feel bad about the loss of the Temple of Jerusalem, at least you should feel bad that you do not feel bad. This itself is a positive step in the right direction."

﴾ 142 / קמב ﴿

ג אֶשְׁפֹּךְ לְפָנָיו שִׂיחִי צָרָתִי לְפָנָיו אַגִּיד:

³ I will pour out before Him the story of what has befallen me. My troubles before Him I will tell.

Verse one states that King David recited this Psalm when he was in a cave hiding from his enemies. Besides taking action to hide from them, he was fully absorbed in praying to Hashem to be saved.

As *Malbim* explains: King David was alone in the cave. No other human being was present, so he could not alleviate his distress by expressing his thoughts and feelings to another person. Nevertheless, King David did not need to bottle up those thoughts and feelings. Rather, as he states here, he poured out his words to Hashem. He described his *tzaros* (troubles) to the Ultimate One.

When we endure difficulties, it is emotionally beneficial to share our thoughts and feelings with another person. It is a great act of kindness to be a good listener, when others experience hardships. Even when we cannot do anything concrete to correct or improve a situation, being there to listen empathetically lightens the burden considerably. The person experiencing difficulties does not have to carry the entire load himself. The listener helps him carry the heavy baggage. Now it is easier for him to cope.

When we pour out our hearts to Hashem upon experiencing difficulties, not only do we benefit from having the Ultimate Listener hearing us, but we are addressing the One Who has the power to improve and transform the entire situation.

Remember a time when something was bothering you and you did not have anyone with whom to share your thoughts and feelings. Now imagine how much better you would have felt if you had found a caring listener. You might remember a situation when this was actually the case. Allow yourself to gain these benefits, when you express yourself to your loving Father and powerful King, Creator and Sustainer of the universe.

Many years ago, I was shocked when my father's doctor told me that his serious illness had reached a stage which was considered incurable. This came a week after I had first learned that my father needed emergency surgery. When the doctor related the grim news, I was in a situation where I was not able to share this with anyone else. Even though this was a long time ago, the feelings of that experience are still vivid in my memory. I remember how strongly I had wished there was someone to whom I could speak. No one I might have spoken to could have done anything more to save my father's life than this highly skilled specialist and the well-trained team of physicians with whom he worked, but I knew that just talking about it would have lessened some of the intense pressure.

After that, I understood better the power and kindness of listening compassionately to the stories of suffering that others felt a need to share. Instead of merely focusing on the frustration of not being able to help to the degree that I would like, I balanced this by gaining an appreciation for the power of helpfulness of being available to listen.

Looking back, I realized, even more, that I could have gained so much by having had a stronger awareness that expressing my feelings to our Creator from a deep place within, has tremendous therapeutic power. Many times since then, I have experienced these benefits. Remembering my father, serves as a continuous reminder for me, that my Heavenly Father is always present and available to hear what I need to express.

⊰ 145 / קמה ⊱

ח חַנּוּן וְרַחוּם יהוה אֶרֶךְ אַפַּיִם וּגְדָל־חָסֶד:
ט טוֹב־יהוה לַכֹּל וְרַחֲמָיו עַל־כָּל־מַעֲשָׂיו:

⁸ **Gracious and merciful is** Hashem, **slow to anger, and great in [bestowing] kindness.**
⁹ Hashem **is good to all; His mercies are on all His works.**

This chapter of Psalms is recited three times daily as part of the *Ashrei* prayer, twice during the morning prayers, and once at the beginning of *Minchah*, the afternoon service. In these two verses we declare our awareness of the kindness and mercy of Hashem.

The Torah tells us to emulate Hashem, to walk in His ways. Just as Hashem is kind and merciful, we too need to develop these qualities within ourselves. As my Rebbe, R' Mordechai Gifter, used to say, "The *mitzvah* of the Torah to emulate Hashem goes beyond the commandment to love other people as yourself. From the *mitzvah* of loving others as yourself, we know that, if we see someone who needs our help, we have an obligation to do acts of kindness for him. The *mitzvah* to emulate Hashem means that just as Hashem created the world in order to bestow kindness, (even though before this creation there was no need for kindness since no one existed), so too, we should be on the lookout for ways that we can be kind to others even before someone's needs come to our attention. This was the level of Abraham who sat outside his tent to look for people to help" (see *Pirkei Torah*).

"Hashem is good to all." How can we be good to all? On a practical level, our resources are limited. No matter how much money someone has, the amount is finite. No matter how much good one does with one's time and energy, those also are finite. Our internal attitude however, should be that we wish to do kindness to everyone we can. Our compassion and inner caring should encompass the entire world.

The Talmud states that too much compassion is not good. Too much compassion can be overwhelming — it will exhaust us. There are individuals who need to learn to be more balanced but, for most people, the problem is not that they have too much compassion, but not enough.

Think about this. Ask yourself, "In what ways could I be kinder to other people?" "In what ways can I be more compassionate?"

On a practical level, it is easier to do acts of kindness than it is to increase compassion. We are kind with our words and with our actions. We can all decide to speak more kindly to others, and to go out of our way to do kind acts. We have greater control over our words and actions than over our thoughts and emotions. Compassion is an inner feeling. How do we increase these feelings?

As you remember past times when you experienced a certain feeling and were in a certain state, your brain begins to put you in that state again — in the present — to some degree. Some people experience this more strongly than others, but almost everyone will feel this to some extent. (Unfortunately, some people are more expert at doing this with angry or distressful memories, than with positive memories.) This is a skill that grows with conscious practice. So, think of a time when you felt compassion, when the plight or suffering of someone, touched your heart. It might have been a friend or relative, or it could have been a story you read. It might be the pain of a single individual, a disaster that affected a large amount of people, or be compassion for an animal that was hurt. As you feel the emotion of compassion, imagine it getting stronger and stronger. Some people find it helpful if they say to themselves, "This feeling will double and double. Double and double. Getting stronger and stronger."

As you feel compassion, be aware that having this quality is a way in which you are emulating Hashem. Think of specific actions you can do, so that your compassion is translated into words and behavior. When you read this verse in the daily prayers, let it serve as a reminder to increase your acts of kindness to more people.

"I loved doing favors for my friends. I would go out of my way to help them as much as I could. Some people used to tell me that I was being abused. 'You should learn to be more assertive and to say, "No" more often,' I was told, but I loved helping others. I did not consider what I did for others a burden. Being kind was one of my biggest pleasures in life.

"I discovered the book **Gateway to Self-knowledge** *which has questions on various character traits. Someone suggested to me that it would be worthwhile to read the questions for the two or three traits that I felt I was the strongest in, and also to read the questions for the two or three traits that I felt were my weakest areas. Since I considered myself to be very kind, I started by reading the section on Kindness.*

"Some of the questions were:

'Towards which people are you kind?'

'Towards which people do you lack kindness?'

'What is your initial reaction when someone asks you for a favor: "Oh, no, someone is making demands on me"? or, "How fortunate that I have an opportunity to do an act of kindness"?

'Are you only kind towards people who are kind to you or are you kind towards everyone with whom you come into contact?'

"These and other questions gave me a more accurate picture of where I really stood in reference to being kind. I was extremely kind to my friends. I would go out of my way to help relatives, even if they were distantly related, but I tried to avoid doing things for people I did not know. In addition, if someone was not grateful to me for the kindness I did for him, I would not do things for him in the future, unless I could not get out of it.

"I had to admit that my kindnesses were limited to my benefiting emotionally from the kind acts I did. I was far from being kind to everyone. I understood that, to be a truly kind person, I needed to be kind to all, to those I liked and those I did not like, to those who were kind to me and to those who were not, and to those who were grateful and to those who were not. I resolved to do at least one act of kindness each day when I did not feel like it. After keeping this up for a few months, I felt that the kindnesses that I had done before had served as a stepping-stone to becoming a truly kind person."

טז פּוֹתֵחַ אֶת־יָדֶךָ וּמַשְׂבִּיעַ לְכָל־חַי רָצוֹן:

16 You open your hand, and satisfy the desire of every living thing.

This well-known verse is part of the daily recited *Ashrei* prayer. Because of the importance of this verse we are obligated to say it with special concentration (*kavanah*). If we did not concentrate on the meaning of what we were saying the first time we said the verse, we are obligated to repeat it (*Shulchan Aruch, Aruch Chaim* 51:7).

The classic work *Yesod Veshoresh HaAvodah* (*Shaar* 3, chapter 5) emphasizes the importance of reciting the entire *Ashrei* prayer with enthusiasm and joy. He cites the Talmud (*Berachos 4b*) which states that whoever recites this chapter of *Tehillim* three times a day, is guaranteed a portion in the world to come. This refers to saying it with proper intent.

The Talmud explains that a major reason for the importance of this entire chapter of Psalms is because of our verse. And the author of *Yesod Veshoresh HaAvodah* writes that, when reciting this verse, we should intensify our joy. In this verse we proclaim our awareness that it is the Almighty Who supplies every living creature, from the largest of animals to the tiniest of insects, with the food that they need.

Every time we eat any sort of food, we make a blessing to thank Hashem for the specific food that He has given us to eat at that time. In this verse we comprehensively assert our understanding that all the food in the world that is for human consumption and all the food that any animal, be it bird, fish, mammal, or insect, ingests, is ultimately from the Creator.

Every living creature needs food to satisfy its appetite; being without food causes physical suffering, and the purpose of this distress is to motivate one to obtain the food that is necessary for health and survival. Every human and animal needs food to maintain all the processes of the body. Food is needed to maintain body temperature and activity. And food is necessary for growth.

Every time you eat, you see the message of this verse in action. Every time you see another human being eating, you see the message of this verse in action. Every time you see food, in your home, in a store, being delivered, or in a picture, you see the message of this verse in action. Every time you see a bird or dog or cat or insect or cow or horse or any other animal eating anything, you see the message of this verse in action. All this serves as a constant reminder of the Creator and His unlimited power.

The kindness of the Almighty is all around you. You see it wherever you go. Open your eyes and observe it. When you attend a Shabbos *kiddush* or meal and see people eating, you are seeing the kindness of the Almighty. When you attend a wedding or bar-mitzvah or any other celebration where food is served, you are seeing the kindness of the Almighty. When you see a parent giving food to a child, you are seeing the kindness of the Almighty. When you see an advertisement for food, you are seeing the kindness of the Almighty, and with every bite of food that you take, you are experiencing the kindness of the Almighty. Be mindful, and the world you see will be transformed into a constant spiritual seminar.

*As an exercise in appreciating the kindness of the Almighty
and His hashgacha pratis (Divine Providence), a group of
young men decided to repeat our verse, "You open your
hand" every time they began eating a different type of food,
on a given day. They also decided to say it when they came
across any person eating and when they saw any creature
eating. They reported that this had a significant positive effect
on them when they said the Ashrei prayer each day. This
constant reminder of the Almighty's benevolence uplifted
them to such a degree that they gained a new understanding
of why the Sages say that reciting this Psalm is a pathway to
the next world.*

◄{ 146 / קמו }►

---

³ אֲהַלְלָה יהוה בְּחַיָּי אֲזַמְּרָה לֵאלֹהַי בְּעוֹדִי:

**² I will praise HASHEM while I am alive, I will
make music to my God while I exist.**

Reciting this verse, which is part of the daily morning
prayers, reminds us that we are only temporary residents
in this world. We will not always be alive. and therefore we
need to make the best use of our time while we are here. So let us
praise and sing to Hashem while we still have the opportunity to do
so.

While the first half of the verse is usually translated as, "while I
am alive," it can be understood to mean, "with my life." That is, my
entire life will be lived in such a way that it is a manifestation of
praise of Hashem.

How do you praise Hashem "with your life"? Constantly praise
Hashem, with all that you do in your life. When a person has one
area of life that is his specialty and he thinks and talks about it the
entire day, we can say that this is what the person "is." This is what
he stands for.

For instance, when it comes to making money or running a
business, some people live their lives and also want to make
money. Their life might be their family, but they also spend time

and effort to make money to support their family. On the other hand, there are people whose essence is making money or running their business. This is always on their minds. This is what they think about all the time. This is what they read about. Their life is their business. The drawbacks of making this one's main focus in life is that, since we are only temporary residents in this world, our eternal soul is not getting the vitamins and minerals that it needs.

There are some people who consider having fun and a good time to be the essence of their lives. There are others who consider food the essence of their lives while some center their lives on winning praise and honor from others. Some people want power, and some people want accomplishment, and their focus is on themselves, their ego, their fame and fortune.

When you make your essence gratitude and praise to Hashem, then this is what you think about, this is what you talk about, this is what you read about — this is you. This is the meaning of your life. Everything you do centers around praising Hashem.

A person whose life is focused on praising Hashem, might also be involved in business, but he constantly praises Hashem for every major and minor success. He cherishes his opportunities to pray to Hashem and to recite blessings thanking Hashem, even more than he cherishes business opportunities. His mind is focused on gratitude to Hashem whether he makes money or loses money. If the stock market goes down, he still keeps praising Hashem for the good in his life, as a higher focus than the financial loss.

Those who are involved with their family day and night, who view the essence of their lives as opportunities to praise Hashem, will praise Hashem for the food and other necessities that they are able to provide with Hashem's help.

Those in school who view the essence of their lives as praising Hashem will be grateful for the brain and mind with which Hashem has blessed them. It is so easy to focus on what you do not remember and what you did not understand as well as you would have wished, but when you view your life's essence as praise for Hashem, you are constantly grateful for everything that you do remember. You are grateful for the magnificent brain with its — at least — 100 billion neurons!

When the essence of your life is praising Hashem, you are free from envy of others. The only benefit of having what anyone has is that it gives us more opportunities to praise Hashem. Since your focus is on praising Hashem with your life, you have exactly what you need to do so. You are alive. That means that you have enough positive things in your life, to be full of praise.

Gratitude and appreciation are the most important ingredients for happiness and joy. You will have this day and night, wherever you are, when you make this verse the motto of your life.

> "I was overweight. I was not obese, but I was noticeably fat. This bothered me and I constantly struggled with one diet after another. I knew that I would look better if I lost weight but, even though I thought I was highly motivated, when I saw food that I liked, all my good intentions were forgotten. Before I knew it, I had binged once again. I would have self-control for a while, but again and again I gave in to temptation.
>
> "Just one cookie," became five and ten and even fifteen. When I managed to refrain from eating all that I would have liked to eat, it was a battle. Throughout the day I was hungry, and the number one thing that I would think about, was food.
>
> "A turning point in my life was when I heard a rabbi say, 'The purpose of food is to praise Hashem.' We praise Hashem for the nutrition and health benefits of the food. We praise Hashem for the energy that food gives us. We praise Hashem for the pleasure of the food. And for this we do not need to eat large amounts. Small amounts are sufficient to serve this goal. He related a well-known statement of R' Aharon of Karlin: 'We do not eat an apple simply because we want to eat, only saying a blessing because that is what we are obligated to do. Rather, the ideal is to want to bless Hashem for everything. When we see an apple, we should appreciate the miracle of how this apple grew on a tree, tastes good and nourishes us. And with these and similar thoughts, we should feel a great desire to praise Hashem. We make the blessing to express our enthusiastic praise, and then we eat the apple as part of the process of praising Hashem.'
>
> "Immediately I realized that this was the solution. I viewed

food as a source of my good feelings. Whenever I felt sad or depressed, I would eat — and it wasn't just fruit and vegetables. The more sugar, the more it served as a substitute for the good feelings that I should have gotten in healthier and more spiritual ways. [1]

"I resolved to view food as part of my life's mission to praise Hashem. I started to view food as fuel to give me energy to live a joyful and productive life. I started to view food as a source of good health. I was dedicated to praising Hashem, not only in the blessings I would say before and after the food, but also with thoughts of gratitude to Hashem while I was eating. This focus on food as a source of energy and health and as my connection with Hashem, the Giver of the food and the Creator of the health-giving properties of food, transformed my life. It increased the spontaneous happiness I experienced, on a regular basis. This alone decreased my need for excessive food, and when I thought about energy and health, I made better choices about what I would eat and how much. I am grateful to Hashem that my gratitude to Him has helped me in so many ways."

◆∥ 148 / קמח ∥◆

א הַלְלוּיָהּ הַלְלוּ אֶת־יהוה מִן־הַשָּׁמַיִם הַלְלוּהוּ בַּמְּרוֹמִים:
ב הַלְלוּהוּ כָל־מַלְאָכָיו הַלְלוּהוּ כָּל־צְבָאָיו:
ג הַלְלוּהוּ שֶׁמֶשׁ וְיָרֵחַ הַלְלוּהוּ כָּל־כּוֹכְבֵי אוֹר:
ד הַלְלוּהוּ שְׁמֵי הַשָּׁמָיִם וְהַמַּיִם אֲשֶׁר מֵעַל הַשָּׁמָיִם:
ה יְהַלְלוּ אֶת־שֵׁם יְהוָה כִּי הוּא צִוָּה וְנִבְרָאוּ:

[1] **Halleluyah! praise HASHEM from the heavens; praise Him in the heights.** [2] **Praise Him, all His angels; praise Him, all His legions.** [3] **Praise Him sun and moon; praise Him, all bright stars.** [4] **Praise Him, heavens of the heavens and the waters that are above the heavens.** [5] **Let them praise the Name of HASHEM, for He commanded and they were created.**

bn Ezra comments on the first verse: "This chapter is highly cherished, and contains deep mystical secrets." We should be aware that there is a depth here beyond our comprehension, even as we try to grasp it on a basic level.

R' Avigdor Miller, of blessed memory, wrote: "There is a secret, or secrets, in the physical world, which the Creator imparted to the phenomena that they should awaken a deep response in the souls of human beings who utilize them properly. They are like the strings of a harp which can produce music which stirs the listener profoundly, but only when someone sets the strings in motion. This chapter signifies the human being's function in setting all Creation in motion to praise its Creator.

"The world is a harp to awaken the greatness in us" (*Praise, My Soul, p.189*).

Verse 3 mentions the sun and moon. R' Miller comments: "The sun has a conspicuous share in the praise of Hashem. 'The heavens declare the glory of God. For the sun He has made a tent therein' (*Psalms*, ch. 19). There the function of the sun is described at length. When the Roman ruler demanded to view the God of the Jews, the Sage told him to gaze at the sun. When the Roman replied that he was unable to, the Sage said, 'If you are unable to view the sun, which is but one of those that serve God, how can you expect to look at *Him?*' (*Chullin* 60a).

"Thus the splendor of the sun is intended as a faint intimation of the greatness of its Creator. Just as the sun's light, direct or indirect is everywhere ('None are hidden from its heat' — *Psalms* 19:7), and the entire earth is prevented from freezing by the warmth which the sun supplies all over the surface of the globe, so also do we take a lesson that Hashem's glory fills the Universe.

"The fact of the sun's vast mass and enormous energy testifies to the greatness of its Designer; and this is a common function of all the huge phenomena, just as the endless profundity of their composition and their operation testifies to His endless wisdom" (*Praise, My Soul*, pp.190-1).

According to Encarta Encyclopedia (2002): "The Sun is large and massive compared to the other objects in the solar system. The Sun's radius (the distance from its center to its surface) is 695,508 km (432,169 miles), 109 times as large as Earth's radius.

If the Sun were hollow, a million Earths could fit inside it. The Sun has a mass of 1,989 x 1027 metric tons. This number is very large. Written out, it would be the digits 1989 followed by 24 zeroes. The Sun is 333,000 times as massive as Earth is. The Sun produces an enormous amount of light. The temperature of the outer, visible part of the Sun is 5500°C (9900°F)."

Each morning when we recite this Psalm in the daily prayers, we call upon the magnificent Sun to praise the Creator.

In the same verse we also call upon the stars to praise the Creator. Encarta Encyclopedia has this to say about the stars:

"The Sun is extremely important to Earth and to our solar system, but on the scale of the galaxy and the universe, the Sun is just an average star. It is one of hundreds of billions of stars in our galaxy, the Milky Way, which is just one of more than 100 billion galaxies in the observable universe."

So when we refer to the stars, we are talking about extremely large objects that exist in enormous numbers. And they, too, have been created to proclaim the glory of their Creator.

Verse 4 states, "Praise Him, heavens of the heavens." R' Miller comments: "The vastness of Space *is intended* as a praise, for it signifies the endless vastness of the power of Hashem" (ibid. p.191).

We might talk about the vastness of space but we mortals living on our small planet have no possible way to TRULY comprehend what this means. We might cite the dry facts, but our limitations prevent us from a true grasp of these facts.

As of March 1998, the most distant galaxy ever found was 12.2 billion light-years from earth. How big is a light year? The speed of light is 186,000 miles per second, which is 300 million meters. Multiply this by 60 for the distance light travels in a minute, then multiply this by 60 again for the distance light travels in one hour. Then multiply this by 24 for the distance light travels in one day. This is certainly a considerable distance. But then you must multiply this by the amount of days in a year for the distance light travels in just one year. Then multiply this by 12.2 billion — billion, not million — that is, 1,000,000,000 multiplied by 12.2. That is still not the entire space of the universe, but only the distance of this faraway galaxy in one direction from earth; we also have the distances of above and below earth and on either side. And we have no idea how many further galaxies there are that have not yet been discovered.

Now let us repeat the last sentence quoted from R' Miller, "The vastness of Space *is intended* as a praise, for it signifies the endless vastness of the power of Hashem." After reading the previous paragraph we can see that the size of even the known universe is the most mind-boggling phenomena that exists in the physical world. And each morning when we recite this Psalm in the daily prayers, we call upon this vast amount of Space to praise the Creator. Reading the previous paragraph daily for a month will have an amazingly expansive effect on our minds.

Keeping the vastness of the universe in mind, we can have a greater understanding of what it would mean to internalize a greatly empowering Talmudic statement. The Talmud (*Sanhedrin* 37a) states, "A person is obligated to say, 'The universe was created for me.' Imagine the self-image we would all have by integrating this consciousness. Without an awareness of the Creator and the value He has given each human being we are but a tiny speck, without intrinsic value. We are nothing in size compared to the size of the world. But realizing that our Heavenly Father created all that exists, and He has given us value, we know that we were put into this world for an important purpose.

⋅≺{ **150 / קנ** }≻⋅

⁶ **כֹּל הַנְּשָׁמָה תְּהַלֵּל יָהּ**

⁶ *Let all souls praise* HASHEM.

T**he** Midrash (*Yalkut Shimoni*) comments on this verse, the last verse of Psalms: "Praise Hashem for each and every breath." The Hebrew word for soul is *neshamah,* similar to the word *neshimah,* breath.

This is a strikingly fitting way to conclude *Tehillim.* We have much to be grateful for. And the gift of being able to breathe oxygen is the biggest gift of them all. Breathing oxygen is life giving. Without fresh oxygen one cannot exist. With each breath you take, you are inhaling the fuel necessary to keep you alive right now.

Even if we do not consciously think at all about breathing, we still breathe day and night. Even when we are asleep at night, the entire time we keep on breathing. Imagine what it would be like if we were required to concentrate on our breathing, to inhale oxygen. People would frequently forget to breathe and constant fainting would be the norm.

However, there is a disadvantage to our breathing without having to be mindful of it — we might forget to be grateful for our breathing. Therefore, we are reminded here to remember to be grateful — do not take breathing for granted.

Slow, deep breathing, calms your entire nervous system. As you breathe slowly and deeply, your muscles become calmer and more relaxed. Your muscles soften; tension and stress melt away. As you think of how fortunate you are to have oxygen to breathe, you will find your entire emotional state improving.

There are many things in this world that can be appreciated. The more appreciation you have for things, the more happiness you will experience. There are many wonders of the world to appreciate: appreciation of music and architecture, appreciation of the complexity of our bodies and the entire world in which we live. When you learn to appreciate breathing, you will live in a constant state of appreciation.

Remembering our Creator brings us to the highest spiritual levels. We remember Him when we pray, we remember Him when we do good deeds, we remember Him when we recite blessings and when we study Torah. And those who remember Him when they breathe, have a constant reminder.

The entire time you have been reading this section, you have been breathing, as you were reading. Be grateful for your very next breath. And be grateful for the breath after that and the breath after that. "Thank you, my loving Father, and powerful King, Creator and Sustainer of the universe for giving me the ability to breath and supplying me with the oxygen I need."

You have been breathing from the first minute of your life until this very moment. Not a minute has gone by without your breathing, several times. Right now, express gratitude for all of your past breaths. "Thank you, my loving Father and powerful King, Creator and Sustainer of the universe, for having given me the oxygen I needed my entire life."

Develop the habit of being grateful for your breathing, a number of times each day. This will have a powerfully positive effect on your spiritual level and your emotional well-being. Resolve to follow through. Your gratitude for your breathing will enable you to integrate and internalize gratitude, as a basic attribute.

We find what we are looking for. When you look for factors for which to be grateful, you will become an expert. This will help you master the realization that "His kindness is forever." This will improve your own life and the lives of the people with whom you interact.

Index

ספר תהלים ⋙

The Book of Psalms

﴾ תפלה קודם אמירת\ תהלים ﴿

יְהִי רָצוֹן מִלְּפָנֶיךָ יהוה אֱלֹהֵינוּ וֵאלֹהֵי אֲבוֹתֵינוּ – הַבּוֹחֵר בְּדָוִד עַבְדּוֹ
וּבְזַרְעוֹ אַחֲרָיו, וְהַבּוֹחֵר בְּשִׁירוֹת וְתִשְׁבָּחוֹת – שֶׁתֵּפֶן
בְּרַחֲמִים אֶל קְרִיאַת מִזְמוֹרֵי תְהִלִּים שֶׁאֶקְרָא כְּאִלּוּ אֲמָרָם דָּוִד הַמֶּלֶךְ
עָלָיו הַשָּׁלוֹם בְּעַצְמוֹ, זְכוּתוֹ יָגֵן עָלֵינוּ. וְתַעֲמוֹד לָנוּ זְכוּת פְּסוּקֵי תְהִלִּים –
וּזְכוּת תֵּבוֹתֵיהֶם וְאוֹתִיּוֹתֵיהֶם וּנְקֻדּוֹתֵיהֶם וְטַעֲמֵיהֶם וְהַשֵּׁמוֹת הַיּוֹצְאִים
מֵהֶם מֵרָאשֵׁי תֵבוֹת וּמִסּוֹפֵי תֵבוֹת – לְכַפֵּר פְּשָׁעֵינוּ וַעֲוֹנוֹתֵינוּ וְחַטֹּאתֵינוּ;
וּלְזַמֵּר עָרִיצִים וּלְהַכְרִית כָּל הַחוֹחִים וְהַקּוֹצִים הַסּוֹבְבִים אֶת הַשּׁוֹשַׁנָּה
הָעֶלְיוֹנָה; וּלְחַבֵּר אֵשֶׁת נְעוּרִים עִם דּוֹדָהּ בְּאַהֲבָה וְאַחֲוָה וְרֵעוּת. וּמִשָּׁם
יִמָּשֵׁךְ לָנוּ שֶׁפַע לְנֶפֶשׁ רוּחַ וּנְשָׁמָה, לְטַהֲרֵנוּ מֵעֲוֹנוֹתֵינוּ וְלִסְלוֹחַ
חַטֹּאתֵינוּ וּלְכַפֵּר פְּשָׁעֵינוּ. כְּמוֹ שֶׁסָּלַחְתָּ לְדָוִד שֶׁאָמַר מִזְמוֹרִים אֵלּוּ
לְפָנֶיךָ – כְּמוֹ שֶׁנֶּאֱמַר: גַּם יהוה הֶעֱבִיר חַטָּאתְךָ לֹא תָמוּת. וְאַל תִּקָּחֵנוּ
מֵהָעוֹלָם הַזֶּה קוֹדֶם זְמַנֵּנוּ עַד מְלֹאת שְׁנוֹתֵינוּ (בָּהֶם שִׁבְעִים שָׁנָה) בְּאוֹפֶן
שֶׁנּוּכַל לְתַקֵּן אֵת אֲשֶׁר שִׁחַתְנוּ. וּזְכוּת דָּוִד הַמֶּלֶךְ עָלָיו הַשָּׁלוֹם יָגֵן עָלֵינוּ
וּבַעֲדֵינוּ, שֶׁתַּאֲרִיךְ אַפְּךָ עַד שׁוּבֵנוּ אֵלֶיךָ בִּתְשׁוּבָה שְׁלֵמָה לְפָנֶיךָ.
וּמֵאוֹצַר מַתְּנַת חִנָּם חָנֵּנוּ, כְּדִכְתִיב: וְחַנֹּתִי אֶת אֲשֶׁר אָחֹן וְרִחַמְתִּי אֵת
אֲשֶׁר אֲרַחֵם. וּכְשֵׁם שֶׁאָנוּ אוֹמְרִים לְפָנֶיךָ שִׁירָה בָּעוֹלָם הַזֶּה, כַּךְ נִזְכֶּה
לוֹמַר לְפָנֶיךָ, יהוה אֱלֹהֵינוּ, שִׁיר וּשְׁבָחָה לָעוֹלָם הַבָּא. וְעַל יְדֵי אֲמִירַת
תְּהִלִּים תִּתְעוֹרֵר חֲבַצֶּלֶת הַשָּׁרוֹן לָשִׁיר בְּקוֹל נָעִים בְּגִילַת וְרַנֵּן, כְּבוֹד
הַלְּבָנוֹן נִתַּן לָהּ, הוֹד וְהָדָר בְּבֵית אֱלֹהֵינוּ בִּמְהֵרָה בְיָמֵינוּ, אָמֵן סֶלָה.

לְכוּ נְרַנְּנָה לַיהוה, נָרִיעָה לְצוּר יִשְׁעֵנוּ. נְקַדְּמָה פָנָיו בְּתוֹדָה, בִּזְמִרוֹת
נָרִיעַ לוֹ. כִּי אֵל גָּדוֹל יהוה, וּמֶלֶךְ גָּדוֹל עַל כָּל אֱלֹהִים.

ספר ראשון / BOOK ONE

﴾ SUNDAY / יום ראשון ﴿

DAY 1 / יום א' לחדש

א א אַשְׁרֵי הָאִישׁ אֲשֶׁר לֹא הָלַךְ בַּעֲצַת רְשָׁעִים, וּבְדֶרֶךְ חַטָּאִים לֹא
עָמָד, וּבְמוֹשַׁב לֵצִים לֹא יָשָׁב. ב כִּי אִם בְּתוֹרַת יהוה חֶפְצוֹ, וּבְתוֹרָתוֹ
יֶהְגֶּה יוֹמָם וָלָיְלָה. ג וְהָיָה כְּעֵץ שָׁתוּל עַל פַּלְגֵי מָיִם; אֲשֶׁר פִּרְיוֹ יִתֵּן בְּעִתּוֹ,
וְעָלֵהוּ לֹא יִבּוֹל, וְכֹל אֲשֶׁר יַעֲשֶׂה יַצְלִיחַ. ד לֹא כֵן הָרְשָׁעִים, כִּי אִם כַּמֹּץ
אֲשֶׁר תִּדְּפֶנּוּ רוּחַ. ה עַל כֵּן לֹא יָקֻמוּ רְשָׁעִים בַּמִּשְׁפָּט, וְחַטָּאִים בַּעֲדַת
צַדִּיקִים. ו כִּי יוֹדֵעַ יהוה דֶּרֶךְ צַדִּיקִים, וְדֶרֶךְ רְשָׁעִים תֹּאבֵד.

ב א לָמָּה רָגְשׁוּ גוֹיִם, וּלְאֻמִּים יֶהְגּוּ רִיק. ב יִתְיַצְּבוּ מַלְכֵי אֶרֶץ, וְרוֹזְנִים נוֹסְדוּ יָחַד, עַל יהוה וְעַל מְשִׁיחוֹ. ג נְנַתְּקָה אֶת מוֹסְרוֹתֵימוֹ, וְנַשְׁלִיכָה מִמֶּנּוּ עֲבֹתֵימוֹ. ד יוֹשֵׁב בַּשָּׁמַיִם יִשְׂחָק, אֲדֹנָי יִלְעַג לָמוֹ. ה אָז יְדַבֵּר אֵלֵימוֹ בְאַפּוֹ, וּבַחֲרוֹנוֹ יְבַהֲלֵמוֹ. ו וַאֲנִי נָסַכְתִּי מַלְכִּי, עַל צִיּוֹן הַר קָדְשִׁי. ז אֲסַפְּרָה אֶל חֹק, יהוה אָמַר אֵלַי בְּנִי אַתָּה, אֲנִי הַיּוֹם יְלִדְתִּיךָ. ח שְׁאַל מִמֶּנִּי וְאֶתְּנָה גוֹיִם נַחֲלָתֶךָ, וַאֲחֻזָּתְךָ אַפְסֵי אָרֶץ. ט תְּרֹעֵם בְּשֵׁבֶט בַּרְזֶל, כִּכְלִי יוֹצֵר תְּנַפְּצֵם. י וְעַתָּה מְלָכִים הַשְׂכִּילוּ, הִוָּסְרוּ שֹׁפְטֵי אָרֶץ. יא עִבְדוּ אֶת יהוה בְּיִרְאָה, וְגִילוּ בִּרְעָדָה. יב נַשְּׁקוּ בַר, פֶּן יֶאֱנַף וְתֹאבְדוּ דֶרֶךְ, כִּי יִבְעַר כִּמְעַט אַפּוֹ; אַשְׁרֵי כָּל חוֹסֵי בוֹ.

ג א מִזְמוֹר לְדָוִד, בְּבָרְחוֹ מִפְּנֵי אַבְשָׁלוֹם בְּנוֹ. ב יהוה, מָה רַבּוּ צָרָי, רַבִּים קָמִים עָלָי. ג רַבִּים אֹמְרִים לְנַפְשִׁי, אֵין יְשׁוּעָתָה לּוֹ בֵאלֹהִים סֶלָה. ד וְאַתָּה יהוה מָגֵן בַּעֲדִי, כְּבוֹדִי וּמֵרִים רֹאשִׁי. ה קוֹלִי אֶל יהוה אֶקְרָא, וַיַּעֲנֵנִי מֵהַר קָדְשׁוֹ סֶלָה. ו אֲנִי שָׁכַבְתִּי וָאִישָׁנָה, הֱקִיצוֹתִי, כִּי יהוה יִסְמְכֵנִי. ז לֹא אִירָא מֵרִבְבוֹת עָם, אֲשֶׁר סָבִיב שָׁתוּ עָלָי. ח קוּמָה יהוה, הוֹשִׁיעֵנִי אֱלֹהַי, כִּי הִכִּיתָ אֶת כָּל אֹיְבַי לֶחִי, שִׁנֵּי רְשָׁעִים שִׁבַּרְתָּ. ט לַיהוה הַיְשׁוּעָה, עַל עַמְּךָ בִרְכָתֶךָ סֶּלָה.

ד א לַמְנַצֵּחַ בִּנְגִינוֹת מִזְמוֹר לְדָוִד. ב בְּקָרְאִי עֲנֵנִי אֱלֹהֵי צִדְקִי, בַּצָּר הִרְחַבְתָּ לִּי, חָנֵּנִי וּשְׁמַע תְּפִלָּתִי. ג בְּנֵי אִישׁ, עַד מֶה כְבוֹדִי לִכְלִמָּה, תֶּאֱהָבוּן רִיק, תְּבַקְשׁוּ כָזָב סֶלָה. ד וּדְעוּ כִּי הִפְלָה יהוה חָסִיד לוֹ, יהוה יִשְׁמַע בְּקָרְאִי אֵלָיו. ה רִגְזוּ וְאַל תֶּחֱטָאוּ, אִמְרוּ בִלְבַבְכֶם עַל מִשְׁכַּבְכֶם, וְדֹמּוּ סֶלָה. ו זִבְחוּ זִבְחֵי צֶדֶק, וּבִטְחוּ אֶל יהוה. ז רַבִּים אֹמְרִים: מִי יַרְאֵנוּ טוֹב, נְסָה עָלֵינוּ אוֹר פָּנֶיךָ, יהוה. ח נָתַתָּה שִׂמְחָה בְלִבִּי, מֵעֵת דְּגָנָם וְתִירוֹשָׁם רָבּוּ. ט בְּשָׁלוֹם יַחְדָּו אֶשְׁכְּבָה וְאִישָׁן, כִּי אַתָּה יהוה לְבָדָד לָבֶטַח תּוֹשִׁיבֵנִי.

ה א לַמְנַצֵּחַ, אֶל הַנְּחִילוֹת, מִזְמוֹר לְדָוִד. ב אֲמָרַי הַאֲזִינָה יהוה, בִּינָה הֲגִיגִי. ג הַקְשִׁיבָה לְקוֹל שַׁוְעִי, מַלְכִּי וֵאלֹהָי, כִּי אֵלֶיךָ אֶתְפַּלָּל. ד יהוה, בֹּקֶר תִּשְׁמַע קוֹלִי, בֹּקֶר אֶעֱרָךְ לְךָ, וַאֲצַפֶּה. ה כִּי לֹא אֵל חָפֵץ רֶשַׁע אָתָּה, לֹא יְגֻרְךָ רָע. ו לֹא יִתְיַצְּבוּ הוֹלְלִים לְנֶגֶד עֵינֶיךָ, שָׂנֵאתָ כָּל פֹּעֲלֵי אָוֶן. ז תְּאַבֵּד דֹּבְרֵי כָזָב, אִישׁ דָּמִים וּמִרְמָה יְתָעֵב יהוה. ח וַאֲנִי בְּרֹב חַסְדְּךָ אָבוֹא בֵיתֶךָ, אֶשְׁתַּחֲוֶה אֶל הֵיכַל קָדְשְׁךָ בְּיִרְאָתֶךָ. ט יהוה, נְחֵנִי בְצִדְקָתֶךָ לְמַעַן שׁוֹרְרָי, הַיְשַׁר לְפָנַי דַּרְכֶּךָ. י כִּי אֵין בְּפִיהוּ נְכוֹנָה, קִרְבָּם הַוּוֹת, קֶבֶר פָּתוּחַ גְּרֹנָם, לְשׁוֹנָם יַחֲלִיקוּן. יא הַאֲשִׁימֵם אֱלֹהִים, יִפְּלוּ מִמֹּעֲצוֹתֵיהֶם; בְּרֹב פִּשְׁעֵיהֶם הַדִּיחֵמוֹ, כִּי מָרוּ בָךְ. יב וְיִשְׂמְחוּ כָל חוֹסֵי בָךְ, לְעוֹלָם יְרַנֵּנוּ,

וַתָּסֶךְ עָלֵימוֹ; וְיַעְלְצוּ בְךָ אֹהֲבֵי שְׁמֶךָ. יג כִּי אַתָּה תְּבָרֵךְ צַדִּיק; יהוה, כַּצִּנָּה
רָצוֹן תַּעְטְרֶנּוּ.

ו א לַמְנַצֵּחַ בִּנְגִינוֹת עַל הַשְּׁמִינִית, מִזְמוֹר לְדָוִד. ב יהוה, אַל בְּאַפְּךָ
תוֹכִיחֵנִי, וְאַל בַּחֲמָתְךָ תְיַסְּרֵנִי. ג חָנֵּנִי יהוה כִּי אֻמְלַל אָנִי, רְפָאֵנִי יהוה
כִּי נִבְהֲלוּ עֲצָמָי. ד וְנַפְשִׁי נִבְהֲלָה מְאֹד, וְאַתָּה יהוה עַד מָתָי. ה שׁוּבָה יהוה
חַלְּצָה נַפְשִׁי, הוֹשִׁיעֵנִי לְמַעַן חַסְדֶּךָ. ו כִּי אֵין בַּמָּוֶת זִכְרֶךָ, בִּשְׁאוֹל מִי יוֹדֶה
לָךְ. ז יָגַעְתִּי בְּאַנְחָתִי, אַשְׂחֶה בְכָל לַיְלָה מִטָּתִי, בְּדִמְעָתִי עַרְשִׂי אַמְסֶה.
ח עָשְׁשָׁה מִכַּעַס עֵינִי, עָתְקָה בְּכָל צוֹרְרָי. ט סוּרוּ מִמֶּנִּי כָּל פֹּעֲלֵי אָוֶן, כִּי
שָׁמַע יהוה קוֹל בִּכְיִי. י שָׁמַע יהוה תְּחִנָּתִי, יהוה תְּפִלָּתִי יִקָּח. יא יֵבֹשׁוּ
וְיִבָּהֲלוּ מְאֹד כָּל אֹיְבָי, יָשֻׁבוּ יֵבֹשׁוּ רָגַע.

ז א שִׁגָּיוֹן לְדָוִד; אֲשֶׁר שָׁר לַיהוה, עַל דִּבְרֵי כוּשׁ בֶּן יְמִינִי. ב יהוה אֱלֹהַי
בְּךָ חָסִיתִי, הוֹשִׁיעֵנִי מִכָּל רֹדְפַי וְהַצִּילֵנִי. ג פֶּן יִטְרֹף כְּאַרְיֵה נַפְשִׁי, פֹּרֵק
וְאֵין מַצִּיל. ד יהוה אֱלֹהַי, אִם עָשִׂיתִי זֹאת, אִם יֶשׁ עָוֶל בְּכַפָּי. ה אִם גָּמַלְתִּי
שׁוֹלְמִי רָע, וָאֲחַלְּצָה צוֹרְרִי רֵיקָם. ו יִרַדֹּף אוֹיֵב נַפְשִׁי וְיַשֵּׂג, וְיִרְמֹס לָאָרֶץ
חַיָּי, וּכְבוֹדִי לֶעָפָר יַשְׁכֵּן סֶלָה. ז קוּמָה יהוה בְּאַפֶּךָ, הִנָּשֵׂא בְּעַבְרוֹת
צוֹרְרָי, וְעוּרָה אֵלַי מִשְׁפָּט צִוִּיתָ. ח וַעֲדַת לְאֻמִּים תְּסוֹבְבֶךָּ, וְעָלֶיהָ לַמָּרוֹם
שׁוּבָה. ט יהוה יָדִין עַמִּים; שָׁפְטֵנִי יהוה, כְּצִדְקִי וּכְתֻמִּי עָלָי. י יִגְמָר נָא רַע
רְשָׁעִים, וּתְכוֹנֵן צַדִּיק; וּבֹחֵן לִבּוֹת וּכְלָיוֹת אֱלֹהִים צַדִּיק. יא מָגִנִּי עַל
אֱלֹהִים, מוֹשִׁיעַ יִשְׁרֵי לֵב. יב אֱלֹהִים שׁוֹפֵט צַדִּיק, וְאֵל זֹעֵם בְּכָל יוֹם. יג אִם
לֹא יָשׁוּב, חַרְבּוֹ יִלְטוֹשׁ, קַשְׁתּוֹ דָרַךְ וַיְכוֹנְנֶהָ. יד וְלוֹ הֵכִין כְּלֵי מָוֶת, חִצָּיו
לְדֹלְקִים יִפְעָל. טו הִנֵּה יְחַבֶּל אָוֶן, וְהָרָה עָמָל וְיָלַד שָׁקֶר. טז בּוֹר כָּרָה
וַיַּחְפְּרֵהוּ, וַיִּפֹּל בְּשַׁחַת יִפְעָל. יז יָשׁוּב עֲמָלוֹ בְרֹאשׁוֹ, וְעַל קָדְקֳדוֹ חֲמָסוֹ
יֵרֵד. יח אוֹדֶה יהוה כְּצִדְקוֹ, וַאֲזַמְּרָה שֵׁם יהוה עֶלְיוֹן.

ח א לַמְנַצֵּחַ עַל הַגִּתִּית, מִזְמוֹר לְדָוִד. ב יהוה אֲדֹנֵינוּ, מָה אַדִּיר שִׁמְךָ בְּכָל
הָאָרֶץ, אֲשֶׁר תְּנָה הוֹדְךָ עַל הַשָּׁמָיִם. ג מִפִּי עוֹלְלִים וְיֹנְקִים יִסַּדְתָּ עֹז;
לְמַעַן צוֹרְרֶיךָ, לְהַשְׁבִּית אוֹיֵב וּמִתְנַקֵּם. ד כִּי אֶרְאֶה שָׁמֶיךָ מַעֲשֵׂה
אֶצְבְּעֹתֶיךָ, יָרֵחַ וְכוֹכָבִים אֲשֶׁר כּוֹנָנְתָּה. ה מָה אֱנוֹשׁ כִּי תִזְכְּרֶנּוּ, וּבֶן אָדָם
כִּי תִפְקְדֶנּוּ. ו וַתְּחַסְּרֵהוּ מְּעַט מֵאֱלֹהִים, וְכָבוֹד וְהָדָר תְּעַטְּרֵהוּ.
ז תַּמְשִׁילֵהוּ בְּמַעֲשֵׂי יָדֶיךָ, כֹּל שַׁתָּה תַחַת רַגְלָיו. ח צֹנֶה וַאֲלָפִים כֻּלָּם,
וְגַם בַּהֲמוֹת שָׂדָי. ט צִפּוֹר שָׁמַיִם וּדְגֵי הַיָּם, עֹבֵר אָרְחוֹת יַמִּים. י יהוה
אֲדֹנֵינוּ, מָה אַדִּיר שִׁמְךָ בְּכָל הָאָרֶץ.

ט א לַמְנַצֵּחַ עַל מוּת לַבֵּן, מִזְמוֹר לְדָוִד. ב אוֹדֶה יהוה בְּכָל לִבִּי, אֲסַפְּרָה

כָּל נִפְלְאוֹתֶיךָ. גּ אֶשְׂמְחָה וְאֶעֶלְצָה בָךְ, אֲזַמְּרָה שִׁמְךָ עֶלְיוֹן. דּ בְּשׁוּב אוֹיְבַי אָחוֹר, יִכָּשְׁלוּ וְיֹאבְדוּ מִפָּנֶיךָ. הּ כִּי עָשִׂיתָ מִשְׁפָּטִי וְדִינִי, יָשַׁבְתָּ לְכִסֵּא שׁוֹפֵט צֶדֶק. וּ גָּעַרְתָּ גוֹיִם, אִבַּדְתָּ רָשָׁע, שְׁמָם מָחִיתָ לְעוֹלָם וָעֶד. זּ הָאוֹיֵב, תַּמּוּ חֳרָבוֹת לָנֶצַח; וְעָרִים נָתַשְׁתָּ, אָבַד זִכְרָם הֵמָּה. חּ וַיהוה לְעוֹלָם יֵשֵׁב, כּוֹנֵן לַמִּשְׁפָּט כִּסְאוֹ. טּ וְהוּא יִשְׁפֹּט תֵּבֵל בְּצֶדֶק, יָדִין לְאֻמִּים בְּמֵישָׁרִים. יּ וִיהִי יהוה מִשְׂגָּב לַדָּךְ, מִשְׂגָּב לְעִתּוֹת בַּצָּרָה. יאּ וְיִבְטְחוּ בְךָ יוֹדְעֵי שְׁמֶךָ, כִּי לֹא עָזַבְתָּ דֹרְשֶׁיךָ, יהוה. יבּ זַמְּרוּ לַיהוה יֹשֵׁב צִיּוֹן, הַגִּידוּ בָעַמִּים עֲלִילוֹתָיו. יגּ כִּי דֹרֵשׁ דָּמִים אוֹתָם זָכָר, לֹא שָׁכַח צַעֲקַת עֲנָוִים. ידּ חָנְנֵנִי יהוה, רְאֵה עָנְיִי מִשֹּׂנְאָי, מְרוֹמְמִי מִשַּׁעֲרֵי מָוֶת. טוּ לְמַעַן אֲסַפְּרָה כָּל תְּהִלָּתֶיךָ, בְּשַׁעֲרֵי בַת צִיּוֹן אָגִילָה בִּישׁוּעָתֶךָ. טזּ טָבְעוּ גוֹיִם בְּשַׁחַת עָשׂוּ, בְּרֶשֶׁת זוּ טָמָנוּ נִלְכְּדָה רַגְלָם. יזּ נוֹדַע יהוה מִשְׁפָּט עָשָׂה, בְּפֹעַל כַּפָּיו נוֹקֵשׁ רָשָׁע, הִגָּיוֹן סֶלָה. יחּ יָשׁוּבוּ רְשָׁעִים לִשְׁאוֹלָה, כָּל גּוֹיִם שְׁכֵחֵי אֱלֹהִים. יטּ כִּי לֹא לָנֶצַח יִשָּׁכַח אֶבְיוֹן, תִּקְוַת עֲנָוִים תֹּאבַד לָעַד. כּ קוּמָה יהוה אַל יָעֹז אֱנוֹשׁ, יִשָּׁפְטוּ גוֹיִם עַל פָּנֶיךָ. כאּ שִׁיתָה יהוה מוֹרָה לָהֶם, יֵדְעוּ גוֹיִם אֱנוֹשׁ הֵמָּה סֶלָה.

יוֹם ב' לַחֹדֶשׁ / DAY 2

י אּ לָמָה יהוה תַּעֲמֹד בְּרָחוֹק, תַּעְלִים לְעִתּוֹת בַּצָּרָה. בּ בְּגַאֲוַת רָשָׁע יִדְלַק עָנִי, יִתָּפְשׂוּ בִּמְזִמּוֹת זוּ חָשָׁבוּ. גּ כִּי הִלֵּל רָשָׁע עַל תַּאֲוַת נַפְשׁוֹ, וּבֹצֵעַ בֵּרֵךְ נִאֵץ יהוה. דּ רָשָׁע, כְּגֹבַהּ אַפּוֹ בַּל יִדְרֹשׁ, אֵין אֱלֹהִים כָּל מְזִמּוֹתָיו. הּ יָחִילוּ דְרָכָיו בְּכָל עֵת, מָרוֹם מִשְׁפָּטֶיךָ מִנֶּגְדּוֹ; כָּל צוֹרְרָיו יָפִיחַ בָּהֶם. וּ אָמַר בְּלִבּוֹ: בַּל אֶמּוֹט, לְדֹר וָדֹר אֲשֶׁר לֹא בְרָע. זּ אָלָה פִּיהוּ מָלֵא וּמִרְמוֹת וָתֹךְ, תַּחַת לְשׁוֹנוֹ עָמָל וָאָוֶן. חּ יֵשֵׁב בְּמַאְרַב חֲצֵרִים, בַּמִּסְתָּרִים יַהֲרֹג נָקִי, עֵינָיו לְחֵלְכָה יִצְפֹּנוּ. טּ יֶאֱרֹב בַּמִּסְתָּר כְּאַרְיֵה בְסֻכֹּה, יֶאֱרֹב לַחֲטוֹף עָנִי; יַחְטֹף עָנִי בְּמָשְׁכוֹ בְרִשְׁתּוֹ. יּ יִדְכֶּה יָשֹׁחַ, וְנָפַל בַּעֲצוּמָיו חֵל כָּאִים. יאּ אָמַר בְּלִבּוֹ שָׁכַח אֵל, הִסְתִּיר פָּנָיו בַּל רָאָה לָנֶצַח. יבּ קוּמָה יהוה, אֵל נְשָׂא יָדֶךָ, אַל תִּשְׁכַּח עֲנָוִים. יגּ עַל מֶה נִאֵץ רָשָׁע אֱלֹהִים, אָמַר בְּלִבּוֹ לֹא תִדְרֹשׁ. ידּ רָאִתָה, כִּי אַתָּה עָמָל וָכַעַס תַּבִּיט, לָתֵת בְּיָדֶךָ; עָלֶיךָ יַעֲזֹב חֵלֵכָה, יָתוֹם אַתָּה הָיִיתָ עוֹזֵר. טוּ שְׁבֹר זְרוֹעַ רָשָׁע; וָרָע, תִּדְרוֹשׁ רִשְׁעוֹ בַל תִּמְצָא. טזּ יהוה מֶלֶךְ עוֹלָם וָעֶד, אָבְדוּ גוֹיִם מֵאַרְצוֹ. יזּ תַּאֲוַת עֲנָוִים שָׁמַעְתָּ, יהוה, תָּכִין לִבָּם תַּקְשִׁיב אָזְנֶךָ. יחּ לִשְׁפֹּט יָתוֹם וָדָךְ; בַּל יוֹסִיף עוֹד, לַעֲרֹץ אֱנוֹשׁ מִן הָאָרֶץ.

יא אּ לַמְנַצֵּחַ לְדָוִד; בַּיהוה חָסִיתִי, אֵיךְ תֹּאמְרוּ לְנַפְשִׁי, נוּדִי הַרְכֶם

צִפּוֹר. בּ כִּי הִנֵּה הָרְשָׁעִים יִדְרְכוּן קֶשֶׁת, כּוֹנְנוּ חִצָּם עַל יֶתֶר, לִירוֹת בְּמוֹ אֹפֶל לְיִשְׁרֵי לֵב. גּ כִּי הַשָּׁתוֹת יֵהָרֵסוּן, צַדִּיק מַה פָּעָל. דּ יְהוָה בְּהֵיכַל קָדְשׁוֹ, יְהוָה בַּשָּׁמַיִם כִּסְאוֹ; עֵינָיו יֶחֱזוּ, עַפְעַפָּיו יִבְחֲנוּ בְּנֵי אָדָם. הּ יְהוָה צַדִּיק יִבְחָן, וְרָשָׁע וְאֹהֵב חָמָס שָׂנְאָה נַפְשׁוֹ. וּ יַמְטֵר עַל רְשָׁעִים פַּחִים; אֵשׁ וְגָפְרִית וְרוּחַ זִלְעָפוֹת מְנָת כּוֹסָם. זּ כִּי צַדִּיק יְהוָה, צְדָקוֹת אָהֵב, יָשָׁר יֶחֱזוּ פָנֵימוֹ.

יב א לַמְנַצֵּחַ עַל הַשְּׁמִינִית, מִזְמוֹר לְדָוִד. בּ הוֹשִׁיעָה יְהוָה כִּי גָמַר חָסִיד, כִּי פַסּוּ אֱמוּנִים מִבְּנֵי אָדָם. גּ שָׁוְא יְדַבְּרוּ אִישׁ אֶת רֵעֵהוּ; שְׂפַת חֲלָקוֹת, בְּלֵב וָלֵב יְדַבֵּרוּ. דּ יַכְרֵת יְהוָה כָּל שִׂפְתֵי חֲלָקוֹת, לָשׁוֹן מְדַבֶּרֶת גְּדֹלוֹת. הּ אֲשֶׁר אָמְרוּ: לִלְשֹׁנֵנוּ נַגְבִּיר, שְׂפָתֵינוּ אִתָּנוּ, מִי אָדוֹן לָנוּ. וּ מִשֹּׁד עֲנִיִּים, מֵאַנְקַת אֶבְיוֹנִים; עַתָּה אָקוּם יֹאמַר יְהוָה, אָשִׁית בְּיֵשַׁע יָפִיחַ לוֹ. זּ אִמְרוֹת יְהוָה אֲמָרוֹת טְהֹרוֹת; כֶּסֶף צָרוּף, בַּעֲלִיל לָאָרֶץ, מְזֻקָּק שִׁבְעָתָיִם. חּ אַתָּה יְהוָה תִּשְׁמְרֵם, תִּצְּרֶנּוּ מִן הַדּוֹר זוּ לְעוֹלָם. טּ סָבִיב רְשָׁעִים יִתְהַלָּכוּן, כְּרֻם זֻלּוּת לִבְנֵי אָדָם.

יג א לַמְנַצֵּחַ מִזְמוֹר לְדָוִד. בּ עַד אָנָה יְהוָה תִּשְׁכָּחֵנִי נֶצַח, עַד אָנָה תַּסְתִּיר אֶת פָּנֶיךָ מִמֶּנִּי. גּ עַד אָנָה אָשִׁית עֵצוֹת בְּנַפְשִׁי, יָגוֹן בִּלְבָבִי יוֹמָם; עַד אָנָה יָרוּם אֹיְבִי עָלָי. דּ הַבִּיטָה עֲנֵנִי יְהוָה אֱלֹהָי, הָאִירָה עֵינַי פֶּן אִישַׁן הַמָּוֶת. הּ פֶּן יֹאמַר אֹיְבִי יְכָלְתִּיו, צָרַי יָגִילוּ כִּי אֶמּוֹט. וּ וַאֲנִי בְּחַסְדְּךָ בָטַחְתִּי, יָגֵל לִבִּי בִּישׁוּעָתֶךָ; אָשִׁירָה לַיהוָה, כִּי גָמַל עָלָי.

יד א לַמְנַצֵּחַ לְדָוִד; אָמַר נָבָל בְּלִבּוֹ אֵין אֱלֹהִים, הִשְׁחִיתוּ הִתְעִיבוּ עֲלִילָה, אֵין עֹשֵׂה טוֹב. בּ יְהוָה מִשָּׁמַיִם הִשְׁקִיף עַל בְּנֵי אָדָם, לִרְאוֹת הֲיֵשׁ מַשְׂכִּיל דֹּרֵשׁ אֶת אֱלֹהִים. גּ הַכֹּל סָר, יַחְדָּו נֶאֱלָחוּ; אֵין עֹשֵׂה טוֹב, אֵין גַּם אֶחָד. דּ הֲלֹא יָדְעוּ כָּל פֹּעֲלֵי אָוֶן; אֹכְלֵי עַמִּי אָכְלוּ לֶחֶם, יְהוָה לֹא קָרָאוּ. הּ שָׁם פָּחֲדוּ פָחַד, כִּי אֱלֹהִים בְּדוֹר צַדִּיק. וּ עֲצַת עָנִי תָבִישׁוּ, כִּי יְהוָה מַחְסֵהוּ. זּ מִי יִתֵּן מִצִּיּוֹן יְשׁוּעַת יִשְׂרָאֵל; בְּשׁוּב יְהוָה שְׁבוּת עַמּוֹ, יָגֵל יַעֲקֹב יִשְׂמַח יִשְׂרָאֵל.

טו א מִזְמוֹר לְדָוִד; יְהוָה מִי יָגוּר בְּאָהֳלֶךָ, מִי יִשְׁכֹּן בְּהַר קָדְשֶׁךָ. בּ הוֹלֵךְ תָּמִים וּפֹעֵל צֶדֶק, וְדֹבֵר אֱמֶת בִּלְבָבוֹ. גּ לֹא רָגַל עַל לְשֹׁנוֹ, לֹא עָשָׂה לְרֵעֵהוּ רָעָה, וְחֶרְפָּה לֹא נָשָׂא עַל קְרֹבוֹ. דּ נִבְזֶה בְּעֵינָיו נִמְאָס, וְאֶת יִרְאֵי יְהוָה יְכַבֵּד, נִשְׁבַּע לְהָרַע וְלֹא יָמִר. הּ כַּסְפּוֹ לֹא נָתַן בְּנֶשֶׁךְ, וְשֹׁחַד עַל נָקִי לֹא לָקָח; עֹשֵׂה אֵלֶּה לֹא יִמּוֹט לְעוֹלָם.

טז א מִכְתָּם לְדָוִד, שָׁמְרֵנִי אֵל כִּי חָסִיתִי בָךְ. בּ אָמַרְתְּ לַיהוָה, אֲדֹנָי אָתָּה,

טוּבָתִי בַּל עָלֶיךָ. ג לִקְדוֹשִׁים אֲשֶׁר בָּאֶרֶץ הֵמָּה, וְאַדִּירֵי כָּל חֶפְצִי בָם.
ד יִרְבּוּ עַצְּבוֹתָם אַחֵר מָהָרוּ; בַּל אַסִּיךְ נִסְכֵּיהֶם מִדָּם, וּבַל אֶשָּׂא אֶת
שְׁמוֹתָם עַל שְׂפָתָי. ה יְהוָה מְנָת חֶלְקִי וְכוֹסִי, אַתָּה תּוֹמִיךְ גּוֹרָלִי. ו חֲבָלִים
נָפְלוּ לִי בַּנְּעִמִים, אַף נַחֲלָת שָׁפְרָה עָלָי. ז אֲבָרֵךְ אֶת יְהוָה אֲשֶׁר יְעָצָנִי, אַף
לֵילוֹת יִסְּרוּנִי כִלְיוֹתָי. ח שִׁוִּיתִי יְהוָה לְנֶגְדִּי תָמִיד, כִּי מִימִינִי, בַּל אֶמּוֹט.
ט לָכֵן שָׂמַח לִבִּי וַיָּגֶל כְּבוֹדִי, אַף בְּשָׂרִי יִשְׁכֹּן לָבֶטַח. י כִּי לֹא תַעֲזֹב נַפְשִׁי
לִשְׁאוֹל, לֹא תִתֵּן חֲסִידְךָ לִרְאוֹת שָׁחַת. יא תּוֹדִיעֵנִי אֹרַח חַיִּים, שֹׂבַע
שְׂמָחוֹת אֶת פָּנֶיךָ, נְעִמוֹת בִּימִינְךָ נֶצַח.

יז א תְּפִלָּה לְדָוִד; שִׁמְעָה יְהוָה צֶדֶק, הַקְשִׁיבָה רִנָּתִי, הַאֲזִינָה תְפִלָּתִי,
בְּלֹא שִׂפְתֵי מִרְמָה. ב מִלְּפָנֶיךָ מִשְׁפָּטִי יֵצֵא, עֵינֶיךָ תֶּחֱזֶינָה מֵישָׁרִים.
ג בָּחַנְתָּ לִבִּי, פָּקַדְתָּ לַּיְלָה, צְרַפְתַּנִי בַל תִּמְצָא; זַמֹּתִי בַּל יַעֲבָר פִּי.
ד לִפְעֻלּוֹת אָדָם בִּדְבַר שְׂפָתֶיךָ, אֲנִי שָׁמַרְתִּי אָרְחוֹת פָּרִיץ. ה תָּמֹךְ אֲשֻׁרַי
בְּמַעְגְּלוֹתֶיךָ, בַּל נָמוֹטוּ פְעָמָי. ו אֲנִי קְרָאתִיךָ כִי תַעֲנֵנִי, אֵל; הַט אָזְנְךָ לִי,
שְׁמַע אִמְרָתִי. ז הַפְלֵה חֲסָדֶיךָ, מוֹשִׁיעַ חוֹסִים, מִמִּתְקוֹמְמִים בִּימִינֶךָ.
ח שָׁמְרֵנִי כְּאִישׁוֹן בַּת עָיִן, בְּצֵל כְּנָפֶיךָ תַּסְתִּירֵנִי. ט מִפְּנֵי רְשָׁעִים זוּ שַׁדּוּנִי,
אֹיְבַי בְּנֶפֶשׁ יַקִּיפוּ עָלָי. י חֶלְבָּמוֹ סָגְרוּ, פִּימוֹ דִּבְּרוּ בְגֵאוּת. יא אַשֻּׁרֵנוּ עַתָּה
סְבָבוּנוּ, עֵינֵיהֶם יָשִׁיתוּ לִנְטוֹת בָּאָרֶץ. יב דִּמְיֹנוֹ כְּאַרְיֵה יִכְסוֹף לִטְרוֹף,
וְכִכְפִיר יֹשֵׁב בְּמִסְתָּרִים. יג קוּמָה יְהוָה, קַדְּמָה פָנָיו הַכְרִיעֵהוּ, פַּלְּטָה נַפְשִׁי
מֵרָשָׁע חַרְבֶּךָ. יד מִמְתִים יָדְךָ יְהוָה, מִמְתִים מֵחֶלֶד, חֶלְקָם בַּחַיִּים וּצְפוּנְךָ
תְּמַלֵּא בִטְנָם; יִשְׂבְּעוּ בָנִים, וְהִנִּיחוּ יִתְרָם לְעוֹלְלֵיהֶם. טו אֲנִי בְּצֶדֶק אֶחֱזֶה
פָנֶיךָ, אֶשְׂבְּעָה בְהָקִיץ תְּמוּנָתֶךָ.

יח א לַמְנַצֵּחַ לְעֶבֶד יְהוָה לְדָוִד; אֲשֶׁר דִּבֶּר לַיהוָה אֶת דִּבְרֵי הַשִּׁירָה
הַזֹּאת, בְּיוֹם הִצִּיל יְהוָה אוֹתוֹ מִכַּף כָּל אֹיְבָיו, וּמִיַּד שָׁאוּל. ב וַיֹּאמַר,
אֶרְחָמְךָ יְהוָה חִזְקִי. ג יְהוָה סַלְעִי וּמְצוּדָתִי וּמְפַלְטִי; אֵלִי צוּרִי אֶחֱסֶה בּוֹ,
מָגִנִּי וְקֶרֶן יִשְׁעִי, מִשְׂגַּבִּי. ד מְהֻלָּל אֶקְרָא יְהוָה, וּמִן אֹיְבַי אִוָּשֵׁעַ. ה אֲפָפוּנִי
חֶבְלֵי מָוֶת, וְנַחֲלֵי בְלִיַּעַל יְבַעֲתוּנִי. ו חֶבְלֵי שְׁאוֹל סְבָבוּנִי, קִדְּמוּנִי מוֹקְשֵׁי
מָוֶת. ז בַּצַּר לִי אֶקְרָא יְהוָה, וְאֶל אֱלֹהַי אֲשַׁוֵּעַ; יִשְׁמַע מֵהֵיכָלוֹ קוֹלִי,
וְשַׁוְעָתִי לְפָנָיו תָּבוֹא בְאָזְנָיו. ח וַתִּגְעַשׁ וַתִּרְעַשׁ הָאָרֶץ, וּמוֹסְדֵי הָרִים
יִרְגָּזוּ; וַיִּתְגָּעֲשׁוּ כִּי חָרָה לוֹ. ט עָלָה עָשָׁן בְּאַפּוֹ, וְאֵשׁ מִפִּיו תֹּאכֵל, גֶּחָלִים
בָּעֲרוּ מִמֶּנּוּ. י וַיֵּט שָׁמַיִם וַיֵּרַד, וַעֲרָפֶל תַּחַת רַגְלָיו. יא וַיִּרְכַּב עַל כְּרוּב
וַיָּעֹף, וַיֵּדֶא עַל כַּנְפֵי רוּחַ. יב יָשֶׁת חֹשֶׁךְ סִתְרוֹ, סְבִיבוֹתָיו סֻכָּתוֹ, חֶשְׁכַת

מַיִם עָבֵי שְׁחָקִים. יג מִנֹּגַהּ נֶגְדּוֹ, עָבָיו עָבְרוּ, בָּרָד וְגַחֲלֵי אֵשׁ. יד וַיַּרְעֵם
בַּשָּׁמַיִם יְהוָה, וְעֶלְיוֹן יִתֵּן קֹלוֹ, בָּרָד וְגַחֲלֵי אֵשׁ. טו וַיִּשְׁלַח חִצָּיו וַיְפִיצֵם,
וּבְרָקִים רָב וַיְהֻמֵּם. טז וַיֵּרָאוּ אֲפִיקֵי מַיִם, וַיִּגָּלוּ מוֹסְדוֹת תֵּבֵל; מִגַּעֲרָתְךָ
יְהוָה, מִנִּשְׁמַת רוּחַ אַפֶּךָ. יז יִשְׁלַח מִמָּרוֹם יִקָּחֵנִי, יַמְשֵׁנִי מִמַּיִם רַבִּים.
יח יַצִּילֵנִי מֵאֹיְבִי עָז, וּמִשֹּׂנְאַי כִּי אָמְצוּ מִמֶּנִּי. יט יְקַדְּמוּנִי בְיוֹם אֵידִי, וַיְהִי
יְהוָה לְמִשְׁעָן לִי. כ וַיּוֹצִיאֵנִי לַמֶּרְחָב, יְחַלְּצֵנִי כִּי חָפֵץ בִּי. כא יִגְמְלֵנִי יְהוָה
כְּצִדְקִי, כְּבֹר יָדַי יָשִׁיב לִי. כב כִּי שָׁמַרְתִּי דַּרְכֵי יְהוָה, וְלֹא רָשַׁעְתִּי מֵאֱלֹהָי.
כג כִּי כָל מִשְׁפָּטָיו לְנֶגְדִּי, וְחֻקֹּתָיו לֹא אָסִיר מֶנִּי. כד וָאֱהִי תָמִים עִמּוֹ,
וָאֶשְׁתַּמֵּר מֵעֲוֹנִי. כה וַיָּשֶׁב יְהוָה לִי כְצִדְקִי, כְּבֹר יָדַי לְנֶגֶד עֵינָיו. כו עִם
חָסִיד תִּתְחַסָּד, עִם גְּבַר תָּמִים תִּתַּמָּם. כז עִם נָבָר תִּתְבָּרָר, וְעִם עִקֵּשׁ
תִּתְפַּתָּל. כח כִּי אַתָּה עַם עָנִי תוֹשִׁיעַ, וְעֵינַיִם רָמוֹת תַּשְׁפִּיל. כט כִּי אַתָּה
תָּאִיר נֵרִי, יְהוָה אֱלֹהַי יַגִּיהַּ חָשְׁכִּי. ל כִּי בְךָ אָרֻץ גְּדוּד, וּבֵאלֹהַי אֲדַלֶּג
שׁוּר. לא הָאֵל תָּמִים דַּרְכּוֹ, אִמְרַת יְהוָה צְרוּפָה, מָגֵן הוּא לְכֹל הַחֹסִים בּוֹ.
לב כִּי מִי אֱלוֹהַּ מִבַּלְעֲדֵי יְהוָה, וּמִי צוּר זוּלָתִי אֱלֹהֵינוּ. לג הָאֵל הַמְאַזְּרֵנִי
חָיִל, וַיִּתֵּן תָּמִים דַּרְכִּי. לד מְשַׁוֶּה רַגְלַי כָּאַיָּלוֹת, וְעַל בָּמֹתַי יַעֲמִידֵנִי.
לה מְלַמֵּד יָדַי לַמִּלְחָמָה, וְנִחֲתָה קֶשֶׁת נְחוּשָׁה זְרוֹעֹתָי. לו וַתִּתֶּן לִי מָגֵן
יִשְׁעֶךָ, וִימִינְךָ תִסְעָדֵנִי, וְעַנְוַתְךָ תַרְבֵּנִי. לז תַּרְחִיב צַעֲדִי תַחְתָּי, וְלֹא מָעֲדוּ
קַרְסֻלָּי. לח אֶרְדּוֹף אוֹיְבַי וְאַשִּׂיגֵם, וְלֹא אָשׁוּב עַד כַּלּוֹתָם. לט אֶמְחָצֵם וְלֹא
יֻכְלוּ קוּם, יִפְּלוּ תַּחַת רַגְלָי. מ וַתְּאַזְּרֵנִי חַיִל לַמִּלְחָמָה, תַּכְרִיעַ קָמַי תַּחְתָּי.
מא וְאֹיְבַי נָתַתָּה לִּי עֹרֶף, וּמְשַׂנְאַי אַצְמִיתֵם. מב יְשַׁוְּעוּ וְאֵין מוֹשִׁיעַ, עַל יְהוָה
וְלֹא עָנָם. מג וְאֶשְׁחָקֵם כְּעָפָר עַל פְּנֵי רוּחַ, כְּטִיט חוּצוֹת אֲרִיקֵם.
מד תְּפַלְּטֵנִי מֵרִיבֵי עָם; תְּשִׂימֵנִי לְרֹאשׁ גּוֹיִם, עַם לֹא יָדַעְתִּי יַעַבְדוּנִי.
מה לְשֵׁמַע אֹזֶן יִשָּׁמְעוּ לִי, בְּנֵי נֵכָר יְכַחֲשׁוּ לִי. מו בְּנֵי נֵכָר יִבֹּלוּ, וְיַחְרְגוּ
מִמִּסְגְּרוֹתֵיהֶם. מז חַי יְהוָה וּבָרוּךְ צוּרִי, וְיָרוּם אֱלוֹהֵי יִשְׁעִי. מח הָאֵל הַנּוֹתֵן
נְקָמוֹת לִי, וַיַּדְבֵּר עַמִּים תַּחְתָּי. מט מְפַלְּטִי מֵאֹיְבָי; אַף מִן קָמַי תְּרוֹמְמֵנִי,
מֵאִישׁ חָמָס תַּצִּילֵנִי. נ עַל כֵּן אוֹדְךָ בַגּוֹיִם יְהוָה, וּלְשִׁמְךָ אֲזַמֵּרָה. נא מַגְדִּל
יְשׁוּעוֹת מַלְכּוֹ; וְעֹשֶׂה חֶסֶד לִמְשִׁיחוֹ, לְדָוִד וּלְזַרְעוֹ עַד עוֹלָם.

יט א לַמְנַצֵּחַ מִזְמוֹר לְדָוִד. ב הַשָּׁמַיִם מְסַפְּרִים כְּבוֹד אֵל, וּמַעֲשֵׂה יָדָיו
מַגִּיד הָרָקִיעַ. ג יוֹם לְיוֹם יַבִּיעַ אֹמֶר, וְלַיְלָה לְּלַיְלָה יְחַוֶּה דָּעַת. ד אֵין
אֹמֶר וְאֵין דְּבָרִים, בְּלִי נִשְׁמָע קוֹלָם. ה בְּכָל הָאָרֶץ יָצָא קַוָּם, וּבִקְצֵה תֵבֵל
מִלֵּיהֶם; לַשֶּׁמֶשׁ שָׂם אֹהֶל בָּהֶם. ו וְהוּא כְּחָתָן יֹצֵא מֵחֻפָּתוֹ, יָשִׂישׂ כְּגִבּוֹר
לָרוּץ אֹרַח. ז מִקְצֵה הַשָּׁמַיִם מוֹצָאוֹ, וּתְקוּפָתוֹ עַל קְצוֹתָם; וְאֵין נִסְתָּר
מֵחַמָּתוֹ. ח תּוֹרַת יְהוָה תְּמִימָה, מְשִׁיבַת נָפֶשׁ; עֵדוּת יְהוָה נֶאֱמָנָה,

מַחְכִּימַת פֶּתִי. ט פִּקּוּדֵי יהוה יְשָׁרִים, מְשַׂמְּחֵי לֵב; מִצְוַת יהוה בָּרָה,
מְאִירַת עֵינָיִם. י יִרְאַת יהוה טְהוֹרָה, עוֹמֶדֶת לָעַד; מִשְׁפְּטֵי יהוה אֱמֶת,
צָדְקוּ יַחְדָּו. יא הַנֶּחֱמָדִים מִזָּהָב וּמִפַּז רָב, וּמְתוּקִים מִדְּבַשׁ וְנֹפֶת צוּפִים.
יב גַּם עַבְדְּךָ נִזְהָר בָּהֶם, בְּשָׁמְרָם עֵקֶב רָב. יג שְׁגִיאוֹת מִי יָבִין, מִנִּסְתָּרוֹת
נַקֵּנִי. יד גַּם מִזֵּדִים חֲשֹׂךְ עַבְדֶּךָ, אַל יִמְשְׁלוּ בִי, אָז אֵיתָם; וְנִקֵּיתִי מִפֶּשַׁע
רָב. טו יִהְיוּ לְרָצוֹן אִמְרֵי פִי וְהֶגְיוֹן לִבִּי לְפָנֶיךָ, יהוה צוּרִי וְגֹאֲלִי.

כ א לַמְנַצֵּחַ מִזְמוֹר לְדָוִד. ב יַעַנְךָ יהוה בְּיוֹם צָרָה; יְשַׂגֶּבְךָ, שֵׁם אֱלֹהֵי
יַעֲקֹב. ג יִשְׁלַח עֶזְרְךָ מִקֹּדֶשׁ, וּמִצִּיּוֹן יִסְעָדֶךָּ. ד יִזְכֹּר כָּל מִנְחֹתֶיךָ,
וְעוֹלָתְךָ יְדַשְּׁנֶה סֶלָה. ה יִתֶּן לְךָ כִלְבָבֶךָ, וְכָל עֲצָתְךָ יְמַלֵּא. ו נְרַנְּנָה
בִּישׁוּעָתֶךָ, וּבְשֵׁם אֱלֹהֵינוּ נִדְגֹּל; יְמַלֵּא יהוה כָּל מִשְׁאֲלוֹתֶיךָ. ז עַתָּה יָדַעְתִּי
כִּי הוֹשִׁיעַ יהוה מְשִׁיחוֹ; יַעֲנֵהוּ מִשְּׁמֵי קָדְשׁוֹ, בִּגְבֻרוֹת יֵשַׁע יְמִינוֹ. ח אֵלֶּה
בָרֶכֶב וְאֵלֶּה בַסּוּסִים, וַאֲנַחְנוּ בְּשֵׁם יהוה אֱלֹהֵינוּ נַזְכִּיר. ט הֵמָּה כָּרְעוּ
וְנָפָלוּ, וַאֲנַחְנוּ קַּמְנוּ וַנִּתְעוֹדָד. י יהוה הוֹשִׁיעָה, הַמֶּלֶךְ יַעֲנֵנוּ בְיוֹם קָרְאֵנוּ.

כא א לַמְנַצֵּחַ מִזְמוֹר לְדָוִד. ב יהוה בְּעָזְּךָ יִשְׂמַח מֶלֶךְ; וּבִישׁוּעָתְךָ מַה יָּגֶל
מְאֹד. ג תַּאֲוַת לִבּוֹ נָתַתָּה לּוֹ, וַאֲרֶשֶׁת שְׂפָתָיו בַּל מָנַעְתָּ סֶּלָה. ד כִּי
תְקַדְּמֶנּוּ בִּרְכוֹת טוֹב, תָּשִׁית לְרֹאשׁוֹ עֲטֶרֶת פָּז. ה חַיִּים שָׁאַל מִמְּךָ נָתַתָּה
לּוֹ, אֹרֶךְ יָמִים עוֹלָם וָעֶד. ו גָּדוֹל כְּבוֹדוֹ בִּישׁוּעָתֶךָ, הוֹד וְהָדָר תְּשַׁוֶּה עָלָיו.
ז כִּי תְשִׁיתֵהוּ בְרָכוֹת לָעַד, תְּחַדֵּהוּ בְשִׂמְחָה אֶת פָּנֶיךָ. ח כִּי הַמֶּלֶךְ בֹּטֵחַ
בַּיהוה, וּבְחֶסֶד עֶלְיוֹן בַּל יִמּוֹט. ט תִּמְצָא יָדְךָ לְכָל אֹיְבֶיךָ, יְמִינְךָ תִּמְצָא
שֹׂנְאֶיךָ. י תְּשִׁיתֵמוֹ כְּתַנּוּר אֵשׁ לְעֵת פָּנֶיךָ; יהוה בְּאַפּוֹ יְבַלְּעֵם, וְתֹאכְלֵם
אֵשׁ. יא פִּרְיָמוֹ מֵאֶרֶץ תְּאַבֵּד, וְזַרְעָם מִבְּנֵי אָדָם. יב כִּי נָטוּ עָלֶיךָ רָעָה,
חָשְׁבוּ מְזִמָּה בַּל יוּכָלוּ. יג כִּי תְּשִׁיתֵמוֹ שֶׁכֶם, בְּמֵיתָרֶיךָ תְּכוֹנֵן עַל פְּנֵיהֶם.
יד רוּמָה יהוה בְעֻזֶּךָ, נָשִׁירָה וּנְזַמְּרָה גְּבוּרָתֶךָ.

כב א לַמְנַצֵּחַ עַל אַיֶּלֶת הַשַּׁחַר, מִזְמוֹר לְדָוִד. ב אֵלִי אֵלִי לָמָה עֲזַבְתָּנִי,
רָחוֹק מִישׁוּעָתִי דִּבְרֵי שַׁאֲגָתִי. ג אֱלֹהַי, אֶקְרָא יוֹמָם וְלֹא תַעֲנֶה,
וְלַיְלָה וְלֹא דוּמִיָּה לִי. ד וְאַתָּה קָדוֹשׁ, יוֹשֵׁב תְּהִלּוֹת יִשְׂרָאֵל. ה בְּךָ בָּטְחוּ
אֲבֹתֵינוּ, בָּטְחוּ וַתְּפַלְּטֵמוֹ. ו אֵלֶיךָ זָעֲקוּ וְנִמְלָטוּ, בְּךָ בָטְחוּ וְלֹא בוֹשׁוּ.
ז וְאָנֹכִי תוֹלַעַת וְלֹא אִישׁ, חֶרְפַּת אָדָם וּבְזוּי עָם. ח כָּל רֹאַי יַלְעִגוּ לִי;
יַפְטִירוּ בְשָׂפָה, יָנִיעוּ רֹאשׁ. ט גֹּל אֶל יהוה יְפַלְּטֵהוּ, יַצִּילֵהוּ כִּי חָפֵץ בּוֹ. י כִּי
אַתָּה גֹחִי מִבָּטֶן, מַבְטִיחִי עַל שְׁדֵי אִמִּי. יא עָלֶיךָ הָשְׁלַכְתִּי מֵרָחֶם, מִבֶּטֶן
אִמִּי אֵלִי אָתָּה. יב אַל תִּרְחַק מִמֶּנִּי כִּי צָרָה קְרוֹבָה, כִּי אֵין עוֹזֵר. יג סְבָבוּנִי
פָּרִים רַבִּים, אַבִּירֵי בָשָׁן כִּתְּרוּנִי. יד פָּצוּ עָלַי פִּיהֶם, אַרְיֵה טֹרֵף וְשֹׁאֵג.

טו כַּמַּיִם נִשְׁפַּכְתִּי, וְהִתְפָּרְדוּ כָּל עַצְמוֹתָי; הָיָה לִבִּי כַּדּוֹנָג, נָמֵס בְּתוֹךְ מֵעָי. טז יָבֵשׁ כַּחֶרֶשׂ כֹּחִי, וּלְשׁוֹנִי מֻדְבָּק מַלְקוֹחָי; וְלַעֲפַר מָוֶת תִּשְׁפְּתֵנִי. יז כִּי סְבָבוּנִי כְּלָבִים; עֲדַת מְרֵעִים הִקִּיפוּנִי, כָּאֲרִי יָדַי וְרַגְלָי. יח אֲסַפֵּר כָּל עַצְמוֹתָי, הֵמָּה יַבִּיטוּ יִרְאוּ בִי. יט יְחַלְּקוּ בְגָדַי לָהֶם, וְעַל לְבוּשִׁי יַפִּילוּ גוֹרָל. כ וְאַתָּה יהוה אַל תִּרְחָק, אֱיָלוּתִי לְעֶזְרָתִי חוּשָׁה. כא הַצִּילָה מֵחֶרֶב נַפְשִׁי, מִיַּד כֶּלֶב יְחִידָתִי. כב הוֹשִׁיעֵנִי מִפִּי אַרְיֵה, וּמִקַּרְנֵי רֵמִים עֲנִיתָנִי. כג אֲסַפְּרָה שִׁמְךָ לְאֶחָי, בְּתוֹךְ קָהָל אֲהַלְלֶךָּ. כד יִרְאֵי יהוה הַלְלוּהוּ, כָּל זֶרַע יַעֲקֹב כַּבְּדוּהוּ, וְגוּרוּ מִמֶּנּוּ כָּל זֶרַע יִשְׂרָאֵל. כה כִּי לֹא בָזָה וְלֹא שִׁקַּץ עֱנוּת עָנִי, וְלֹא הִסְתִּיר פָּנָיו מִמֶּנּוּ; וּבְשַׁוְּעוֹ אֵלָיו שָׁמֵעַ. כו מֵאִתְּךָ תְהִלָּתִי בְּקָהָל רָב, נְדָרַי אֲשַׁלֵּם נֶגֶד יְרֵאָיו. כז יֹאכְלוּ עֲנָוִים וְיִשְׂבָּעוּ, יְהַלְלוּ יהוה דֹּרְשָׁיו; יְחִי לְבַבְכֶם לָעַד. כח יִזְכְּרוּ וְיָשֻׁבוּ אֶל יהוה כָּל אַפְסֵי אָרֶץ, וְיִשְׁתַּחֲווּ לְפָנֶיךָ כָּל מִשְׁפְּחוֹת גּוֹיִם. כט כִּי לַיהוה הַמְּלוּכָה, וּמֹשֵׁל בַּגּוֹיִם. ל אָכְלוּ וַיִּשְׁתַּחֲווּ כָּל דִּשְׁנֵי אֶרֶץ, לְפָנָיו יִכְרְעוּ כָּל יוֹרְדֵי עָפָר, וְנַפְשׁוֹ לֹא חִיָּה. לא זֶרַע יַעַבְדֶנּוּ, יְסֻפַּר לַאדֹנָי לַדּוֹר. לב יָבֹאוּ וְיַגִּידוּ צִדְקָתוֹ, לְעַם נוֹלָד כִּי עָשָׂה.

יום ד' לחדש / DAY 4

כג א מִזְמוֹר לְדָוִד, יהוה רֹעִי, לֹא אֶחְסָר. ב בִּנְאוֹת דֶּשֶׁא יַרְבִּיצֵנִי, עַל מֵי מְנֻחוֹת יְנַהֲלֵנִי. ג נַפְשִׁי יְשׁוֹבֵב, יַנְחֵנִי בְמַעְגְּלֵי צֶדֶק לְמַעַן שְׁמוֹ. ד גַּם כִּי אֵלֵךְ בְּגֵיא צַלְמָוֶת, לֹא אִירָא רָע כִּי אַתָּה עִמָּדִי; שִׁבְטְךָ וּמִשְׁעַנְתֶּךָ הֵמָּה יְנַחֲמֻנִי. ה תַּעֲרֹךְ לְפָנַי שֻׁלְחָן נֶגֶד צֹרְרָי; דִּשַּׁנְתָּ בַשֶּׁמֶן רֹאשִׁי, כּוֹסִי רְוָיָה. ו אַךְ טוֹב וָחֶסֶד יִרְדְּפוּנִי כָּל יְמֵי חַיָּי, וְשַׁבְתִּי בְּבֵית יהוה לְאֹרֶךְ יָמִים.

כד א לְדָוִד מִזְמוֹר; לַיהוה הָאָרֶץ וּמְלוֹאָהּ, תֵּבֵל וְיֹשְׁבֵי בָהּ. ב כִּי הוּא עַל יַמִּים יְסָדָהּ, וְעַל נְהָרוֹת יְכוֹנְנֶהָ. ג מִי יַעֲלֶה בְהַר יהוה, וּמִי יָקוּם בִּמְקוֹם קָדְשׁוֹ. ד נְקִי כַפַּיִם וּבַר לֵבָב; אֲשֶׁר לֹא נָשָׂא לַשָּׁוְא נַפְשִׁי, וְלֹא נִשְׁבַּע לְמִרְמָה. ה יִשָּׂא בְרָכָה מֵאֵת יהוה, וּצְדָקָה מֵאֱלֹהֵי יִשְׁעוֹ. ו זֶה דוֹר דֹּרְשָׁיו, מְבַקְשֵׁי פָנֶיךָ יַעֲקֹב סֶלָה. ז שְׂאוּ שְׁעָרִים רָאשֵׁיכֶם, וְהִנָּשְׂאוּ פִּתְחֵי עוֹלָם, וְיָבוֹא מֶלֶךְ הַכָּבוֹד. ח מִי זֶה מֶלֶךְ הַכָּבוֹד, יהוה עִזּוּז וְגִבּוֹר, יהוה גִּבּוֹר מִלְחָמָה. ט שְׂאוּ שְׁעָרִים רָאשֵׁיכֶם, וּשְׂאוּ פִּתְחֵי עוֹלָם, וְיָבֹא מֶלֶךְ הַכָּבוֹד. י מִי הוּא זֶה מֶלֶךְ הַכָּבוֹד, יהוה צְבָאוֹת הוּא מֶלֶךְ הַכָּבוֹד סֶלָה.

כה א לְדָוִד, אֵלֶיךָ יהוה נַפְשִׁי אֶשָּׂא. ב אֱלֹהַי, בְּךָ בָטַחְתִּי אַל אֵבוֹשָׁה, אַל יַעַלְצוּ אוֹיְבַי לִי. ג גַּם כָּל קֹוֶיךָ לֹא יֵבֹשׁוּ, יֵבֹשׁוּ הַבּוֹגְדִים רֵיקָם. ד דְּרָכֶיךָ יהוה הוֹדִיעֵנִי, אֹרְחוֹתֶיךָ לַמְּדֵנִי. ה הַדְרִיכֵנִי בַאֲמִתֶּךָ וְלַמְּדֵנִי, כִּי

אַתָּה אֱלֹהֵי יִשְׁעִי, אוֹתְךָ קִוִּיתִי כָּל הַיּוֹם. וּ זְכֹר רַחֲמֶיךָ יהוה וַחֲסָדֶיךָ, כִּי מֵעוֹלָם הֵמָּה. זּ חַטֹּאות נְעוּרַי וּפְשָׁעַי אַל תִּזְכֹּר; כְּחַסְדְּךָ זְכָר לִי אַתָּה, לְמַעַן טוּבְךָ יהוה. חּ טוֹב וְיָשָׁר יהוה, עַל כֵּן יוֹרֶה חַטָּאִים בַּדָּרֶךְ. טּ יַדְרֵךְ עֲנָוִים בַּמִּשְׁפָּט, וִילַמֵּד עֲנָוִים דַּרְכּוֹ. כָּל אָרְחוֹת יהוה חֶסֶד וֶאֱמֶת, לְנֹצְרֵי בְרִיתוֹ וְעֵדֹתָיו. יאּ לְמַעַן שִׁמְךָ יהוה, וְסָלַחְתָּ לַעֲוֹנִי כִּי רַב הוּא. יבּ מִי זֶה הָאִישׁ יְרֵא יהוה, יוֹרֶנּוּ בְּדֶרֶךְ יִבְחָר. יגּ נַפְשׁוֹ בְּטוֹב תָּלִין, וְזַרְעוֹ יִירַשׁ אָרֶץ. ידּ סוֹד יהוה לִירֵאָיו, וּבְרִיתוֹ לְהוֹדִיעָם. טוּ עֵינַי תָּמִיד אֶל יהוה, כִּי הוּא יוֹצִיא מֵרֶשֶׁת רַגְלָי. טזּ פְּנֵה אֵלַי וְחָנֵּנִי, כִּי יָחִיד וְעָנִי אָנִי. יזּ צָרוֹת לְבָבִי הִרְחִיבוּ, מִמְּצוּקוֹתַי הוֹצִיאֵנִי. יחּ רְאֵה עָנְיִי וַעֲמָלִי, וְשָׂא לְכָל חַטֹּאותָי. יטּ רְאֵה אֹיְבַי כִּי רָבּוּ, וְשִׂנְאַת חָמָס שְׂנֵאוּנִי. כּ שָׁמְרָה נַפְשִׁי וְהַצִּילֵנִי, אַל אֵבוֹשׁ כִּי חָסִיתִי בָךְ. כאּ תֹּם וָיֹשֶׁר יִצְּרוּנִי, כִּי קִוִּיתִיךָ. כבּ פְּדֵה אֱלֹהִים אֶת יִשְׂרָאֵל מִכֹּל צָרוֹתָיו.

כו אּ לְדָוִד, שָׁפְטֵנִי יהוה, כִּי אֲנִי בְּתֻמִּי הָלַכְתִּי; וּבַיהוה בָּטַחְתִּי לֹא אֶמְעָד. בּ בְּחָנֵנִי יהוה וְנַסֵּנִי, צָרְפָה כִלְיוֹתַי וְלִבִּי. גּ כִּי חַסְדְּךָ לְנֶגֶד עֵינָי, וְהִתְהַלַּכְתִּי בַּאֲמִתֶּךָ. דּ לֹא יָשַׁבְתִּי עִם מְתֵי שָׁוְא, וְעִם נַעֲלָמִים לֹא אָבוֹא. הּ שָׂנֵאתִי קְהַל מְרֵעִים, וְעִם רְשָׁעִים לֹא אֵשֵׁב. וּ אֶרְחַץ בְּנִקָּיוֹן כַּפָּי, וַאֲסֹבְבָה אֶת מִזְבַּחֲךָ יהוה. זּ לַשְׁמִעַ בְּקוֹל תּוֹדָה, וּלְסַפֵּר כָּל נִפְלְאוֹתֶיךָ. חּ יהוה, אָהַבְתִּי מְעוֹן בֵּיתֶךָ, וּמְקוֹם מִשְׁכַּן כְּבוֹדֶךָ. טּ אַל תֶּאֱסֹף עִם חַטָּאִים נַפְשִׁי, וְעִם אַנְשֵׁי דָמִים חַיָּי. יּ אֲשֶׁר בִּידֵיהֶם זִמָּה, וִימִינָם מָלְאָה שֹּׁחַד. יאּ וַאֲנִי בְּתֻמִּי אֵלֵךְ, פְּדֵנִי וְחָנֵּנִי. יבּ רַגְלִי עָמְדָה בְמִישׁוֹר, בְּמַקְהֵלִים אֲבָרֵךְ יהוה.

כז אּ לְדָוִד, יהוה אוֹרִי וְיִשְׁעִי, מִמִּי אִירָא; יהוה מָעוֹז חַיַּי, מִמִּי אֶפְחָד. בּ בִּקְרֹב עָלַי מְרֵעִים לֶאֱכֹל אֶת בְּשָׂרִי, צָרַי וְאֹיְבַי לִי, הֵמָּה כָשְׁלוּ וְנָפָלוּ. גּ אִם תַּחֲנֶה עָלַי מַחֲנֶה, לֹא יִירָא לִבִּי; אִם תָּקוּם עָלַי מִלְחָמָה, בְּזֹאת אֲנִי בוֹטֵחַ. דּ אַחַת שָׁאַלְתִּי מֵאֵת יהוה, אוֹתָהּ אֲבַקֵּשׁ; שִׁבְתִּי בְּבֵית יהוה כָּל יְמֵי חַיַּי, לַחֲזוֹת בְּנֹעַם יהוה, וּלְבַקֵּר בְּהֵיכָלוֹ. הּ כִּי יִצְפְּנֵנִי בְּסֻכֹּה בְּיוֹם רָעָה; יַסְתִּרֵנִי בְּסֵתֶר אָהֳלוֹ, בְּצוּר יְרוֹמְמֵנִי. וּ וְעַתָּה יָרוּם רֹאשִׁי עַל אֹיְבַי סְבִיבוֹתַי, וְאֶזְבְּחָה בְאָהֳלוֹ זִבְחֵי תְרוּעָה; אָשִׁירָה וַאֲזַמְּרָה לַיהוה. זּ שְׁמַע יהוה קוֹלִי אֶקְרָא, וְחָנֵּנִי וַעֲנֵנִי. חּ לְךָ אָמַר לִבִּי בַּקְּשׁוּ פָנָי, אֶת פָּנֶיךָ יהוה אֲבַקֵּשׁ. טּ אַל תַּסְתֵּר פָּנֶיךָ מִמֶּנִּי, אַל תַּט בְּאַף עַבְדֶּךָ; עֶזְרָתִי הָיִיתָ, אַל תִּטְּשֵׁנִי וְאַל תַּעַזְבֵנִי, אֱלֹהֵי יִשְׁעִי. יּ כִּי אָבִי וְאִמִּי עֲזָבוּנִי, וַיהוה יַאַסְפֵנִי. יאּ הוֹרֵנִי יהוה דַּרְכֶּךָ; וּנְחֵנִי בְּאֹרַח מִישׁוֹר, לְמַעַן שׁוֹרְרָי. יבּ אַל תִּתְּנֵנִי בְּנֶפֶשׁ צָרָי, כִּי קָמוּ בִי עֵדֵי שֶׁקֶר, וִיפֵחַ חָמָס. יגּ לוּלֵא הֶאֱמַנְתִּי

לִרְאוֹת בְּטוּב יְהוֹה בְּאֶרֶץ חַיִּים. יד קַוֵּה אֶל יְהוֹה; חֲזַק וְיַאֲמֵץ לִבֶּךָ, וְקַוֵּה אֶל יְהוֹה.

כח א לְדָוִד, אֵלֶיךָ יְהוֹה אֶקְרָא, צוּרִי אַל תֶּחֱרַשׁ מִמֶּנִּי; פֶּן תֶּחֱשֶׁה מִמֶּנִּי, וְנִמְשַׁלְתִּי עִם יוֹרְדֵי בוֹר. ב שְׁמַע קוֹל תַּחֲנוּנַי בְּשַׁוְּעִי אֵלֶיךָ, בְּנָשְׂאִי יָדַי אֶל דְּבִיר קָדְשֶׁךָ. ג אַל תִּמְשְׁכֵנִי עִם רְשָׁעִים וְעִם פֹּעֲלֵי אָוֶן, דֹּבְרֵי שָׁלוֹם עִם רֵעֵיהֶם, וְרָעָה בִּלְבָבָם. ד תֶּן לָהֶם כְּפָעֳלָם וּכְרֹעַ מַעַלְלֵיהֶם; כְּמַעֲשֵׂה יְדֵיהֶם תֵּן לָהֶם, הָשֵׁב גְּמוּלָם לָהֶם. ה כִּי לֹא יָבִינוּ אֶל פְּעֻלֹּת יְהוֹה וְאֶל מַעֲשֵׂה יָדָיו, יֶהֶרְסֵם וְלֹא יִבְנֵם. ו בָּרוּךְ יְהוֹה, כִּי שָׁמַע קוֹל תַּחֲנוּנָי. ז יְהוֹה עֻזִּי וּמָגִנִּי, בּוֹ בָטַח לִבִּי וְנֶעֱזָרְתִּי; וַיַּעֲלֹז לִבִּי, וּמִשִּׁירִי אֲהוֹדֶנּוּ. ח יְהוֹה עֹז לָמוֹ, וּמָעוֹז יְשׁוּעוֹת מְשִׁיחוֹ הוּא. ט הוֹשִׁיעָה אֶת עַמֶּךָ, וּבָרֵךְ אֶת נַחֲלָתֶךָ; וּרְעֵם וְנַשְּׂאֵם עַד הָעוֹלָם.

יום ה' לחדש / DAY 5

כט א מִזְמוֹר לְדָוִד; הָבוּ לַיהוֹה בְּנֵי אֵלִים, הָבוּ לַיהוֹה כָּבוֹד וָעֹז. ב הָבוּ לַיהוֹה כְּבוֹד שְׁמוֹ, הִשְׁתַּחֲווּ לַיהוֹה בְּהַדְרַת קֹדֶשׁ. ג קוֹל יְהוֹה עַל הַמָּיִם, אֵל הַכָּבוֹד הִרְעִים, יְהוֹה עַל מַיִם רַבִּים. ד קוֹל יְהוֹה בַּכֹּחַ, קוֹל יְהוֹה בֶּהָדָר. ה קוֹל יְהוֹה שֹׁבֵר אֲרָזִים, וַיְשַׁבֵּר יְהוֹה אֶת אַרְזֵי הַלְּבָנוֹן. ו וַיַּרְקִידֵם כְּמוֹ עֵגֶל, לְבָנוֹן וְשִׂרְיֹן כְּמוֹ בֶן רְאֵמִים. ז קוֹל יְהוֹה חֹצֵב לַהֲבוֹת אֵשׁ. ח קוֹל יְהוֹה יָחִיל מִדְבָּר, יָחִיל יְהוֹה מִדְבַּר קָדֵשׁ. ט קוֹל יְהוֹה יְחוֹלֵל אַיָּלוֹת, וַיֶּחֱשֹׂף יְעָרוֹת; וּבְהֵיכָלוֹ כֻּלּוֹ אֹמֵר כָּבוֹד. י יְהוֹה לַמַּבּוּל יָשָׁב, וַיֵּשֶׁב יְהוֹה מֶלֶךְ לְעוֹלָם. יא יְהוֹה עֹז לְעַמּוֹ יִתֵּן, יְהוֹה יְבָרֵךְ אֶת עַמּוֹ בַשָּׁלוֹם.

יום שני / MONDAY

ל א מִזְמוֹר שִׁיר חֲנֻכַּת הַבַּיִת לְדָוִד. ב אֲרוֹמִמְךָ יְהוֹה כִּי דִלִּיתָנִי, וְלֹא שִׂמַּחְתָּ אֹיְבַי לִי. ג יְהוֹה אֱלֹהָי, שִׁוַּעְתִּי אֵלֶיךָ וַתִּרְפָּאֵנִי. ד יְהוֹה, הֶעֱלִיתָ מִן שְׁאוֹל נַפְשִׁי, חִיִּיתַנִי מִיָּרְדִי בוֹר. ה זַמְּרוּ לַיהוֹה חֲסִידָיו, וְהוֹדוּ לְזֵכֶר קָדְשׁוֹ. ו כִּי רֶגַע בְּאַפּוֹ, חַיִּים בִּרְצוֹנוֹ; בָּעֶרֶב יָלִין בֶּכִי וְלַבֹּקֶר רִנָּה. ז וַאֲנִי אָמַרְתִּי בְשַׁלְוִי, בַּל אֶמּוֹט לְעוֹלָם. ח יְהוֹה, בִּרְצוֹנְךָ הֶעֱמַדְתָּה לְהַרְרִי עֹז, הִסְתַּרְתָּ פָנֶיךָ הָיִיתִי נִבְהָל. ט אֵלֶיךָ יְהוֹה אֶקְרָא, וְאֶל אֲדֹנָי אֶתְחַנָּן. י מַה בֶּצַע בְּדָמִי, בְּרִדְתִּי אֶל שָׁחַת; הֲיוֹדְךָ עָפָר, הֲיַגִּיד אֲמִתֶּךָ. יא שְׁמַע יְהוֹה וְחָנֵּנִי, יְהוֹה הֱיֵה עֹזֵר לִי. יב הָפַכְתָּ מִסְפְּדִי לְמָחוֹל לִי, פִּתַּחְתָּ שַׂקִּי וַתְּאַזְּרֵנִי שִׂמְחָה. יג לְמַעַן יְזַמֶּרְךָ כָבוֹד וְלֹא יִדֹּם, יְהוֹה אֱלֹהַי לְעוֹלָם אוֹדֶךָּ.

לא א לַמְנַצֵּחַ מִזְמוֹר לְדָוִד. ב בְּךָ יְהוֹה חָסִיתִי, אַל אֵבוֹשָׁה לְעוֹלָם; בְּצִדְקָתְךָ פַלְּטֵנִי. ג הַטֵּה אֵלַי אָזְנְךָ, מְהֵרָה הַצִּילֵנִי; הֱיֵה לִי לְצוּר

מָעוֹז, לְבֵית מְצוּדוֹת לְהוֹשִׁיעֵנִי. ד כִּי סַלְעִי וּמְצוּדָתִי אָתָּה, וּלְמַעַן שִׁמְךָ תַּנְחֵנִי וּתְנַהֲלֵנִי. ה תּוֹצִיאֵנִי מֵרֶשֶׁת זוּ טָמְנוּ לִי, כִּי אַתָּה מָעוּזִי. ו בְּיָדְךָ אַפְקִיד רוּחִי, פָּדִיתָה אוֹתִי יהוה, אֵל אֱמֶת. ז שָׂנֵאתִי הַשֹּׁמְרִים הַבְלֵי שָׁוְא, וַאֲנִי אֶל יהוה בָּטָחְתִּי. ח אָגִילָה וְאֶשְׂמְחָה בְּחַסְדֶּךָ; אֲשֶׁר רָאִיתָ אֶת עָנְיִי, יָדַעְתָּ בְּצָרוֹת נַפְשִׁי. ט וְלֹא הִסְגַּרְתַּנִי בְּיַד אוֹיֵב, הֶעֱמַדְתָּ בַמֶּרְחָב רַגְלָי. י חָנֵּנִי יהוה כִּי צַר לִי, עָשְׁשָׁה בְכַעַס עֵינִי נַפְשִׁי וּבִטְנִי. יא כִּי כָלוּ בְיָגוֹן חַיַּי, וּשְׁנוֹתַי בַּאֲנָחָה; כָּשַׁל בַּעֲוֹנִי כֹחִי, וַעֲצָמַי עָשֵׁשׁוּ. יב מִכָּל צֹרְרַי הָיִיתִי חֶרְפָּה, וְלִשְׁכֵנַי מְאֹד, וּפַחַד לִמְיֻדָּעָי; רֹאַי בַּחוּץ נָדְדוּ מִמֶּנִּי. יג נִשְׁכַּחְתִּי כְּמֵת מִלֵּב, הָיִיתִי כִּכְלִי אֹבֵד. יד כִּי שָׁמַעְתִּי דִּבַּת רַבִּים, מָגוֹר מִסָּבִיב; בְּהִוָּסְדָם יַחַד עָלַי, לָקַחַת נַפְשִׁי זָמָמוּ. טו וַאֲנִי, עָלֶיךָ בָטַחְתִּי יהוה, אָמַרְתִּי: אֱלֹהַי אָתָּה. טז בְּיָדְךָ עִתֹּתָי, הַצִּילֵנִי מִיַּד אוֹיְבַי וּמֵרֹדְפָי. יז הָאִירָה פָנֶיךָ עַל עַבְדֶּךָ, הוֹשִׁיעֵנִי בְחַסְדֶּךָ. יח יהוה, אַל אֵבוֹשָׁה כִּי קְרָאתִיךָ; יֵבֹשׁוּ רְשָׁעִים, יִדְּמוּ לִשְׁאוֹל. יט תֵּאָלַמְנָה שִׂפְתֵי שָׁקֶר, הַדֹּבְרוֹת עַל צַדִּיק עָתָק בְּגַאֲוָה וָבוּז. כ מָה רַב טוּבְךָ אֲשֶׁר צָפַנְתָּ לִּירֵאֶיךָ, פָּעַלְתָּ לַחֹסִים בָּךְ נֶגֶד בְּנֵי אָדָם. כא תַּסְתִּירֵם בְּסֵתֶר פָּנֶיךָ מֵרֻכְסֵי אִישׁ, תִּצְפְּנֵם בְּסֻכָּה מֵרִיב לְשֹׁנוֹת. כב בָּרוּךְ יהוה, כִּי הִפְלִיא חַסְדּוֹ לִי בְּעִיר מָצוֹר. כג וַאֲנִי אָמַרְתִּי בְחָפְזִי נִגְרַזְתִּי מִנֶּגֶד עֵינֶיךָ, אָכֵן שָׁמַעְתָּ קוֹל תַּחֲנוּנַי בְּשַׁוְּעִי אֵלֶיךָ. כד אֶהֱבוּ אֶת יהוה כָּל חֲסִידָיו, אֱמוּנִים נֹצֵר יהוה, וּמְשַׁלֵּם עַל יֶתֶר עֹשֵׂה גַאֲוָה. כה חִזְקוּ וְיַאֲמֵץ לְבַבְכֶם, כָּל הַמְיַחֲלִים לַיהוה.

לב א לְדָוִד מַשְׂכִּיל; אַשְׁרֵי נְשׂוּי פֶּשַׁע, כְּסוּי חֲטָאָה. ב אַשְׁרֵי אָדָם לֹא יַחְשֹׁב יהוה לוֹ עָוֹן, וְאֵין בְּרוּחוֹ רְמִיָּה. ג כִּי הֶחֱרַשְׁתִּי בָּלוּ עֲצָמָי, בְּשַׁאֲגָתִי כָּל הַיּוֹם. ד כִּי יוֹמָם וָלַיְלָה תִּכְבַּד עָלַי יָדֶךָ, נֶהְפַּךְ לְשַׁדִּי בְּחַרְבֹנֵי קַיִץ סֶלָה. ה חַטָּאתִי אוֹדִיעֲךָ, וַעֲוֹנִי לֹא כִסִּיתִי, אָמַרְתִּי, אוֹדֶה עֲלֵי פְשָׁעַי לַיהוה; וְאַתָּה נָשָׂאתָ עֲוֹן חַטָּאתִי סֶלָה. ו עַל זֹאת יִתְפַּלֵּל כָּל חָסִיד אֵלֶיךָ לְעֵת מְצֹא, רַק לְשֵׁטֶף מַיִם רַבִּים אֵלָיו לֹא יַגִּיעוּ. ז אַתָּה סֵתֶר לִי, מִצַּר תִּצְּרֵנִי; רָנֵּי פַלֵּט תְּסוֹבְבֵנִי סֶלָה. ח אַשְׂכִּילְךָ וְאוֹרְךָ בְּדֶרֶךְ זוּ תֵלֵךְ, אִיעֲצָה עָלֶיךָ עֵינִי. ט אַל תִּהְיוּ כְּסוּס כְּפֶרֶד אֵין הָבִין; בְּמֶתֶג וָרֶסֶן עֶדְיוֹ לִבְלוֹם, בַּל קְרֹב אֵלֶיךָ. י רַבִּים מַכְאוֹבִים לָרָשָׁע, וְהַבּוֹטֵחַ בַּיהוה חֶסֶד יְסוֹבְבֶנּוּ. יא שִׂמְחוּ בַיהוה וְגִילוּ צַדִּיקִים, וְהַרְנִינוּ כָּל יִשְׁרֵי לֵב.

לג א רַנְּנוּ צַדִּיקִים בַּיהוה, לַיְשָׁרִים נָאוָה תְהִלָּה. ב הוֹדוּ לַיהוה בְּכִנּוֹר, בְּנֵבֶל עָשׂוֹר זַמְּרוּ לוֹ. ג שִׁירוּ לוֹ שִׁיר חָדָשׁ, הֵיטִיבוּ נַגֵּן בִּתְרוּעָה. ד כִּי יָשָׁר דְּבַר יהוה, וְכָל מַעֲשֵׂהוּ בֶּאֱמוּנָה. ה אֹהֵב צְדָקָה וּמִשְׁפָּט, חֶסֶד יהוה מָלְאָה הָאָרֶץ. ו בִּדְבַר יהוה שָׁמַיִם נַעֲשׂוּ, וּבְרוּחַ פִּיו כָּל צְבָאָם. ז כֹּנֵס כַּנֵּד

מֵי הַיָּם, נֹתֵן בְּאוֹצָרוֹת תְּהוֹמוֹת. ח יִירְאוּ מֵיהוה כָּל הָאָרֶץ, מִמֶּנּוּ יָגוּרוּ כָּל יֹשְׁבֵי תֵבֵל. ט כִּי הוּא אָמַר וַיֶּהִי, הוּא צִוָּה וַיַּעֲמֹד. י יהוה הֵפִיר עֲצַת גּוֹיִם, הֵנִיא מַחְשְׁבוֹת עַמִּים. יא עֲצַת יהוה לְעוֹלָם תַּעֲמֹד, מַחְשְׁבוֹת לִבּוֹ לְדֹר וָדֹר. יב אַשְׁרֵי הַגּוֹי אֲשֶׁר יהוה אֱלֹהָיו, הָעָם בָּחַר לְנַחֲלָה לוֹ. יג מִשָּׁמַיִם הִבִּיט יהוה, רָאָה אֶת כָּל בְּנֵי הָאָדָם. יד מִמְּכוֹן שִׁבְתּוֹ הִשְׁגִּיחַ, אֶל כָּל יֹשְׁבֵי הָאָרֶץ. טו הַיֹּצֵר יַחַד לִבָּם, הַמֵּבִין אֶל כָּל מַעֲשֵׂיהֶם. טז אֵין הַמֶּלֶךְ נוֹשָׁע בְּרָב חָיִל, גִּבּוֹר לֹא יִנָּצֵל בְּרָב כֹּחַ. יז שֶׁקֶר הַסּוּס לִתְשׁוּעָה, וּבְרֹב חֵילוֹ לֹא יְמַלֵּט. יח הִנֵּה עֵין יהוה אֶל יְרֵאָיו, לַמְיַחֲלִים לְחַסְדּוֹ. יט לְהַצִּיל מִמָּוֶת נַפְשָׁם, וּלְחַיּוֹתָם בָּרָעָב. כ נַפְשֵׁנוּ חִכְּתָה לַיהוה, עֶזְרֵנוּ וּמָגִנֵּנוּ הוּא. כא כִּי בוֹ יִשְׂמַח לִבֵּנוּ, כִּי בְשֵׁם קָדְשׁוֹ בָטָחְנוּ. כב יְהִי חַסְדְּךָ יהוה עָלֵינוּ, כַּאֲשֶׁר יִחַלְנוּ לָךְ.

לד א לְדָוִד, בְּשַׁנּוֹתוֹ אֶת טַעְמוֹ לִפְנֵי אֲבִימֶלֶךְ, וַיְגָרְשֵׁהוּ וַיֵּלַךְ. ב אֲבָרְכָה אֶת יהוה בְּכָל עֵת, תָּמִיד תְּהִלָּתוֹ בְּפִי. ג בַּיהוה תִּתְהַלֵּל נַפְשִׁי, יִשְׁמְעוּ עֲנָוִים וְיִשְׂמָחוּ. ד גַּדְּלוּ לַיהוה אִתִּי, וּנְרוֹמְמָה שְׁמוֹ יַחְדָּו. ה דָּרַשְׁתִּי אֶת יהוה וְעָנָנִי, וּמִכָּל מְגוּרוֹתַי הִצִּילָנִי. ו הִבִּיטוּ אֵלָיו וְנָהָרוּ, וּפְנֵיהֶם אַל יֶחְפָּרוּ. ז זֶה עָנִי קָרָא וַיהוה שָׁמֵעַ, וּמִכָּל צָרוֹתָיו הוֹשִׁיעוֹ. ח חֹנֶה מַלְאַךְ יהוה סָבִיב לִירֵאָיו, וַיְחַלְּצֵם. ט טַעֲמוּ וּרְאוּ כִּי טוֹב יהוה, אַשְׁרֵי הַגֶּבֶר יֶחֱסֶה בּוֹ. י יְראוּ אֶת יהוה קְדֹשָׁיו, כִּי אֵין מַחְסוֹר לִירֵאָיו. יא כְּפִירִים רָשׁוּ וְרָעֵבוּ, וְדֹרְשֵׁי יהוה לֹא יַחְסְרוּ כָל טוֹב. יב לְכוּ בָנִים שִׁמְעוּ לִי, יִרְאַת יהוה אֲלַמֶּדְכֶם. יג מִי הָאִישׁ הֶחָפֵץ חַיִּים, אֹהֵב יָמִים לִרְאוֹת טוֹב. יד נְצֹר לְשׁוֹנְךָ מֵרָע, וּשְׂפָתֶיךָ מִדַּבֵּר מִרְמָה. טו סוּר מֵרָע וַעֲשֵׂה טוֹב, בַּקֵּשׁ שָׁלוֹם וְרָדְפֵהוּ. טז עֵינֵי יהוה אֶל צַדִּיקִים, וְאָזְנָיו אֶל שַׁוְעָתָם. יז פְּנֵי יהוה בְּעֹשֵׂי רָע, לְהַכְרִית מֵאֶרֶץ זִכְרָם. יח צָעֲקוּ וַיהוה שָׁמֵעַ, וּמִכָּל צָרוֹתָם הִצִּילָם. יט קָרוֹב יהוה לְנִשְׁבְּרֵי לֵב, וְאֶת דַּכְּאֵי רוּחַ יוֹשִׁיעַ. כ רַבּוֹת רָעוֹת צַדִּיק, וּמִכֻּלָּם יַצִּילֶנּוּ יהוה. כא שֹׁמֵר כָּל עַצְמוֹתָיו, אַחַת מֵהֵנָּה לֹא נִשְׁבָּרָה. כב תְּמוֹתֵת רָשָׁע רָעָה, וְשֹׂנְאֵי צַדִּיק יֶאְשָׁמוּ. כג פּוֹדֶה יהוה נֶפֶשׁ עֲבָדָיו, וְלֹא יֶאְשְׁמוּ כָּל הַחֹסִים בּוֹ.

לה א לְדָוִד, רִיבָה יהוה אֶת יְרִיבַי, לְחַם אֶת לֹחֲמָי. ב הַחֲזֵק מָגֵן וְצִנָּה, וְקוּמָה בְּעֶזְרָתִי. ג וְהָרֵק חֲנִית וּסְגֹר לִקְרַאת רֹדְפָי, אֱמֹר לְנַפְשִׁי יְשֻׁעָתֵךְ אָנִי. ד יֵבֹשׁוּ וְיִכָּלְמוּ מְבַקְשֵׁי נַפְשִׁי; יִסֹּגוּ אָחוֹר וְיַחְפְּרוּ, חֹשְׁבֵי רָעָתִי. ה יִהְיוּ כְּמֹץ לִפְנֵי רוּחַ, וּמַלְאַךְ יהוה דּוֹחֶה. ו יְהִי דַרְכָּם חֹשֶׁךְ

וַחֲלַקְלַקֹּת, וּמַלְאַךְ יהוה רֹדְפָם. ז כִּי חִנָּם טָמְנוּ לִי שַׁחַת רִשְׁתָּם, חִנָּם חָפְרוּ לְנַפְשִׁי. ח תְּבוֹאֵהוּ שׁוֹאָה לֹא יֵדָע; וְרִשְׁתּוֹ אֲשֶׁר טָמַן תִּלְכְּדוֹ, בְּשׁוֹאָה יִפָּל בָּהּ. ט וְנַפְשִׁי תָּגִיל בַּיהוה, תָּשִׂישׂ בִּישׁוּעָתוֹ. י כָּל עַצְמוֹתַי תֹּאמַרְנָה, יהוה מִי כָמוֹךָ; מַצִּיל עָנִי מֵחָזָק מִמֶּנּוּ, וְעָנִי וְאֶבְיוֹן מִגֹּזְלוֹ. יא יְקוּמוּן עֵדֵי חָמָס, אֲשֶׁר לֹא יָדַעְתִּי יִשְׁאָלוּנִי. יב יְשַׁלְּמוּנִי רָעָה תַּחַת טוֹבָה, שְׁכוֹל לְנַפְשִׁי. יג וַאֲנִי בַּחֲלוֹתָם לְבוּשִׁי שָׂק, עִנֵּיתִי בַצּוֹם נַפְשִׁי; וּתְפִלָּתִי עַל חֵיקִי תָשׁוּב. יד כְּרֵעַ כְּאָח לִי הִתְהַלָּכְתִּי, כַּאֲבֶל אֵם קֹדֵר שַׁחוֹתִי. טו וּבְצַלְעִי שָׂמְחוּ וְנֶאֱסָפוּ; נֶאֶסְפוּ עָלַי נֵכִים וְלֹא יָדַעְתִּי, קָרְעוּ וְלֹא דָמּוּ. טז בְּחַנְפֵי לַעֲגֵי מָעוֹג, חָרֹק עָלַי שִׁנֵּימוֹ. יז אֲדֹנָי, כַּמָּה תִרְאֶה, הָשִׁיבָה נַפְשִׁי מִשֹּׁאֵיהֶם, מִכְּפִירִים יְחִידָתִי. יח אוֹדְךָ בְּקָהָל רָב, בְּעַם עָצוּם אֲהַלְלֶךָּ. יט אַל יִשְׂמְחוּ לִי אֹיְבַי שֶׁקֶר, שֹׂנְאַי חִנָּם יִקְרְצוּ עָיִן. כ כִּי לֹא שָׁלוֹם יְדַבֵּרוּ; וְעַל רִגְעֵי אֶרֶץ, דִּבְרֵי מִרְמוֹת יַחֲשֹׁבוּן. כא וַיַּרְחִיבוּ עָלַי פִּיהֶם; אָמְרוּ: הֶאָח הֶאָח, רָאֲתָה עֵינֵנוּ. כב רָאִיתָה, יהוה, אַל תֶּחֱרַשׁ; אֲדֹנָי, אַל תִּרְחַק מִמֶּנִּי. כג הָעִירָה וְהָקִיצָה לְמִשְׁפָּטִי, אֱלֹהַי וַאדֹנָי לְרִיבִי. כד שָׁפְטֵנִי כְצִדְקְךָ יהוה אֱלֹהָי, וְאַל יִשְׂמְחוּ לִי. כה אַל יֹאמְרוּ בְלִבָּם הֶאָח נַפְשֵׁנוּ, אַל יֹאמְרוּ בִּלַּעֲנוּהוּ. כו יֵבֹשׁוּ וְיַחְפְּרוּ יַחְדָּו שְׂמֵחֵי רָעָתִי; יִלְבְּשׁוּ בֹשֶׁת וּכְלִמָּה, הַמַּגְדִּילִים עָלָי. כז יָרֹנּוּ וְיִשְׂמְחוּ חֲפֵצֵי צִדְקִי; וְיֹאמְרוּ תָמִיד: יִגְדַּל יהוה, הֶחָפֵץ שְׁלוֹם עַבְדּוֹ. כח וּלְשׁוֹנִי תֶּהְגֶּה צִדְקֶךָ, כָּל הַיּוֹם תְּהִלָּתֶךָ.

לו א לַמְנַצֵּחַ לְעֶבֶד יהוה לְדָוִד. ב נְאֻם פֶּשַׁע לָרָשָׁע בְּקֶרֶב לִבִּי, אֵין פַּחַד אֱלֹהִים לְנֶגֶד עֵינָיו. ג כִּי הֶחֱלִיק אֵלָיו בְּעֵינָיו, לִמְצֹא עֲוֹנוֹ לִשְׂנֹא. ד דִּבְרֵי פִיו אָוֶן וּמִרְמָה, חָדַל לְהַשְׂכִּיל לְהֵיטִיב. ה אָוֶן יַחְשֹׁב עַל מִשְׁכָּבוֹ; יִתְיַצֵּב עַל דֶּרֶךְ לֹא טוֹב, רָע לֹא יִמְאָס. ו יהוה בְּהַשָּׁמַיִם חַסְדֶּךָ, אֱמוּנָתְךָ עַד שְׁחָקִים. ז צִדְקָתְךָ כְּהַרְרֵי אֵל, מִשְׁפָּטֶיךָ תְּהוֹם רַבָּה; אָדָם וּבְהֵמָה תוֹשִׁיעַ יהוה. ח מַה יָּקָר חַסְדְּךָ אֱלֹהִים, וּבְנֵי אָדָם בְּצֵל כְּנָפֶיךָ יֶחֱסָיוּן. ט יִרְוְיֻן מִדֶּשֶׁן בֵּיתֶךָ, וְנַחַל עֲדָנֶיךָ תַשְׁקֵם. י כִּי עִמְּךָ מְקוֹר חַיִּים, בְּאוֹרְךָ נִרְאֶה אוֹר. יא מְשֹׁךְ חַסְדְּךָ לְיֹדְעֶיךָ, וְצִדְקָתְךָ לְיִשְׁרֵי לֵב. יב אַל תְּבוֹאֵנִי רֶגֶל גַּאֲוָה, וְיַד רְשָׁעִים אַל תְּנִדֵנִי. יג שָׁם נָפְלוּ פֹּעֲלֵי אָוֶן, דֹּחוּ וְלֹא יָכְלוּ קוּם.

לז א לְדָוִד, אַל תִּתְחַר בַּמְּרֵעִים, אַל תְּקַנֵּא בְּעֹשֵׂי עַוְלָה. ב כִּי כֶחָצִיר מְהֵרָה יִמָּלוּ, וּכְיֶרֶק דֶּשֶׁא יִבּוֹלוּן. ג בְּטַח בַּיהוה וַעֲשֵׂה טוֹב, שְׁכָן אֶרֶץ וּרְעֵה אֱמוּנָה. ד וְהִתְעַנַּג עַל יהוה, וְיִתֶּן לְךָ מִשְׁאֲלֹת לִבֶּךָ. ה גּוֹל עַל יהוה דַּרְכֶּךָ, וּבְטַח עָלָיו וְהוּא יַעֲשֶׂה. ו וְהוֹצִיא כָאוֹר צִדְקֶךָ, וּמִשְׁפָּטֶךָ כַּצָּהֳרָיִם. ז דּוֹם לַיהוה וְהִתְחוֹלֵל לוֹ; אַל תִּתְחַר בְּמַצְלִיחַ דַּרְכּוֹ, בְּאִישׁ עֹשֶׂה מְזִמּוֹת. ח הֶרֶף מֵאַף וַעֲזֹב חֵמָה; אַל תִּתְחַר אַךְ לְהָרֵעַ. ט כִּי מְרֵעִים

יִכָּרֵתוּן, וְקֹוֵי יהוה הֵמָּה יִירְשׁוּ אָרֶץ. וְעוֹד מְעַט וְאֵין רָשָׁע, וְהִתְבּוֹנַנְתָּ עַל מְקוֹמוֹ וְאֵינֶנּוּ. יֹא וַעֲנָוִים יִירְשׁוּ אָרֶץ, וְהִתְעַנְּגוּ עַל רֹב שָׁלוֹם. יֹב זֹמֵם רָשָׁע לַצַּדִּיק, וְחֹרֵק עָלָיו שִׁנָּיו. יֹג אֲדֹנָי יִשְׂחַק לוֹ, כִּי רָאָה כִּי יָבֹא יוֹמוֹ. יֹד חֶרֶב פָּתְחוּ רְשָׁעִים וְדָרְכוּ קַשְׁתָּם, לְהַפִּיל עָנִי וְאֶבְיוֹן, לִטְבוֹחַ יִשְׁרֵי דָרֶךְ. יֹה חַרְבָּם תָּבוֹא בְלִבָּם, וְקַשְּׁתוֹתָם תִּשָּׁבַרְנָה. יֹו טוֹב מְעַט לַצַּדִּיק, מֵהֲמוֹן רְשָׁעִים רַבִּים. יֹז כִּי זְרוֹעוֹת רְשָׁעִים תִּשָּׁבַרְנָה, וְסוֹמֵךְ צַדִּיקִים יהוה. יֹח יוֹדֵעַ יהוה יְמֵי תְמִימִם, וְנַחֲלָתָם לְעוֹלָם תִּהְיֶה. יֹט לֹא יֵבֹשׁוּ בְּעֵת רָעָה, וּבִימֵי רְעָבוֹן יִשְׂבָּעוּ. כ כִּי רְשָׁעִים יֹאבֵדוּ, וְאֹיְבֵי יהוה כִּיקַר כָּרִים, כָּלוּ בֶעָשָׁן כָּלוּ. כֹא לֹוֶה רָשָׁע וְלֹא יְשַׁלֵּם, וְצַדִּיק חוֹנֵן וְנוֹתֵן. כֹב כִּי מְבֹרָכָיו יִירְשׁוּ אָרֶץ, וּמְקֻלָּלָיו יִכָּרֵתוּ. כֹג מֵיהוה מִצְעֲדֵי גֶבֶר כּוֹנָנוּ, וְדַרְכּוֹ יֶחְפָּץ. כֹד כִּי יִפֹּל לֹא יוּטָל, כִּי יהוה סוֹמֵךְ יָדוֹ. כֹה נַעַר הָיִיתִי גַם זָקַנְתִּי, וְלֹא רָאִיתִי צַדִּיק נֶעֱזָב, וְזַרְעוֹ מְבַקֶּשׁ לָחֶם. כֹו כָּל הַיּוֹם חוֹנֵן וּמַלְוֶה, וְזַרְעוֹ לִבְרָכָה. כֹז סוּר מֵרָע וַעֲשֵׂה טוֹב, וּשְׁכֹן לְעוֹלָם. כֹח כִּי יהוה אֹהֵב מִשְׁפָּט, וְלֹא יַעֲזֹב אֶת חֲסִידָיו, לְעוֹלָם נִשְׁמָרוּ; וְזֶרַע רְשָׁעִים נִכְרָת. כֹט צַדִּיקִים יִירְשׁוּ אָרֶץ, וְיִשְׁכְּנוּ לָעַד עָלֶיהָ. ל פִּי צַדִּיק יֶהְגֶּה חָכְמָה, וּלְשׁוֹנוֹ תְּדַבֵּר מִשְׁפָּט. לֹא תּוֹרַת אֱלֹהָיו בְּלִבּוֹ, לֹא תִמְעַד אֲשֻׁרָיו. לֹב צוֹפֶה רָשָׁע לַצַּדִּיק, וּמְבַקֵּשׁ לַהֲמִיתוֹ. לֹג יהוה לֹא יַעַזְבֶנּוּ בְיָדוֹ, וְלֹא יַרְשִׁיעֶנּוּ בְּהִשָּׁפְטוֹ. לֹד קַוֵּה אֶל יהוה וּשְׁמֹר דַּרְכּוֹ, וִירוֹמִמְךָ לָרֶשֶׁת אָרֶץ; בְּהִכָּרֵת רְשָׁעִים תִּרְאֶה. לֹה רָאִיתִי רָשָׁע עָרִיץ, וּמִתְעָרֶה כְּאֶזְרָח רַעֲנָן. לֹו וַיַּעֲבֹר וְהִנֵּה אֵינֶנּוּ, וָאֲבַקְשֵׁהוּ וְלֹא נִמְצָא. לֹז שְׁמָר תָּם וּרְאֵה יָשָׁר, כִּי אַחֲרִית לְאִישׁ שָׁלוֹם. לֹח וּפֹשְׁעִים נִשְׁמְדוּ יַחְדָּו, אַחֲרִית רְשָׁעִים נִכְרָתָה. לֹט וּתְשׁוּעַת צַדִּיקִים מֵיהוה, מָעוּזָּם בְּעֵת צָרָה. מ וַיַּעְזְרֵם יהוה וַיְפַלְּטֵם; יְפַלְּטֵם מֵרְשָׁעִים וְיוֹשִׁיעֵם, כִּי חָסוּ בוֹ.

לח א מִזְמוֹר לְדָוִד לְהַזְכִּיר. ב יהוה אַל בְּקֶצְפְּךָ תוֹכִיחֵנִי, וּבַחֲמָתְךָ תְיַסְּרֵנִי. ג כִּי חִצֶּיךָ נִחֲתוּ בִי, וַתִּנְחַת עָלַי יָדֶךָ. ד אֵין מְתֹם בִּבְשָׂרִי מִפְּנֵי זַעְמֶךָ, אֵין שָׁלוֹם בַּעֲצָמַי מִפְּנֵי חַטָּאתִי. ה כִּי עֲוֹנֹתַי עָבְרוּ רֹאשִׁי, כְּמַשָּׂא כָבֵד יִכְבְּדוּ מִמֶּנִּי. ו הִבְאִישׁוּ נָמַקּוּ חַבּוּרֹתָי, מִפְּנֵי אִוַּלְתִּי. ז נַעֲוֵיתִי שַׁחֹתִי עַד מְאֹד, כָּל הַיּוֹם קֹדֵר הִלָּכְתִּי. ח כִּי כְסָלַי מָלְאוּ נִקְלֶה, וְאֵין מְתֹם בִּבְשָׂרִי. ט נְפוּגֹתִי וְנִדְכֵּיתִי עַד מְאֹד, שָׁאַגְתִּי מִנַּהֲמַת לִבִּי. י אֲדֹנָי, נֶגְדְּךָ כָל תַּאֲוָתִי, וְאַנְחָתִי מִמְּךָ לֹא נִסְתָּרָה. יֹא לִבִּי סְחַרְחַר, עֲזָבַנִי כֹחִי; וְאוֹר עֵינַי גַּם הֵם אֵין אִתִּי. יֹב אֹהֲבַי וְרֵעַי מִנֶּגֶד נִגְעִי יַעֲמֹדוּ, וּקְרוֹבַי מֵרָחֹק עָמָדוּ. יֹג וַיְנַקְשׁוּ מְבַקְשֵׁי נַפְשִׁי, וְדֹרְשֵׁי רָעָתִי דִּבְּרוּ הַוּוֹת, וּמִרְמוֹת כָּל הַיּוֹם יֶהְגּוּ. יֹד וַאֲנִי כְחֵרֵשׁ לֹא אֶשְׁמָע, וּכְאִלֵּם לֹא יִפְתַּח פִּיו. יֹה וָאֱהִי כְּאִישׁ אֲשֶׁר לֹא שֹׁמֵעַ, וְאֵין בְּפִיו תּוֹכָחוֹת. יֹו כִּי לְךָ יהוה הוֹחָלְתִּי; אַתָּה תַעֲנֶה, אֲדֹנָי

אֱלֹהָי. יז כִּי אָמַרְתִּי פֶּן יִשְׂמְחוּ לִי, בְּמוֹט רַגְלִי עָלַי הִגְדִּילוּ. יח כִּי אֲנִי לְצֶלַע נָכוֹן, וּמַכְאוֹבִי נֶגְדִּי תָמִיד. יט כִּי עֲוֹנִי אַגִּיד, אֶדְאַג מֵחַטָּאתִי. כ וְאֹיְבַי חַיִּים עָצֵמוּ, וְרַבּוּ שֹׂנְאַי שָׁקֶר. כא וּמְשַׁלְּמֵי רָעָה תַּחַת טוֹבָה, יִשְׂטְנוּנִי תַּחַת רָדְפִי טוֹב. כב אַל תַּעַזְבֵנִי יהוה, אֱלֹהַי אַל תִּרְחַק מִמֶּנִּי. כג חוּשָׁה לְעֶזְרָתִי, אֲדֹנָי תְּשׁוּעָתִי.

יום ז' לחודש / DAY 7

לט א לַמְנַצֵּחַ לידיתון, מִזְמוֹר לְדָוִד. ב אָמַרְתִּי אֶשְׁמְרָה דְרָכַי מֵחֲטוֹא בִלְשׁוֹנִי, אֶשְׁמְרָה לְפִי מַחְסוֹם בְּעֹד רָשָׁע לְנֶגְדִּי. ג נֶאֱלַמְתִּי דוּמִיָּה, הֶחֱשֵׁיתִי מִטּוֹב, וּכְאֵבִי נֶעְכָּר. ד חַם לִבִּי בְּקִרְבִּי, בַּהֲגִיגִי תִבְעַר אֵשׁ; דִּבַּרְתִּי בִּלְשׁוֹנִי. ה הוֹדִיעֵנִי יהוה קִצִּי, וּמִדַּת יָמַי מַה הִיא; אֵדְעָה מֶה חָדֵל אָנִי. ו הִנֵּה טְפָחוֹת נָתַתָּה יָמַי, וְחֶלְדִּי כְאַיִן נֶגְדֶּךָ; אַךְ כָּל הֶבֶל כָּל אָדָם נִצָּב סֶלָה. ז אַךְ בְּצֶלֶם יִתְהַלֶּךְ אִישׁ, אַךְ הֶבֶל יֶהֱמָיוּן; יִצְבֹּר, וְלֹא יֵדַע מִי אֹסְפָם. ח וְעַתָּה מַה קִּוִּיתִי אֲדֹנָי, תּוֹחַלְתִּי לְךָ הִיא. ט מִכָּל פְּשָׁעַי הַצִּילֵנִי, חֶרְפַּת נָבָל אַל תְּשִׂימֵנִי. י נֶאֱלַמְתִּי לֹא אֶפְתַּח פִּי, כִּי אַתָּה עָשִׂיתָ. יא הָסֵר מֵעָלַי נִגְעֶךָ, מִתִּגְרַת יָדְךָ אֲנִי כָלִיתִי. יב בְּתוֹכָחוֹת עַל עָוֹן יִסַּרְתָּ אִישׁ, וַתֶּמֶס כָּעָשׁ חֲמוּדוֹ; אַךְ הֶבֶל כָּל אָדָם סֶלָה. יג שִׁמְעָה תְפִלָּתִי יהוה, וְשַׁוְעָתִי הַאֲזִינָה, אֶל דִּמְעָתִי אַל תֶּחֱרַשׁ; כִּי גֵר אָנֹכִי עִמָּךְ, תּוֹשָׁב כְּכָל אֲבוֹתָי. יד הָשַׁע מִמֶּנִּי וְאַבְלִיגָה, בְּטֶרֶם אֵלֵךְ וְאֵינֶנִּי.

מ א לַמְנַצֵּחַ לְדָוִד מִזְמוֹר. ב קַוֹּה קִוִּיתִי יהוה, וַיֵּט אֵלַי וַיִּשְׁמַע שַׁוְעָתִי. ג וַיַּעֲלֵנִי מִבּוֹר שָׁאוֹן מִטִּיט הַיָּוֵן; וַיָּקֶם עַל סֶלַע רַגְלַי, כּוֹנֵן אֲשֻׁרָי. ד וַיִּתֵּן בְּפִי שִׁיר חָדָשׁ, תְּהִלָּה לֵאלֹהֵינוּ; יִרְאוּ רַבִּים וְיִירָאוּ, וְיִבְטְחוּ בַּיהוה. ה אַשְׁרֵי הַגֶּבֶר אֲשֶׁר שָׂם יהוה מִבְטַחוֹ, וְלֹא פָנָה אֶל רְהָבִים וְשָׂטֵי כָזָב. ו רַבּוֹת עָשִׂיתָ אַתָּה יהוה אֱלֹהַי, נִפְלְאֹתֶיךָ וּמַחְשְׁבֹתֶיךָ אֵלֵינוּ; אֵין עֲרֹךְ אֵלֶיךָ, אַגִּידָה וַאֲדַבֵּרָה, עָצְמוּ מִסַּפֵּר. ז זֶבַח וּמִנְחָה לֹא חָפַצְתָּ, אָזְנַיִם כָּרִיתָ לִּי; עוֹלָה וַחֲטָאָה לֹא שָׁאָלְתָּ. ח אָז אָמַרְתִּי הִנֵּה בָאתִי, בִּמְגִלַּת סֵפֶר כָּתוּב עָלָי. ט לַעֲשׂוֹת רְצוֹנְךָ אֱלֹהַי חָפָצְתִּי; וְתוֹרָתְךָ בְּתוֹךְ מֵעָי. י בִּשַּׂרְתִּי צֶדֶק בְּקָהָל רָב, הִנֵּה שְׂפָתַי לֹא אֶכְלָא; יהוה, אַתָּה יָדָעְתָּ. יא צִדְקָתְךָ לֹא כִסִּיתִי בְּתוֹךְ לִבִּי, אֱמוּנָתְךָ וּתְשׁוּעָתְךָ אָמָרְתִּי; לֹא כִחַדְתִּי חַסְדְּךָ וַאֲמִתְּךָ לְקָהָל רָב. יב אַתָּה יהוה לֹא תִכְלָא רַחֲמֶיךָ מִמֶּנִּי, חַסְדְּךָ וַאֲמִתְּךָ תָּמִיד יִצְּרוּנִי. יג כִּי אָפְפוּ עָלַי רָעוֹת עַד אֵין מִסְפָּר, הִשִּׂיגוּנִי עֲוֹנֹתַי וְלֹא יָכֹלְתִּי לִרְאוֹת; עָצְמוּ מִשַּׂעֲרוֹת רֹאשִׁי, וְלִבִּי עֲזָבָנִי. יד רְצֵה יהוה לְהַצִּילֵנִי, יהוה לְעֶזְרָתִי חוּשָׁה. טו יֵבֹשׁוּ וְיַחְפְּרוּ יַחַד מְבַקְשֵׁי נַפְשִׁי לִסְפּוֹתָהּ, יִסֹּגוּ אָחוֹר

וַיְכַלְמוּ חֲפֵצֵי רָעָתִי. טו יָשֹׁמּוּ עַל עֵקֶב בָּשְׁתָּם, הָאֹמְרִים לִי הֶאָח הֶאָח. טז יָשִׂישׂוּ וְיִשְׂמְחוּ בְּךָ כָּל מְבַקְשֶׁיךָ; יֹאמְרוּ תָמִיד יִגְדַּל יהוה, אֹהֲבֵי תְּשׁוּעָתֶךָ. יז וַאֲנִי עָנִי וְאֶבְיוֹן, אֲדֹנָי יַחֲשָׁב לִי; עֶזְרָתִי וּמְפַלְטִי אַתָּה, אֱלֹהַי אַל תְּאַחַר.

מא א לַמְנַצֵּחַ מִזְמוֹר לְדָוִד. ב אַשְׁרֵי מַשְׂכִּיל אֶל דָּל, בְּיוֹם רָעָה יְמַלְּטֵהוּ יהוה. ג יהוה יִשְׁמְרֵהוּ וִיחַיֵּהוּ, וְאֻשַּׁר בָּאָרֶץ, וְאַל תִּתְּנֵהוּ בְּנֶפֶשׁ אֹיְבָיו. ד יהוה יִסְעָדֶנּוּ עַל עֶרֶשׂ דְּוָי, כָּל מִשְׁכָּבוֹ הָפַכְתָּ בְחָלְיוֹ. ה אֲנִי אָמַרְתִּי: יהוה חָנֵּנִי, רְפָאָה נַפְשִׁי, כִּי חָטָאתִי לָךְ. ו אוֹיְבַי יֹאמְרוּ רַע לִי, מָתַי יָמוּת וְאָבַד שְׁמוֹ. ז וְאִם בָּא לִרְאוֹת שָׁוְא יְדַבֵּר, לִבּוֹ יִקְבָּץ אָוֶן לוֹ; יֵצֵא לַחוּץ יְדַבֵּר. ח יַחַד עָלַי יִתְלַחֲשׁוּ כָּל שֹׂנְאָי, עָלַי יַחְשְׁבוּ רָעָה לִי. ט דְּבַר בְּלִיַּעַל יָצוּק בּוֹ, וַאֲשֶׁר שָׁכַב לֹא יוֹסִיף לָקוּם. י גַּם אִישׁ שְׁלוֹמִי אֲשֶׁר בָּטַחְתִּי בוֹ, אוֹכֵל לַחְמִי, הִגְדִּיל עָלַי עָקֵב. יא וְאַתָּה יהוה חָנֵּנִי וַהֲקִימֵנִי, וַאֲשַׁלְּמָה לָהֶם. יב בְּזֹאת יָדַעְתִּי כִּי חָפַצְתָּ בִּי, כִּי לֹא יָרִיעַ אֹיְבִי עָלָי. יג וַאֲנִי בְּתֻמִּי תָּמַכְתָּ בִּי, וַתַּצִּיבֵנִי לְפָנֶיךָ לְעוֹלָם. יד בָּרוּךְ יהוה אֱלֹהֵי יִשְׂרָאֵל מֵהָעוֹלָם וְעַד הָעוֹלָם, אָמֵן וְאָמֵן.

ספר שני / BOOK TWO

מב א לַמְנַצֵּחַ מַשְׂכִּיל לִבְנֵי קֹרַח. ב כְּאַיָּל תַּעֲרֹג עַל אֲפִיקֵי מָיִם, כֵּן נַפְשִׁי תַעֲרֹג אֵלֶיךָ אֱלֹהִים. ג צָמְאָה נַפְשִׁי לֵאלֹהִים, לְאֵל חָי; מָתַי אָבוֹא וְאֵרָאֶה פְּנֵי אֱלֹהִים. ד הָיְתָה לִּי דִמְעָתִי לֶחֶם יוֹמָם וָלָיְלָה, בֶּאֱמֹר אֵלַי כָּל הַיּוֹם: אַיֵּה אֱלֹהֶיךָ. ה אֵלֶּה אֶזְכְּרָה וְאֶשְׁפְּכָה עָלַי נַפְשִׁי, כִּי אֶעֱבֹר בַּסָּךְ, אֶדַּדֵּם עַד בֵּית אֱלֹהִים; בְּקוֹל רִנָּה וְתוֹדָה הָמוֹן חוֹגֵג. ו מַה תִּשְׁתּוֹחֲחִי נַפְשִׁי, וַתֶּהֱמִי עָלָי; הוֹחִלִי לֵאלֹהִים, כִּי עוֹד אוֹדֶנּוּ יְשׁוּעוֹת פָּנָיו. ז אֱלֹהַי, עָלַי נַפְשִׁי תִשְׁתּוֹחָח, עַל כֵּן אֶזְכָּרְךָ מֵאֶרֶץ יַרְדֵּן וְחֶרְמוֹנִים, מֵהַר מִצְעָר. ח תְּהוֹם אֶל תְּהוֹם קוֹרֵא לְקוֹל צִנּוֹרֶיךָ, כָּל מִשְׁבָּרֶיךָ וְגַלֶּיךָ עָלַי עָבָרוּ. ט יוֹמָם יְצַוֶּה יהוה חַסְדּוֹ, וּבַלַּיְלָה שִׁירֹה עִמִּי; תְּפִלָּה לְאֵל חַיָּי. י אוֹמְרָה לְאֵל סַלְעִי, לָמָה שְׁכַחְתָּנִי, לָמָה קֹדֵר אֵלֵךְ בְּלַחַץ אוֹיֵב. יא בְּרֶצַח בְּעַצְמוֹתַי חֵרְפוּנִי צוֹרְרָי, בְּאָמְרָם אֵלַי כָּל הַיּוֹם: אַיֵּה אֱלֹהֶיךָ. יב מַה תִּשְׁתּוֹחֲחִי נַפְשִׁי, וּמַה תֶּהֱמִי עָלָי; הוֹחִילִי לֵאלֹהִים, כִּי עוֹד אוֹדֶנּוּ יְשׁוּעֹת פָּנַי וֵאלֹהָי.

מג א שָׁפְטֵנִי אֱלֹהִים וְרִיבָה רִיבִי מִגּוֹי לֹא חָסִיד, מֵאִישׁ מִרְמָה וְעַוְלָה תְפַלְּטֵנִי. ב כִּי אַתָּה אֱלֹהֵי מָעוּזִּי, לָמָה זְנַחְתָּנִי, לָמָה קֹדֵר אֶתְהַלֵּךְ בְּלַחַץ אוֹיֵב. ג שְׁלַח אוֹרְךָ וַאֲמִתְּךָ, הֵמָּה יַנְחוּנִי, יְבִיאוּנִי אֶל הַר קָדְשְׁךָ

וְאֶל מִשְׁכְּנוֹתֶיךָ. דּ וְאָבוֹאָה אֶל מִזְבַּח אֱלֹהִים, אֶל אֵל שִׂמְחַת גִּילִי; וְאוֹדְךָ
בְכִנּוֹר, אֱלֹהִים אֱלֹהָי. הּ מַה תִּשְׁתּוֹחֲחִי נַפְשִׁי, וּמַה תֶּהֱמִי עָלָי; הוֹחִילִי
לֵאלֹהִים, כִּי עוֹד אוֹדֶנּוּ יְשׁוּעֹת פָּנַי וֵאלֹהָי.

יוֹם ח' לַחֹדֶשׁ / DAY 8

מד א לַמְנַצֵּחַ לִבְנֵי קֹרַח מַשְׂכִּיל. בּ אֱלֹהִים בְּאָזְנֵינוּ שָׁמַעְנוּ, אֲבוֹתֵינוּ
סִפְּרוּ לָנוּ, פֹּעַל פָּעַלְתָּ בִימֵיהֶם בִּימֵי קֶדֶם. גּ אַתָּה, יָדְךָ גּוֹיִם הוֹרַשְׁתָּ
וַתִּטָּעֵם, תָּרַע לְאֻמִּים וַתְּשַׁלְּחֵם. דּ כִּי לֹא בְחַרְבָּם יָרְשׁוּ אָרֶץ, וּזְרוֹעָם לֹא
הוֹשִׁיעָה לָּמוֹ; כִּי יְמִינְךָ וּזְרוֹעֲךָ וְאוֹר פָּנֶיךָ כִּי רְצִיתָם. הּ אַתָּה הוּא מַלְכִּי
אֱלֹהִים, צַוֵּה יְשׁוּעוֹת יַעֲקֹב. וּ בְּךָ צָרֵינוּ נְנַגֵּחַ, בְּשִׁמְךָ נָבוּס קָמֵינוּ. זּ כִּי לֹא
בְקַשְׁתִּי אֶבְטָח, וְחַרְבִּי לֹא תוֹשִׁיעֵנִי. חּ כִּי הוֹשַׁעְתָּנוּ מִצָּרֵינוּ, וּמְשַׂנְאֵינוּ
הֱבִישׁוֹתָ. טּ בֵּאלֹהִים הִלַּלְנוּ כָל הַיּוֹם, וְשִׁמְךָ לְעוֹלָם נוֹדֶה סֶלָה. יּ אַף זָנַחְתָּ
וַתַּכְלִימֵנוּ, וְלֹא תֵצֵא בְּצִבְאוֹתֵינוּ. יא תְּשִׁיבֵנוּ אָחוֹר מִנִּי צָר, וּמְשַׂנְאֵינוּ
שָׁסוּ לָמוֹ. יב תִּתְּנֵנוּ כְּצֹאן מַאֲכָל, וּבַגּוֹיִם זֵרִיתָנוּ. יג תִּמְכֹּר עַמְּךָ בְלֹא הוֹן,
וְלֹא רִבִּיתָ בִּמְחִירֵיהֶם. יד תְּשִׂימֵנוּ חֶרְפָּה לִשְׁכֵנֵינוּ, לַעַג וָקֶלֶס
לִסְבִיבוֹתֵינוּ. טו תְּשִׂימֵנוּ מָשָׁל בַּגּוֹיִם, מְנוֹד רֹאשׁ בַּל־אֻמִּים. טז כָּל הַיּוֹם
כְּלִמָּתִי נֶגְדִּי, וּבֹשֶׁת פָּנַי כִּסָּתְנִי. יז מִקּוֹל מְחָרֵף וּמְגַדֵּף, מִפְּנֵי אוֹיֵב
וּמִתְנַקֵּם. יח כָּל זֹאת בָּאַתְנוּ וְלֹא שְׁכַחֲנוּךָ, וְלֹא שִׁקַּרְנוּ בִּבְרִיתֶךָ. יט לֹא
נָסוֹג אָחוֹר לִבֵּנוּ, וַתֵּט אֲשֻׁרֵינוּ מִנִּי אָרְחֶךָ. כּ כִּי דִכִּיתָנוּ בִּמְקוֹם תַּנִּים,
וַתְּכַס עָלֵינוּ בְצַלְמָוֶת. כא אִם שָׁכַחְנוּ שֵׁם אֱלֹהֵינוּ, וַנִּפְרֹשׂ כַּפֵּינוּ לְאֵל זָר.
כב הֲלֹא אֱלֹהִים יַחֲקָר זֹאת, כִּי הוּא יֹדֵעַ תַּעֲלֻמוֹת לֵב. כג כִּי עָלֶיךָ הֹרַגְנוּ כָל
הַיּוֹם, נֶחְשַׁבְנוּ כְּצֹאן טִבְחָה. כד עוּרָה לָמָּה תִישַׁן, אֲדֹנָי; הָקִיצָה, אַל תִּזְנַח
לָנֶצַח. כה לָמָּה פָנֶיךָ תַסְתִּיר, תִּשְׁכַּח עָנְיֵנוּ וְלַחֲצֵנוּ. כו כִּי שָׁחָה לֶעָפָר
נַפְשֵׁנוּ, דָּבְקָה לָאָרֶץ בִּטְנֵנוּ. כז קוּמָה עֶזְרָתָה לָּנוּ, וּפְדֵנוּ לְמַעַן חַסְדֶּךָ.

מה א לַמְנַצֵּחַ עַל שֹׁשַׁנִּים לִבְנֵי קֹרַח, מַשְׂכִּיל שִׁיר יְדִידֹת. בּ רָחַשׁ לִבִּי
דָּבָר טוֹב, אֹמֵר אָנִי מַעֲשַׂי לְמֶלֶךְ, לְשׁוֹנִי עֵט סוֹפֵר מָהִיר. גּ יָפְיָפִיתָ
מִבְּנֵי אָדָם, הוּצַק חֵן בְּשִׂפְתוֹתֶיךָ, עַל כֵּן בֵּרַכְךָ אֱלֹהִים לְעוֹלָם. דּ חֲגוֹר
חַרְבְּךָ עַל יָרֵךְ, גִּבּוֹר, הוֹדְךָ וַהֲדָרֶךָ. הּ וַהֲדָרְךָ, צְלַח רְכַב עַל דְּבַר אֱמֶת
וְעַנְוָה צֶדֶק, וְתוֹרְךָ נוֹרָאוֹת יְמִינֶךָ. וּ חִצֶּיךָ שְׁנוּנִים, עַמִּים תַּחְתֶּיךָ יִפְּלוּ,
בְּלֵב אוֹיְבֵי הַמֶּלֶךְ. זּ כִּסְאֲךָ אֱלֹהִים עוֹלָם וָעֶד, שֵׁבֶט מִישֹׁר שֵׁבֶט מַלְכוּתֶךָ.
חּ אָהַבְתָּ צֶּדֶק וַתִּשְׂנָא רֶשַׁע; עַל כֵּן מְשָׁחֲךָ אֱלֹהִים אֱלֹהֶיךָ, שֶׁמֶן שָׂשׂוֹן
מֵחֲבֵרֶךָ. טּ מֹר וַאֲהָלוֹת קְצִיעוֹת כָּל בִּגְדֹתֶיךָ, מִן הֵיכְלֵי שֵׁן מִנִּי שִׂמְּחוּךָ.
יּ בְּנוֹת מְלָכִים בְּיִקְּרוֹתֶיךָ, נִצְּבָה שֵׁגַל לִימִינְךָ בְּכֶתֶם אוֹפִיר. יא שִׁמְעִי בַת

וּרְאִי, וְהַטִּי אָזְנֵךְ; וְשִׁכְחִי עַמֵּךְ וּבֵית אָבִיךְ. יב וְיִתְאָו הַמֶּלֶךְ יָפְיֵךְ; כִּי הוּא אֲדֹנַיִךְ, וְהִשְׁתַּחֲוִי לוֹ. יג וּבַת צֹר, בְּמִנְחָה פָּנַיִךְ יְחַלּוּ עֲשִׁירֵי עָם. יד כָּל כְּבוּדָּה בַת מֶלֶךְ פְּנִימָה, מִמִּשְׁבְּצוֹת זָהָב לְבוּשָׁהּ. טו לִרְקָמוֹת תּוּבַל לַמֶּלֶךְ; בְּתוּלוֹת אַחֲרֶיהָ רֵעוֹתֶיהָ, מוּבָאוֹת לָךְ. טז תּוּבַלְנָה בִּשְׂמָחֹת וָגִיל, תְּבֹאֶינָה בְּהֵיכַל מֶלֶךְ. יז תַּחַת אֲבֹתֶיךָ יִהְיוּ בָנֶיךָ, תְּשִׁיתֵמוֹ לְשָׂרִים בְּכָל הָאָרֶץ. יח אַזְכִּירָה שִׁמְךָ בְּכָל דֹּר וָדֹר, עַל כֵּן עַמִּים יְהוֹדֻךָ לְעֹלָם וָעֶד.

מו א לַמְנַצֵּחַ לִבְנֵי קֹרַח, עַל עֲלָמוֹת שִׁיר. ב אֱלֹהִים לָנוּ מַחֲסֶה וָעֹז, עֶזְרָה בְצָרוֹת, נִמְצָא מְאֹד. ג עַל כֵּן לֹא נִירָא בְּהָמִיר אָרֶץ, וּבְמוֹט הָרִים בְּלֵב יַמִּים. ד יֶהֱמוּ יֶחְמְרוּ מֵימָיו, יִרְעֲשׁוּ הָרִים בְּגַאֲוָתוֹ סֶלָה. ה נָהָר, פְּלָגָיו יְשַׂמְּחוּ עִיר אֱלֹהִים, קְדֹשׁ מִשְׁכְּנֵי עֶלְיוֹן. ו אֱלֹהִים בְּקִרְבָּהּ, בַּל תִּמּוֹט, יַעְזְרֶהָ אֱלֹהִים לִפְנוֹת בֹּקֶר. ז הָמוּ גוֹיִם מָטוּ מַמְלָכוֹת, נָתַן בְּקוֹלוֹ תָּמוּג אָרֶץ. ח יְהוָה צְבָאוֹת עִמָּנוּ, מִשְׂגָּב לָנוּ אֱלֹהֵי יַעֲקֹב סֶלָה. ט לְכוּ חֲזוּ מִפְעֲלוֹת יְהוָה, אֲשֶׁר שָׂם שַׁמּוֹת בָּאָרֶץ. י מַשְׁבִּית מִלְחָמוֹת עַד קְצֵה הָאָרֶץ; קֶשֶׁת יְשַׁבֵּר וְקִצֵּץ חֲנִית, עֲגָלוֹת יִשְׂרֹף בָּאֵשׁ. יא הַרְפּוּ וּדְעוּ כִּי אָנֹכִי אֱלֹהִים; אָרוּם בַּגּוֹיִם, אָרוּם בָּאָרֶץ. יב יְהוָה צְבָאוֹת עִמָּנוּ, מִשְׂגָּב לָנוּ אֱלֹהֵי יַעֲקֹב סֶלָה.

מז א לַמְנַצֵּחַ לִבְנֵי קֹרַח מִזְמוֹר. ב כָּל הָעַמִּים תִּקְעוּ כָף, הָרִיעוּ לֵאלֹהִים בְּקוֹל רִנָּה. ג כִּי יְהוָה עֶלְיוֹן נוֹרָא, מֶלֶךְ גָּדוֹל עַל כָּל הָאָרֶץ. ד יַדְבֵּר עַמִּים תַּחְתֵּינוּ, וּלְאֻמִּים תַּחַת רַגְלֵינוּ. ה יִבְחַר לָנוּ אֶת נַחֲלָתֵנוּ, אֶת גְּאוֹן יַעֲקֹב אֲשֶׁר אָהֵב סֶלָה. ו עָלָה אֱלֹהִים בִּתְרוּעָה, יְהוָה בְּקוֹל שׁוֹפָר. ז זַמְּרוּ אֱלֹהִים זַמֵּרוּ, זַמְּרוּ לְמַלְכֵּנוּ זַמֵּרוּ. ח כִּי מֶלֶךְ כָּל הָאָרֶץ אֱלֹהִים, זַמְּרוּ מַשְׂכִּיל. ט מָלַךְ אֱלֹהִים עַל גּוֹיִם, אֱלֹהִים יָשַׁב עַל כִּסֵּא קָדְשׁוֹ. י נְדִיבֵי עַמִּים נֶאֱסָפוּ, עַם אֱלֹהֵי אַבְרָהָם; כִּי לֵאלֹהִים מָגִנֵּי אֶרֶץ, מְאֹד נַעֲלָה.

מח א שִׁיר מִזְמוֹר לִבְנֵי קֹרַח. ב גָּדוֹל יְהוָה וּמְהֻלָּל מְאֹד, בְּעִיר אֱלֹהֵינוּ, הַר קָדְשׁוֹ. ג יְפֵה נוֹף, מְשׂוֹשׂ כָּל הָאָרֶץ, הַר צִיּוֹן יַרְכְּתֵי צָפוֹן, קִרְיַת מֶלֶךְ רָב. ד אֱלֹהִים בְּאַרְמְנוֹתֶיהָ נוֹדַע לְמִשְׂגָּב. ה כִּי הִנֵּה הַמְּלָכִים נוֹעֲדוּ, עָבְרוּ יַחְדָּו. ו הֵמָּה רָאוּ כֵּן תָּמָהוּ, נִבְהֲלוּ נֶחְפָּזוּ. ז רְעָדָה אֲחָזָתַם שָׁם, חִיל כַּיּוֹלֵדָה. ח בְּרוּחַ קָדִים תְּשַׁבֵּר אֳנִיּוֹת תַּרְשִׁישׁ. ט כַּאֲשֶׁר שָׁמַעְנוּ כֵּן רָאִינוּ בְּעִיר יְהוָה צְבָאוֹת, בְּעִיר אֱלֹהֵינוּ, אֱלֹהִים יְכוֹנְנֶהָ עַד עוֹלָם סֶלָה. י דִּמִּינוּ אֱלֹהִים חַסְדֶּךָ, בְּקֶרֶב הֵיכָלֶךָ. יא כְּשִׁמְךָ אֱלֹהִים, כֵּן תְּהִלָּתְךָ עַל קַצְוֵי אֶרֶץ; צֶדֶק מָלְאָה יְמִינֶךָ. יב יִשְׂמַח הַר צִיּוֹן, תָּגֵלְנָה בְּנוֹת יְהוּדָה, לְמַעַן מִשְׁפָּטֶיךָ. יג סֹבּוּ צִיּוֹן וְהַקִּיפוּהָ, סִפְרוּ מִגְדָּלֶיהָ. יד שִׁיתוּ לִבְּכֶם לְחֵילָה,

פִּסְגּוּ אַרְמְנוֹתֶיהָ, לְמַעַן תְּסַפְּרוּ לְדוֹר אַחֲרוֹן. טּ כִּי זֶה אֱלֹהִים אֱלֹהֵינוּ
עוֹלָם וָעֶד, הוּא יְנַהֲגֵנוּ עַל־מוּת.

DAY 9 / יוֹם ט' לַחֹדֶשׁ

מט א לַמְנַצֵּחַ לִבְנֵי קֹרַח מִזְמוֹר. ב שִׁמְעוּ זֹאת כָּל הָעַמִּים, הַאֲזִינוּ כָּל
יֹשְׁבֵי חָלֶד. ג גַּם בְּנֵי אָדָם, גַּם בְּנֵי אִישׁ; יַחַד עָשִׁיר וְאֶבְיוֹן. ד פִּי יְדַבֵּר
חָכְמוֹת, וְהָגוּת לִבִּי תְבוּנוֹת. ה אַטֶּה לְמָשָׁל אָזְנִי, אֶפְתַּח בְּכִנּוֹר חִידָתִי.
ו לָמָּה אִירָא בִּימֵי רָע, עֲוֹן עֲקֵבַי יְסוּבֵּנִי. ז הַבֹּטְחִים עַל חֵילָם, וּבְרֹב
עָשְׁרָם יִתְהַלָּלוּ. ח אָח לֹא פָדֹה יִפְדֶּה אִישׁ, לֹא יִתֵּן לֵאלֹהִים כָּפְרוֹ. ט וְיֵקַר
פִּדְיוֹן נַפְשָׁם, וְחָדַל לְעוֹלָם. י וִיחִי עוֹד לָנֶצַח, לֹא יִרְאֶה הַשָּׁחַת. יא כִּי
יִרְאֶה חֲכָמִים יָמוּתוּ, יַחַד כְּסִיל וָבַעַר יֹאבֵדוּ, וְעָזְבוּ לַאֲחֵרִים חֵילָם.
יב קִרְבָּם בָּתֵּימוֹ לְעוֹלָם, מִשְׁכְּנֹתָם לְדוֹר וָדֹר; קָרְאוּ בִשְׁמוֹתָם עֲלֵי אֲדָמוֹת.
יג וְאָדָם בִּיקָר בַּל יָלִין, נִמְשַׁל כַּבְּהֵמוֹת נִדְמוּ. יד זֶה דַרְכָּם כֵּסֶל לָמוֹ,
וְאַחֲרֵיהֶם בְּפִיהֶם יִרְצוּ סֶלָה. טו כַּצֹּאן לִשְׁאוֹל שַׁתּוּ, מָוֶת יִרְעֵם; וַיִּרְדּוּ בָם
יְשָׁרִים לַבֹּקֶר, וְצוּרָם לְבַלּוֹת שְׁאוֹל מִזְּבֻל לוֹ. טז אַךְ אֱלֹהִים יִפְדֶּה נַפְשִׁי
מִיַּד שְׁאוֹל, כִּי יִקָּחֵנִי סֶלָה. יז אַל תִּירָא כִּי יַעֲשִׁר אִישׁ, כִּי יִרְבֶּה כְּבוֹד
בֵּיתוֹ. יח כִּי לֹא בְמוֹתוֹ יִקַּח הַכֹּל, לֹא יֵרֵד אַחֲרָיו כְּבוֹדוֹ. יט כִּי נַפְשׁוֹ בְּחַיָּיו
יְבָרֵךְ, וְיוֹדֻךָ כִּי תֵיטִיב לָךְ. כ תָּבוֹא עַד דּוֹר אֲבוֹתָיו, עַד נֵצַח לֹא יִרְאוּ אוֹר.
כא אָדָם בִּיקָר וְלֹא יָבִין, נִמְשַׁל כַּבְּהֵמוֹת נִדְמוּ.

נ א מִזְמוֹר לְאָסָף; אֵל אֱלֹהִים יהוה, דִּבֶּר וַיִּקְרָא אָרֶץ, מִמִּזְרַח שֶׁמֶשׁ עַד
מְבֹאוֹ. ב מִצִּיּוֹן מִכְלַל יֹפִי, אֱלֹהִים הוֹפִיעַ. ג יָבֹא אֱלֹהֵינוּ וְאַל יֶחֱרַשׁ; אֵשׁ
לְפָנָיו תֹּאכֵל, וּסְבִיבָיו נִשְׂעֲרָה מְאֹד. ד יִקְרָא אֶל הַשָּׁמַיִם מֵעָל, וְאֶל הָאָרֶץ
לָדִין עַמּוֹ. ה אִסְפוּ לִי חֲסִידָי, כֹּרְתֵי בְרִיתִי עֲלֵי זָבַח. ו וַיַּגִּידוּ שָׁמַיִם צִדְקוֹ,
כִּי אֱלֹהִים שֹׁפֵט הוּא סֶלָה. ז שִׁמְעָה עַמִּי וַאֲדַבֵּרָה, יִשְׂרָאֵל וְאָעִידָה בָּךְ,
אֱלֹהִים אֱלֹהֶיךָ אָנֹכִי. ח לֹא עַל זְבָחֶיךָ אוֹכִיחֶךָ, וְעוֹלֹתֶיךָ לְנֶגְדִּי תָמִיד.
ט לֹא אֶקַּח מִבֵּיתְךָ פָר, מִמִּכְלְאֹתֶיךָ עַתּוּדִים. י כִּי לִי כָל חַיְתוֹ יָעַר, בְּהֵמוֹת
בְּהַרְרֵי אָלֶף. יא יָדַעְתִּי כָּל עוֹף הָרִים, וְזִיז שָׂדַי עִמָּדִי. יב אִם אֶרְעַב לֹא
אֹמַר לָךְ, כִּי לִי תֵבֵל וּמְלֹאָהּ. יג הַאוֹכַל בְּשַׂר אַבִּירִים, וְדַם עַתּוּדִים
אֶשְׁתֶּה. יד זְבַח לֵאלֹהִים תּוֹדָה, וְשַׁלֵּם לְעֶלְיוֹן נְדָרֶיךָ. טו וּקְרָאֵנִי בְּיוֹם צָרָה,
אֲחַלֶּצְךָ וּתְכַבְּדֵנִי. טז וְלָרָשָׁע אָמַר אֱלֹהִים: מַה לְּךָ לְסַפֵּר חֻקָּי, וַתִּשָּׂא
בְרִיתִי עֲלֵי פִיךָ. יז וְאַתָּה שָׂנֵאתָ מוּסָר, וַתַּשְׁלֵךְ דְּבָרַי אַחֲרֶיךָ. יח אִם רָאִיתָ
גַנָּב וַתִּרֶץ עִמּוֹ, וְעִם מְנָאֲפִים חֶלְקֶךָ. יט פִּיךָ שָׁלַחְתָּ בְרָעָה, וּלְשׁוֹנְךָ
תַּצְמִיד מִרְמָה. כ תֵּשֵׁב בְּאָחִיךָ תְדַבֵּר, בְּבֶן אִמְּךָ תִּתֶּן דֹּפִי. כא אֵלֶּה עָשִׂיתָ

וְהֶחֱרַשְׁתִּי, דִּמִּיתָ הֱיוֹת אֶהְיֶה כָמוֹךָ, אוֹכִיחֲךָ וְאֶעֶרְכָה לְעֵינֶיךָ. כּב בִּינוּ נָא זֹאת שֹׁכְחֵי אֱלוֹהַּ, פֶּן אֶטְרֹף וְאֵין מַצִּיל. כג זֹבֵחַ תּוֹדָה יְכַבְּדָנְנִי; וְשָׂם דֶּרֶךְ, אַרְאֶנּוּ בְּיֵשַׁע אֱלֹהִים.

﴾ יום שלישי / TUESDAY ﴿

נא א לַמְנַצֵּחַ מִזְמוֹר לְדָוִד. ב בְּבוֹא אֵלָיו נָתָן הַנָּבִיא, כַּאֲשֶׁר בָּא אֶל בַּת שֶׁבַע. ג חָנֵּנִי אֱלֹהִים כְּחַסְדֶּךָ, כְּרֹב רַחֲמֶיךָ מְחֵה פְשָׁעָי. ד הֶרֶב כַּבְּסֵנִי מֵעֲוֹנִי, וּמֵחַטָּאתִי טַהֲרֵנִי. ה כִּי פְשָׁעַי אֲנִי אֵדָע, וְחַטָּאתִי נֶגְדִּי תָמִיד. ו לְךָ לְבַדְּךָ חָטָאתִי, וְהָרַע בְּעֵינֶיךָ עָשִׂיתִי; לְמַעַן תִּצְדַּק בְּדָבְרֶךָ, תִּזְכֶּה בְשָׁפְטֶךָ. ז הֵן בְּעָווֹן חוֹלָלְתִּי, וּבְחֵטְא יֶחֱמַתְנִי אִמִּי. ח הֵן אֱמֶת חָפַצְתָּ בַטֻּחוֹת, וּבְסָתֻם חָכְמָה תוֹדִיעֵנִי. ט תְּחַטְּאֵנִי בְאֵזוֹב וְאֶטְהָר, תְּכַבְּסֵנִי וּמִשֶּׁלֶג אַלְבִּין. י תַּשְׁמִיעֵנִי שָׂשׂוֹן וְשִׂמְחָה, תָּגֵלְנָה עֲצָמוֹת דִּכִּיתָ. יא הַסְתֵּר פָּנֶיךָ מֵחֲטָאָי, וְכָל עֲוֹנֹתַי מְחֵה. יב לֵב טָהוֹר בְּרָא לִי אֱלֹהִים, וְרוּחַ נָכוֹן חַדֵּשׁ בְּקִרְבִּי. יג אַל תַּשְׁלִיכֵנִי מִלְּפָנֶיךָ, וְרוּחַ קָדְשְׁךָ אַל תִּקַּח מִמֶּנִּי. יד הָשִׁיבָה לִּי שְׂשׂוֹן יִשְׁעֶךָ, וְרוּחַ נְדִיבָה תִסְמְכֵנִי. טו אֲלַמְּדָה פֹשְׁעִים דְּרָכֶיךָ, וְחַטָּאִים אֵלֶיךָ יָשׁוּבוּ. טז הַצִּילֵנִי מִדָּמִים, אֱלֹהִים אֱלֹהֵי תְּשׁוּעָתִי, תְּרַנֵּן לְשׁוֹנִי צִדְקָתֶךָ. יז אֲדֹנָי שְׂפָתַי תִּפְתָּח, וּפִי יַגִּיד תְּהִלָּתֶךָ. יח כִּי לֹא תַחְפֹּץ זֶבַח וְאֶתֵּנָה, עוֹלָה לֹא תִרְצֶה. יט זִבְחֵי אֱלֹהִים רוּחַ נִשְׁבָּרָה; לֵב נִשְׁבָּר וְנִדְכֶּה, אֱלֹהִים לֹא תִבְזֶה. כ הֵיטִיבָה בִרְצוֹנְךָ אֶת צִיּוֹן, תִּבְנֶה חוֹמוֹת יְרוּשָׁלָיִם. כא אָז תַּחְפֹּץ זִבְחֵי צֶדֶק, עוֹלָה וְכָלִיל; אָז יַעֲלוּ עַל מִזְבַּחֲךָ פָרִים.

נב א לַמְנַצֵּחַ מַשְׂכִּיל לְדָוִד. ב בְּבוֹא דּוֹאֵג הָאֲדֹמִי וַיַּגֵּד לְשָׁאוּל, וַיֹּאמֶר לוֹ, בָּא דָוִד אֶל בֵּית אֲחִימֶלֶךְ. ג מַה תִּתְהַלֵּל בְּרָעָה, הַגִּבּוֹר; חֶסֶד אֵל כָּל הַיּוֹם. ד הַוּוֹת תַּחְשֹׁב לְשׁוֹנֶךָ, כְּתַעַר מְלֻטָּשׁ עֹשֵׂה רְמִיָּה. ה אָהַבְתָּ רָע מִטּוֹב, שֶׁקֶר מִדַּבֵּר צֶדֶק סֶלָה. ו אָהַבְתָּ כָל דִּבְרֵי בָלַע, לְשׁוֹן מִרְמָה. ז גַּם אֵל יִתָּצְךָ לָנֶצַח; יַחְתְּךָ וְיִסָּחֲךָ מֵאֹהֶל, וְשֵׁרֶשְׁךָ מֵאֶרֶץ חַיִּים סֶלָה. ח וְיִרְאוּ צַדִּיקִים וְיִירָאוּ, וְעָלָיו יִשְׂחָקוּ. ט הִנֵּה הַגֶּבֶר לֹא יָשִׂים אֱלֹהִים מָעוּזּוֹ; וַיִּבְטַח בְּרֹב עָשְׁרוֹ, יָעֹז בְּהַוָּתוֹ. י וַאֲנִי כְּזַיִת רַעֲנָן בְּבֵית אֱלֹהִים, בָּטַחְתִּי בְחֶסֶד אֱלֹהִים עוֹלָם וָעֶד. יא אוֹדְךָ לְעוֹלָם כִּי עָשִׂיתָ, וַאֲקַוֶּה שִׁמְךָ כִי טוֹב נֶגֶד חֲסִידֶיךָ.

נג א לַמְנַצֵּחַ עַל מָחֲלַת מַשְׂכִּיל לְדָוִד. ב אָמַר נָבָל בְּלִבּוֹ אֵין אֱלֹהִים; הִשְׁחִיתוּ וְהִתְעִיבוּ עָוֶל, אֵין עֹשֵׂה טוֹב. ג אֱלֹהִים מִשָּׁמַיִם הִשְׁקִיף עַל בְּנֵי אָדָם, לִרְאוֹת הֲיֵשׁ מַשְׂכִּיל דֹּרֵשׁ אֶת אֱלֹהִים. ד כֻּלּוֹ סָג, יַחְדָּו נֶאֱלָחוּ;

אֵין עֹשֵׂה טוֹב, אֵין גַּם אֶחָד. ‏ה הֲלֹא יָדְעוּ פֹּעֲלֵי אָוֶן, אֹכְלֵי עַמִּי אָכְלוּ
לֶחֶם, אֱלֹהִים לֹא קָרָאוּ. ‏ו שָׁם פָּחֲדוּ פַחַד לֹא הָיָה פָחַד; כִּי אֱלֹהִים פִּזַּר
עַצְמוֹת חֹנָךְ, הֱבִשֹׁתָה, כִּי אֱלֹהִים מְאָסָם. ‏ז מִי יִתֵּן מִצִּיּוֹן יְשֻׁעוֹת יִשְׂרָאֵל;
בְּשׁוּב אֱלֹהִים שְׁבוּת עַמּוֹ, יָגֵל יַעֲקֹב יִשְׂמַח יִשְׂרָאֵל.

נד ‏א לַמְנַצֵּחַ בִּנְגִינֹת מַשְׂכִּיל לְדָוִד. ‏ב בְּבוֹא הַזִּיפִים וַיֹּאמְרוּ לְשָׁאוּל: הֲלֹא
דָוִד מִסְתַּתֵּר עִמָּנוּ. ‏ג אֱלֹהִים, בְּשִׁמְךָ הוֹשִׁיעֵנִי, וּבִגְבוּרָתְךָ תְדִינֵנִי.
‏ד אֱלֹהִים, שְׁמַע תְּפִלָּתִי, הַאֲזִינָה לְאִמְרֵי פִי. ‏ה כִּי זָרִים קָמוּ עָלַי, וְעָרִיצִים
בִּקְשׁוּ נַפְשִׁי, לֹא שָׂמוּ אֱלֹהִים לְנֶגְדָּם סֶלָה. ‏ו הִנֵּה אֱלֹהִים עֹזֵר לִי, אֲדֹנָי
בְּסֹמְכֵי נַפְשִׁי. ‏ז יָשִׁיב הָרַע לְשֹׁרְרָי, בַּאֲמִתְּךָ הַצְמִיתֵם. ‏ח בִּנְדָבָה אֶזְבְּחָה
לָּךְ, אוֹדֶה שִּׁמְךָ יהוה כִּי טוֹב. ‏ט כִּי מִכָּל צָרָה הִצִּילָנִי, וּבְאֹיְבַי רָאֲתָה עֵינִי.

נה ‏א לַמְנַצֵּחַ בִּנְגִינֹת מַשְׂכִּיל לְדָוִד. ‏ב הַאֲזִינָה אֱלֹהִים תְּפִלָּתִי, וְאַל
תִּתְעַלַּם מִתְּחִנָּתִי. ‏ג הַקְשִׁיבָה לִּי וַעֲנֵנִי, אָרִיד בְּשִׂיחִי וְאָהִימָה. ‏ד מִקּוֹל
אוֹיֵב, מִפְּנֵי עָקַת רָשָׁע; כִּי יָמִיטוּ עָלַי אָוֶן, וּבְאַף יִשְׂטְמוּנִי. ‏ה לִבִּי יָחִיל
בְּקִרְבִּי, וְאֵימוֹת מָוֶת נָפְלוּ עָלָי. ‏ו יִרְאָה וָרַעַד יָבֹא בִי, וַתְּכַסֵּנִי פַּלָּצוּת.
‏ז וָאֹמַר, מִי יִתֶּן לִי אֵבֶר כַּיּוֹנָה, אָעוּפָה וְאֶשְׁכֹּנָה. ‏ח הִנֵּה אַרְחִיק נְדֹד, אָלִין
בַּמִּדְבָּר סֶלָה. ‏ט אָחִישָׁה מִפְלָט לִי, מֵרוּחַ סֹעָה מִסָּעַר. ‏י בַּלַּע אֲדֹנָי, פַּלַּג
לְשׁוֹנָם; כִּי רָאִיתִי חָמָס וְרִיב בָּעִיר. ‏יא יוֹמָם וָלַיְלָה יְסוֹבְבֻהָ עַל חוֹמֹתֶיהָ,
וְאָוֶן וְעָמָל בְּקִרְבָּהּ. ‏יב הַוּוֹת בְּקִרְבָּהּ, וְלֹא יָמִישׁ מֵרְחֹבָהּ תֹּךְ וּמִרְמָה. ‏יג כִּי
לֹא אוֹיֵב יְחָרְפֵנִי וְאֶשָּׂא, לֹא מְשַׂנְאִי עָלַי הִגְדִּיל וְאֶסָּתֵר מִמֶּנּוּ. ‏יד וְאַתָּה,
אֱנוֹשׁ כְּעֶרְכִּי, אַלּוּפִי וּמְיֻדָּעִי. ‏טו אֲשֶׁר יַחְדָּו נַמְתִּיק סוֹד, בְּבֵית אֱלֹהִים
נְהַלֵּךְ בְּרָגֶשׁ. ‏טז יַשִּׁי מָוֶת עָלֵימוֹ, יֵרְדוּ שְׁאוֹל חַיִּים; כִּי רָעוֹת בִּמְגוּרָם
בְּקִרְבָּם. ‏יז אֲנִי אֶל אֱלֹהִים אֶקְרָא, וַיהוה יוֹשִׁיעֵנִי. ‏יח עֶרֶב וָבֹקֶר וְצָהֳרַיִם
אָשִׂיחָה וְאֶהֱמֶה, וַיִּשְׁמַע קוֹלִי. ‏יט פָּדָה בְשָׁלוֹם נַפְשִׁי מִקְּרָב לִי, כִּי בְרַבִּים
הָיוּ עִמָּדִי. ‏כ יִשְׁמַע אֵל וְיַעֲנֵם, וְיֹשֵׁב קֶדֶם סֶלָה; אֲשֶׁר אֵין חֲלִיפוֹת לָמוֹ,
וְלֹא יָרְאוּ אֱלֹהִים. ‏כא שָׁלַח יָדָיו בִּשְׁלֹמָיו, חִלֵּל בְּרִיתוֹ. ‏כב חָלְקוּ מַחְמָאֹת
פִּיו וּקְרָב לִבּוֹ, רַכּוּ דְבָרָיו מִשֶּׁמֶן, וְהֵמָּה פְתִחוֹת. ‏כג הַשְׁלֵךְ עַל יהוה יְהָבְךָ,
וְהוּא יְכַלְכְּלֶךָ; לֹא יִתֵּן לְעוֹלָם מוֹט לַצַּדִּיק. ‏כד וְאַתָּה אֱלֹהִים, תּוֹרִדֵם
לִבְאֵר שַׁחַת, אַנְשֵׁי דָמִים וּמִרְמָה לֹא יֶחֱצוּ יְמֵיהֶם; וַאֲנִי אֶבְטַח בָּךְ.

נו ‏א לַמְנַצֵּחַ עַל יוֹנַת אֵלֶם רְחֹקִים, לְדָוִד מִכְתָּם, בֶּאֱחֹז אֹתוֹ פְלִשְׁתִּים
בְּגַת. ‏ב חָנֵּנִי אֱלֹהִים כִּי שְׁאָפַנִי אֱנוֹשׁ, כָּל הַיּוֹם לֹחֵם יִלְחָצֵנִי. ‏ג שָׁאֲפוּ
שׁוֹרְרַי כָּל הַיּוֹם, כִּי רַבִּים לֹחֲמִים לִי, מָרוֹם. ‏ד יוֹם אִירָא, אֲנִי אֵלֶיךָ אֶבְטָח.

ה בֵּאלֹהִים אֲהַלֵּל דְּבָרוֹ; בֵּאלֹהִים בָּטַחְתִּי לֹא אִירָא, מַה יַּעֲשֶׂה בָשָׂר לִי.
ו כָּל הַיּוֹם דְּבָרַי יְעַצֵּבוּ, עָלַי כָּל מַחְשְׁבֹתָם לָרָע. ז יָגוּרוּ יִצְפֹּנוּ, הֵמָּה עֲקֵבַי
יִשְׁמֹרוּ, כַּאֲשֶׁר קִוּוּ נַפְשִׁי. ח עַל אָוֶן פַּלֶּט לָמוֹ; בְּאַף עַמִּים הוֹרֵד, אֱלֹהִים.
ט נֹדִי סָפַרְתָּה אָתָּה; שִׂימָה דִמְעָתִי בְנֹאדֶךָ, הֲלֹא בְּסִפְרָתֶךָ. י אָז יָשׁוּבוּ
אוֹיְבַי אָחוֹר בְּיוֹם אֶקְרָא; זֶה יָדַעְתִּי כִּי אֱלֹהִים לִי. יא בֵּאלֹהִים אֲהַלֵּל
דָּבָר, בַּיהוה אֲהַלֵּל דָּבָר. יב בֵּאלֹהִים בָּטַחְתִּי לֹא אִירָא, מַה יַּעֲשֶׂה אָדָם
לִי. יג עָלַי אֱלֹהִים נְדָרֶיךָ, אֲשַׁלֵּם תּוֹדֹת לָךְ. יד כִּי הִצַּלְתָּ נַפְשִׁי מִמָּוֶת, הֲלֹא
רַגְלַי מִדֶּחִי; לְהִתְהַלֵּךְ לִפְנֵי אֱלֹהִים בְּאוֹר הַחַיִּים.

נז א לַמְנַצֵּחַ אַל תַּשְׁחֵת, לְדָוִד מִכְתָּם, בְּבָרְחוֹ מִפְּנֵי שָׁאוּל בַּמְּעָרָה.
ב חָנֵּנִי אֱלֹהִים חָנֵּנִי, כִּי בְךָ חָסָיָה נַפְשִׁי; וּבְצֵל כְּנָפֶיךָ אֶחְסֶה עַד יַעֲבֹר
הַוּוֹת. ג אֶקְרָא לֵאלֹהִים עֶלְיוֹן, לָאֵל גֹּמֵר עָלָי. ד יִשְׁלַח מִשָּׁמַיִם וְיוֹשִׁיעֵנִי
חֵרֵף שֹׁאֲפִי סֶלָה, יִשְׁלַח אֱלֹהִים חַסְדּוֹ וַאֲמִתּוֹ. ה נַפְשִׁי בְּתוֹךְ לְבָאִם,
אֶשְׁכְּבָה לֹהֲטִים; בְּנֵי אָדָם שִׁנֵּיהֶם חֲנִית וְחִצִּים, וּלְשׁוֹנָם חֶרֶב חַדָּה.
ו רוּמָה עַל הַשָּׁמַיִם אֱלֹהִים, עַל כָּל הָאָרֶץ כְּבוֹדֶךָ. ז רֶשֶׁת הֵכִינוּ לִפְעָמַי,
כָּפַף נַפְשִׁי; כָּרוּ לְפָנַי שִׁיחָה, נָפְלוּ בְתוֹכָהּ סֶלָה. ח נָכוֹן לִבִּי, אֱלֹהִים, נָכוֹן
לִבִּי, אָשִׁירָה וַאֲזַמֵּרָה. ט עוּרָה כְבוֹדִי, עוּרָה הַנֵּבֶל וְכִנּוֹר, אָעִירָה שָּׁחַר.
י אוֹדְךָ בָעַמִּים, אֲדֹנָי; אֲזַמֶּרְךָ בַּלְאֻמִּים. יא כִּי גָדֹל עַד שָׁמַיִם חַסְדֶּךָ, וְעַד
שְׁחָקִים אֲמִתֶּךָ. יב רוּמָה עַל שָׁמַיִם, אֱלֹהִים; עַל כָּל הָאָרֶץ כְּבוֹדֶךָ.

נח א לַמְנַצֵּחַ אַל תַּשְׁחֵת, לְדָוִד מִכְתָּם. ב הַאֻמְנָם אֵלֶם צֶדֶק תְּדַבֵּרוּן,
מֵישָׁרִים תִּשְׁפְּטוּ בְּנֵי אָדָם. ג אַף בְּלֵב עוֹלֹת תִּפְעָלוּן, בָּאָרֶץ חֲמַס
יְדֵיכֶם תְּפַלֵּסוּן. ד זֹרוּ רְשָׁעִים מֵרָחֶם, תָּעוּ מִבֶּטֶן דֹּבְרֵי כָזָב. ה חֲמַת לָמוֹ
כִּדְמוּת חֲמַת נָחָשׁ, כְּמוֹ פֶתֶן חֵרֵשׁ יַאְטֵם אָזְנוֹ. ו אֲשֶׁר לֹא יִשְׁמַע לְקוֹל
מְלַחֲשִׁים, חוֹבֵר חֲבָרִים מְחֻכָּם. ז אֱלֹהִים, הֲרָס שִׁנֵּימוֹ בְּפִימוֹ; מַלְתְּעוֹת
כְּפִירִים נְתֹץ, יהוה. ח יִמָּאֲסוּ כְמוֹ מַיִם יִתְהַלְּכוּ לָמוֹ, יִדְרֹךְ חִצָּו כְּמוֹ
יִתְמֹלָלוּ. ט כְּמוֹ שַׁבְּלוּל תֶּמֶס יַהֲלֹךְ, נֵפֶל אֵשֶׁת בַּל חָזוּ שָׁמֶשׁ. י בְּטֶרֶם יָבִינוּ
סִּירֹתֵיכֶם אָטָד, כְּמוֹ חַי כְּמוֹ חָרוֹן יִשְׂעָרֶנּוּ. יא יִשְׂמַח צַדִּיק כִּי חָזָה נָקָם,
פְּעָמָיו יִרְחַץ בְּדַם הָרָשָׁע. יב וְיֹאמַר אָדָם: אַךְ פְּרִי לַצַּדִּיק, אַךְ יֵשׁ אֱלֹהִים
שֹׁפְטִים בָּאָרֶץ.

נט א לַמְנַצֵּחַ אַל תַּשְׁחֵת, לְדָוִד מִכְתָּם; בִּשְׁלֹחַ שָׁאוּל, וַיִּשְׁמְרוּ אֶת הַבַּיִת
לַהֲמִיתוֹ. ב הַצִּילֵנִי מֵאֹיְבַי, אֱלֹהָי; מִמִּתְקוֹמְמַי תְּשַׂגְּבֵנִי. ג הַצִּילֵנִי
מִפֹּעֲלֵי אָוֶן, וּמֵאַנְשֵׁי דָמִים הוֹשִׁיעֵנִי. ד כִּי הִנֵּה אָרְבוּ לְנַפְשִׁי, יָגוּרוּ עָלַי
עַזִּים; לֹא פִשְׁעִי וְלֹא חַטָּאתִי, יהוה. ה בְּלִי עָוֹן יְרֻצוּן וְיִכּוֹנָנוּ, עוּרָה
לִקְרָאתִי וּרְאֵה. ו וְאַתָּה יהוה אֱלֹהִים צְבָאוֹת אֱלֹהֵי יִשְׂרָאֵל, הָקִיצָה

לִפְקֹד כָּל הַגּוֹיִם, אַל תָּחֹן כָּל בֹּגְדֵי אָוֶן סֶלָה. ז יָשׁוּבוּ לָעֶרֶב, יֶהֱמוּ כַכָּלֶב, וִיסוֹבְבוּ עִיר. ח הִנֵּה יַבִּיעוּן בְּפִיהֶם, חֲרָבוֹת בְּשִׂפְתוֹתֵיהֶם, כִּי מִי שֹׁמֵעַ. ט וְאַתָּה יהוה תִּשְׂחַק לָמוֹ, תִּלְעַג לְכָל גּוֹיִם. י עֻזּוֹ, אֵלֶיךָ אֶשְׁמֹרָה, כִּי אֱלֹהִים מִשְׂגַּבִּי. יא אֱלֹהֵי חַסְדִּי יְקַדְּמֵנִי, אֱלֹהִים יַרְאֵנִי בְשֹׁרְרָי. יב אַל תַּהַרְגֵם פֶּן יִשְׁכְּחוּ עַמִּי; הֲנִיעֵמוֹ בְחֵילְךָ וְהוֹרִידֵמוֹ, מָגִנֵּנוּ אֲדֹנָי. יג חַטַּאת פִּימוֹ דְּבַר שְׂפָתֵימוֹ, וְיִלָּכְדוּ בִגְאוֹנָם, וּמֵאָלָה וּמִכַּחַשׁ יְסַפֵּרוּ. יד כַּלֵּה בְחֵמָה, כַּלֵּה וְאֵינֵמוֹ; וְיֵדְעוּ כִּי אֱלֹהִים מֹשֵׁל בְּיַעֲקֹב, לְאַפְסֵי הָאָרֶץ סֶלָה. טו וְיָשֻׁבוּ לָעֶרֶב, יֶהֱמוּ כַכָּלֶב, וִיסוֹבְבוּ עִיר. טז הֵמָּה יְנִיעוּן לֶאֱכֹל, אִם לֹא יִשְׂבְּעוּ וַיָּלִינוּ. יז וַאֲנִי אָשִׁיר עֻזֶּךָ, וַאֲרַנֵּן לַבֹּקֶר חַסְדֶּךָ; כִּי הָיִיתָ מִשְׂגָּב לִי, וּמָנוֹס בְּיוֹם צַר לִי. יח עֻזִּי, אֵלֶיךָ אֲזַמֵּרָה; כִּי אֱלֹהִים מִשְׂגַּבִּי, אֱלֹהֵי חַסְדִּי.

יוֹם י״א לְחֹדֶשׁ / DAY 11

ס א לַמְנַצֵּחַ עַל שׁוּשַׁן עֵדוּת, מִכְתָּם לְדָוִד לְלַמֵּד. ב בְּהַצּוֹתוֹ אֶת אֲרַם נַהֲרַיִם וְאֶת אֲרַם צוֹבָה; וַיָּשָׁב יוֹאָב וַיַּךְ אֶת אֱדוֹם בְּגֵיא מֶלַח, שְׁנֵים עָשָׂר אָלֶף. ג אֱלֹהִים, זְנַחְתָּנוּ פְרַצְתָּנוּ; אָנַפְתָּ, תְּשׁוֹבֵב לָנוּ. ד הִרְעַשְׁתָּה אֶרֶץ פְּצַמְתָּהּ, רְפָה שְׁבָרֶיהָ כִי מָטָה. ה הִרְאִיתָ עַמְּךָ קָשָׁה, הִשְׁקִיתָנוּ יַיִן תַּרְעֵלָה. ו נָתַתָּה לִּירֵאֶיךָ נֵּס לְהִתְנוֹסֵס, מִפְּנֵי קֹשֶׁט סֶלָה. ז לְמַעַן יֵחָלְצוּן יְדִידֶיךָ, הוֹשִׁיעָה יְמִינְךָ וַעֲנֵנִי. ח אֱלֹהִים דִּבֶּר בְּקָדְשׁוֹ אֶעְלֹזָה; אֲחַלְּקָה שְׁכֶם, וְעֵמֶק סֻכּוֹת אֲמַדֵּד. ט לִי גִלְעָד וְלִי מְנַשֶּׁה, וְאֶפְרַיִם מָעוֹז רֹאשִׁי, יְהוּדָה מְחֹקְקִי. י מוֹאָב סִיר רַחְצִי, עַל אֱדוֹם אַשְׁלִיךְ נַעֲלִי, עָלַי פְּלֶשֶׁת הִתְרוֹעָעִי. יא מִי יֹבִלֵנִי עִיר מָצוֹר, מִי נָחַנִי עַד אֱדוֹם. יב הֲלֹא אַתָּה אֱלֹהִים זְנַחְתָּנוּ, וְלֹא תֵצֵא אֱלֹהִים בְּצִבְאוֹתֵינוּ. יג הָבָה לָּנוּ עֶזְרָת מִצָּר, וְשָׁוְא תְּשׁוּעַת אָדָם. יד בֵּאלֹהִים נַעֲשֶׂה חָיִל, וְהוּא יָבוּס צָרֵינוּ.

סא א לַמְנַצֵּחַ עַל נְגִינַת לְדָוִד. ב שִׁמְעָה אֱלֹהִים רִנָּתִי, הַקְשִׁיבָה תְּפִלָּתִי. ג מִקְצֵה הָאָרֶץ אֵלֶיךָ אֶקְרָא בַּעֲטֹף לִבִּי, בְּצוּר יָרוּם מִמֶּנִּי תַנְחֵנִי. ד כִּי הָיִיתָ מַחְסֶה לִי, מִגְדַּל עֹז מִפְּנֵי אוֹיֵב. ה אָגוּרָה בְאָהָלְךָ עוֹלָמִים, אֶחֱסֶה בְסֵתֶר כְּנָפֶיךָ סֶּלָה. ו כִּי אַתָּה אֱלֹהִים שָׁמַעְתָּ לִנְדָרָי, נָתַתָּ יְרֻשַּׁת יִרְאֵי שְׁמֶךָ. ז יָמִים עַל יְמֵי מֶלֶךְ תּוֹסִיף, שְׁנוֹתָיו כְּמוֹ דֹר וָדֹר. ח יֵשֵׁב עוֹלָם לִפְנֵי אֱלֹהִים, חֶסֶד וֶאֱמֶת מַן יִנְצְרֻהוּ. ט כֵּן אֲזַמְּרָה שִׁמְךָ לָעַד, לְשַׁלְּמִי נְדָרַי יוֹם יוֹם.

סב א לַמְנַצֵּחַ עַל יְדוּתוּן מִזְמוֹר לְדָוִד. ב אַךְ אֶל אֱלֹהִים דּוּמִיָּה נַפְשִׁי, מִמֶּנּוּ יְשׁוּעָתִי. ג אַךְ הוּא צוּרִי וִישׁוּעָתִי; מִשְׂגַּבִּי, לֹא אֶמּוֹט רַבָּה. ד עַד אָנָה תְּהוֹתְתוּ עַל אִישׁ, תְּרָצְּחוּ כֻלְּכֶם; כְּקִיר נָטוּי, גָּדֵר הַדְּחוּיָה.

ה אַךְ מִשְּׂאֵתוֹ יָעֲצוּ לְהַדִּיחַ, יִרְצוּ כָזָב; בְּפִיו יְבָרֵכוּ, וּבְקִרְבָּם יְקַלְלוּ סֶלָה. ו אַךְ לֵאלֹהִים דּוֹמִּי נַפְשִׁי, כִּי מִמֶּנּוּ תִּקְוָתִי. ז אַךְ הוּא צוּרִי וִישׁוּעָתִי; מִשְׂגַּבִּי, לֹא אֶמּוֹט. ח עַל אֱלֹהִים יִשְׁעִי וּכְבוֹדִי; צוּר עֻזִּי מַחְסִי, בֵּאלֹהִים. ט בִּטְחוּ בוֹ בְכָל עֵת, עָם, שִׁפְכוּ לְפָנָיו לְבַבְכֶם; אֱלֹהִים מַחֲסֶה לָּנוּ סֶלָה. י אַךְ הֶבֶל בְּנֵי אָדָם, כָּזָב בְּנֵי אִישׁ; בְּמֹאזְנַיִם לַעֲלוֹת, הֵמָּה מֵהֶבֶל יָחַד. יא אַל תִּבְטְחוּ בְעֹשֶׁק, וּבְגָזֵל אַל תֶּהְבָּלוּ; חַיִל כִּי יָנוּב, אַל תָּשִׁיתוּ לֵב. יב אַחַת דִּבֶּר אֱלֹהִים, שְׁתַּיִם זוּ שָׁמָעְתִּי, כִּי עֹז לֵאלֹהִים. יג וּלְךָ אֲדֹנָי חָסֶד, כִּי אַתָּה תְשַׁלֵּם לְאִישׁ כְּמַעֲשֵׂהוּ.

סג א מִזְמוֹר לְדָוִד, בִּהְיוֹתוֹ בְּמִדְבַּר יְהוּדָה. ב אֱלֹהִים אֵלִי אַתָּה, אֲשַׁחֲרֶךָּ; צָמְאָה לְךָ נַפְשִׁי, כָּמַהּ לְךָ בְשָׂרִי, בְּאֶרֶץ צִיָּה וְעָיֵף בְּלִי מָיִם. ג כֵּן בַּקֹּדֶשׁ חֲזִיתִךָ, לִרְאוֹת עֻזְּךָ וּכְבוֹדֶךָ. ד כִּי טוֹב חַסְדְּךָ מֵחַיִּים, שְׂפָתַי יְשַׁבְּחוּנְךָ. ה כֵּן אֲבָרֶכְךָ בְחַיָּי, בְּשִׁמְךָ אֶשָּׂא כַפָּי. ו כְּמוֹ חֵלֶב וָדֶשֶׁן תִּשְׂבַּע נַפְשִׁי, וְשִׂפְתֵי רְנָנוֹת יְהַלֶּל פִּי. ז אִם זְכַרְתִּיךָ עַל יְצוּעָי, בְּאַשְׁמֻרוֹת אֶהְגֶּה בָּךְ. ח כִּי הָיִיתָ עֶזְרָתָה לִּי, וּבְצֵל כְּנָפֶיךָ אֲרַנֵּן. ט דָּבְקָה נַפְשִׁי אַחֲרֶיךָ, בִּי תָּמְכָה יְמִינֶךָ. י וְהֵמָּה לְשׁוֹאָה יְבַקְשׁוּ נַפְשִׁי, יָבֹאוּ בְּתַחְתִּיּוֹת הָאָרֶץ. יא יַגִּירֻהוּ עַל יְדֵי חָרֶב, מְנָת שֻׁעָלִים יִהְיוּ. יב וְהַמֶּלֶךְ יִשְׂמַח בֵּאלֹהִים; יִתְהַלֵּל כָּל הַנִּשְׁבָּע בּוֹ, כִּי יִסָּכֵר פִּי דוֹבְרֵי שָׁקֶר.

סד א לַמְנַצֵּחַ מִזְמוֹר לְדָוִד. ב שְׁמַע אֱלֹהִים קוֹלִי בְשִׂיחִי, מִפַּחַד אוֹיֵב תִּצֹּר חַיָּי. ג תַּסְתִּירֵנִי מִסּוֹד מְרֵעִים, מֵרִגְשַׁת פֹּעֲלֵי אָוֶן. ד אֲשֶׁר שָׁנְנוּ כַחֶרֶב לְשׁוֹנָם, דָּרְכוּ חִצָּם דָּבָר מָר. ה לִירוֹת בַּמִּסְתָּרִים תָּם, פִּתְאֹם יֹרֻהוּ וְלֹא יִירָאוּ. ו יְחַזְּקוּ לָמוֹ דָּבָר רָע, יְסַפְּרוּ לִטְמוֹן מוֹקְשִׁים; אָמְרוּ, מִי יִרְאֶה לָּמוֹ. ז יַחְפְּשׂוּ עוֹלֹת, תַּמְנוּ חֵפֶשׂ מְחֻפָּשׂ, וְקֶרֶב אִישׁ וְלֵב עָמֹק. ח וַיֹּרֵם אֱלֹהִים; חֵץ פִּתְאוֹם הָיוּ מַכּוֹתָם. ט וַיַּכְשִׁילֻהוּ עָלֵימוֹ לְשׁוֹנָם, יִתְנֹדְדוּ כָּל רֹאֵה בָם. י וַיִּירְאוּ כָּל אָדָם; וַיַּגִּידוּ פֹּעַל אֱלֹהִים, וּמַעֲשֵׂהוּ הִשְׂכִּילוּ. יא יִשְׂמַח צַדִּיק בַּיהוה וְחָסָה בוֹ, וְיִתְהַלְלוּ כָּל יִשְׁרֵי לֵב.

סה א לַמְנַצֵּחַ מִזְמוֹר, לְדָוִד שִׁיר. ב לְךָ דֻמִיָּה תְהִלָּה, אֱלֹהִים בְּצִיּוֹן; וּלְךָ יְשֻׁלַּם נֶדֶר. ג שֹׁמֵעַ תְּפִלָּה, עָדֶיךָ כָּל בָּשָׂר יָבֹאוּ. ד דִּבְרֵי עֲוֹנֹת גָּבְרוּ מֶנִּי, פְּשָׁעֵינוּ אַתָּה תְכַפְּרֵם. ה אַשְׁרֵי תִּבְחַר וּתְקָרֵב יִשְׁכֹּן חֲצֵרֶיךָ; נִשְׂבְּעָה בְּטוּב בֵּיתֶךָ, קְדֹשׁ הֵיכָלֶךָ. ו נוֹרָאוֹת בְּצֶדֶק תַּעֲנֵנוּ, אֱלֹהֵי יִשְׁעֵנוּ; מִבְטָח כָּל קַצְוֵי אֶרֶץ וְיָם רְחֹקִים. ז מֵכִין הָרִים בְּכֹחוֹ, נֶאְזָר בִּגְבוּרָה. ח מַשְׁבִּיחַ שְׁאוֹן יַמִּים, שְׁאוֹן גַּלֵּיהֶם, וַהֲמוֹן לְאֻמִּים. ט וַיִּירְאוּ יֹשְׁבֵי קְצָוֹת מֵאוֹתֹתֶיךָ, מוֹצָאֵי בֹקֶר וָעֶרֶב תַּרְנִין. י פָּקַדְתָּ הָאָרֶץ וַתְּשֹׁקְקֶהָ, רַבַּת תַּעְשְׁרֶנָּה פֶּלֶג

אֱלֹהִים מָלֵא מַיִם, תָּכִין דְּגָנָם כִּי כֵן תְּכִינֶהָ. יא תְּלָמֶיהָ רַוֵּה, נַחֵת גְּדוּדֶהָ;
בִּרְבִיבִים תְּמֹגְגֶנָּה, צִמְחָהּ תְּבָרֵךְ; יב עִטַּרְתָּ שְׁנַת טוֹבָתֶךָ, וּמַעְגָּלֶיךָ יִרְעֲפוּן
דָּשֶׁן. יג יִרְעֲפוּ נְאוֹת מִדְבָּר, וְגִיל גְּבָעוֹת תַּחְגֹּרְנָה. יד לָבְשׁוּ כָרִים הַצֹּאן,
וַעֲמָקִים יַעַטְפוּ בָר, יִתְרוֹעֲעוּ אַף יָשִׁירוּ.

יוֹם י״ב לַחֹדֶשׁ / DAY 12

סו א לַמְנַצֵּחַ שִׁיר מִזְמוֹר, הָרִיעוּ לֵאלֹהִים כָּל הָאָרֶץ. ב זַמְּרוּ כְבוֹד שְׁמוֹ,
שִׂימוּ כָבוֹד תְּהִלָּתוֹ. ג אִמְרוּ לֵאלֹהִים: מַה נּוֹרָא מַעֲשֶׂיךָ, בְּרֹב עֻזְּךָ
יְכַחֲשׁוּ לְךָ אֹיְבֶיךָ. ד כָּל הָאָרֶץ יִשְׁתַּחֲווּ לְךָ וִיזַמְּרוּ לָךְ, יְזַמְּרוּ שִׁמְךָ סֶלָה.
ה לְכוּ וּרְאוּ מִפְעֲלוֹת אֱלֹהִים, נוֹרָא עֲלִילָה עַל בְּנֵי אָדָם. ו הָפַךְ יָם לְיַבָּשָׁה,
בַּנָּהָר יַעַבְרוּ בְרָגֶל; שָׁם נִשְׂמְחָה בּוֹ. ז מֹשֵׁל בִּגְבוּרָתוֹ עוֹלָם, עֵינָיו בַּגּוֹיִם
תִּצְפֶּינָה, הַסּוֹרְרִים אַל יָרִימוּ לָמוֹ סֶלָה. ח בָּרְכוּ עַמִּים אֱלֹהֵינוּ, וְהַשְׁמִיעוּ
קוֹל תְּהִלָּתוֹ. ט הַשָּׂם נַפְשֵׁנוּ בַּחַיִּים, וְלֹא נָתַן לַמּוֹט רַגְלֵנוּ. י כִּי בְחַנְתָּנוּ,
אֱלֹהִים; צְרַפְתָּנוּ כִּצְרָף כָּסֶף. יא הֲבֵאתָנוּ בַמְּצוּדָה, שַׂמְתָּ מוּעָקָה
בְמָתְנֵינוּ. יב הִרְכַּבְתָּ אֱנוֹשׁ לְרֹאשֵׁנוּ; בָּאנוּ בָאֵשׁ וּבַמַּיִם, וַתּוֹצִיאֵנוּ
לָרְוָיָה. יג אָבוֹא בֵיתְךָ בְעוֹלוֹת, אֲשַׁלֵּם לְךָ נְדָרָי. יד אֲשֶׁר פָּצוּ שְׂפָתָי,
וְדִבֶּר פִּי בַּצַּר לִי. טו עֹלוֹת מֵחִים אַעֲלֶה לָּךְ עִם קְטֹרֶת אֵילִים, אֶעֱשֶׂה בָקָר
עִם עַתּוּדִים סֶלָה. טז לְכוּ שִׁמְעוּ וַאֲסַפְּרָה כָּל יִרְאֵי אֱלֹהִים, אֲשֶׁר עָשָׂה
לְנַפְשִׁי. יז אֵלָיו, פִּי קָרָאתִי; וְרוֹמַם תַּחַת לְשׁוֹנִי. יח אָוֶן אִם רָאִיתִי בְלִבִּי,
לֹא יִשְׁמַע אֲדֹנָי. יט אָכֵן שָׁמַע אֱלֹהִים, הִקְשִׁיב בְּקוֹל תְּפִלָּתִי. כ בָּרוּךְ
אֱלֹהִים, אֲשֶׁר לֹא הֵסִיר תְּפִלָּתִי וְחַסְדּוֹ מֵאִתִּי.

סז א לַמְנַצֵּחַ בִּנְגִינֹת מִזְמוֹר שִׁיר. ב אֱלֹהִים יְחָנֵּנוּ וִיבָרְכֵנוּ, יָאֵר פָּנָיו אִתָּנוּ
סֶלָה. ג לָדַעַת בָּאָרֶץ דַּרְכֶּךָ, בְּכָל גּוֹיִם יְשׁוּעָתֶךָ. ד יוֹדוּךָ עַמִּים,
אֱלֹהִים; יוֹדוּךָ עַמִּים כֻּלָּם. ה יִשְׂמְחוּ וִירַנְּנוּ לְאֻמִּים, כִּי תִשְׁפֹּט עַמִּים
מִישֹׁר, וּלְאֻמִּים בָּאָרֶץ תַּנְחֵם סֶלָה. ו יוֹדוּךָ עַמִּים, אֱלֹהִים; יוֹדוּךָ עַמִּים
כֻּלָּם. ז אֶרֶץ נָתְנָה יְבוּלָהּ, יְבָרְכֵנוּ אֱלֹהִים אֱלֹהֵינוּ. ח יְבָרְכֵנוּ אֱלֹהִים,
וְיִירְאוּ אוֹתוֹ כָּל אַפְסֵי אָרֶץ.

סח א לַמְנַצֵּחַ לְדָוִד מִזְמוֹר שִׁיר. ב יָקוּם אֱלֹהִים, יָפוּצוּ אוֹיְבָיו, וְיָנוּסוּ
מְשַׂנְאָיו מִפָּנָיו. ג כְּהִנְדֹּף עָשָׁן תִּנְדֹּף; כְּהִמֵּס דּוֹנַג מִפְּנֵי אֵשׁ, יֹאבְדוּ
רְשָׁעִים מִפְּנֵי אֱלֹהִים. ד וְצַדִּיקִים יִשְׂמְחוּ, יַעַלְצוּ לִפְנֵי אֱלֹהִים; וְיָשִׂישׂוּ
בְשִׂמְחָה. ה שִׁירוּ לֵאלֹהִים זַמְּרוּ שְׁמוֹ; סֹלּוּ לָרֹכֵב בָּעֲרָבוֹת בְּיָהּ שְׁמוֹ,
וְעִלְזוּ לְפָנָיו. ו אֲבִי יְתוֹמִים וְדַיַּן אַלְמָנוֹת, אֱלֹהִים בִּמְעוֹן קָדְשׁוֹ. ז אֱלֹהִים
מוֹשִׁיב יְחִידִים בַּיְתָה, מוֹצִיא אֲסִירִים בַּכּוֹשָׁרוֹת אַךְ סוֹרְרִים שָׁכְנוּ

צְחִיחָה. ח אֱלֹהִים, בְּצֵאתְךָ לִפְנֵי עַמֶּךָ, בְּצַעְדְּךָ בִישִׁימוֹן סֶלָה. ט אֶרֶץ
רָעָשָׁה, אַף שָׁמַיִם נָטְפוּ מִפְּנֵי אֱלֹהִים; זֶה סִינַי, מִפְּנֵי אֱלֹהִים אֱלֹהֵי יִשְׂרָאֵל.
י גֶּשֶׁם נְדָבוֹת תָּנִיף אֱלֹהִים; נַחֲלָתְךָ וְנִלְאָה אַתָּה כוֹנַנְתָּהּ. יא חַיָּתְךָ יָשְׁבוּ
בָהּ; תָּכִין בְּטוֹבָתְךָ לֶעָנִי, אֱלֹהִים. יב אֲדֹנָי יִתֶּן אֹמֶר, הַמְבַשְּׂרוֹת צָבָא רָב.
יג מַלְכֵי צְבָאוֹת יִדְּדוּן יִדֹּדוּן, וּנְוַת בַּיִת תְּחַלֵּק שָׁלָל. יד אִם תִּשְׁכְּבוּן בֵּין
שְׁפַתָּיִם; כַּנְפֵי יוֹנָה נֶחְפָּה בַכֶּסֶף, וְאֶבְרוֹתֶיהָ בִּירַקְרַק חָרוּץ. טו בְּפָרֵשׂ שַׁדַּי
מְלָכִים בָּהּ, תַּשְׁלֵג בְּצַלְמוֹן. טז הַר אֱלֹהִים הַר בָּשָׁן, הַר גַּבְנֻנִּים הַר בָּשָׁן.
יז לָמָּה תְּרַצְּדוּן הָרִים גַּבְנֻנִּים; הָהָר חָמַד אֱלֹהִים לְשִׁבְתּוֹ, אַף יהוה יִשְׁכֹּן
לָנֶצַח. יח רֶכֶב אֱלֹהִים רִבֹּתַיִם אַלְפֵי שִׁנְאָן, אֲדֹנָי בָם סִינַי בַּקֹּדֶשׁ. יט עָלִיתָ
לַמָּרוֹם, שָׁבִיתָ שֶּׁבִי, לָקַחְתָּ מַתָּנוֹת בָּאָדָם; וְאַף סוֹרְרִים לִשְׁכֹּן יָהּ אֱלֹהִים.
כ בָּרוּךְ אֲדֹנָי, יוֹם יוֹם יַעֲמָס לָנוּ, הָאֵל יְשׁוּעָתֵנוּ סֶלָה. כא הָאֵל לָנוּ אֵל
לְמוֹשָׁעוֹת; וְלֵיהוִה אֲדֹנָי, לַמָּוֶת תֹּצָאוֹת. כב אַךְ אֱלֹהִים יִמְחַץ רֹאשׁ
אֹיְבָיו, קָדְקֹד שֵׂעָר מִתְהַלֵּךְ בַּאֲשָׁמָיו. כג אָמַר אֲדֹנָי: מִבָּשָׁן אָשִׁיב, אָשִׁיב
מִמְּצֻלוֹת יָם. כד לְמַעַן תִּמְחַץ רַגְלְךָ בְּדָם; לְשׁוֹן כְּלָבֶיךָ, מֵאֹיְבִים מִנֵּהוּ.
כה רָאוּ הֲלִיכוֹתֶיךָ, אֱלֹהִים; הֲלִיכוֹת אֵלִי, מַלְכִּי בַקֹּדֶשׁ. כו קִדְּמוּ שָׁרִים
אַחַר נֹגְנִים, בְּתוֹךְ עֲלָמוֹת תּוֹפֵפוֹת. כז בְּמַקְהֵלוֹת בָּרְכוּ אֱלֹהִים, אֲדֹנָי
מִמְּקוֹר יִשְׂרָאֵל. כח שָׁם בִּנְיָמִן צָעִיר רֹדֵם, שָׂרֵי יְהוּדָה רִגְמָתָם; שָׂרֵי זְבֻלוּן
שָׂרֵי נַפְתָּלִי. כט צִוָּה אֱלֹהֶיךָ עֻזֶּךָ; עוּזָּה אֱלֹהִים, זוּ פָּעַלְתָּ לָּנוּ. ל מֵהֵיכָלֶךָ עַל
יְרוּשָׁלָ͏ִם, לְךָ יוֹבִילוּ מְלָכִים שָׁי. לא גְּעַר חַיַּת קָנֶה, עֲדַת אַבִּירִים בְּעֶגְלֵי
עַמִּים, מִתְרַפֵּס בְּרַצֵּי כָסֶף; בִּזַּר עַמִּים קְרָבוֹת יֶחְפָּצוּ. לב יֶאֱתָיוּ חַשְׁמַנִּים
מִנִּי מִצְרָיִם, כּוּשׁ תָּרִיץ יָדָיו לֵאלֹהִים. לג מַמְלְכוֹת הָאָרֶץ שִׁירוּ לֵאלֹהִים,
זַמְּרוּ אֲדֹנָי סֶלָה. לד לָרֹכֵב בִּשְׁמֵי שְׁמֵי קֶדֶם, הֵן יִתֵּן בְּקוֹלוֹ קוֹל עֹז. לה תְּנוּ עֹז
לֵאלֹהִים; עַל יִשְׂרָאֵל גַּאֲוָתוֹ, וְעֻזּוֹ בַּשְּׁחָקִים. לו נוֹרָא אֱלֹהִים, מִמִּקְדָּשֶׁיךָ;
אֵל יִשְׂרָאֵל הוּא נֹתֵן עֹז וְתַעֲצֻמוֹת לָעָם, בָּרוּךְ אֱלֹהִים.

יום י"ג לחודש / DAY 13

סט א לַמְנַצֵּחַ עַל שׁוֹשַׁנִּים לְדָוִד. ב הוֹשִׁיעֵנִי אֱלֹהִים, כִּי בָאוּ מַיִם עַד
נָפֶשׁ. ג טָבַעְתִּי בִּיוֵן מְצוּלָה וְאֵין מָעֳמָד; בָּאתִי בְמַעֲמַקֵּי מַיִם, וְשִׁבֹּלֶת
שְׁטָפָתְנִי. ד יָגַעְתִּי בְקָרְאִי, נִחַר גְּרוֹנִי; כָּלוּ עֵינַי מְיַחֵל לֵאלֹהָי. ה רַבּוּ
מִשַּׂעֲרוֹת רֹאשִׁי שֹׂנְאַי חִנָּם; עָצְמוּ מַצְמִיתַי אֹיְבַי שֶׁקֶר, אֲשֶׁר לֹא גָזַלְתִּי
אָז אָשִׁיב. ו אֱלֹהִים, אַתָּה יָדַעְתָּ לְאִוַּלְתִּי, וְאַשְׁמוֹתַי מִמְּךָ לֹא נִכְחָדוּ. ז אַל
יֵבֹשׁוּ בִי קֹוֶיךָ, אֲדֹנָי יֱהוִה צְבָאוֹת; אַל יִכָּלְמוּ בִי מְבַקְשֶׁיךָ, אֱלֹהֵי יִשְׂרָאֵל.
ח כִּי עָלֶיךָ נָשָׂאתִי חֶרְפָּה, כִּסְּתָה כְלִמָּה פָנָי. ט מוּזָר הָיִיתִי לְאֶחָי, וְנָכְרִי
לִבְנֵי אִמִּי. י כִּי קִנְאַת בֵּיתְךָ אֲכָלָתְנִי, וְחֶרְפּוֹת חוֹרְפֶיךָ נָפְלוּ עָלָי.

יא וָאֶבְכֶּה בַצּוֹם נַפְשִׁי, וַתְּהִי לַחֲרָפוֹת לִי. יב וָאֶתְּנָה לְבוּשִׁי שָׂק, וָאֱהִי לָהֶם לְמָשָׁל. יג יָשִׂיחוּ בִי יֹשְׁבֵי שָׁעַר, וּנְגִינוֹת שׁוֹתֵי שֵׁכָר. יד וַאֲנִי, תְפִלָּתִי לְךָ יהוה, עֵת רָצוֹן, אֱלֹהִים, בְּרָב חַסְדֶּךָ, עֲנֵנִי בֶּאֱמֶת יִשְׁעֶךָ. טו הַצִּילֵנִי מִטִּיט וְאַל אֶטְבָּעָה, אִנָּצְלָה מִשֹּׂנְאַי וּמִמַּעֲמַקֵּי מָיִם. טז אַל תִּשְׁטְפֵנִי שִׁבֹּלֶת מַיִם, וְאַל תִּבְלָעֵנִי מְצוּלָה, וְאַל תֶּאְטַר עָלַי בְּאֵר פִּיהָ. יז עֲנֵנִי יהוה כִּי טוֹב חַסְדֶּךָ, כְּרֹב רַחֲמֶיךָ פְּנֵה אֵלָי. יח וְאַל תַּסְתֵּר פָּנֶיךָ מֵעַבְדֶּךָ, כִּי צַר לִי, מַהֵר עֲנֵנִי. יט קָרְבָה אֶל נַפְשִׁי גְאָלָהּ, לְמַעַן אֹיְבַי פְּדֵנִי. כ אַתָּה יָדַעְתָּ חֶרְפָּתִי וּבָשְׁתִּי וּכְלִמָּתִי, נֶגְדְּךָ כָּל צוֹרְרָי. כא חֶרְפָּה שָׁבְרָה לִבִּי וָאָנוּשָׁה, וָאֲקַוֶּה לָנוּד וָאַיִן, וְלַמְנַחֲמִים וְלֹא מָצָאתִי. כב וַיִּתְּנוּ בְּבָרוּתִי רֹאשׁ, וְלִצְמָאִי יַשְׁקוּנִי חֹמֶץ. כג יְהִי שֻׁלְחָנָם לִפְנֵיהֶם לְפָח, וְלִשְׁלוֹמִים לְמוֹקֵשׁ. כד תֶּחְשַׁכְנָה עֵינֵיהֶם מֵרְאוֹת, וּמָתְנֵיהֶם תָּמִיד הַמְעַד. כה שְׁפָךְ עֲלֵיהֶם זַעְמֶךָ, וַחֲרוֹן אַפְּךָ יַשִּׂיגֵם. כו תְּהִי טִירָתָם נְשַׁמָּה, בְּאָהֳלֵיהֶם אַל יְהִי יֹשֵׁב. כז כִּי אַתָּה אֲשֶׁר הִכִּיתָ רָדָפוּ, וְאֶל מַכְאוֹב חֲלָלֶיךָ יְסַפֵּרוּ. כח תְּנָה עָוֹן עַל עֲוֹנָם, וְאַל יָבֹאוּ בְּצִדְקָתֶךָ. כט יִמָּחוּ מִסֵּפֶר חַיִּים, וְעִם צַדִּיקִים אַל יִכָּתֵבוּ. ל וַאֲנִי עָנִי וְכוֹאֵב, יְשׁוּעָתְךָ אֱלֹהִים תְּשַׂגְּבֵנִי. לא אֲהַלְלָה שֵׁם אֱלֹהִים בְּשִׁיר, וַאֲגַדְּלֶנּוּ בְתוֹדָה. לב וְתִיטַב לַיהוה מִשּׁוֹר פָּר מַקְרִן מַפְרִיס. לג רָאוּ עֲנָוִים יִשְׂמָחוּ, דֹּרְשֵׁי אֱלֹהִים וִיחִי לְבַבְכֶם. לד כִּי שֹׁמֵעַ אֶל אֶבְיוֹנִים, יהוה, וְאֶת אֲסִירָיו לֹא בָזָה. לה יְהַלְלוּהוּ שָׁמַיִם וָאָרֶץ, יַמִּים וְכָל רֹמֵשׂ בָּם. לו כִּי אֱלֹהִים יוֹשִׁיעַ צִיּוֹן, וְיִבְנֶה עָרֵי יְהוּדָה, וְיָשְׁבוּ שָׁם וִירֵשׁוּהָ. לז וְזֶרַע עֲבָדָיו יִנְחָלוּהָ, וְאֹהֲבֵי שְׁמוֹ יִשְׁכְּנוּ בָהּ.

ע א לַמְנַצֵּחַ לְדָוִד לְהַזְכִּיר. ב אֱלֹהִים לְהַצִּילֵנִי, יהוה, לְעֶזְרָתִי חוּשָׁה. ג יֵבֹשׁוּ וְיַחְפְּרוּ מְבַקְשֵׁי נַפְשִׁי, יִסֹּגוּ אָחוֹר וְיִכָּלְמוּ חֲפֵצֵי רָעָתִי. ד יָשׁוּבוּ עַל עֵקֶב בָּשְׁתָּם, הָאֹמְרִים הֶאָח הֶאָח. ה יָשִׂישׂוּ וְיִשְׂמְחוּ בְּךָ כָּל מְבַקְשֶׁיךָ, וְיֹאמְרוּ תָמִיד יִגְדַּל אֱלֹהִים, אֹהֲבֵי יְשׁוּעָתֶךָ. ו וַאֲנִי עָנִי וְאֶבְיוֹן, אֱלֹהִים חוּשָׁה לִּי, עֶזְרִי וּמְפַלְטִי אַתָּה, יהוה, אַל תְּאַחַר.

עא א בְּךָ יהוה חָסִיתִי, אַל אֵבוֹשָׁה לְעוֹלָם. ב בְּצִדְקָתְךָ תַּצִּילֵנִי וּתְפַלְּטֵנִי, הַטֵּה אֵלַי אָזְנְךָ וְהוֹשִׁיעֵנִי. ג הֱיֵה לִי לְצוּר מָעוֹן לָבוֹא תָּמִיד, צִוִּיתָ לְהוֹשִׁיעֵנִי, כִּי סַלְעִי וּמְצוּדָתִי אָתָּה. ד אֱלֹהַי, פַּלְּטֵנִי מִיַּד רָשָׁע, מִכַּף מְעַוֵּל וְחוֹמֵץ. ה כִּי אַתָּה תִקְוָתִי, אֲדֹנָי יֱהוִה, מִבְטַחִי מִנְּעוּרָי. ו עָלֶיךָ נִסְמַכְתִּי מִבֶּטֶן, מִמְּעֵי אִמִּי אַתָּה גוֹזִי, בְּךָ תְהִלָּתִי תָמִיד. ז כְּמוֹפֵת הָיִיתִי לְרַבִּים, וְאַתָּה מַחֲסִי עֹז. ח יִמָּלֵא פִי תְּהִלָּתֶךָ, כָּל הַיּוֹם תִּפְאַרְתֶּךָ. ט אַל תַּשְׁלִיכֵנִי לְעֵת זִקְנָה, כִּכְלוֹת כֹּחִי אַל תַּעַזְבֵנִי. י כִּי אָמְרוּ אוֹיְבַי לִי, וְשֹׁמְרֵי נַפְשִׁי נוֹעֲצוּ יַחְדָּו. יא לֵאמֹר: אֱלֹהִים עֲזָבוֹ, רִדְפוּ וְתִפְשׂוּהוּ כִּי אֵין מַצִּיל.

יב אֱלֹהִים אַל־תִּרְחַק מִמֶּנִּי, אֱלֹהַי לְעֶזְרָתִי חוּשָׁה. יג יֵבֹשׁוּ יִכְלוּ שֹׂטְנֵי נַפְשִׁי; יַעֲטוּ חֶרְפָּה וּכְלִמָּה, מְבַקְשֵׁי רָעָתִי. יד וַאֲנִי תָּמִיד אֲיַחֵל, וְהוֹסַפְתִּי עַל־כָּל־תְּהִלָּתֶךָ. טו פִּי יְסַפֵּר צִדְקָתֶךָ, כָּל־הַיּוֹם תְּשׁוּעָתֶךָ, כִּי לֹא יָדַעְתִּי סְפֹרוֹת. טז אָבוֹא בִּגְבֻרוֹת אֲדֹנָי יֱהֹוִה, אַזְכִּיר צִדְקָתְךָ לְבַדֶּךָ. יז אֱלֹהִים, לִמַּדְתַּנִי מִנְּעוּרָי; וְעַד־הֵנָּה אַגִּיד נִפְלְאוֹתֶיךָ. יח וְגַם עַד־זִקְנָה וְשֵׂיבָה, אֱלֹהִים אַל־תַּעַזְבֵנִי; עַד־אַגִּיד זְרוֹעֲךָ לְדוֹר, לְכָל־יָבוֹא גְּבוּרָתֶךָ. יט וְצִדְקָתְךָ אֱלֹהִים עַד־מָרוֹם; אֲשֶׁר־עָשִׂיתָ גְדֹלוֹת, אֱלֹהִים מִי כָמוֹךָ. כ אֲשֶׁר הִרְאִיתַנִי צָרוֹת רַבּוֹת וְרָעוֹת, תָּשׁוּב תְּחַיֵּנִי, וּמִתְּהֹמוֹת הָאָרֶץ תָּשׁוּב תַּעֲלֵנִי. כא תֶּרֶב גְּדֻלָּתִי, וְתִסֹּב תְּנַחֲמֵנִי. כב גַּם אֲנִי אוֹדְךָ בִכְלִי־נֶבֶל אֲמִתְּךָ אֱלֹהָי; אֲזַמְּרָה לְךָ בְכִנּוֹר, קְדוֹשׁ יִשְׂרָאֵל. כג תְּרַנֵּנָּה שְׂפָתַי כִּי אֲזַמְּרָה־לָּךְ, וְנַפְשִׁי אֲשֶׁר פָּדִיתָ. כד גַּם־לְשׁוֹנִי כָּל־הַיּוֹם תֶּהְגֶּה צִדְקָתֶךָ, כִּי־בֹשׁוּ כִי־חָפְרוּ מְבַקְשֵׁי רָעָתִי.

יום י״ד לחדש / DAY 14

עב א לִשְׁלֹמֹה, אֱלֹהִים מִשְׁפָּטֶיךָ לְמֶלֶךְ תֵּן, וְצִדְקָתְךָ לְבֶן־מֶלֶךְ. ב יָדִין עַמְּךָ בְצֶדֶק, וַעֲנִיֶּיךָ בְמִשְׁפָּט. ג יִשְׂאוּ הָרִים שָׁלוֹם לָעָם, וּגְבָעוֹת בִּצְדָקָה. ד יִשְׁפֹּט עֲנִיֵּי־עָם, יוֹשִׁיעַ לִבְנֵי אֶבְיוֹן, וִידַכֵּא עוֹשֵׁק. ה יִירָאוּךָ עִם־שָׁמֶשׁ, וְלִפְנֵי יָרֵחַ, דּוֹר דּוֹרִים. ו יֵרֵד כְּמָטָר עַל־גֵּז, כִּרְבִיבִים זַרְזִיף אָרֶץ. ז יִפְרַח־בְּיָמָיו צַדִּיק, וְרֹב שָׁלוֹם עַד־בְּלִי יָרֵחַ. ח וְיֵרְדְּ מִיָּם עַד־יָם, וּמִנָּהָר עַד־אַפְסֵי־אָרֶץ. ט לְפָנָיו יִכְרְעוּ צִיִּים, וְאֹיְבָיו עָפָר יְלַחֵכוּ. י מַלְכֵי תַרְשִׁישׁ וְאִיִּים מִנְחָה יָשִׁיבוּ, מַלְכֵי שְׁבָא וּסְבָא אֶשְׁכָּר יַקְרִיבוּ. יא וְיִשְׁתַּחֲווּ־לוֹ כָל־מְלָכִים, כָּל־גּוֹיִם יַעַבְדוּהוּ. יב כִּי־יַצִּיל אֶבְיוֹן מְשַׁוֵּעַ, וְעָנִי וְאֵין עֹזֵר לוֹ. יג יָחֹס עַל־דַּל וְאֶבְיוֹן, וְנַפְשׁוֹת אֶבְיוֹנִים יוֹשִׁיעַ. יד מִתּוֹךְ וּמֵחָמָס יִגְאַל נַפְשָׁם, וְיֵיקַר דָּמָם בְּעֵינָיו. טו וִיחִי, וְיִתֶּן־לוֹ מִזְּהַב שְׁבָא, וְיִתְפַּלֵּל בַּעֲדוֹ תָמִיד, כָּל־הַיּוֹם יְבָרְכֶנְהוּ. טז יְהִי פִסַּת־בַּר בָּאָרֶץ בְּרֹאשׁ הָרִים, יִרְעַשׁ כַּלְּבָנוֹן פִּרְיוֹ, וְיָצִיצוּ מֵעִיר כְּעֵשֶׂב הָאָרֶץ. יז יְהִי שְׁמוֹ לְעוֹלָם, לִפְנֵי־שֶׁמֶשׁ יִנּוֹן שְׁמוֹ; וְיִתְבָּרְכוּ בוֹ, כָּל־גּוֹיִם יְאַשְּׁרוּהוּ. יח בָּרוּךְ יְהוָה אֱלֹהִים אֱלֹהֵי יִשְׂרָאֵל, עֹשֵׂה נִפְלָאוֹת לְבַדּוֹ. יט וּבָרוּךְ שֵׁם כְּבוֹדוֹ לְעוֹלָם, וְיִמָּלֵא כְבוֹדוֹ אֶת־כֹּל הָאָרֶץ, אָמֵן וְאָמֵן. כ כָּלּוּ תְפִלּוֹת, דָּוִד בֶּן־יִשָׁי.

ספר שלישי / BOOK THREE
יום רביעי / WEDNESDAY ﴾

עג א מִזְמוֹר לְאָסָף, אַךְ טוֹב לְיִשְׂרָאֵל אֱלֹהִים, לְבָרֵי לֵבָב. ב וַאֲנִי כִּמְעַט נָטָיוּ רַגְלָי, כְּאַיִן שֻׁפְּכוּ אֲשֻׁרָי. ג כִּי־קִנֵּאתִי בַּהוֹלְלִים, שְׁלוֹם רְשָׁעִים אֶרְאֶה. ד כִּי אֵין חַרְצֻבּוֹת לְמוֹתָם, וּבָרִיא אוּלָם. ה בַּעֲמַל אֱנוֹשׁ אֵינֵמוֹ, וְעִם

אָדָם לֹא יְנֻגָּעוּ. ו לָכֵן עֲנָקַתְמוֹ גַאֲוָה, יַעֲטָף שִׁית חָמָס לָמוֹ. ז יָצָא מֵחֵלֶב
עֵינֵמוֹ, עָבְרוּ מַשְׂכִּיּוֹת לֵבָב. ח יָמִיקוּ וִידַבְּרוּ בְרָע עֹשֶׁק, מִמָּרוֹם יְדַבֵּרוּ.
ט שַׁתּוּ בַשָּׁמַיִם פִּיהֶם, וּלְשׁוֹנָם תִּהֲלַךְ בָּאָרֶץ. י לָכֵן יָשׁוּב עַמּוֹ הֲלֹם, וּמֵי
מָלֵא יִמָּצוּ לָמוֹ. יא וְאָמְרוּ: אֵיכָה יָדַע אֵל, וְיֵשׁ דֵּעָה בְעֶלְיוֹן. יב הִנֵּה אֵלֶּה
רְשָׁעִים, וְשַׁלְוֵי עוֹלָם הִשְׂגּוּ חָיִל. יג אַךְ רִיק זִכִּיתִי לְבָבִי, וָאֶרְחַץ בְּנִקָּיוֹן
כַּפָּי. יד וָאֱהִי נָגוּעַ כָּל הַיּוֹם, וְתוֹכַחְתִּי לַבְּקָרִים. טו אִם אָמַרְתִּי אֲסַפְּרָה כְמוֹ,
הִנֵּה דוֹר בָּנֶיךָ בָגָדְתִּי. טז וָאֲחַשְּׁבָה לָדַעַת זֹאת, עָמָל הוּא בְעֵינָי. יז עַד
אָבוֹא אֶל מִקְדְּשֵׁי אֵל, אָבִינָה לְאַחֲרִיתָם. יח אַךְ בַּחֲלָקוֹת תָּשִׁית לָמוֹ,
הִפַּלְתָּם לְמַשּׁוּאוֹת. יט אֵיךְ הָיוּ לְשַׁמָּה כְרָגַע, סָפוּ תַמּוּ מִן בַּלָּהוֹת.
כ כַּחֲלוֹם מֵהָקִיץ; אֲדֹנָי, בָּעִיר צַלְמָם תִּבְזֶה. כא כִּי יִתְחַמֵּץ לְבָבִי, וְכִלְיוֹתַי
אֶשְׁתּוֹנָן. כב וַאֲנִי בַעַר וְלֹא אֵדָע, בְּהֵמוֹת הָיִיתִי עִמָּךְ. כג וַאֲנִי תָמִיד עִמָּךְ,
אָחַזְתָּ בְּיַד יְמִינִי. כד בַּעֲצָתְךָ תַנְחֵנִי; וְאַחַר, כָּבוֹד תִּקָּחֵנִי. כה מִי לִי בַשָּׁמַיִם,
וְעִמְּךָ לֹא חָפַצְתִּי בָאָרֶץ. כו כָּלָה שְׁאֵרִי וּלְבָבִי, צוּר לְבָבִי וְחֶלְקִי אֱלֹהִים
לְעוֹלָם. כז כִּי הִנֵּה רְחֵקֶיךָ יֹאבֵדוּ, הִצְמַתָּה כָּל זוֹנֶה מִמֶּךָּ. כח וַאֲנִי, קִרֲבַת
אֱלֹהִים לִי טוֹב; שַׁתִּי בַּאדֹנָי יֱהֹוִה מַחְסִי, לְסַפֵּר כָּל מַלְאֲכוֹתֶיךָ.

עד א מַשְׂכִּיל לְאָסָף, לָמָה אֱלֹהִים זָנַחְתָּ לָנֶצַח, יֶעְשַׁן אַפְּךָ בְּצֹאן
מַרְעִיתֶךָ. ב זְכֹר עֲדָתְךָ קָנִיתָ קֶּדֶם, גָּאַלְתָּ שֵׁבֶט נַחֲלָתֶךָ; הַר צִיּוֹן, זֶה
שָׁכַנְתָּ בּוֹ. ג הָרִימָה פְעָמֶיךָ לְמַשֻּׁאוֹת נֶצַח, כָּל הֵרַע אוֹיֵב בַּקֹּדֶשׁ. ד שָׁאֲגוּ
צֹרְרֶיךָ בְּקֶרֶב מוֹעֲדֶךָ, שָׂמוּ אוֹתֹתָם אֹתוֹת. ה יִוָּדַע כְּמֵבִיא לְמָעְלָה, בִּסְבָךְ
עֵץ קַרְדֻּמּוֹת. ו וְעַתָּ פִּתּוּחֶיהָ יָּחַד, בְּכַשִּׁיל וְכֵילַפּוֹת יַהֲלֹמוּן. ז שִׁלְחוּ בָאֵשׁ
מִקְדָּשֶׁךָ, לָאָרֶץ חִלְּלוּ מִשְׁכַּן שְׁמֶךָ. ח אָמְרוּ בְלִבָּם, נִינָם יָחַד, שָׂרְפוּ כָל
מוֹעֲדֵי אֵל בָּאָרֶץ. ט אוֹתֹתֵינוּ לֹא רָאִינוּ, אֵין עוֹד נָבִיא, וְלֹא אִתָּנוּ יֹדֵעַ עַד
מָה. י עַד מָתַי אֱלֹהִים יְחָרֶף צָר, יְנָאֵץ אוֹיֵב שִׁמְךָ לָנֶצַח. יא לָמָּה תָשִׁיב
יָדְךָ וִימִינֶךָ, מִקֶּרֶב חֵיקְךָ כַלֵּה. יב וֵאלֹהִים מַלְכִּי מִקֶּדֶם, פֹּעֵל יְשׁוּעוֹת
בְּקֶרֶב הָאָרֶץ. יג אַתָּה פוֹרַרְתָּ בְעָזְּךָ יָם, שִׁבַּרְתָּ רָאשֵׁי תַנִּינִים עַל הַמָּיִם.
יד אַתָּה רִצַּצְתָּ רָאשֵׁי לִוְיָתָן, תִּתְּנֶנּוּ מַאֲכָל לְעָם לְצִיִּים. טו אַתָּה בָקַעְתָּ
מַעְיָן וָנָחַל, אַתָּה הוֹבַשְׁתָּ נַהֲרוֹת אֵיתָן. טז לְךָ יוֹם אַף לְךָ לָיְלָה, אַתָּה
הֲכִינוֹתָ מָאוֹר וָשָׁמֶשׁ. יז אַתָּה הִצַּבְתָּ כָּל גְּבוּלוֹת אָרֶץ, קַיִץ וָחֹרֶף אַתָּה
יְצַרְתָּם. יח זְכָר זֹאת: אוֹיֵב חֵרֵף יְהֹוָה, וְעַם נָבָל נִאֲצוּ שְׁמֶךָ. יט אַל תִּתֵּן
לְחַיַּת נֶפֶשׁ תּוֹרֶךָ, חַיַּת עֲנִיֶּיךָ אַל תִּשְׁכַּח לָנֶצַח. כ הַבֵּט לַבְּרִית, כִּי מָלְאוּ
מַחֲשַׁכֵּי אֶרֶץ נְאוֹת חָמָס. כא אַל יָשֹׁב דַּךְ נִכְלָם, עָנִי וְאֶבְיוֹן יְהַלְלוּ שְׁמֶךָ.
כב קוּמָה אֱלֹהִים רִיבָה רִיבֶךָ, זְכֹר חֶרְפָּתְךָ מִנִּי נָבָל כָּל הַיּוֹם. כג אַל תִּשְׁכַּח
קוֹל צֹרְרֶיךָ, שְׁאוֹן קָמֶיךָ עֹלֶה תָמִיד.

עה א לַמְנַצֵּחַ אַל תַּשְׁחֵת, מִזְמוֹר לְאָסָף שִׁיר. ב הוֹדִינוּ לְךָ אֱלֹהִים, הוֹדִינוּ וְקָרוֹב שְׁמֶךָ, סִפְּרוּ נִפְלְאוֹתֶיךָ. ג כִּי אֶקַּח מוֹעֵד, אֲנִי מֵישָׁרִים אֶשְׁפֹּט. ד נְמוֹגִים אֶרֶץ וְכָל יֹשְׁבֶיהָ, אָנֹכִי תִכַּנְתִּי עַמּוּדֶיהָ סֶּלָה. ה אָמַרְתִּי לַהוֹלְלִים אַל תָּהֹלּוּ, וְלָרְשָׁעִים אַל תָּרִימוּ קָרֶן. ו אַל תָּרִימוּ לַמָּרוֹם קַרְנְכֶם, תְּדַבְּרוּ בְצַוָּאר עָתָק. ז כִּי לֹא מִמּוֹצָא וּמִמַּעֲרָב, וְלֹא מִמִּדְבָּר הָרִים. ח כִּי אֱלֹהִים שֹׁפֵט, זֶה יַשְׁפִּיל וְזֶה יָרִים. ט כִּי כוֹס בְּיַד יהוה, וְיַיִן חָמַר מָלֵא מֶסֶךְ, וַיַּגֵּר מִזֶּה; אַךְ שְׁמָרֶיהָ יִמְצוּ יִשְׁתּוּ כֹּל רִשְׁעֵי אָרֶץ. י וַאֲנִי אַגִּיד לְעֹלָם, אֲזַמְּרָה לֵאלֹהֵי יַעֲקֹב. יא וְכָל קַרְנֵי רְשָׁעִים אֲגַדֵּעַ, תְּרוֹמַמְנָה קַרְנוֹת צַדִּיק.

עו א לַמְנַצֵּחַ בִּנְגִינֹת, מִזְמוֹר לְאָסָף שִׁיר. ב נוֹדָע בִּיהוּדָה אֱלֹהִים, בְּיִשְׂרָאֵל גָּדוֹל שְׁמוֹ. ג וַיְהִי בְשָׁלֵם סוּכּוֹ, וּמְעוֹנָתוֹ בְצִיּוֹן. ד שָׁמָּה שִׁבַּר רִשְׁפֵי קָשֶׁת, מָגֵן וְחֶרֶב וּמִלְחָמָה סֶלָה. ה נָאוֹר אַתָּה, אַדִּיר מֵהַרְרֵי טָרֶף. ו אֶשְׁתּוֹלְלוּ אַבִּירֵי לֵב, נָמוּ שְׁנָתָם, וְלֹא מָצְאוּ כָל אַנְשֵׁי חַיִל יְדֵיהֶם. ז מִגַּעֲרָתְךָ אֱלֹהֵי יַעֲקֹב, נִרְדָּם וְרֶכֶב וָסוּס. ח אַתָּה נוֹרָא אַתָּה, וּמִי יַעֲמֹד לְפָנֶיךָ מֵאָז אַפֶּךָ. ט מִשָּׁמַיִם הִשְׁמַעְתָּ דִּין, אֶרֶץ יָרְאָה וְשָׁקָטָה. י בְּקוּם לַמִּשְׁפָּט אֱלֹהִים, לְהוֹשִׁיעַ כָּל עַנְוֵי אֶרֶץ סֶלָה. יא כִּי חֲמַת אָדָם תּוֹדֶךָּ, שְׁאֵרִית חֵמֹת תַּחְגֹּר. יב נִדְרוּ וְשַׁלְּמוּ לַיהוה אֱלֹהֵיכֶם; כָּל סְבִיבָיו, יֹבִילוּ שַׁי לַמּוֹרָא. יג יִבְצֹר רוּחַ נְגִידִים, נוֹרָא לְמַלְכֵי אָרֶץ.

יום ט"ו לחודש / DAY 15

עז א לַמְנַצֵּחַ עַל יְדוּתוּן לְאָסָף מִזְמוֹר. ב קוֹלִי אֶל אֱלֹהִים וְאֶצְעָקָה; קוֹלִי אֶל אֱלֹהִים, וְהַאֲזִין אֵלָי. ג בְּיוֹם צָרָתִי אֲדֹנָי דָּרָשְׁתִּי; יָדִי לַיְלָה נִגְּרָה וְלֹא תָפוּג, מֵאֲנָה הִנָּחֵם נַפְשִׁי. ד אֶזְכְּרָה אֱלֹהִים וְאֶהֱמָיָה, אָשִׂיחָה וְתִתְעַטֵּף רוּחִי סֶלָה. ה אָחַזְתָּ שְׁמֻרוֹת עֵינָי, נִפְעַמְתִּי וְלֹא אֲדַבֵּר. ו חִשַּׁבְתִּי יָמִים מִקֶּדֶם, שְׁנוֹת עוֹלָמִים. ז אֶזְכְּרָה נְגִינָתִי בַּלָּיְלָה; עִם לְבָבִי אָשִׂיחָה, וַיְחַפֵּשׂ רוּחִי. ח הַלְעוֹלָמִים יִזְנַח אֲדֹנָי, וְלֹא יֹסִיף לִרְצוֹת עוֹד. ט הֶאָפֵס לָנֶצַח חַסְדּוֹ, גָּמַר אֹמֶר לְדֹר וָדֹר. י הֲשָׁכַח חַנּוֹת אֵל, אִם קָפַץ בְּאַף רַחֲמָיו סֶלָה. יא וָאֹמַר: חַלּוֹתִי הִיא, שְׁנוֹת יְמִין עֶלְיוֹן. יב אֶזְכּוֹר מַעַלְלֵי יָהּ, כִּי אֶזְכְּרָה מִקֶּדֶם פִּלְאֶךָ. יג וְהָגִיתִי בְכָל פָּעֳלֶךָ, וּבַעֲלִילוֹתֶיךָ אָשִׂיחָה. יד אֱלֹהִים בַּקֹּדֶשׁ דַּרְכֶּךָ, מִי אֵל גָּדוֹל כֵּאלֹהִים. טו אַתָּה הָאֵל עֹשֵׂה פֶלֶא, הוֹדַעְתָּ בָעַמִּים עֻזֶּךָ. טז גָּאַלְתָּ בִּזְרוֹעַ עַמֶּךָ, בְּנֵי יַעֲקֹב וְיוֹסֵף סֶלָה. יז רָאוּךָ מַּיִם אֱלֹהִים, רָאוּךָ מַּיִם יָחִילוּ, אַף יִרְגְּזוּ תְהֹמוֹת. יח זֹרְמוּ מַיִם עָבוֹת, קוֹל נָתְנוּ שְׁחָקִים, אַף חֲצָצֶיךָ יִתְהַלָּכוּ. יט קוֹל רַעַמְךָ בַּגַּלְגַּל, הֵאִירוּ בְרָקִים

תֵּבֵל, רָגְזָה וַתִּרְעַשׁ הָאָרֶץ. כ בַּיָּם דַּרְכֶּךָ, וּשְׁבִילְךָ בְּמַיִם רַבִּים; וְעִקְּבוֹתֶיךָ לֹא נֹדָעוּ. כא נָחִיתָ כַצֹּאן עַמֶּךָ, בְּיַד מֹשֶׁה וְאַהֲרֹן.

עח א מַשְׂכִּיל לְאָסָף, הַאֲזִינָה עַמִּי תּוֹרָתִי, הַטּוּ אָזְנְכֶם לְאִמְרֵי פִי. ב אֶפְתְּחָה בְמָשָׁל פִּי, אַבִּיעָה חִידוֹת מִנִּי קֶדֶם. ג אֲשֶׁר שָׁמַעְנוּ וַנֵּדָעֵם, וַאֲבוֹתֵינוּ סִפְּרוּ לָנוּ. ד לֹא נְכַחֵד מִבְּנֵיהֶם, לְדוֹר אַחֲרוֹן מְסַפְּרִים תְּהִלּוֹת יְהוָה, וֶעֱזוּזוֹ וְנִפְלְאוֹתָיו אֲשֶׁר עָשָׂה. ה וַיָּקֶם עֵדוּת בְּיַעֲקֹב, וְתוֹרָה שָׂם בְּיִשְׂרָאֵל, אֲשֶׁר צִוָּה אֶת אֲבוֹתֵינוּ לְהוֹדִיעָם לִבְנֵיהֶם. ו לְמַעַן יֵדְעוּ דּוֹר אַחֲרוֹן, בָּנִים יִוָּלֵדוּ, יָקֻמוּ וִיסַפְּרוּ לִבְנֵיהֶם. ז וְיָשִׂימוּ בֵאלֹהִים כִּסְלָם, וְלֹא יִשְׁכְּחוּ מַעַלְלֵי אֵל, וּמִצְוֹתָיו יִנְצֹרוּ. ח וְלֹא יִהְיוּ כַּאֲבוֹתָם, דּוֹר סוֹרֵר וּמֹרֶה; דּוֹר לֹא הֵכִין לִבּוֹ, וְלֹא נֶאֶמְנָה אֶת אֵל רוּחוֹ. ט בְּנֵי אֶפְרַיִם נוֹשְׁקֵי רוֹמֵי קָשֶׁת, הָפְכוּ בְּיוֹם קְרָב. י לֹא שָׁמְרוּ בְּרִית אֱלֹהִים, וּבְתוֹרָתוֹ מֵאֲנוּ לָלֶכֶת. יא וַיִּשְׁכְּחוּ עֲלִילוֹתָיו, וְנִפְלְאוֹתָיו אֲשֶׁר הֶרְאָם. יב נֶגֶד אֲבוֹתָם עָשָׂה פֶלֶא, בְּאֶרֶץ מִצְרַיִם שְׂדֵה צֹעַן. יג בָּקַע יָם וַיַּעֲבִירֵם, וַיַּצֶּב מַיִם כְּמוֹ נֵד. יד וַיַּנְחֵם בֶּעָנָן יוֹמָם, וְכָל הַלַּיְלָה בְּאוֹר אֵשׁ. טו יְבַקַּע צֻרִים בַּמִּדְבָּר, וַיַּשְׁקְ כִּתְהֹמוֹת רַבָּה. טז וַיּוֹצִא נוֹזְלִים מִסָּלַע, וַיּוֹרֶד כַּנְּהָרוֹת מָיִם. יז וַיּוֹסִיפוּ עוֹד לַחֲטֹא לוֹ, לַמְרוֹת עֶלְיוֹן בַּצִּיָּה. יח וַיְנַסּוּ אֵל בִּלְבָבָם, לִשְׁאָל אֹכֶל לְנַפְשָׁם. יט וַיְדַבְּרוּ בֵּאלֹהִים; אָמְרוּ, הֲיוּכַל אֵל לַעֲרֹךְ שֻׁלְחָן בַּמִּדְבָּר. כ הֵן הִכָּה צוּר וַיָּזוּבוּ מַיִם, וּנְחָלִים יִשְׁטֹפוּ; הֲגַם לֶחֶם יוּכַל תֵּת, אִם יָכִין שְׁאֵר לְעַמּוֹ. כא לָכֵן שָׁמַע יְהוָה וַיִּתְעַבָּר; וְאֵשׁ נִשְּׂקָה בְיַעֲקֹב, וְגַם אַף עָלָה בְיִשְׂרָאֵל. כב כִּי לֹא הֶאֱמִינוּ בֵּאלֹהִים, וְלֹא בָטְחוּ בִּישׁוּעָתוֹ. כג וַיְצַו שְׁחָקִים מִמָּעַל, וְדַלְתֵי שָׁמַיִם פָּתָח. כד וַיַּמְטֵר עֲלֵיהֶם מָן לֶאֱכֹל, וּדְגַן שָׁמַיִם נָתַן לָמוֹ. כה לֶחֶם אַבִּירִים אָכַל אִישׁ, צֵידָה שָׁלַח לָהֶם לָשֹׂבַע. כו יַסַּע קָדִים בַּשָּׁמָיִם, וַיְנַהֵג בְּעֻזּוֹ תֵימָן. כז וַיַּמְטֵר עֲלֵיהֶם כֶּעָפָר שְׁאֵר, וּכְחוֹל יַמִּים עוֹף כָּנָף. כח וַיַּפֵּל בְּקֶרֶב מַחֲנֵהוּ, סָבִיב לְמִשְׁכְּנֹתָיו. כט וַיֹּאכְלוּ וַיִּשְׂבְּעוּ מְאֹד, וְתַאֲוָתָם יָבִא לָהֶם. ל לֹא זָרוּ מִתַּאֲוָתָם, עוֹד אָכְלָם בְּפִיהֶם. לא וְאַף אֱלֹהִים עָלָה בָהֶם, וַיַּהֲרֹג בְּמִשְׁמַנֵּיהֶם, וּבַחוּרֵי יִשְׂרָאֵל הִכְרִיעַ. לב בְּכָל זֹאת חָטְאוּ עוֹד, וְלֹא הֶאֱמִינוּ בְּנִפְלְאוֹתָיו. לג וַיְכַל בַּהֶבֶל יְמֵיהֶם, וּשְׁנוֹתָם בַּבֶּהָלָה. לד אִם הֲרָגָם וּדְרָשׁוּהוּ, וְשָׁבוּ וְשִׁחֲרוּ אֵל. לה וַיִּזְכְּרוּ כִּי אֱלֹהִים צוּרָם, וְאֵל עֶלְיוֹן גֹּאֲלָם. לו וַיְפַתּוּהוּ בְּפִיהֶם, וּבִלְשׁוֹנָם יְכַזְּבוּ לוֹ. לז וְלִבָּם לֹא נָכוֹן עִמּוֹ, וְלֹא נֶאֶמְנוּ בִּבְרִיתוֹ. לח וְהוּא רַחוּם, יְכַפֵּר עָוֹן וְלֹא יַשְׁחִית; וְהִרְבָּה לְהָשִׁיב אַפּוֹ, וְלֹא יָעִיר כָּל חֲמָתוֹ. לט וַיִּזְכֹּר כִּי בָשָׂר הֵמָּה, רוּחַ הוֹלֵךְ וְלֹא יָשׁוּב. מ כַּמָּה יַמְרוּהוּ בַמִּדְבָּר, יַעֲצִיבוּהוּ בִּישִׁימוֹן. מא וַיָּשׁוּבוּ וַיְנַסּוּ אֵל, וּקְדוֹשׁ יִשְׂרָאֵל הִתְווּ. מב לֹא זָכְרוּ אֶת יָדוֹ, יוֹם אֲשֶׁר פָּדָם מִנִּי צָר. מג אֲשֶׁר שָׂם בְּמִצְרַיִם

אֹתוֹתָיו, וּמוֹפְתָיו בִּשְׂדֵה צֹעַן. מד וַיַּהֲפֹךְ לְדָם יְאֹרֵיהֶם, וְנֹזְלֵיהֶם בַּל יִשְׁתָּיוּן. מה יְשַׁלַּח בָּהֶם עָרֹב וַיֹּאכְלֵם, וּצְפַרְדֵּעַ וַתַּשְׁחִיתֵם. מו וַיִּתֵּן לֶחָסִיל יְבוּלָם, וִיגִיעָם לָאַרְבֶּה. מז יַהֲרֹג בַּבָּרָד גַּפְנָם, וְשִׁקְמוֹתָם בַּחֲנָמַל. מח וַיַּסְגֵּר לַבָּרָד בְּעִירָם, וּמִקְנֵיהֶם לָרְשָׁפִים. מט יְשַׁלַּח בָּם חֲרוֹן אַפּוֹ, עֶבְרָה וָזַעַם וְצָרָה, מִשְׁלַחַת מַלְאֲכֵי רָעִים. נ יְפַלֵּס נָתִיב לְאַפּוֹ; לֹא חָשַׂךְ מִמָּוֶת נַפְשָׁם, וְחַיָּתָם לַדֶּבֶר הִסְגִּיר. נא וַיַּךְ כָּל בְּכוֹר בְּמִצְרָיִם, רֵאשִׁית אוֹנִים בְּאָהֳלֵי חָם. נב וַיַּסַּע כַּצֹּאן עַמּוֹ, וַיְנַהֲגֵם כַּעֵדֶר בַּמִּדְבָּר. נג וַיַּנְחֵם לָבֶטַח וְלֹא פָחָדוּ, וְאֶת אוֹיְבֵיהֶם כִּסָּה הַיָּם. נד וַיְבִיאֵם אֶל גְּבוּל קָדְשׁוֹ, הַר זֶה קָנְתָה יְמִינוֹ. נה וַיְגָרֶשׁ מִפְּנֵיהֶם גּוֹיִם, וַיַּפִּילֵם בְּחֶבֶל נַחֲלָה, וַיַּשְׁכֵּן בְּאָהֳלֵיהֶם שִׁבְטֵי יִשְׂרָאֵל. נו וַיְנַסּוּ וַיַּמְרוּ אֶת אֱלֹהִים עֶלְיוֹן, וְעֵדוֹתָיו לֹא שָׁמָרוּ. נז וַיִּסֹּגוּ וַיִּבְגְּדוּ כַּאֲבוֹתָם, נֶהְפְּכוּ כְּקֶשֶׁת רְמִיָּה. נח וַיַּכְעִיסוּהוּ בְּבָמוֹתָם, וּבִפְסִילֵיהֶם יַקְנִיאוּהוּ. נט שָׁמַע אֱלֹהִים וַיִּתְעַבָּר, וַיִּמְאַס מְאֹד בְּיִשְׂרָאֵל. ס וַיִּטֹּשׁ מִשְׁכַּן שִׁלוֹ, אֹהֶל שִׁכֵּן בָּאָדָם. סא וַיִּתֵּן לַשְּׁבִי עֻזּוֹ, וְתִפְאַרְתּוֹ בְיַד צָר. סב וַיַּסְגֵּר לַחֶרֶב עַמּוֹ, וּבְנַחֲלָתוֹ הִתְעַבָּר. סג בַּחוּרָיו אָכְלָה אֵשׁ, וּבְתוּלֹתָיו לֹא הוּלָּלוּ. סד כֹּהֲנָיו בַּחֶרֶב נָפָלוּ, וְאַלְמְנֹתָיו לֹא תִבְכֶּינָה. סה וַיִּקַץ כְּיָשֵׁן אֲדֹנָי, כְּגִבּוֹר מִתְרוֹנֵן מִיָּיִן. סו וַיַּךְ צָרָיו אָחוֹר, חֶרְפַּת עוֹלָם נָתַן לָמוֹ. סז וַיִּמְאַס בְּאֹהֶל יוֹסֵף, וּבְשֵׁבֶט אֶפְרַיִם לֹא בָחָר. סח וַיִּבְחַר אֶת שֵׁבֶט יְהוּדָה, אֶת הַר צִיּוֹן אֲשֶׁר אָהֵב. סט וַיִּבֶן כְּמוֹ רָמִים מִקְדָּשׁוֹ, כְּאֶרֶץ יְסָדָהּ לְעוֹלָם. ע וַיִּבְחַר בְּדָוִד עַבְדּוֹ, וַיִּקָּחֵהוּ מִמִּכְלְאֹת צֹאן. עא מֵאַחַר עָלוֹת הֱבִיאוֹ, לִרְעוֹת בְּיַעֲקֹב עַמּוֹ, וּבְיִשְׂרָאֵל נַחֲלָתוֹ. עב וַיִּרְעֵם כְּתֹם לְבָבוֹ, וּבִתְבוּנוֹת כַּפָּיו יַנְחֵם.

יום ט"ז לחדש / DAY 16

עט א מִזְמוֹר לְאָסָף; אֱלֹהִים בָּאוּ גוֹיִם בְּנַחֲלָתֶךָ, טִמְּאוּ אֶת הֵיכַל קָדְשֶׁךָ, שָׂמוּ אֶת יְרוּשָׁלַיִם לְעִיִּים. ב נָתְנוּ אֶת נִבְלַת עֲבָדֶיךָ מַאֲכָל לְעוֹף הַשָּׁמָיִם, בְּשַׂר חֲסִידֶיךָ לְחַיְתוֹ אָרֶץ. ג שָׁפְכוּ דָמָם כַּמַּיִם, סְבִיבוֹת יְרוּשָׁלַיִם, וְאֵין קוֹבֵר. ד הָיִינוּ חֶרְפָּה לִשְׁכֵנֵינוּ, לַעַג וָקֶלֶס לִסְבִיבוֹתֵינוּ. ה עַד מָה יהוה תֶּאֱנַף לָנֶצַח, תִּבְעַר כְּמוֹ אֵשׁ קִנְאָתֶךָ. ו שְׁפֹךְ חֲמָתְךָ אֶל הַגּוֹיִם אֲשֶׁר לֹא יְדָעוּךָ; וְעַל מַמְלָכוֹת, אֲשֶׁר בְּשִׁמְךָ לֹא קָרָאוּ. ז כִּי אָכַל אֶת יַעֲקֹב, וְאֶת נָוֵהוּ הֵשַׁמּוּ. ח אַל תִּזְכָּר לָנוּ עֲוֹנֹת רִאשֹׁנִים; מַהֵר יְקַדְּמוּנוּ רַחֲמֶיךָ, כִּי דַלּוֹנוּ מְאֹד. ט עָזְרֵנוּ אֱלֹהֵי יִשְׁעֵנוּ עַל דְּבַר כְּבוֹד שְׁמֶךָ, וְהַצִּילֵנוּ וְכַפֵּר עַל חַטֹּאתֵינוּ לְמַעַן שְׁמֶךָ. י לָמָּה יֹאמְרוּ הַגּוֹיִם: אַיֵּה אֱלֹהֵיהֶם; יִוָּדַע בַּגּוֹיִם לְעֵינֵינוּ, נִקְמַת דַּם עֲבָדֶיךָ הַשָּׁפוּךְ. יא תָּבוֹא לְפָנֶיךָ אֶנְקַת אָסִיר; כְּגֹדֶל זְרוֹעֲךָ, הוֹתֵר בְּנֵי תְמוּתָה. יב וְהָשֵׁב לִשְׁכֵנֵינוּ שִׁבְעָתַיִם אֶל חֵיקָם,

חֵרְפוּךָ אֲשֶׁר חֵרְפוּ, אֲדֹנָי. יג וַאֲנַחְנוּ עַמְּךָ וְצֹאן מַרְעִיתֶךָ, נוֹדֶה לְךָ לְעוֹלָם; לְדוֹר וָדֹר נְסַפֵּר תְּהִלָּתֶךָ.

פ א לַמְנַצֵּחַ אֶל שֹׁשַׁנִּים, עֵדוּת לְאָסָף מִזְמוֹר. ב רֹעֵה יִשְׂרָאֵל הַאֲזִינָה, נֹהֵג כַּצֹּאן יוֹסֵף; יֹשֵׁב הַכְּרוּבִים הוֹפִיעָה. ג לִפְנֵי אֶפְרַיִם וּבִנְיָמִן וּמְנַשֶּׁה עוֹרְרָה אֶת גְּבוּרָתֶךָ, וּלְכָה לִישֻׁעָתָה לָּנוּ. ד אֱלֹהִים הֲשִׁיבֵנוּ, וְהָאֵר פָּנֶיךָ וְנִוָּשֵׁעָה. ה יהוה אֱלֹהִים צְבָאוֹת, עַד מָתַי עָשַׁנְתָּ בִּתְפִלַּת עַמֶּךָ. ו הֶאֱכַלְתָּם לֶחֶם דִּמְעָה, וַתַּשְׁקֵמוֹ בִּדְמָעוֹת שָׁלִישׁ. ז תְּשִׂימֵנוּ מָדוֹן לִשְׁכֵנֵינוּ, וְאֹיְבֵינוּ יִלְעֲגוּ לָמוֹ. ח אֱלֹהִים צְבָאוֹת הֲשִׁיבֵנוּ, וְהָאֵר פָּנֶיךָ וְנִוָּשֵׁעָה. ט גֶּפֶן מִמִּצְרַיִם תַּסִּיעַ, תְּגָרֵשׁ גּוֹיִם וַתִּטָּעֶהָ. י פִּנִּיתָ לְפָנֶיהָ, וַתַּשְׁרֵשׁ שָׁרָשֶׁיהָ, וַתְּמַלֵּא אָרֶץ. יא כָּסּוּ הָרִים צִלָּהּ, וַעֲנָפֶיהָ אַרְזֵי אֵל. יב תְּשַׁלַּח קְצִירֶהָ עַד יָם, וְאֶל נָהָר יוֹנְקוֹתֶיהָ. יג לָמָּה פָּרַצְתָּ גְדֵרֶיהָ, וְאָרוּהָ כָּל עֹבְרֵי דָרֶךְ. יד יְכַרְסְמֶנָּה חֲזִיר מִיָּעַר, וְזִיז שָׂדַי יִרְעֶנָּה. טו אֱלֹהִים צְבָאוֹת שׁוּב נָא; הַבֵּט מִשָּׁמַיִם וּרְאֵה, וּפְקֹד גֶּפֶן זֹאת. טז וְכַנָּה אֲשֶׁר נָטְעָה יְמִינֶךָ, וְעַל בֵּן אִמַּצְתָּה לָּךְ. יז שְׂרֻפָה בָאֵשׁ כְּסוּחָה, מִגַּעֲרַת פָּנֶיךָ יֹאבֵדוּ. יח תְּהִי יָדְךָ עַל אִישׁ יְמִינֶךָ, עַל בֶּן אָדָם אִמַּצְתָּ לָּךְ. יט וְלֹא נָסוֹג מִמֶּךָּ, תְּחַיֵּנוּ וּבְשִׁמְךָ נִקְרָא. כ יהוה אֱלֹהִים צְבָאוֹת הֲשִׁיבֵנוּ, הָאֵר פָּנֶיךָ וְנִוָּשֵׁעָה.

פא א לַמְנַצֵּחַ עַל הַגִּתִּית לְאָסָף. ב הַרְנִינוּ לֵאלֹהִים עוּזֵּנוּ, הָרִיעוּ לֵאלֹהֵי יַעֲקֹב. ג שְׂאוּ זִמְרָה וּתְנוּ תֹף, כִּנּוֹר נָעִים עִם נָבֶל. ד תִּקְעוּ בַחֹדֶשׁ שׁוֹפָר, בַּכֵּסֶה לְיוֹם חַגֵּנוּ. ה כִּי חֹק לְיִשְׂרָאֵל הוּא, מִשְׁפָּט לֵאלֹהֵי יַעֲקֹב. ו עֵדוּת בִּיהוֹסֵף שָׂמוֹ, בְּצֵאתוֹ עַל אֶרֶץ מִצְרָיִם, שְׂפַת לֹא יָדַעְתִּי אֶשְׁמָע. ז הֲסִירוֹתִי מִסֵּבֶל שִׁכְמוֹ, כַּפָּיו מִדּוּד תַּעֲבֹרְנָה. ח בַּצָּרָה קָרָאתָ וָאֲחַלְּצֶךָּ; אֶעֶנְךָ בְּסֵתֶר רַעַם, אֶבְחָנְךָ עַל מֵי מְרִיבָה סֶלָה. ט שְׁמַע עַמִּי וְאָעִידָה בָּךְ, יִשְׂרָאֵל אִם תִּשְׁמַע לִי. י לֹא יִהְיֶה בְךָ אֵל זָר, וְלֹא תִשְׁתַּחֲוֶה לְאֵל נֵכָר. יא אָנֹכִי יהוה אֱלֹהֶיךָ הַמַּעַלְךָ מֵאֶרֶץ מִצְרָיִם, הַרְחֶב פִּיךָ וַאֲמַלְאֵהוּ. יב וְלֹא שָׁמַע עַמִּי לְקוֹלִי, וְיִשְׂרָאֵל לֹא אָבָה לִי. יג וָאֲשַׁלְּחֵהוּ בִּשְׁרִירוּת לִבָּם, יֵלְכוּ בְּמוֹעֲצוֹתֵיהֶם. יד לוּ עַמִּי שֹׁמֵעַ לִי, יִשְׂרָאֵל בִּדְרָכַי יְהַלֵּכוּ. טו כִּמְעַט אוֹיְבֵיהֶם אַכְנִיעַ, וְעַל צָרֵיהֶם אָשִׁיב יָדִי. טז מְשַׂנְאֵי יהוה יְכַחֲשׁוּ לוֹ, וִיהִי עִתָּם לְעוֹלָם. יז וַיַּאֲכִילֵהוּ מֵחֵלֶב חִטָּה; וּמִצּוּר, דְּבַשׁ אַשְׂבִּיעֶךָ.

פב א מִזְמוֹר לְאָסָף; אֱלֹהִים נִצָּב בַּעֲדַת אֵל, בְּקֶרֶב אֱלֹהִים יִשְׁפֹּט. ב עַד מָתַי תִּשְׁפְּטוּ עָוֶל, וּפְנֵי רְשָׁעִים תִּשְׂאוּ סֶלָה. ג שִׁפְטוּ דַל וְיָתוֹם, עָנִי וָרָשׁ הַצְדִּיקוּ. ד פַּלְּטוּ דַל וְאֶבְיוֹן, מִיַּד רְשָׁעִים הַצִּילוּ. ה לֹא יָדְעוּ וְלֹא יָבִינוּ, בַּחֲשֵׁכָה יִתְהַלָּכוּ; יִמּוֹטוּ כָּל מוֹסְדֵי אָרֶץ. ו אֲנִי אָמַרְתִּי אֱלֹהִים

אַתֶּם, וּבְנֵי עֶלְיוֹן כֻּלְּכֶם. ז אָכֵן כְּאָדָם תְּמוּתוּן, וּכְאַחַד הַשָּׂרִים תִּפֹּלוּ. ח קוּמָה אֱלֹהִים שָׁפְטָה הָאָרֶץ, כִּי אַתָּה תִנְחַל בְּכָל הַגּוֹיִם.

יום יז לחודש / DAY 17

פג א שִׁיר מִזְמוֹר לְאָסָף. ב אֱלֹהִים אַל דֳּמִי לָךְ, אַל תֶּחֱרַשׁ וְאַל תִּשְׁקֹט אֵל. ג כִּי הִנֵּה אוֹיְבֶיךָ יֶהֱמָיוּן, וּמְשַׂנְאֶיךָ נָשְׂאוּ רֹאשׁ. ד עַל עַמְּךָ יַעֲרִימוּ סוֹד, וְיִתְיָעֲצוּ עַל צְפוּנֶיךָ. ה אָמְרוּ: לְכוּ וְנַכְחִידֵם מִגּוֹי, וְלֹא יִזָּכֵר שֵׁם יִשְׂרָאֵל עוֹד. ו כִּי נוֹעֲצוּ לֵב יַחְדָּו, עָלֶיךָ בְּרִית יִכְרֹתוּ. ז אָהֳלֵי אֱדוֹם וְיִשְׁמְעֵאלִים, מוֹאָב וְהַגְרִים. ח גְּבָל וְעַמּוֹן וַעֲמָלֵק, פְּלֶשֶׁת עִם יֹשְׁבֵי צוֹר. ט גַּם אַשּׁוּר נִלְוָה עִמָּם, הָיוּ זְרוֹעַ לִבְנֵי לוֹט סֶלָה. י עֲשֵׂה לָהֶם כְּמִדְיָן, כְּסִיסְרָא כְיָבִין בְּנַחַל קִישׁוֹן. יא נִשְׁמְדוּ בְעֵין דֹּאר, הָיוּ דֹּמֶן לָאֲדָמָה. יב שִׁיתֵמוֹ נְדִיבֵמוֹ כְּעֹרֵב וְכִזְאֵב, וּכְזֶבַח וּכְצַלְמֻנָּע כָּל נְסִיכֵמוֹ. יג אֲשֶׁר אָמְרוּ: נִירְשָׁה לָּנוּ, אֵת נְאוֹת אֱלֹהִים. יד אֱלֹהַי, שִׁיתֵמוֹ כַגַּלְגַּל, כְּקַשׁ לִפְנֵי רוּחַ. טו כְּאֵשׁ תִּבְעַר יָעַר, וּכְלֶהָבָה תְּלַהֵט הָרִים. טז כֵּן תִּרְדְּפֵם בְּסַעֲרֶךָ, וּבְסוּפָתְךָ תְבַהֲלֵם. יז מַלֵּא פְנֵיהֶם קָלוֹן, וִיבַקְשׁוּ שִׁמְךָ יהוה. יח יֵבֹשׁוּ וְיִבָּהֲלוּ עֲדֵי עַד, וְיַחְפְּרוּ וְיֹאבֵדוּ. יט וְיֵדְעוּ כִּי אַתָּה שִׁמְךָ יהוה לְבַדֶּךָ, עֶלְיוֹן עַל כָּל הָאָרֶץ.

פד א לַמְנַצֵּחַ עַל הַגִּתִּית, לִבְנֵי קֹרַח מִזְמוֹר. ב מַה יְּדִידוֹת מִשְׁכְּנוֹתֶיךָ יהוה צְבָאוֹת. ג נִכְסְפָה וְגַם כָּלְתָה נַפְשִׁי לְחַצְרוֹת יהוה, לִבִּי וּבְשָׂרִי, יְרַנְּנוּ אֶל אֵל חָי. ד גַּם צִפּוֹר מָצְאָה בַיִת, וּדְרוֹר קֵן לָהּ אֲשֶׁר שָׁתָה אֶפְרֹחֶיהָ; אֶת מִזְבְּחוֹתֶיךָ יהוה צְבָאוֹת, מַלְכִּי וֵאלֹהָי. ה אַשְׁרֵי יוֹשְׁבֵי בֵיתֶךָ, עוֹד יְהַלְלוּךָ סֶּלָה. ו אַשְׁרֵי אָדָם עוֹז לוֹ בָךְ, מְסִלּוֹת בִּלְבָבָם. ז עֹבְרֵי בְּעֵמֶק הַבָּכָא מַעְיָן יְשִׁיתוּהוּ, גַּם בְּרָכוֹת יַעְטֶה מוֹרֶה. ח יֵלְכוּ מֵחַיִל אֶל חָיִל, יֵרָאֶה אֶל אֱלֹהִים בְּצִיּוֹן. ט יהוה אֱלֹהִים צְבָאוֹת שִׁמְעָה תְפִלָּתִי, הַאֲזִינָה אֱלֹהֵי יַעֲקֹב סֶלָה. י מָגִנֵּנוּ רְאֵה, אֱלֹהִים; וְהַבֵּט פְּנֵי מְשִׁיחֶךָ. יא כִּי טוֹב יוֹם בַּחֲצֵרֶיךָ מֵאָלֶף, בָּחַרְתִּי הִסְתּוֹפֵף בְּבֵית אֱלֹהַי, מִדּוּר בְּאָהֳלֵי רֶשַׁע. יב כִּי שֶׁמֶשׁ וּמָגֵן יהוה אֱלֹהִים; חֵן וְכָבוֹד יִתֵּן יהוה, לֹא יִמְנַע טוֹב לַהֹלְכִים בְּתָמִים. יג יהוה צְבָאוֹת, אַשְׁרֵי אָדָם בֹּטֵחַ בָּךְ.

פה א לַמְנַצֵּחַ לִבְנֵי קֹרַח מִזְמוֹר. ב רָצִיתָ יהוה אַרְצֶךָ, שַׁבְתָּ שְׁבִית יַעֲקֹב. ג נָשָׂאתָ עֲוֹן עַמֶּךָ, כִּסִּיתָ כָל חַטָּאתָם סֶלָה. ד אָסַפְתָּ כָל עֶבְרָתֶךָ, הֱשִׁיבוֹתָ מֵחֲרוֹן אַפֶּךָ. ה שׁוּבֵנוּ אֱלֹהֵי יִשְׁעֵנוּ, וְהָפֵר כַּעַסְךָ עִמָּנוּ. ו הַלְעוֹלָם תֶּאֱנַף בָּנוּ, תִּמְשֹׁךְ אַפְּךָ לְדֹר וָדֹר. ז הֲלֹא אַתָּה תָּשׁוּב תְּחַיֵּנוּ, וְעַמְּךָ יִשְׂמְחוּ בָךְ. ח הַרְאֵנוּ יהוה חַסְדֶּךָ, וְיֶשְׁעֲךָ תִּתֶּן לָנוּ. ט אֶשְׁמְעָה מַה יְדַבֵּר

הָאֵל יהוה; כִּי יְדַבֵּר שָׁלוֹם אֶל עַמּוֹ וְאֶל חֲסִידָיו, וְאַל יָשׁוּבוּ לְכִסְלָה. ‏ד אַךְ קָרוֹב לִירֵאָיו יִשְׁעוֹ, לִשְׁכֹּן כָּבוֹד בְּאַרְצֵנוּ. ‏יא חֶסֶד וֶאֱמֶת נִפְגָּשׁוּ, צֶדֶק וְשָׁלוֹם נָשָׁקוּ. ‏יב אֱמֶת מֵאֶרֶץ תִּצְמָח, וְצֶדֶק מִשָּׁמַיִם נִשְׁקָף. ‏יג גַּם יהוה יִתֵּן הַטּוֹב, וְאַרְצֵנוּ תִּתֵּן יְבוּלָהּ. ‏יד צֶדֶק לְפָנָיו יְהַלֵּךְ, וְיָשֵׂם לְדֶרֶךְ פְּעָמָיו.

פו א תְּפִלָּה לְדָוִד, הַטֵּה יהוה אָזְנְךָ עֲנֵנִי, כִּי עָנִי וְאֶבְיוֹן אָנִי. ‏ב שָׁמְרָה נַפְשִׁי כִּי חָסִיד אָנִי; הוֹשַׁע עַבְדְּךָ אַתָּה אֱלֹהַי, הַבּוֹטֵחַ אֵלֶיךָ. ‏ג חָנֵּנִי אֲדֹנָי, כִּי אֵלֶיךָ אֶקְרָא כָּל הַיּוֹם. ‏ד שַׂמֵּחַ נֶפֶשׁ עַבְדֶּךָ, כִּי אֵלֶיךָ אֲדֹנָי נַפְשִׁי אֶשָּׂא. ‏ה כִּי אַתָּה אֲדֹנָי טוֹב וְסַלָּח, וְרַב חֶסֶד לְכָל קֹרְאֶיךָ. ‏ו הַאֲזִינָה יהוה תְּפִלָּתִי, וְהַקְשִׁיבָה בְּקוֹל תַּחֲנוּנוֹתָי. ‏ז בְּיוֹם צָרָתִי אֶקְרָאֶךָּ כִּי תַעֲנֵנִי. ‏ח אֵין כָּמוֹךָ בָאֱלֹהִים אֲדֹנָי, וְאֵין כְּמַעֲשֶׂיךָ. ‏ט כָּל גּוֹיִם אֲשֶׁר עָשִׂיתָ יָבוֹאוּ וְיִשְׁתַּחֲווּ לְפָנֶיךָ, אֲדֹנָי; וִיכַבְּדוּ לִשְׁמֶךָ. ‏י כִּי גָדוֹל אַתָּה וְעֹשֵׂה נִפְלָאוֹת, אַתָּה אֱלֹהִים לְבַדֶּךָ. ‏יא הוֹרֵנִי יהוה דַּרְכֶּךָ, אֲהַלֵּךְ בַּאֲמִתֶּךָ, יַחֵד לְבָבִי לְיִרְאָה שְׁמֶךָ. ‏יב אוֹדְךָ אֲדֹנָי אֱלֹהַי בְּכָל לְבָבִי, וַאֲכַבְּדָה שִׁמְךָ לְעוֹלָם. ‏יג כִּי חַסְדְּךָ גָּדוֹל עָלָי, וְהִצַּלְתָּ נַפְשִׁי מִשְּׁאוֹל תַּחְתִּיָּה. ‏יד אֱלֹהִים, זֵדִים קָמוּ עָלַי, וַעֲדַת עָרִיצִים בִּקְשׁוּ נַפְשִׁי; וְלֹא שָׂמוּךָ לְנֶגְדָּם. ‏טו וְאַתָּה אֲדֹנָי אֵל רַחוּם וְחַנּוּן, אֶרֶךְ אַפַּיִם וְרַב חֶסֶד וֶאֱמֶת. ‏טז פְּנֵה אֵלַי וְחָנֵּנִי; תְּנָה עֻזְּךָ לְעַבְדֶּךָ, וְהוֹשִׁיעָה לְבֶן אֲמָתֶךָ. ‏יז עֲשֵׂה עִמִּי אוֹת לְטוֹבָה; וְיִרְאוּ שֹׂנְאַי וְיֵבֹשׁוּ, כִּי אַתָּה יהוה עֲזַרְתַּנִי וְנִחַמְתָּנִי:

פז א לִבְנֵי קֹרַח מִזְמוֹר שִׁיר, יְסוּדָתוֹ בְּהַרְרֵי קֹדֶשׁ. ‏ב אֹהֵב יהוה שַׁעֲרֵי צִיּוֹן, מִכֹּל מִשְׁכְּנוֹת יַעֲקֹב. ‏ג נִכְבָּדוֹת מְדֻבָּר בָּךְ, עִיר הָאֱלֹהִים סֶלָה. ‏ד אַזְכִּיר רַהַב וּבָבֶל לְיֹדְעָי, הִנֵּה פְלֶשֶׁת וְצֹר עִם כּוּשׁ, זֶה יֻלַּד שָׁם. ‏ה וּלְצִיּוֹן יֵאָמַר: אִישׁ וְאִישׁ יֻלַּד בָּהּ, וְהוּא יְכוֹנְנֶהָ עֶלְיוֹן. ‏ו יהוה יִסְפֹּר בִּכְתוֹב עַמִּים, זֶה יֻלַּד שָׁם סֶלָה. ‏ז וְשָׁרִים כְּחֹלְלִים, כָּל מַעְיָנַי בָּךְ.

פח א שִׁיר מִזְמוֹר לִבְנֵי קֹרַח, לַמְנַצֵּחַ עַל מָחֲלַת לְעַנּוֹת, מַשְׂכִּיל לְהֵימָן הָאֶזְרָחִי. ‏ב יהוה אֱלֹהֵי יְשׁוּעָתִי, יוֹם צָעַקְתִּי בַלַּיְלָה נֶגְדֶּךָ. ‏ג תָּבוֹא לְפָנֶיךָ תְּפִלָּתִי, הַטֵּה אָזְנְךָ לְרִנָּתִי. ‏ד כִּי שָׂבְעָה בְרָעוֹת נַפְשִׁי, וְחַיַּי לִשְׁאוֹל הִגִּיעוּ. ‏ה נֶחְשַׁבְתִּי עִם יוֹרְדֵי בוֹר, הָיִיתִי כְּגֶבֶר אֵין אֱיָל. ‏ו בַּמֵּתִים חָפְשִׁי; כְּמוֹ חֲלָלִים שֹׁכְבֵי קֶבֶר אֲשֶׁר לֹא זְכַרְתָּם עוֹד, וְהֵמָּה מִיָּדְךָ נִגְזָרוּ. ‏ז שַׁתַּנִי בְּבוֹר תַּחְתִּיּוֹת, בְּמַחֲשַׁכִּים בִּמְצֹלוֹת. ‏ח עָלַי סָמְכָה חֲמָתֶךָ, וְכָל מִשְׁבָּרֶיךָ עִנִּיתָ סֶּלָה. ‏ט הִרְחַקְתָּ מְיֻדָּעַי מִמֶּנִּי; שַׁתַּנִי תוֹעֵבוֹת לָמוֹ, כָּלֻא וְלֹא אֵצֵא. ‏י עֵינִי דָאֲבָה מִנִּי עֹנִי; קְרָאתִיךָ יהוה בְּכָל יוֹם, שִׁטַּחְתִּי אֵלֶיךָ כַפָּי.

יא הֲלַמֵּתִים תַּעֲשֶׂה פֶּלֶא, אִם רְפָאִים יָקוּמוּ יוֹדוּךָ סֶּלָה. יב הַיְסֻפַּר בַּקֶּבֶר חַסְדֶּךָ, אֱמוּנָתְךָ בָּאֲבַדּוֹן. יג הֲיִוָּדַע בַּחֹשֶׁךְ פִּלְאֶךָ, וְצִדְקָתְךָ בְּאֶרֶץ נְשִׁיָּה. יד וַאֲנִי אֵלֶיךָ יהוה שִׁוַּעְתִּי, וּבַבֹּקֶר תְּפִלָּתִי תְקַדְּמֶךָּ. טו לָמָה יהוה תִּזְנַח נַפְשִׁי, תַּסְתִּיר פָּנֶיךָ מִמֶּנִּי. טז עָנִי אֲנִי וְגֹוֵעַ מִנֹּעַר, נָשָׂאתִי אֵמֶיךָ אָפוּנָה. יז עָלַי עָבְרוּ חֲרוֹנֶיךָ, בִּעוּתֶיךָ צִמְּתֻתוּנִי. יח סַבּוּנִי כַמַּיִם כָּל הַיּוֹם, הִקִּיפוּ עָלַי יָחַד. יט הִרְחַקְתָּ מִמֶּנִּי אֹהֵב וָרֵעַ, מְיֻדָּעַי מַחְשָׁךְ:

פט א מַשְׂכִּיל לְאֵיתָן הָאֶזְרָחִי. ב חַסְדֵי יהוה עוֹלָם אָשִׁירָה, לְדֹר וָדֹר אוֹדִיעַ אֱמוּנָתְךָ בְּפִי. ג כִּי אָמַרְתִּי, עוֹלָם חֶסֶד יִבָּנֶה, שָׁמַיִם תָּכִן אֱמוּנָתְךָ בָהֶם. ד כָּרַתִּי בְרִית לִבְחִירִי, נִשְׁבַּעְתִּי לְדָוִד עַבְדִּי. ה עַד עוֹלָם אָכִין זַרְעֶךָ, וּבָנִיתִי לְדֹר וָדוֹר כִּסְאֲךָ סֶלָה. ו וְיוֹדוּ שָׁמַיִם פִּלְאֲךָ יהוה, אַף אֱמוּנָתְךָ בִּקְהַל קְדֹשִׁים. ז כִּי מִי בַשַּׁחַק יַעֲרֹךְ לַיהוה, יִדְמֶה לַיהוה בִּבְנֵי אֵלִים. ח אֵל נַעֲרָץ בְּסוֹד קְדֹשִׁים רַבָּה, וְנוֹרָא עַל כָּל סְבִיבָיו. ט יהוה אֱלֹהֵי צְבָאוֹת, מִי כָמוֹךָ, חֲסִין יָהּ, וֶאֱמוּנָתְךָ סְבִיבוֹתֶיךָ. י אַתָּה מוֹשֵׁל בְּגֵאוּת הַיָּם, בְּשׂוֹא גַלָּיו אַתָּה תְשַׁבְּחֵם. יא אַתָּה דִכִּאתָ כֶחָלָל רָהַב, בִּזְרוֹעַ עֻזְּךָ פִּזַּרְתָּ אוֹיְבֶיךָ. יב לְךָ שָׁמַיִם אַף לְךָ אָרֶץ, תֵּבֵל וּמְלֹאָהּ אַתָּה יְסַדְתָּם. יג צָפוֹן וְיָמִין אַתָּה בְרָאתָם, תָּבוֹר וְחֶרְמוֹן בְּשִׁמְךָ יְרַנֵּנוּ. יד לְךָ זְרוֹעַ עִם גְּבוּרָה, תָּעֹז יָדְךָ תָּרוּם יְמִינֶךָ. טו צֶדֶק וּמִשְׁפָּט מְכוֹן כִּסְאֶךָ, חֶסֶד וֶאֱמֶת יְקַדְּמוּ פָנֶיךָ. טז אַשְׁרֵי הָעָם יוֹדְעֵי תְרוּעָה, יהוה בְּאוֹר פָּנֶיךָ יְהַלֵּכוּן. יז בְּשִׁמְךָ יְגִילוּן כָּל הַיּוֹם, וּבְצִדְקָתְךָ יָרוּמוּ. יח כִּי תִפְאֶרֶת עֻזָּמוֹ אָתָּה, וּבִרְצוֹנְךָ תָּרוּם קַרְנֵנוּ. יט כִּי לַיהוה מָגִנֵּנוּ, וְלִקְדוֹשׁ יִשְׂרָאֵל מַלְכֵּנוּ. כ אָז דִּבַּרְתָּ בְחָזוֹן לַחֲסִידֶיךָ, וַתֹּאמֶר שִׁוִּיתִי עֵזֶר עַל גִּבּוֹר, הֲרִימוֹתִי בָחוּר מֵעָם. כא מָצָאתִי דָּוִד עַבְדִּי, בְּשֶׁמֶן קָדְשִׁי מְשַׁחְתִּיו. כב אֲשֶׁר יָדִי תִּכּוֹן עִמּוֹ, אַף זְרוֹעִי תְאַמְּצֶנּוּ. כג לֹא יַשִּׁיא אוֹיֵב בּוֹ, וּבֶן עַוְלָה לֹא יְעַנֶּנּוּ. כד וְכַתּוֹתִי מִפָּנָיו צָרָיו, וּמְשַׂנְאָיו אֶגּוֹף. כה וֶאֱמוּנָתִי וְחַסְדִּי עִמּוֹ, וּבִשְׁמִי תָּרוּם קַרְנוֹ. כו וְשַׂמְתִּי בַיָּם יָדוֹ, וּבַנְּהָרוֹת יְמִינוֹ. כז הוּא יִקְרָאֵנִי אָבִי אָתָּה, אֵלִי וְצוּר יְשׁוּעָתִי. כח אַף אָנִי בְּכוֹר אֶתְּנֵהוּ, עֶלְיוֹן לְמַלְכֵי אָרֶץ. כט לְעוֹלָם אֶשְׁמָר לוֹ חַסְדִּי, וּבְרִיתִי נֶאֱמֶנֶת לוֹ. ל וְשַׂמְתִּי לָעַד זַרְעוֹ, וְכִסְאוֹ כִּימֵי שָׁמָיִם. לא אִם יַעַזְבוּ בָנָיו תּוֹרָתִי, וּבְמִשְׁפָּטַי לֹא יֵלֵכוּן. לב אִם חֻקֹּתַי יְחַלֵּלוּ, וּמִצְוֹתַי לֹא יִשְׁמֹרוּ. לג וּפָקַדְתִּי בְשֵׁבֶט פִּשְׁעָם, וּבִנְגָעִים עֲוֹנָם. לד וְחַסְדִּי לֹא אָפִיר מֵעִמּוֹ, וְלֹא אֲשַׁקֵּר בֶּאֱמוּנָתִי. לה לֹא אֲחַלֵּל בְּרִיתִי, וּמוֹצָא שְׂפָתַי לֹא אֲשַׁנֶּה. לו אַחַת נִשְׁבַּעְתִּי בְקָדְשִׁי, אִם לְדָוִד אֲכַזֵּב. לז זַרְעוֹ לְעוֹלָם יִהְיֶה, וְכִסְאוֹ כַשֶּׁמֶשׁ נֶגְדִּי. לח כְּיָרֵחַ יִכּוֹן עוֹלָם, וְעֵד בַּשַּׁחַק נֶאֱמָן סֶלָה. לט וְאַתָּה זָנַחְתָּ וַתִּמְאָס, הִתְעַבַּרְתָּ עִם מְשִׁיחֶךָ. מ נֵאַרְתָּה בְּרִית עַבְדֶּךָ, חִלַּלְתָּ לָאָרֶץ נִזְרוֹ. מא פָּרַצְתָּ כָל גְּדֵרֹתָיו, שַׂמְתָּ

מִבְצָרָיו מְחִתָּה. מב שַׁסֻּהוּ כָּל עֹבְרֵי דָרֶךְ, הָיָה חֶרְפָּה לִשְׁכֵנָיו. מג הֲרִימוֹתָ יְמִין צָרָיו, הִשְׂמַחְתָּ כָּל אוֹיְבָיו. מד אַף תָּשִׁיב צוּר חַרְבּוֹ, וְלֹא הֲקֵמֹתוֹ בַּמִּלְחָמָה. מה הִשְׁבַּתָּ מִטְּהָרוֹ, וְכִסְאוֹ לָאָרֶץ מִגַּרְתָּה. מו הִקְצַרְתָּ יְמֵי עֲלוּמָיו, הֶעֱטִיתָ עָלָיו בּוּשָׁה סֶלָה. מז עַד מָה יהוה תִּסָּתֵר לָנֶצַח, תִּבְעַר כְּמוֹ אֵשׁ חֲמָתֶךָ. מח זְכָר אֲנִי מֶה חָלֶד, עַל מַה שָּׁוְא בָּרָאתָ כָל בְּנֵי אָדָם. מט מִי גֶבֶר יִחְיֶה וְלֹא יִרְאֶה מָּוֶת, יְמַלֵּט נַפְשׁוֹ מִיַּד שְׁאוֹל סֶלָה. נ אַיֵּה חֲסָדֶיךָ הָרִאשֹׁנִים אֲדֹנָי, נִשְׁבַּעְתָּ לְדָוִד בֶּאֱמוּנָתֶךָ. נא זְכֹר אֲדֹנָי חֶרְפַּת עֲבָדֶיךָ, שְׂאֵתִי בְחֵיקִי כָּל רַבִּים עַמִּים. נב אֲשֶׁר חֵרְפוּ אוֹיְבֶיךָ יהוה, אֲשֶׁר חֵרְפוּ עִקְּבוֹת מְשִׁיחֶךָ. נג בָּרוּךְ יהוה לְעוֹלָם, אָמֵן וְאָמֵן:

סֵפֶר רְבִיעִי / BOOK FOUR

יוֹם חֲמִישִׁי / THURSDAY

DAY 19 / יוֹם י״ט לַחוֹדֶשׁ

צ א תְּפִלָּה לְמֹשֶׁה אִישׁ הָאֱלֹהִים; אֲדֹנָי, מָעוֹן אַתָּה הָיִיתָ לָּנוּ בְּדֹר וָדֹר. ב בְּטֶרֶם הָרִים יֻלָּדוּ, וַתְּחוֹלֵל אֶרֶץ וְתֵבֵל, וּמֵעוֹלָם עַד עוֹלָם אַתָּה אֵל. ג תָּשֵׁב אֱנוֹשׁ עַד דַּכָּא, וַתֹּאמֶר: שׁוּבוּ בְנֵי אָדָם. ד כִּי אֶלֶף שָׁנִים בְּעֵינֶיךָ כְּיוֹם אֶתְמוֹל כִּי יַעֲבֹר, וְאַשְׁמוּרָה בַלָּיְלָה. ה זְרַמְתָּם, שֵׁנָה יִהְיוּ, בַּבֹּקֶר כֶּחָצִיר יַחֲלֹף. ו בַּבֹּקֶר יָצִיץ וְחָלָף, לָעֶרֶב יְמוֹלֵל וְיָבֵשׁ. ז כִּי כָלִינוּ בְאַפֶּךָ, וּבַחֲמָתְךָ נִבְהָלְנוּ. ח שַׁתָּה עֲוֺנֹתֵינוּ לְנֶגְדֶּךָ, עֲלֻמֵנוּ לִמְאוֹר פָּנֶיךָ. ט כִּי כָל יָמֵינוּ פָּנוּ בְעֶבְרָתֶךָ, כִּלִּינוּ שָׁנֵינוּ כְמוֹ הֶגֶה. י יְמֵי שְׁנוֹתֵינוּ בָהֶם שִׁבְעִים שָׁנָה, וְאִם בִּגְבוּרֹת שְׁמוֹנִים שָׁנָה, וְרָהְבָּם עָמָל וָאָוֶן, כִּי גָז חִישׁ וַנָּעֻפָה. יא מִי יוֹדֵעַ עֹז אַפֶּךָ, וּכְיִרְאָתְךָ עֶבְרָתֶךָ. יב לִמְנוֹת יָמֵינוּ כֵּן הוֹדַע, וְנָבִא לְבַב חָכְמָה. יג שׁוּבָה יהוה עַד מָתָי, וְהִנָּחֵם עַל עֲבָדֶיךָ. יד שַׂבְּעֵנוּ בַבֹּקֶר חַסְדֶּךָ, וּנְרַנְּנָה וְנִשְׂמְחָה בְּכָל יָמֵינוּ. טו שַׂמְּחֵנוּ כִּימוֹת עִנִּיתָנוּ, שְׁנוֹת רָאִינוּ רָעָה. טז יֵרָאֶה אֶל עֲבָדֶיךָ פָעֳלֶךָ, וַהֲדָרְךָ עַל בְּנֵיהֶם. יז וִיהִי נֹעַם אֲדֹנָי אֱלֹהֵינוּ עָלֵינוּ; וּמַעֲשֵׂה יָדֵינוּ כּוֹנְנָה עָלֵינוּ, וּמַעֲשֵׂה יָדֵינוּ כּוֹנְנֵהוּ.

צא א יֹשֵׁב בְּסֵתֶר עֶלְיוֹן, בְּצֵל שַׁדַּי יִתְלוֹנָן. ב אֹמַר לַיהוה: מַחְסִי וּמְצוּדָתִי, אֱלֹהַי אֶבְטַח בּוֹ. ג כִּי הוּא יַצִּילְךָ מִפַּח יָקוּשׁ, מִדֶּבֶר הַוּוֹת. ד בְּאֶבְרָתוֹ יָסֶךְ לָךְ, וְתַחַת כְּנָפָיו תֶּחְסֶה; צִנָּה וְסֹחֵרָה אֲמִתּוֹ. ה לֹא תִירָא מִפַּחַד לָיְלָה, מֵחֵץ יָעוּף יוֹמָם. ו מִדֶּבֶר בָּאֹפֶל יַהֲלֹךְ, מִקֶּטֶב יָשׁוּד צָהֳרָיִם. ז יִפֹּל מִצִּדְּךָ אֶלֶף, וּרְבָבָה מִימִינֶךָ, אֵלֶיךָ לֹא יִגָּשׁ. ח רַק בְּעֵינֶיךָ תַבִּיט, וְשִׁלֻּמַת רְשָׁעִים תִּרְאֶה. ט כִּי אַתָּה יהוה מַחְסִי, עֶלְיוֹן שַׂמְתָּ מְעוֹנֶךָ. י לֹא תְאֻנֶּה אֵלֶיךָ רָעָה, וְנֶגַע לֹא יִקְרַב בְּאָהֳלֶךָ. יא כִּי מַלְאָכָיו יְצַוֶּה לָּךְ,

לִשְׁמָרְךָ בְּכָל דְּרָכֶיךָ. יב עַל כַּפַּיִם יִשָּׂאוּנְךָ, פֶּן תִּגֹּף בָּאֶבֶן רַגְלֶךָ. יג עַל שַׁחַל וָפֶתֶן תִּדְרֹךְ, תִּרְמֹס כְּפִיר וְתַנִּין. יד כִּי בִי חָשַׁק וַאֲפַלְּטֵהוּ, אֲשַׂגְּבֵהוּ כִּי יָדַע שְׁמִי. טו יִקְרָאֵנִי וְאֶעֱנֵהוּ, עִמּוֹ אָנֹכִי בְצָרָה; אֲחַלְּצֵהוּ וַאֲכַבְּדֵהוּ. טז אֹרֶךְ יָמִים אַשְׂבִּיעֵהוּ, וְאַרְאֵהוּ בִּישׁוּעָתִי.

צב א מִזְמוֹר שִׁיר לְיוֹם הַשַּׁבָּת. ב טוֹב לְהֹדוֹת לַיהוה, וּלְזַמֵּר לְשִׁמְךָ עֶלְיוֹן. ג לְהַגִּיד בַּבֹּקֶר חַסְדֶּךָ, וֶאֱמוּנָתְךָ בַּלֵּילוֹת. ד עֲלֵי עָשׂוֹר וַעֲלֵי נָבֶל, עֲלֵי הִגָּיוֹן בְּכִנּוֹר. ה כִּי שִׂמַּחְתַּנִי יהוה בְּפָעֳלֶךָ, בְּמַעֲשֵׂי יָדֶיךָ אֲרַנֵּן. ו מַה גָּדְלוּ מַעֲשֶׂיךָ יהוה, מְאֹד עָמְקוּ מַחְשְׁבֹתֶיךָ. ז אִישׁ בַּעַר לֹא יֵדָע, וּכְסִיל לֹא יָבִין אֶת זֹאת. ח בִּפְרֹחַ רְשָׁעִים כְּמוֹ עֵשֶׂב, וַיָּצִיצוּ כָּל פֹּעֲלֵי אָוֶן, לְהִשָּׁמְדָם עֲדֵי עַד. ט וְאַתָּה מָרוֹם לְעֹלָם, יהוה. י כִּי הִנֵּה אֹיְבֶיךָ יהוה, כִּי הִנֵּה אֹיְבֶיךָ יֹאבֵדוּ, יִתְפָּרְדוּ כָּל פֹּעֲלֵי אָוֶן. יא וַתָּרֶם כִּרְאֵים קַרְנִי, בַּלֹּתִי בְּשֶׁמֶן רַעֲנָן. יב וַתַּבֵּט עֵינִי בְּשׁוּרָי; בַּקָּמִים עָלַי מְרֵעִים, תִּשְׁמַעְנָה אָזְנָי. יג צַדִּיק כַּתָּמָר יִפְרָח, כְּאֶרֶז בַּלְּבָנוֹן יִשְׂגֶּה. יד שְׁתוּלִים בְּבֵית יהוה, בְּחַצְרוֹת אֱלֹהֵינוּ יַפְרִיחוּ. טו עוֹד יְנוּבוּן בְּשֵׂיבָה, דְּשֵׁנִים וְרַעֲנַנִּים יִהְיוּ. טז לְהַגִּיד כִּי יָשָׁר יהוה, צוּרִי וְלֹא עַוְלָתָה בּוֹ.

צג א יהוה מָלָךְ גֵּאוּת לָבֵשׁ; לָבֵשׁ יהוה עֹז הִתְאַזָּר, אַף תִּכּוֹן תֵּבֵל בַּל תִּמּוֹט. ב נָכוֹן כִּסְאֲךָ מֵאָז, מֵעוֹלָם אָתָּה. ג נָשְׂאוּ נְהָרוֹת, יהוה, נָשְׂאוּ נְהָרוֹת קוֹלָם; יִשְׂאוּ נְהָרוֹת דָּכְיָם. ד מִקֹּלוֹת מַיִם רַבִּים אַדִּירִים מִשְׁבְּרֵי יָם, אַדִּיר בַּמָּרוֹם יהוה. ה עֵדֹתֶיךָ נֶאֶמְנוּ מְאֹד לְבֵיתְךָ נַאֲוָה קֹדֶשׁ, יהוה לְאֹרֶךְ יָמִים.

צד א אֵל נְקָמוֹת יהוה, אֵל נְקָמוֹת הוֹפִיעַ. ב הִנָּשֵׂא שֹׁפֵט הָאָרֶץ, הָשֵׁב גְּמוּל עַל גֵּאִים. ג עַד מָתַי רְשָׁעִים יהוה, עַד מָתַי רְשָׁעִים יַעֲלֹזוּ. ד יַבִּיעוּ יְדַבְּרוּ עָתָק, יִתְאַמְּרוּ כָּל פֹּעֲלֵי אָוֶן. ה עַמְּךָ יהוה יְדַכְּאוּ, וְנַחֲלָתְךָ יְעַנּוּ. ו אַלְמָנָה וְגֵר יַהֲרֹגוּ, וִיתוֹמִים יְרַצֵּחוּ. ז וַיֹּאמְרוּ, לֹא יִרְאֶה יָּהּ, וְלֹא יָבִין אֱלֹהֵי יַעֲקֹב. ח בִּינוּ בֹּעֲרִים בָּעָם, וּכְסִילִים מָתַי תַּשְׂכִּילוּ. ט הֲנֹטַע אֹזֶן הֲלֹא יִשְׁמָע, אִם יֹצֵר עַיִן הֲלֹא יַבִּיט. י הֲיֹסֵר גּוֹיִם הֲלֹא יוֹכִיחַ, הַמְלַמֵּד אָדָם דָּעַת. יא יהוה יֹדֵעַ מַחְשְׁבוֹת אָדָם, כִּי הֵמָּה הָבֶל. יב אַשְׁרֵי הַגֶּבֶר אֲשֶׁר תְּיַסְּרֶנּוּ יָּהּ, וּמִתּוֹרָתְךָ תְלַמְּדֶנּוּ. יג לְהַשְׁקִיט לוֹ מִימֵי רָע, עַד יִכָּרֶה לָרָשָׁע שָׁחַת. יד כִּי לֹא יִטֹּשׁ יהוה עַמּוֹ, וְנַחֲלָתוֹ לֹא יַעֲזֹב. טו כִּי עַד צֶדֶק יָשׁוּב מִשְׁפָּט, וְאַחֲרָיו כָּל יִשְׁרֵי לֵב. טז מִי יָקוּם לִי עִם מְרֵעִים, מִי יִתְיַצֵּב לִי עִם פֹּעֲלֵי אָוֶן. יז לוּלֵי יהוה עֶזְרָתָה לִּי, כִּמְעַט שָׁכְנָה דוּמָה נַפְשִׁי. יח אִם אָמַרְתִּי מָטָה רַגְלִי, חַסְדְּךָ יהוה יִסְעָדֵנִי. יט בְּרֹב שַׂרְעַפַּי בְּקִרְבִּי, תַּנְחוּמֶיךָ

יְשַׁעְשְׁעוּ נַפְשִׁי. כ הַיְחָבְרְךָ כִּסֵּא הַוּוֹת, יֹצֵר עָמָל עֲלֵי חֹק. כא יָגוֹדּוּ עַל נֶפֶשׁ צַדִּיק, וְדָם נָקִי יַרְשִׁיעוּ. כב וַיְהִי יהוה לִי לְמִשְׂגָּב, וֵאלֹהַי לְצוּר מַחְסִי. כג וַיָּשֶׁב עֲלֵיהֶם אֶת אוֹנָם, וּבְרָעָתָם יַצְמִיתֵם; יַצְמִיתֵם יהוה אֱלֹהֵינוּ.

צה א לְכוּ נְרַנְּנָה לַיהוה, נָרִיעָה לְצוּר יִשְׁעֵנוּ. ב נְקַדְּמָה פָנָיו בְּתוֹדָה, בִּזְמִרוֹת נָרִיעַ לוֹ. ג כִּי אֵל גָּדוֹל יהוה, וּמֶלֶךְ גָּדוֹל עַל כָּל אֱלֹהִים. ד אֲשֶׁר בְּיָדוֹ מֶחְקְרֵי אָרֶץ, וְתוֹעֲפֹת הָרִים לוֹ. ה אֲשֶׁר לוֹ הַיָּם וְהוּא עָשָׂהוּ, וְיַבֶּשֶׁת יָדָיו יָצָרוּ. ו בֹּאוּ נִשְׁתַּחֲוֶה וְנִכְרָעָה, נִבְרְכָה לִפְנֵי יהוה עֹשֵׂנוּ. ז כִּי הוּא אֱלֹהֵינוּ, וַאֲנַחְנוּ עַם מַרְעִיתוֹ וְצֹאן יָדוֹ, הַיּוֹם אִם בְּקֹלוֹ תִשְׁמָעוּ. ח אַל תַּקְשׁוּ לְבַבְכֶם כִּמְרִיבָה, כְּיוֹם מַסָּה בַּמִּדְבָּר. ט אֲשֶׁר נִסּוּנִי אֲבוֹתֵיכֶם, בְּחָנוּנִי גַּם רָאוּ פָעֳלִי. י אַרְבָּעִים שָׁנָה אָקוּט בְּדוֹר, וָאֹמַר עַם תֹּעֵי לֵבָב הֵם, וְהֵם לֹא יָדְעוּ דְרָכָי. יא אֲשֶׁר נִשְׁבַּעְתִּי בְאַפִּי, אִם יְבֹאוּן אֶל מְנוּחָתִי.

צו א שִׁירוּ לַיהוה שִׁיר חָדָשׁ, שִׁירוּ לַיהוה כָּל הָאָרֶץ. ב שִׁירוּ לַיהוה בָּרְכוּ שְׁמוֹ, בַּשְּׂרוּ מִיּוֹם לְיוֹם יְשׁוּעָתוֹ. ג סַפְּרוּ בַגּוֹיִם כְּבוֹדוֹ, בְּכָל הָעַמִּים נִפְלְאוֹתָיו. ד כִּי גָדוֹל יהוה וּמְהֻלָּל מְאֹד, נוֹרָא הוּא עַל כָּל אֱלֹהִים. ה כִּי, כָּל אֱלֹהֵי הָעַמִּים אֱלִילִים, וַיהוה שָׁמַיִם עָשָׂה. ו הוֹד וְהָדָר לְפָנָיו, עֹז וְתִפְאֶרֶת בְּמִקְדָּשׁוֹ. ז הָבוּ לַיהוה מִשְׁפְּחוֹת עַמִּים, הָבוּ לַיהוה כָּבוֹד וָעֹז. ח הָבוּ לַיהוה כְּבוֹד שְׁמוֹ, שְׂאוּ מִנְחָה וּבֹאוּ לְחַצְרוֹתָיו. ט הִשְׁתַּחֲווּ לַיהוה בְּהַדְרַת קֹדֶשׁ, חִילוּ מִפָּנָיו כָּל הָאָרֶץ. י אִמְרוּ בַגּוֹיִם יהוה מָלָךְ, אַף תִּכּוֹן תֵּבֵל בַּל תִּמּוֹט, יָדִין עַמִּים בְּמֵישָׁרִים. יא יִשְׂמְחוּ הַשָּׁמַיִם וְתָגֵל הָאָרֶץ, יִרְעַם הַיָּם וּמְלֹאוֹ. יב יַעֲלֹז שָׂדַי וְכָל אֲשֶׁר בּוֹ, אָז יְרַנְּנוּ כָּל עֲצֵי יָעַר. יג לִפְנֵי יהוה כִּי בָא, כִּי בָא לִשְׁפֹּט הָאָרֶץ; יִשְׁפֹּט תֵּבֵל בְּצֶדֶק, וְעַמִּים בֶּאֱמוּנָתוֹ.

צז א יהוה מָלָךְ תָּגֵל הָאָרֶץ, יִשְׂמְחוּ אִיִּים רַבִּים. ב עָנָן וַעֲרָפֶל סְבִיבָיו, צֶדֶק וּמִשְׁפָּט מְכוֹן כִּסְאוֹ. ג אֵשׁ לְפָנָיו תֵּלֵךְ, וּתְלַהֵט סָבִיב צָרָיו. ד הֵאִירוּ בְרָקָיו תֵּבֵל, רָאֲתָה וַתָּחֵל הָאָרֶץ. ה הָרִים כַּדּוֹנַג נָמַסּוּ מִלִּפְנֵי יהוה, מִלִּפְנֵי אֲדוֹן כָּל הָאָרֶץ. ו הִגִּידוּ הַשָּׁמַיִם צִדְקוֹ, וְרָאוּ כָל הָעַמִּים כְּבוֹדוֹ. ז יֵבֹשׁוּ כָּל עֹבְדֵי פֶסֶל, הַמִּתְהַלְלִים בָּאֱלִילִים; הִשְׁתַּחֲווּ לוֹ כָּל אֱלֹהִים. ח שָׁמְעָה וַתִּשְׂמַח צִיּוֹן, וַתָּגֵלְנָה בְּנוֹת יְהוּדָה, לְמַעַן מִשְׁפָּטֶיךָ יהוה. ט כִּי אַתָּה יהוה עֶלְיוֹן עַל כָּל הָאָרֶץ, מְאֹד נַעֲלֵיתָ עַל כָּל אֱלֹהִים. י אֹהֲבֵי יהוה שִׂנְאוּ רָע; שֹׁמֵר נַפְשׁוֹת חֲסִידָיו, מִיַּד רְשָׁעִים יַצִּילֵם. יא אוֹר

זֶרַע לַצַּדִּיק, וּלְיִשְׁרֵי לֵב שִׂמְחָה. יב שִׂמְחוּ צַדִּיקִים בַּיהוה, וְהוֹדוּ לְזֵכֶר
קָדְשׁוֹ.

צח א מִזְמוֹר, שִׁירוּ לַיהוה שִׁיר חָדָשׁ, כִּי נִפְלָאוֹת עָשָׂה; הוֹשִׁיעָה לּוֹ יְמִינוֹ
וּזְרוֹעַ קָדְשׁוֹ. ב הוֹדִיעַ יהוה יְשׁוּעָתוֹ, לְעֵינֵי הַגּוֹיִם גִּלָּה צִדְקָתוֹ. ג זָכַר
חַסְדּוֹ וֶאֱמוּנָתוֹ לְבֵית יִשְׂרָאֵל, רָאוּ כָל אַפְסֵי אָרֶץ אֵת יְשׁוּעַת אֱלֹהֵינוּ.
ד הָרִיעוּ לַיהוה כָּל הָאָרֶץ, פִּצְחוּ וְרַנְּנוּ וְזַמֵּרוּ. ה זַמְּרוּ לַיהוה בְּכִנּוֹר, בְּכִנּוֹר
וְקוֹל זִמְרָה. ו בַּחֲצֹצְרוֹת וְקוֹל שׁוֹפָר, הָרִיעוּ לִפְנֵי הַמֶּלֶךְ יהוה. ז יִרְעַם הַיָּם
וּמְלֹאוֹ, תֵּבֵל וְיֹשְׁבֵי בָהּ. ח נְהָרוֹת יִמְחֲאוּ כָף, יַחַד הָרִים יְרַנֵּנוּ. ט לִפְנֵי יהוה
כִּי בָא לִשְׁפֹּט הָאָרֶץ; יִשְׁפֹּט תֵּבֵל בְּצֶדֶק, וְעַמִּים בְּמֵישָׁרִים.

צט א יהוה מָלָךְ יִרְגְּזוּ עַמִּים, יֹשֵׁב כְּרוּבִים תָּנוּט הָאָרֶץ. ב יהוה בְּצִיּוֹן
גָּדוֹל, וְרָם הוּא עַל כָּל הָעַמִּים. ג יוֹדוּ שִׁמְךָ גָּדוֹל וְנוֹרָא, קָדוֹשׁ הוּא.
ד וְעֹז מֶלֶךְ מִשְׁפָּט אָהֵב; אַתָּה כּוֹנַנְתָּ מֵישָׁרִים, מִשְׁפָּט וּצְדָקָה בְּיַעֲקֹב אַתָּה
עָשִׂיתָ. ה רוֹמְמוּ יהוה אֱלֹהֵינוּ, וְהִשְׁתַּחֲווּ לַהֲדֹם רַגְלָיו, קָדוֹשׁ הוּא. ו מֹשֶׁה
וְאַהֲרֹן בְּכֹהֲנָיו, וּשְׁמוּאֵל בְּקֹרְאֵי שְׁמוֹ, קֹרִאים אֶל יהוה וְהוּא יַעֲנֵם.
ז בְּעַמּוּד עָנָן יְדַבֵּר אֲלֵיהֶם, שָׁמְרוּ עֵדֹתָיו וְחֹק נָתַן לָמוֹ. ח יהוה אֱלֹהֵינוּ
אַתָּה עֲנִיתָם; אֵל נֹשֵׂא הָיִיתָ לָהֶם, וְנֹקֵם עַל עֲלִילוֹתָם. ט רוֹמְמוּ יהוה
אֱלֹהֵינוּ, וְהִשְׁתַּחֲווּ לְהַר קָדְשׁוֹ; כִּי קָדוֹשׁ יהוה אֱלֹהֵינוּ.

ק א מִזְמוֹר לְתוֹדָה, הָרִיעוּ לַיהוה כָּל הָאָרֶץ. ב עִבְדוּ אֶת יהוה בְּשִׂמְחָה,
בֹּאוּ לְפָנָיו בִּרְנָנָה. ג דְּעוּ כִּי יהוה הוּא אֱלֹהִים, הוּא עָשָׂנוּ, וְלוֹ אֲנַחְנוּ,
עַמּוֹ וְצֹאן מַרְעִיתוֹ. ד בֹּאוּ שְׁעָרָיו בְּתוֹדָה, חֲצֵרֹתָיו בִּתְהִלָּה; הוֹדוּ לוֹ,
בָּרְכוּ שְׁמוֹ. ה כִּי טוֹב יהוה, לְעוֹלָם חַסְדּוֹ, וְעַד דֹּר וָדֹר אֱמוּנָתוֹ.

קא א לְדָוִד מִזְמוֹר; חֶסֶד וּמִשְׁפָּט אָשִׁירָה, לְךָ יהוה אֲזַמֵּרָה. ב אַשְׂכִּילָה
בְּדֶרֶךְ תָּמִים, מָתַי תָּבוֹא אֵלָי; אֶתְהַלֵּךְ בְּתָם לְבָבִי בְּקֶרֶב בֵּיתִי. ג לֹא
אָשִׁית לְנֶגֶד עֵינַי דְּבַר בְּלִיָּעַל; עֲשֹׂה סֵטִים שָׂנֵאתִי, לֹא יִדְבַּק בִּי. ד לֵבָב
עִקֵּשׁ יָסוּר מִמֶּנִּי, רָע לֹא אֵדָע. ה מְלָשְׁנִי בַסֵּתֶר רֵעֵהוּ, אוֹתוֹ אַצְמִית; גְּבַהּ
עֵינַיִם וּרְחַב לֵבָב, אֹתוֹ לֹא אוּכָל. ו עֵינַי בְּנֶאֶמְנֵי אֶרֶץ לָשֶׁבֶת עִמָּדִי; הֹלֵךְ
בְּדֶרֶךְ תָּמִים, הוּא יְשָׁרְתֵנִי. ז לֹא יֵשֵׁב בְּקֶרֶב בֵּיתִי עֹשֵׂה רְמִיָּה; דֹּבֵר
שְׁקָרִים, לֹא יִכּוֹן לְנֶגֶד עֵינָי. ח לַבְּקָרִים אַצְמִית כָּל רִשְׁעֵי אָרֶץ, לְהַכְרִית
מֵעִיר יהוה כָּל פֹּעֲלֵי אָוֶן.

קב א תְּפִלָּה לְעָנִי כִי יַעֲטֹף, וְלִפְנֵי יהוה יִשְׁפֹּךְ שִׂיחוֹ. ב יהוה שִׁמְעָה
תְפִלָּתִי, וְשַׁוְעָתִי אֵלֶיךָ תָבוֹא. ג אַל תַּסְתֵּר פָּנֶיךָ מִמֶּנִּי בְּיוֹם צַר לִי;
הַטֵּה אֵלַי אָזְנֶךָ, בְּיוֹם אֶקְרָא, מַהֵר עֲנֵנִי. ד כִּי כָלוּ בְעָשָׁן יָמָי, וְעַצְמוֹתַי

כְּמוֹקֵד נִחָרוּ. ה הוּכָּה כָעֵשֶׂב וַיִּבַשׁ לִבִּי, כִּי שָׁכַחְתִּי מֵאֲכֹל לַחְמִי. ו מִקּוֹל אַנְחָתִי, דָּבְקָה עַצְמִי לִבְשָׂרִי. ז דָּמִיתִי לִקְאַת מִדְבָּר, הָיִיתִי כְּכוֹס חֳרָבוֹת. ח שָׁקַדְתִּי וָאֶהְיֶה, כְּצִפּוֹר בּוֹדֵד עַל גָּג. ט כָּל הַיּוֹם חֵרְפוּנִי אוֹיְבָי, מְהוֹלָלַי בִּי נִשְׁבָּעוּ. י כִּי אֵפֶר כַּלֶּחֶם אָכָלְתִּי, וְשִׁקֻּוַי בִּבְכִי מָסָכְתִּי. יא מִפְּנֵי זַעַמְךָ וְקִצְפֶּךָ, כִּי נְשָׂאתַנִי וַתַּשְׁלִיכֵנִי. יב יָמַי כְּצֵל נָטוּי, וַאֲנִי כָּעֵשֶׂב אִיבָשׁ. יג וְאַתָּה יהוה לְעוֹלָם תֵּשֵׁב, וְזִכְרְךָ לְדֹר וָדֹר. יד אַתָּה תָקוּם תְּרַחֵם צִיּוֹן, כִּי עֵת לְחֶנְנָהּ כִּי בָא מוֹעֵד. טו כִּי רָצוּ עֲבָדֶיךָ אֶת אֲבָנֶיהָ, וְאֶת עֲפָרָהּ יְחֹנֵנוּ. טז וְיִירְאוּ גוֹיִם אֶת שֵׁם יהוה, וְכָל מַלְכֵי הָאָרֶץ אֶת כְּבוֹדֶךָ. יז כִּי בָנָה יהוה צִיּוֹן, נִרְאָה בִּכְבוֹדוֹ. יח פָּנָה אֶל תְּפִלַּת הָעַרְעָר, וְלֹא בָזָה אֶת תְּפִלָּתָם. יט תִּכָּתֶב זֹאת לְדוֹר אַחֲרוֹן, וְעַם נִבְרָא יְהַלֶּל יָהּ. כ כִּי הִשְׁקִיף מִמְּרוֹם קָדְשׁוֹ, יהוה מִשָּׁמַיִם אֶל אֶרֶץ הִבִּיט. כא לִשְׁמֹעַ אֶנְקַת אָסִיר, לְפַתֵּחַ בְּנֵי תְמוּתָה. כב לְסַפֵּר בְּצִיּוֹן שֵׁם יהוה, וּתְהִלָּתוֹ בִּירוּשָׁלָיִם. כג בְּהִקָּבֵץ עַמִּים יַחְדָּו, וּמַמְלָכוֹת לַעֲבֹד אֶת יהוה. כד עִנָּה בַדֶּרֶךְ כֹּחִי, קִצַּר יָמָי. כה אֹמַר: אֵלִי, אַל תַּעֲלֵנִי בַּחֲצִי יָמָי, בְּדוֹר דּוֹרִים שְׁנוֹתֶיךָ. כו לְפָנִים הָאָרֶץ יָסַדְתָּ, וּמַעֲשֵׂה יָדֶיךָ שָׁמָיִם. כז הֵמָּה יֹאבֵדוּ, וְאַתָּה תַעֲמֹד; וְכֻלָּם כַּבֶּגֶד יִבְלוּ, כַּלְּבוּשׁ תַּחֲלִיפֵם וְיַחֲלֹפוּ. כח וְאַתָּה הוּא, וּשְׁנוֹתֶיךָ לֹא יִתָּמּוּ. כט בְּנֵי עֲבָדֶיךָ יִשְׁכּוֹנוּ, וְזַרְעָם לְפָנֶיךָ יִכּוֹן.

קג א לְדָוִד, בָּרְכִי נַפְשִׁי אֶת יהוה, וְכָל קְרָבַי אֶת שֵׁם קָדְשׁוֹ. ב בָּרְכִי נַפְשִׁי אֶת יהוה, וְאַל תִּשְׁכְּחִי כָּל גְּמוּלָיו. ג הַסֹּלֵחַ לְכָל עֲוֹנֵכִי, הָרֹפֵא לְכָל תַּחֲלֻאָיְכִי. ד הַגּוֹאֵל מִשַּׁחַת חַיָּיְכִי, הַמְעַטְּרֵכִי חֶסֶד וְרַחֲמִים. ה הַמַּשְׂבִּיעַ בַּטּוֹב עֶדְיֵךְ, תִּתְחַדֵּשׁ כַּנֶּשֶׁר נְעוּרָיְכִי. ו עֹשֵׂה צְדָקוֹת יהוה, וּמִשְׁפָּטִים לְכָל עֲשׁוּקִים. ז יוֹדִיעַ דְּרָכָיו לְמֹשֶׁה, לִבְנֵי יִשְׂרָאֵל עֲלִילוֹתָיו. ח רַחוּם וְחַנּוּן יהוה, אֶרֶךְ אַפַּיִם וְרַב חָסֶד. ט לֹא לָנֶצַח יָרִיב, וְלֹא לְעוֹלָם יִטּוֹר. י לֹא כַחֲטָאֵינוּ עָשָׂה לָנוּ, וְלֹא כַעֲוֹנֹתֵינוּ גָּמַל עָלֵינוּ. יא כִּי כִגְבֹהַּ שָׁמַיִם עַל הָאָרֶץ, גָּבַר חַסְדּוֹ עַל יְרֵאָיו. יב כִּרְחֹק מִזְרָח מִמַּעֲרָב, הִרְחִיק מִמֶּנּוּ אֶת פְּשָׁעֵינוּ. יג כְּרַחֵם אָב עַל בָּנִים, רִחַם יהוה עַל יְרֵאָיו. יד כִּי הוּא יָדַע יִצְרֵנוּ, זָכוּר כִּי עָפָר אֲנָחְנוּ. טו אֱנוֹשׁ כֶּחָצִיר יָמָיו, כְּצִיץ הַשָּׂדֶה כֵּן יָצִיץ. טז כִּי רוּחַ עָבְרָה בּוֹ וְאֵינֶנּוּ, וְלֹא יַכִּירֶנּוּ עוֹד מְקוֹמוֹ. יז וְחֶסֶד יהוה מֵעוֹלָם וְעַד עוֹלָם עַל יְרֵאָיו, וְצִדְקָתוֹ לִבְנֵי בָנִים. יח לְשֹׁמְרֵי בְרִיתוֹ, וּלְזֹכְרֵי פִקֻּדָיו לַעֲשׂוֹתָם. יט יהוה בַּשָּׁמַיִם הֵכִין כִּסְאוֹ, וּמַלְכוּתוֹ בַּכֹּל מָשָׁלָה. כ בָּרְכוּ יהוה מַלְאָכָיו; גִּבֹּרֵי כֹחַ עֹשֵׂי דְבָרוֹ, לִשְׁמֹעַ בְּקוֹל דְּבָרוֹ. כא בָּרְכוּ יהוה כָּל צְבָאָיו, מְשָׁרְתָיו עֹשֵׂי רְצוֹנוֹ. כב בָּרְכוּ יהוה כָּל מַעֲשָׂיו, בְּכָל מְקֹמוֹת מֶמְשַׁלְתּוֹ, בָּרְכִי נַפְשִׁי אֶת יהוה.

קד א בָּרְכִי נַפְשִׁי אֶת יהוה; יהוה אֱלֹהַי גָּדַלְתָּ מְּאֹד, הוֹד וְהָדָר לָבָשְׁתָּ. ב עֹטֶה אוֹר כַּשַּׂלְמָה, נוֹטֶה שָׁמַיִם כַּיְרִיעָה. ג הַמְקָרֶה בַמַּיִם עֲלִיּוֹתָיו; הַשָּׂם עָבִים רְכוּבוֹ, הַמְהַלֵּךְ עַל כַּנְפֵי רוּחַ. ד עֹשֶׂה מַלְאָכָיו רוּחוֹת, מְשָׁרְתָיו אֵשׁ לֹהֵט. ה יָסַד אֶרֶץ עַל מְכוֹנֶיהָ, בַּל תִּמּוֹט עוֹלָם וָעֶד. ו תְּהוֹם כַּלְּבוּשׁ כִּסִּיתוֹ, עַל הָרִים יַעַמְדוּ מָיִם. ז מִן גַּעֲרָתְךָ יְנוּסוּן, מִן קוֹל רַעַמְךָ יֵחָפֵזוּן. ח יַעֲלוּ הָרִים, יֵרְדוּ בְקָעוֹת, אֶל מְקוֹם זֶה יָסַדְתָּ לָהֶם. ט גְּבוּל שַׂמְתָּ בַּל יַעֲבֹרוּן, בַּל יְשׁוּבוּן לְכַסּוֹת הָאָרֶץ. י הַמְשַׁלֵּחַ מַעְיָנִים בַּנְּחָלִים, בֵּין הָרִים יְהַלֵּכוּן. יא יַשְׁקוּ כָּל חַיְתוֹ שָׂדָי, יִשְׁבְּרוּ פְרָאִים צְמָאָם. יב עֲלֵיהֶם עוֹף הַשָּׁמַיִם יִשְׁכּוֹן, מִבֵּין עֳפָאיִם יִתְּנוּ קוֹל. יג מַשְׁקֶה הָרִים מֵעֲלִיּוֹתָיו, מִפְּרִי מַעֲשֶׂיךָ תִּשְׂבַּע הָאָרֶץ. יד מַצְמִיחַ חָצִיר לַבְּהֵמָה, וְעֵשֶׂב לַעֲבֹדַת הָאָדָם; לְהוֹצִיא לֶחֶם מִן הָאָרֶץ. טו וְיַיִן יְשַׂמַּח לְבַב אֱנוֹשׁ, לְהַצְהִיל פָּנִים מִשָּׁמֶן, וְלֶחֶם לְבַב אֱנוֹשׁ יִסְעָד. טז יִשְׂבְּעוּ עֲצֵי יהוה, אַרְזֵי לְבָנוֹן אֲשֶׁר נָטָע. יז אֲשֶׁר שָׁם צִפֳּרִים יְקַנֵּנוּ, חֲסִידָה בְּרוֹשִׁים בֵּיתָהּ. יח הָרִים הַגְּבֹהִים לַיְּעֵלִים, סְלָעִים מַחְסֶה לַשְׁפַנִּים. יט עָשָׂה יָרֵחַ לְמוֹעֲדִים, שֶׁמֶשׁ יָדַע מְבוֹאוֹ. כ תָּשֶׁת חֹשֶׁךְ וִיהִי לָיְלָה, בּוֹ תִרְמֹשׂ כָּל חַיְתוֹ יָעַר. כא הַכְּפִירִים שֹׁאֲגִים לַטָּרֶף, וּלְבַקֵּשׁ מֵאֵל אָכְלָם. כב תִּזְרַח הַשֶּׁמֶשׁ יֵאָסֵפוּן, וְאֶל מְעוֹנֹתָם יִרְבָּצוּן. כג יֵצֵא אָדָם לְפָעֳלוֹ, וְלַעֲבֹדָתוֹ עֲדֵי עָרֶב. כד מָה רַבּוּ מַעֲשֶׂיךָ יהוה, כֻּלָּם בְּחָכְמָה עָשִׂיתָ, מָלְאָה הָאָרֶץ קִנְיָנֶךָ. כה זֶה הַיָּם, גָּדוֹל וּרְחַב יָדָיִם; שָׁם רֶמֶשׂ וְאֵין מִסְפָּר, חַיּוֹת קְטַנּוֹת עִם גְּדֹלוֹת. כו שָׁם אֳנִיּוֹת יְהַלֵּכוּן, לִוְיָתָן זֶה יָצַרְתָּ לְשַׂחֶק בּוֹ. כז כֻּלָּם אֵלֶיךָ יְשַׂבֵּרוּן, לָתֵת אָכְלָם בְּעִתּוֹ. כח תִּתֵּן לָהֶם, יִלְקֹטוּן; תִּפְתַּח יָדְךָ, יִשְׂבְּעוּן טוֹב. כט תַּסְתִּיר פָּנֶיךָ יִבָּהֵלוּן; תֹּסֵף רוּחָם יִגְוָעוּן, וְאֶל עֲפָרָם יְשׁוּבוּן. ל תְּשַׁלַּח רוּחֲךָ יִבָּרֵאוּן, וּתְחַדֵּשׁ פְּנֵי אֲדָמָה. לא יְהִי כְבוֹד יהוה לְעוֹלָם, יִשְׂמַח יהוה בְּמַעֲשָׂיו. לב הַמַּבִּיט לָאָרֶץ וַתִּרְעָד, יִגַּע בֶּהָרִים וְיֶעֱשָׁנוּ. לג אָשִׁירָה לַיהוה בְּחַיָּי, אֲזַמְּרָה לֵאלֹהַי בְּעוֹדִי. לד יֶעֱרַב עָלָיו שִׂיחִי, אָנֹכִי אֶשְׂמַח בַּיהוה. לה יִתַּמּוּ חַטָּאִים מִן הָאָרֶץ, וּרְשָׁעִים עוֹד אֵינָם, בָּרְכִי נַפְשִׁי אֶת יהוה, הַלְלוּיָהּ.

קה א הוֹדוּ לַיהוה קִרְאוּ בִשְׁמוֹ, הוֹדִיעוּ בָעַמִּים עֲלִילוֹתָיו. ב שִׁירוּ לוֹ זַמְּרוּ לוֹ, שִׂיחוּ בְּכָל נִפְלְאוֹתָיו. ג הִתְהַלְלוּ בְּשֵׁם קָדְשׁוֹ, יִשְׂמַח לֵב מְבַקְשֵׁי יהוה. ד דִּרְשׁוּ יהוה וְעֻזּוֹ, בַּקְּשׁוּ פָנָיו תָּמִיד. ה זִכְרוּ נִפְלְאוֹתָיו אֲשֶׁר עָשָׂה, מֹפְתָיו וּמִשְׁפְּטֵי פִיו. ו זֶרַע אַבְרָהָם עַבְדּוֹ, בְּנֵי יַעֲקֹב בְּחִירָיו. ז הוּא יהוה אֱלֹהֵינוּ, בְּכָל הָאָרֶץ מִשְׁפָּטָיו. ח זָכַר לְעוֹלָם בְּרִיתוֹ, דָּבָר צִוָּה לְאֶלֶף דּוֹר. ט אֲשֶׁר כָּרַת אֶת אַבְרָהָם, וּשְׁבוּעָתוֹ לְיִשְׂחָק. י וַיַּעֲמִידֶהָ לְיַעֲקֹב לְחֹק,

לְיִשְׂרָאֵל בְּרִית עוֹלָם. יא לֵאמֹר לְךָ אֶתֵּן אֶת אֶרֶץ כְּנָעַן, חֶבֶל נַחֲלַתְכֶם.
יב בִּהְיוֹתָם מְתֵי מִסְפָּר, כִּמְעַט וְגָרִים בָּהּ. יג וַיִּתְהַלְּכוּ מִגּוֹי אֶל גּוֹי,
מִמַּמְלָכָה אֶל עַם אַחֵר. יד לֹא הִנִּיחַ אָדָם לְעָשְׁקָם, וַיּוֹכַח עֲלֵיהֶם מְלָכִים.
טו אַל תִּגְּעוּ בִמְשִׁיחָי, וְלִנְבִיאַי אַל תָּרֵעוּ. טז וַיִּקְרָא רָעָב עַל הָאָרֶץ, כָּל
מַטֵּה לֶחֶם שָׁבָר. יז שָׁלַח לִפְנֵיהֶם אִישׁ, לְעֶבֶד נִמְכַּר יוֹסֵף. יח עִנּוּ בַכֶּבֶל
רַגְלוֹ, בַּרְזֶל בָּאָה נַפְשׁוֹ. יט עַד עֵת בֹּא דְבָרוֹ, אִמְרַת יהוה צְרָפָתְהוּ. כ שָׁלַח
מֶלֶךְ וַיַּתִּירֵהוּ, מֹשֵׁל עַמִּים וַיְפַתְּחֵהוּ. כא שָׂמוֹ אָדוֹן לְבֵיתוֹ, וּמֹשֵׁל בְּכָל
קִנְיָנוֹ. כב לֶאְסֹר שָׂרָיו בְּנַפְשׁוֹ, וּזְקֵנָיו יְחַכֵּם. כג וַיָּבֹא יִשְׂרָאֵל מִצְרָיִם, וְיַעֲקֹב
גָּר בְּאֶרֶץ חָם. כד וַיֶּפֶר אֶת עַמּוֹ מְאֹד, וַיַּעֲצִמֵהוּ מִצָּרָיו. כה הָפַךְ לִבָּם לִשְׂנֹא
עַמּוֹ, לְהִתְנַכֵּל בַּעֲבָדָיו. כו שָׁלַח מֹשֶׁה עַבְדּוֹ, אַהֲרֹן אֲשֶׁר בָּחַר בּוֹ. כז שָׂמוּ
בָם דִּבְרֵי אֹתוֹתָיו, וּמֹפְתִים בְּאֶרֶץ חָם. כח שָׁלַח חֹשֶׁךְ וַיַּחְשִׁךְ, וְלֹא מָרוּ
אֶת דְּבָרוֹ. כט הָפַךְ אֶת מֵימֵיהֶם לְדָם, וַיָּמֶת אֶת דְּגָתָם. ל שָׁרַץ אַרְצָם
צְפַרְדְּעִים, בְּחַדְרֵי מַלְכֵיהֶם. לא אָמַר וַיָּבֹא עָרֹב, כִּנִּים בְּכָל גְּבוּלָם. לב נָתַן
גִּשְׁמֵיהֶם בָּרָד, אֵשׁ לֶהָבוֹת בְּאַרְצָם. לג וַיַּךְ גַּפְנָם וּתְאֵנָתָם, וַיְשַׁבֵּר עֵץ
גְּבוּלָם. לד אָמַר וַיָּבֹא אַרְבֶּה, וְיֶלֶק וְאֵין מִסְפָּר. לה וַיֹּאכַל כָּל עֵשֶׂב בְּאַרְצָם,
וַיֹּאכַל פְּרִי אַדְמָתָם. לו וַיַּךְ כָּל בְּכוֹר בְּאַרְצָם, רֵאשִׁית לְכָל אוֹנָם.
לז וַיּוֹצִיאֵם בְּכֶסֶף וְזָהָב, וְאֵין בִּשְׁבָטָיו כּוֹשֵׁל. לח שָׂמַח מִצְרַיִם בְּצֵאתָם, כִּי
נָפַל פַּחְדָּם עֲלֵיהֶם. לט פָּרַשׂ עָנָן לְמָסָךְ, וְאֵשׁ לְהָאִיר לָיְלָה. מ שָׁאַל וַיָּבֵא
שְׂלָו, וְלֶחֶם שָׁמַיִם יַשְׂבִּיעֵם. מא פָּתַח צוּר וַיָּזוּבוּ מָיִם, הָלְכוּ בַּצִּיּוֹת נָהָר.
מב כִּי זָכַר אֶת דְּבַר קָדְשׁוֹ, אֶת אַבְרָהָם עַבְדּוֹ. מג וַיּוֹצִא עַמּוֹ בְשָׂשׂוֹן, בְּרִנָּה
אֶת בְּחִירָיו. מד וַיִּתֵּן לָהֶם אַרְצוֹת גּוֹיִם, וַעֲמַל לְאֻמִּים יִירָשׁוּ. מה בַּעֲבוּר
יִשְׁמְרוּ חֻקָּיו, וְתוֹרֹתָיו יִנְצֹרוּ, הַלְלוּיָהּ.

DAY 9 / יוֹם כ"ב לַחֹדֶשׁ

קו א הַלְלוּיָהּ, הוֹדוּ לַיהוה כִּי טוֹב, כִּי לְעוֹלָם חַסְדּוֹ. ב מִי יְמַלֵּל גְּבוּרוֹת
יהוה, יַשְׁמִיעַ כָּל תְּהִלָּתוֹ. ג אַשְׁרֵי שֹׁמְרֵי מִשְׁפָּט, עֹשֵׂה צְדָקָה בְּכָל
עֵת. ד זָכְרֵנִי יהוה בִּרְצוֹן עַמֶּךָ, פָּקְדֵנִי בִּישׁוּעָתֶךָ. ה לִרְאוֹת בְּטוֹבַת
בְּחִירֶיךָ, לִשְׂמֹחַ בְּשִׂמְחַת גּוֹיֶךָ; לְהִתְהַלֵּל עִם נַחֲלָתֶךָ. ו חָטָאנוּ עִם
אֲבוֹתֵינוּ, הֶעֱוִינוּ הִרְשָׁעְנוּ. ז אֲבוֹתֵינוּ בְמִצְרַיִם לֹא הִשְׂכִּילוּ נִפְלְאוֹתֶיךָ, לֹא
זָכְרוּ אֶת רֹב חֲסָדֶיךָ, וַיַּמְרוּ עַל יָם בְּיַם סוּף. ח וַיּוֹשִׁיעֵם לְמַעַן שְׁמוֹ,
לְהוֹדִיעַ אֶת גְּבוּרָתוֹ. ט וַיִּגְעַר בְּיַם סוּף וַיֶּחֱרָב, וַיּוֹלִיכֵם בַּתְּהֹמוֹת כַּמִּדְבָּר.
י וַיּוֹשִׁיעֵם מִיַּד שׂוֹנֵא, וַיִּגְאָלֵם מִיַּד אוֹיֵב. יא וַיְכַסּוּ מַיִם צָרֵיהֶם, אֶחָד מֵהֶם
לֹא נוֹתָר. יב וַיַּאֲמִינוּ בִדְבָרָיו, יָשִׁירוּ תְּהִלָּתוֹ. יג מִהֲרוּ שָׁכְחוּ מַעֲשָׂיו, לֹא
חִכּוּ לַעֲצָתוֹ. יד וַיִּתְאַוּוּ תַאֲוָה בַּמִּדְבָּר, וַיְנַסּוּ אֵל בִּישִׁימוֹן. טו וַיִּתֵּן לָהֶם

שְׁאֵלָתָם, וַיְשַׁלַּח רָזוֹן בְּנַפְשָׁם. טז וַיְקַנְאוּ לְמֹשֶׁה בַּמַּחֲנֶה, לְאַהֲרֹן קְדוֹשׁ
יהוה. יז תִּפְתַּח אֶרֶץ וַתִּבְלַע דָּתָן, וַתְּכַס עַל עֲדַת אֲבִירָם. יח וַתִּבְעַר אֵשׁ
בַּעֲדָתָם, לֶהָבָה תְּלַהֵט רְשָׁעִים. יט יַעֲשׂוּ עֵגֶל בְּחֹרֵב, וַיִּשְׁתַּחֲווּ לְמַסֵּכָה.
כ וַיָּמִירוּ אֶת כְּבוֹדָם, בְּתַבְנִית שׁוֹר אֹכֵל עֵשֶׂב. כא שָׁכְחוּ אֵל מוֹשִׁיעָם,
עֹשֶׂה גְדֹלוֹת בְּמִצְרָיִם. כב נִפְלָאוֹת בְּאֶרֶץ חָם, נוֹרָאוֹת עַל יַם סוּף.
כג וַיֹּאמֶר לְהַשְׁמִידָם; לוּלֵי מֹשֶׁה בְחִירוֹ עָמַד בַּפֶּרֶץ לְפָנָיו, לְהָשִׁיב חֲמָתוֹ
מֵהַשְׁחִית. כד וַיִּמְאֲסוּ בְּאֶרֶץ חֶמְדָּה, לֹא הֶאֱמִינוּ לִדְבָרוֹ. כה וַיֵּרָגְנוּ
בְאָהֳלֵיהֶם, לֹא שָׁמְעוּ בְּקוֹל יהוה. כו וַיִּשָּׂא יָדוֹ לָהֶם, לְהַפִּיל אוֹתָם
בַּמִּדְבָּר. כז וּלְהַפִּיל זַרְעָם בַּגּוֹיִם, וּלְזָרוֹתָם בָּאֲרָצוֹת. כח וַיִּצָּמְדוּ לְבַעַל
פְּעוֹר, וַיֹּאכְלוּ זִבְחֵי מֵתִים. כט וַיַּכְעִיסוּ בְּמַעַלְלֵיהֶם, וַתִּפְרָץ בָּם מַגֵּפָה.
ל וַיַּעֲמֹד פִּינְחָס וַיְפַלֵּל, וַתֵּעָצַר הַמַּגֵּפָה. לא וַתֵּחָשֶׁב לוֹ לִצְדָקָה, לְדֹר וָדֹר
עַד עוֹלָם. לב וַיַּקְצִיפוּ עַל מֵי מְרִיבָה, וַיֵּרַע לְמֹשֶׁה בַּעֲבוּרָם. לג כִּי הִמְרוּ אֶת
רוּחוֹ, וַיְבַטֵּא בִּשְׂפָתָיו. לד לֹא הִשְׁמִידוּ אֶת הָעַמִּים, אֲשֶׁר אָמַר יהוה לָהֶם.
לה וַיִּתְעָרְבוּ בַגּוֹיִם, וַיִּלְמְדוּ מַעֲשֵׂיהֶם. לו וַיַּעַבְדוּ אֶת עֲצַבֵּיהֶם, וַיִּהְיוּ לָהֶם
לְמוֹקֵשׁ. לז וַיִּזְבְּחוּ אֶת בְּנֵיהֶם וְאֶת בְּנוֹתֵיהֶם לַשֵּׁדִים. לח וַיִּשְׁפְּכוּ דָם נָקִי,
דַּם בְּנֵיהֶם וּבְנוֹתֵיהֶם, אֲשֶׁר זִבְּחוּ לַעֲצַבֵּי כְנָעַן; וַתֶּחֱנַף הָאָרֶץ בַּדָּמִים.
לט וַיִּטְמְאוּ בְמַעֲשֵׂיהֶם, וַיִּזְנוּ בְּמַעַלְלֵיהֶם. מ וַיִּחַר אַף יהוה בְּעַמּוֹ, וַיְתָעֵב
אֶת נַחֲלָתוֹ. מא וַיִּתְּנֵם בְּיַד גּוֹיִם, וַיִּמְשְׁלוּ בָהֶם שֹׂנְאֵיהֶם. מב וַיִּלְחָצוּם
אוֹיְבֵיהֶם, וַיִּכָּנְעוּ תַּחַת יָדָם. מג פְּעָמִים רַבּוֹת יַצִּילֵם; וְהֵמָּה יַמְרוּ בַעֲצָתָם,
וַיָּמֹכּוּ בַּעֲוֹנָם. מד וַיַּרְא בַּצַּר לָהֶם, בְּשָׁמְעוֹ אֶת רִנָּתָם. מה וַיִּזְכֹּר לָהֶם בְּרִיתוֹ,
וַיִּנָּחֵם כְּרֹב חֲסָדָיו. מו וַיִּתֵּן אוֹתָם לְרַחֲמִים, לִפְנֵי כָּל שׁוֹבֵיהֶם. מז הוֹשִׁיעֵנוּ
יהוה אֱלֹהֵינוּ, וְקַבְּצֵנוּ מִן הַגּוֹיִם; לְהֹדוֹת לְשֵׁם קָדְשֶׁךָ, לְהִשְׁתַּבֵּחַ
בִּתְהִלָּתֶךָ. מח בָּרוּךְ יהוה אֱלֹהֵי יִשְׂרָאֵל מִן הָעוֹלָם וְעַד הָעוֹלָם, וְאָמַר כָּל
הָעָם אָמֵן, הַלְלוּיָהּ.

BOOK FIVE / ספר חמישי

﹛ FRIDAY / יום ששי ﹜

קז א הֹדוּ לַיהוה כִּי טוֹב, כִּי לְעוֹלָם חַסְדּוֹ. ב יֹאמְרוּ גְּאוּלֵי יהוה, אֲשֶׁר
גְּאָלָם מִיַּד צָר. ג וּמֵאֲרָצוֹת קִבְּצָם; מִמִּזְרָח וּמִמַּעֲרָב, מִצָּפוֹן וּמִיָּם.
ד תָּעוּ בַמִּדְבָּר בִּישִׁימוֹן דָּרֶךְ, עִיר מוֹשָׁב לֹא מָצָאוּ. ה רְעֵבִים גַּם צְמֵאִים,
נַפְשָׁם בָּהֶם תִּתְעַטָּף. ו וַיִּצְעֲקוּ אֶל יהוה בַּצַּר לָהֶם, מִמְּצוּקוֹתֵיהֶם יַצִּילֵם.
ז וַיַּדְרִיכֵם בְּדֶרֶךְ יְשָׁרָה, לָלֶכֶת אֶל עִיר מוֹשָׁב. ח יוֹדוּ לַיהוה חַסְדּוֹ,
וְנִפְלְאוֹתָיו לִבְנֵי אָדָם. ט כִּי הִשְׂבִּיעַ נֶפֶשׁ שֹׁקֵקָה, וְנֶפֶשׁ רְעֵבָה מִלֵּא טוֹב.
י יֹשְׁבֵי חֹשֶׁךְ וְצַלְמָוֶת, אֲסִירֵי עֳנִי וּבַרְזֶל. יא כִּי הִמְרוּ אִמְרֵי אֵל, וַעֲצַת

עֶלְיוֹן נָאָצוּ. יבוַיַּכְנַע בֶּעָמָל לִבָּם, כָּשְׁלוּ וְאֵין עֹזֵר. יגוַיִּזְעֲקוּ אֶל יהוה בַּצַּר לָהֶם, מִמְּצֻקוֹתֵיהֶם יוֹשִׁיעֵם. ידיוֹצִיאֵם מֵחֹשֶׁךְ וְצַלְמָוֶת, וּמוֹסְרוֹתֵיהֶם יְנַתֵּק. טויוֹדוּ לַיהוה חַסְדּוֹ, וְנִפְלְאוֹתָיו לִבְנֵי אָדָם. טזכִּי שִׁבַּר דַּלְתוֹת נְחֹשֶׁת, וּבְרִיחֵי בַרְזֶל גִּדֵּעַ. יזאֱוִלִים מִדֶּרֶךְ פִּשְׁעָם, וּמֵעֲוֹנֹתֵיהֶם יִתְעַנּוּ. יחכָּל אֹכֶל תְּתַעֵב נַפְשָׁם, וַיַּגִּיעוּ עַד שַׁעֲרֵי מָוֶת. יטוַיִּזְעֲקוּ אֶל יהוה בַּצַּר לָהֶם, מִמְּצֻקוֹתֵיהֶם יוֹשִׁיעֵם. כיִשְׁלַח דְּבָרוֹ וְיִרְפָּאֵם, וִימַלֵּט מִשְּׁחִיתוֹתָם. כאיוֹדוּ לַיהוה חַסְדּוֹ, וְנִפְלְאוֹתָיו לִבְנֵי אָדָם. כבוְיִזְבְּחוּ זִבְחֵי תוֹדָה, וִיסַפְּרוּ מַעֲשָׂיו בְּרִנָּה. כגיוֹרְדֵי הַיָּם בָּאֳנִיּוֹת, עֹשֵׂי מְלָאכָה בְּמַיִם רַבִּים. כדהֵמָּה רָאוּ מַעֲשֵׂי יהוה, וְנִפְלְאוֹתָיו בִּמְצוּלָה. כהוַיֹּאמֶר וַיַּעֲמֵד רוּחַ סְעָרָה, וַתְּרוֹמֵם גַּלָּיו. כוֹיַעֲלוּ שָׁמַיִם יֵרְדוּ תְהוֹמוֹת, נַפְשָׁם בְּרָעָה תִתְמוֹגָג. כזיָחוֹגּוּ וְיָנוּעוּ כַּשִּׁכּוֹר, וְכָל חָכְמָתָם תִּתְבַּלָּע. כחוַיִּצְעֲקוּ אֶל יהוה בַּצַּר לָהֶם, וּמִמְּצוּקֹתֵיהֶם יוֹצִיאֵם. כטיָקֵם סְעָרָה לִדְמָמָה, וַיֶּחֱשׁוּ גַּלֵּיהֶם. לוַיִּשְׂמְחוּ כִי יִשְׁתֹּקוּ, וַיַּנְחֵם אֶל מְחוֹז חֶפְצָם. לאיוֹדוּ לַיהוה חַסְדּוֹ, וְנִפְלְאוֹתָיו לִבְנֵי אָדָם. לבוִירוֹמְמוּהוּ בִּקְהַל עָם, וּבְמוֹשַׁב זְקֵנִים יְהַלְלוּהוּ. לגיָשֵׂם נְהָרוֹת לְמִדְבָּר, וּמֹצָאֵי מַיִם לְצִמָּאוֹן. לדאֶרֶץ פְּרִי לִמְלֵחָה, מֵרָעַת יֹשְׁבֵי בָהּ. להיָשֵׂם מִדְבָּר לַאֲגַם מַיִם, וְאֶרֶץ צִיָּה לְמֹצָאֵי מָיִם. לווַיּוֹשֶׁב שָׁם רְעֵבִים, וַיְכוֹנְנוּ עִיר מוֹשָׁב. לזוַיִּזְרְעוּ שָׂדוֹת, וַיִּטְּעוּ כְרָמִים, וַיַּעֲשׂוּ פְּרִי תְבוּאָה. לחוַיְבָרְכֵם וַיִּרְבּוּ מְאֹד, וּבְהֶמְתָּם לֹא יַמְעִיט. לטוַיִּמְעֲטוּ וַיָּשֹׁחוּ, מֵעֹצֶר רָעָה וְיָגוֹן. משֹׁפֵךְ בּוּז עַל נְדִיבִים, וַיַּתְעֵם בְּתֹהוּ לֹא דָרֶךְ. מאוַיְשַׂגֵּב אֶבְיוֹן מֵעוֹנִי, וַיָּשֶׂם כַּצֹּאן מִשְׁפָּחוֹת. מביִרְאוּ יְשָׁרִים וְיִשְׂמָחוּ, וְכָל עַוְלָה קָפְצָה פִּיהָ. מגמִי חָכָם וְיִשְׁמָר אֵלֶּה, וְיִתְבּוֹנְנוּ חַסְדֵי יהוה.

DAY 23 / יוֹם כ״ג לַחוֹדֶשׁ

קח אשִׁיר מִזְמוֹר לְדָוִד. בנָכוֹן לִבִּי אֱלֹהִים, אָשִׁירָה וַאֲזַמְּרָה אַף כְּבוֹדִי. געוּרָה הַנֵּבֶל וְכִנּוֹר, אָעִירָה שָּׁחַר. דאוֹדְךָ בָעַמִּים יהוה, וַאֲזַמֶּרְךָ בַּלְאֻמִּים. הכִּי גָדֹל מֵעַל שָׁמַיִם חַסְדֶּךָ, וְעַד שְׁחָקִים אֲמִתֶּךָ. ורוּמָה עַל שָׁמַיִם אֱלֹהִים; וְעַל כָּל הָאָרֶץ כְּבוֹדֶךָ. זלְמַעַן יֵחָלְצוּן יְדִידֶיךָ, הוֹשִׁיעָה יְמִינְךָ וַעֲנֵנִי. חאֱלֹהִים דִּבֶּר בְּקָדְשׁוֹ אֶעְלֹזָה; אֲחַלְּקָה שְׁכֶם, וְעֵמֶק סֻכּוֹת אֲמַדֵּד. טלִי גִלְעָד לִי מְנַשֶּׁה, וְאֶפְרַיִם מָעוֹז רֹאשִׁי, יְהוּדָה מְחֹקְקִי. ימוֹאָב סִיר רַחְצִי, עַל אֱדוֹם אַשְׁלִיךְ נַעֲלִי, עֲלֵי פְלֶשֶׁת אֶתְרוֹעָע. יאמִי יֹבִלֵנִי עִיר מִבְצָר, מִי נָחַנִי עַד אֱדוֹם. יבהֲלֹא אֱלֹהִים זְנַחְתָּנוּ, וְלֹא תֵצֵא אֱלֹהִים בְּצִבְאֹתֵינוּ. יגהָבָה לָּנוּ עֶזְרָת מִצָּר, וְשָׁוְא תְּשׁוּעַת אָדָם. ידבֵּאלֹהִים נַעֲשֶׂה חָיִל, וְהוּא יָבוּס צָרֵינוּ.

קט א לַמְנַצֵּחַ לְדָוִד מִזְמוֹר, אֱלֹהֵי תְהִלָּתִי אַל תֶּחֱרַשׁ. ב כִּי פִי רָשָׁע וּפִי מִרְמָה עָלַי פָּתֵחוּ, דִּבְּרוּ אִתִּי לְשׁוֹן שָׁקֶר. ג וְדִבְרֵי שִׂנְאָה סְבָבוּנִי, וַיִּלָּחֲמוּנִי חִנָּם. ד תַּחַת אַהֲבָתִי יִשְׂטְנוּנִי, וַאֲנִי תְפִלָּה. ה וַיָּשִׂימוּ עָלַי רָעָה תַּחַת טוֹבָה, וְשִׂנְאָה תַּחַת אַהֲבָתִי. ו הַפְקֵד עָלָיו רָשָׁע, וְשָׂטָן יַעֲמֹד עַל יְמִינוֹ. ז בְּהִשָּׁפְטוֹ יֵצֵא רָשָׁע, וּתְפִלָּתוֹ תִּהְיֶה לַחֲטָאָה. ח יִהְיוּ יָמָיו מְעַטִּים, פְּקֻדָּתוֹ יִקַּח אַחֵר. ט יִהְיוּ בָנָיו יְתוֹמִים, וְאִשְׁתּוֹ אַלְמָנָה. י וְנוֹעַ יָנוּעוּ בָנָיו וְשִׁאֵלוּ, וְדָרְשׁוּ מֵחָרְבוֹתֵיהֶם. יא יְנַקֵּשׁ נוֹשֶׁה לְכָל אֲשֶׁר לוֹ, וְיָבֹזּוּ זָרִים יְגִיעוֹ. יב אַל יְהִי לוֹ מֹשֵׁךְ חָסֶד, וְאַל יְהִי חוֹנֵן לִיתוֹמָיו. יג יְהִי אַחֲרִיתוֹ לְהַכְרִית, בְּדוֹר אַחֵר יִמַּח שְׁמָם. יד יִזָּכֵר עֲוֹן אֲבֹתָיו אֶל יְהוָה, וְחַטַּאת אִמּוֹ אַל תִּמָּח. טו יִהְיוּ נֶגֶד יְהוָה תָּמִיד, וְיַכְרֵת מֵאֶרֶץ זִכְרָם. טז יַעַן אֲשֶׁר לֹא זָכַר עֲשׂוֹת חָסֶד; וַיִּרְדֹּף אִישׁ עָנִי וְאֶבְיוֹן, וְנִכְאֵה לֵבָב לְמוֹתֵת. יז וַיֶּאֱהַב קְלָלָה וַתְּבוֹאֵהוּ; וְלֹא חָפֵץ בִּבְרָכָה, וַתִּרְחַק מִמֶּנּוּ. יח וַיִּלְבַּשׁ קְלָלָה כְּמַדּוֹ; וַתָּבֹא כַמַּיִם בְּקִרְבּוֹ, וְכַשֶּׁמֶן בְּעַצְמוֹתָיו. יט תְּהִי לוֹ כְּבֶגֶד יַעְטֶה, וּלְמֵזַח תָּמִיד יַחְגְּרֶהָ. כ זֹאת פְּעֻלַּת שֹׂטְנַי מֵאֵת יְהוָה, וְהַדֹּבְרִים רָע עַל נַפְשִׁי. כא וְאַתָּה יְהוִה אֲדֹנָי עֲשֵׂה אִתִּי לְמַעַן שְׁמֶךָ, כִּי טוֹב חַסְדְּךָ הַצִּילֵנִי. כב כִּי עָנִי וְאֶבְיוֹן אָנֹכִי, וְלִבִּי חָלַל בְּקִרְבִּי. כג כְּצֵל כִּנְטוֹתוֹ נֶהֱלָכְתִּי, נִנְעַרְתִּי כָּאַרְבֶּה. כד בִּרְכַּי כָּשְׁלוּ מִצּוֹם, וּבְשָׂרִי כָּחַשׁ מִשָּׁמֶן. כה וַאֲנִי הָיִיתִי חֶרְפָּה לָהֶם, יִרְאוּנִי יְנִיעוּן רֹאשָׁם. כו עָזְרֵנִי יְהוָה אֱלֹהָי, הוֹשִׁיעֵנִי כְחַסְדֶּךָ. כז וְיֵדְעוּ כִּי יָדְךָ זֹּאת, אַתָּה יְהוָה עֲשִׂיתָהּ. כח יְקַלְלוּ הֵמָּה וְאַתָּה תְבָרֵךְ; קָמוּ וַיֵּבֹשׁוּ, וְעַבְדְּךָ יִשְׂמָח. כט יִלְבְּשׁוּ שׂוֹטְנַי כְּלִמָּה, וְיַעֲטוּ כַמְעִיל בָּשְׁתָּם. ל אוֹדֶה יְהוָה מְאֹד בְּפִי, וּבְתוֹךְ רַבִּים אֲהַלְלֶנּוּ. לא כִּי יַעֲמֹד לִימִין אֶבְיוֹן, לְהוֹשִׁיעַ מִשֹּׁפְטֵי נַפְשׁוֹ.

קי א לְדָוִד מִזְמוֹר; נְאֻם יְהוָה לַאדֹנִי: שֵׁב לִימִינִי, עַד אָשִׁית אֹיְבֶיךָ הֲדֹם לְרַגְלֶיךָ. ב מַטֵּה עֻזְּךָ יִשְׁלַח יְהוָה מִצִּיּוֹן, רְדֵה בְּקֶרֶב אֹיְבֶיךָ. ג עַמְּךָ נְדָבֹת בְּיוֹם חֵילֶךָ; בְּהַדְרֵי קֹדֶשׁ מֵרֶחֶם מִשְׁחָר, לְךָ טַל יַלְדֻתֶיךָ. ד נִשְׁבַּע יְהוָה וְלֹא יִנָּחֵם, אַתָּה כֹהֵן לְעוֹלָם, עַל דִּבְרָתִי מַלְכִּי צֶדֶק. ה אֲדֹנָי עַל יְמִינְךָ, מָחַץ בְּיוֹם אַפּוֹ מְלָכִים. ו יָדִין בַּגּוֹיִם מָלֵא גְוִיּוֹת, מָחַץ רֹאשׁ עַל אֶרֶץ רַבָּה. ז מִנַּחַל בַּדֶּרֶךְ יִשְׁתֶּה, עַל כֵּן יָרִים רֹאשׁ.

קיא א הַלְלוּיָהּ, אוֹדֶה יְהוָה בְּכָל לֵבָב, בְּסוֹד יְשָׁרִים וְעֵדָה. ב גְּדֹלִים מַעֲשֵׂי יְהוָה, דְּרוּשִׁים לְכָל חֶפְצֵיהֶם. ג הוֹד וְהָדָר פָּעֳלוֹ, וְצִדְקָתוֹ עֹמֶדֶת לָעַד. ד זֵכֶר עָשָׂה לְנִפְלְאֹתָיו, חַנּוּן וְרַחוּם יְהוָה. ה טֶרֶף נָתַן לִירֵאָיו, יִזְכֹּר לְעוֹלָם בְּרִיתוֹ. ו כֹּחַ מַעֲשָׂיו הִגִּיד לְעַמּוֹ, לָתֵת לָהֶם נַחֲלַת גּוֹיִם. ז מַעֲשֵׂי יָדָיו אֱמֶת וּמִשְׁפָּט, נֶאֱמָנִים כָּל פִּקּוּדָיו. ח סְמוּכִים לָעַד

לְעוֹלָם, עֲשׂוּיִם בֶּאֱמֶת וְיָשָׁר. טפְּדוּת שָׁלַח לְעַמּוֹ, צִוָּה לְעוֹלָם בְּרִיתוֹ; קָדוֹשׁ וְנוֹרָא שְׁמוֹ. ירֵאשִׁית חָכְמָה יִרְאַת יהוה, שֵׂכֶל טוֹב לְכָל עֹשֵׂיהֶם; תְּהִלָּתוֹ עֹמֶדֶת לָעַד.

קיב אהַלְלוּיָהּ, אַשְׁרֵי אִישׁ יָרֵא אֶת יהוה, בְּמִצְוֹתָיו חָפֵץ מְאֹד. בגִּבּוֹר בָּאָרֶץ יִהְיֶה זַרְעוֹ, דּוֹר יְשָׁרִים יְבֹרָךְ. גהוֹן וָעֹשֶׁר בְּבֵיתוֹ, וְצִדְקָתוֹ עֹמֶדֶת לָעַד. דזָרַח בַּחֹשֶׁךְ אוֹר לַיְשָׁרִים, חַנּוּן וְרַחוּם וְצַדִּיק. הטוֹב אִישׁ חוֹנֵן וּמַלְוֶה, יְכַלְכֵּל דְּבָרָיו בְּמִשְׁפָּט. וכִּי לְעוֹלָם לֹא יִמּוֹט, לְזֵכֶר עוֹלָם יִהְיֶה צַדִּיק. זמִשְּׁמוּעָה רָעָה לֹא יִירָא, נָכוֹן לִבּוֹ בָּטֻחַ בַּיהוה. חסָמוּךְ לִבּוֹ לֹא יִירָא, עַד אֲשֶׁר יִרְאֶה בְצָרָיו. טפִּזַּר נָתַן לָאֶבְיוֹנִים, צִדְקָתוֹ עֹמֶדֶת לָעַד; קַרְנוֹ תָּרוּם בְּכָבוֹד. ירָשָׁע יִרְאֶה וְכָעָס, שִׁנָּיו יַחֲרֹק וְנָמָס; תַּאֲוַת רְשָׁעִים תֹּאבֵד.

קיג אהַלְלוּיָהּ, הַלְלוּ עַבְדֵי יהוה, הַלְלוּ אֶת שֵׁם יהוה. ביְהִי שֵׁם יהוה מְבֹרָךְ, מֵעַתָּה וְעַד עוֹלָם. גמִמִּזְרַח שֶׁמֶשׁ עַד מְבוֹאוֹ, מְהֻלָּל שֵׁם יהוה. דרָם עַל כָּל גּוֹיִם יהוה, עַל הַשָּׁמַיִם כְּבוֹדוֹ. המִי כַּיהוה אֱלֹהֵינוּ, הַמַּגְבִּיהִי לָשָׁבֶת. והַמַּשְׁפִּילִי לִרְאוֹת, בַּשָּׁמַיִם וּבָאָרֶץ. זמְקִימִי מֵעָפָר דָּל, מֵאַשְׁפֹּת יָרִים אֶבְיוֹן. חלְהוֹשִׁיבִי עִם נְדִיבִים, עִם נְדִיבֵי עַמּוֹ. טמוֹשִׁיבִי עֲקֶרֶת הַבַּיִת, אֵם הַבָּנִים שְׂמֵחָה, הַלְלוּיָהּ.

קיד אבְּצֵאת יִשְׂרָאֵל מִמִּצְרָיִם, בֵּית יַעֲקֹב מֵעַם לֹעֵז. בהָיְתָה יְהוּדָה לְקָדְשׁוֹ, יִשְׂרָאֵל מַמְשְׁלוֹתָיו. גהַיָּם רָאָה וַיָּנֹס, הַיַּרְדֵּן יִסֹּב לְאָחוֹר. דהֶהָרִים רָקְדוּ כְאֵילִים, גְּבָעוֹת כִּבְנֵי צֹאן. המַה לְּךָ הַיָּם כִּי תָנוּס, הַיַּרְדֵּן תִּסֹּב לְאָחוֹר. והֶהָרִים תִּרְקְדוּ כְאֵילִים, גְּבָעוֹת כִּבְנֵי צֹאן. זמִלִּפְנֵי אָדוֹן חוּלִי אָרֶץ, מִלִּפְנֵי אֱלוֹהַּ יַעֲקֹב. חהַהֹפְכִי הַצּוּר אֲגַם מָיִם, חַלָּמִישׁ לְמַעְיְנוֹ מָיִם.

קטו אלֹא לָנוּ, יהוה, לֹא לָנוּ; כִּי לְשִׁמְךָ תֵּן כָּבוֹד, עַל חַסְדְּךָ עַל אֲמִתֶּךָ. בלָמָּה יֹאמְרוּ הַגּוֹיִם, אַיֵּה נָא אֱלֹהֵיהֶם. גוֵאלֹהֵינוּ בַשָּׁמָיִם, כֹּל אֲשֶׁר חָפֵץ עָשָׂה. דעֲצַבֵּיהֶם כֶּסֶף וְזָהָב, מַעֲשֵׂה יְדֵי אָדָם. הפֶּה לָהֶם וְלֹא יְדַבֵּרוּ, עֵינַיִם לָהֶם וְלֹא יִרְאוּ. ואָזְנַיִם לָהֶם וְלֹא יִשְׁמָעוּ, אַף לָהֶם וְלֹא יְרִיחוּן. זיְדֵיהֶם וְלֹא יְמִישׁוּן, רַגְלֵיהֶם וְלֹא יְהַלֵּכוּ, לֹא יֶהְגּוּ בִּגְרוֹנָם. חכְּמוֹהֶם יִהְיוּ עֹשֵׂיהֶם, כֹּל אֲשֶׁר בֹּטֵחַ בָּהֶם. טיִשְׂרָאֵל בְּטַח בַּיהוה, עֶזְרָם וּמָגִנָּם הוּא. יבֵּית אַהֲרֹן בִּטְחוּ בַיהוה, עֶזְרָם וּמָגִנָּם הוּא. יאיִרְאֵי יהוה בִּטְחוּ בַיהוה, עֶזְרָם וּמָגִנָּם הוּא. יביהוה זְכָרָנוּ יְבָרֵךְ; יְבָרֵךְ אֶת בֵּית יִשְׂרָאֵל, יְבָרֵךְ אֶת

בֵּית אַהֲרֹן. יג יְבָרֵךְ יִרְאֵי יהוה, הַקְּטַנִּים עִם הַגְּדֹלִים. יד יֹסֵף יהוה עֲלֵיכֶם, עֲלֵיכֶם וְעַל בְּנֵיכֶם. טו בְּרוּכִים אַתֶּם לַיהוה, עֹשֵׂה שָׁמַיִם וָאָרֶץ. טז הַשָּׁמַיִם שָׁמַיִם לַיהוה, וְהָאָרֶץ נָתַן לִבְנֵי אָדָם. יז לֹא הַמֵּתִים יְהַלְלוּ יָהּ, וְלֹא כָּל יֹרְדֵי דוּמָה. יח וַאֲנַחְנוּ נְבָרֵךְ יָהּ, מֵעַתָּה וְעַד עוֹלָם, הַלְלוּיָהּ.

קטז א אָהַבְתִּי כִּי יִשְׁמַע יהוה, אֶת קוֹלִי תַּחֲנוּנָי. ב כִּי הִטָּה אָזְנוֹ לִי, וּבְיָמַי אֶקְרָא. ג אֲפָפוּנִי חֶבְלֵי מָוֶת, וּמְצָרֵי שְׁאוֹל מְצָאוּנִי; צָרָה וְיָגוֹן אֶמְצָא. ד וּבְשֵׁם יהוה אֶקְרָא, אָנָּה יהוה מַלְּטָה נַפְשִׁי. ה חַנּוּן יהוה וְצַדִּיק, וֵאלֹהֵינוּ מְרַחֵם. ו שֹׁמֵר פְּתָאיִם יהוה, דַּלּוֹתִי וְלִי יְהוֹשִׁיעַ. ז שׁוּבִי נַפְשִׁי לִמְנוּחָיְכִי, כִּי יהוה גָּמַל עָלָיְכִי. ח כִּי חִלַּצְתָּ נַפְשִׁי מִמָּוֶת; אֶת עֵינִי מִן דִּמְעָה, אֶת רַגְלִי מִדֶּחִי. ט אֶתְהַלֵּךְ לִפְנֵי יהוה, בְּאַרְצוֹת הַחַיִּים. י הֶאֱמַנְתִּי כִּי אֲדַבֵּר, אֲנִי עָנִיתִי מְאֹד. יא אֲנִי אָמַרְתִּי בְחָפְזִי, כָּל הָאָדָם כֹּזֵב. יב מָה אָשִׁיב לַיהוה, כָּל תַּגְמוּלוֹהִי עָלָי. יג כּוֹס יְשׁוּעוֹת אֶשָּׂא, וּבְשֵׁם יהוה אֶקְרָא. יד נְדָרַי לַיהוה אֲשַׁלֵּם, נֶגְדָה נָּא לְכָל עַמּוֹ. טו יָקָר בְּעֵינֵי יהוה, הַמָּוְתָה לַחֲסִידָיו. טז אָנָּה יהוה כִּי אֲנִי עַבְדֶּךָ; אֲנִי עַבְדְּךָ בֶּן אֲמָתֶךָ, פִּתַּחְתָּ לְמוֹסֵרָי. יז לְךָ אֶזְבַּח זֶבַח תּוֹדָה, וּבְשֵׁם יהוה אֶקְרָא. יח נְדָרַי לַיהוה אֲשַׁלֵּם, נֶגְדָה נָּא לְכָל עַמּוֹ. יט בְּחַצְרוֹת בֵּית יהוה, בְּתוֹכֵכִי יְרוּשָׁלָיִם, הַלְלוּיָהּ.

קיז א הַלְלוּ אֶת יהוה, כָּל גּוֹיִם; שַׁבְּחוּהוּ כָּל הָאֻמִּים. ב כִּי גָבַר עָלֵינוּ חַסְדּוֹ, וֶאֱמֶת יהוה לְעוֹלָם, הַלְלוּיָהּ.

קיח א הוֹדוּ לַיהוה כִּי טוֹב, כִּי לְעוֹלָם חַסְדּוֹ. ב יֹאמַר נָא יִשְׂרָאֵל, כִּי לְעוֹלָם חַסְדּוֹ. ג יֹאמְרוּ נָא בֵית אַהֲרֹן, כִּי לְעוֹלָם חַסְדּוֹ. ד יֹאמְרוּ נָא יִרְאֵי יהוה, כִּי לְעוֹלָם חַסְדּוֹ. ה מִן הַמֵּצַר קָרָאתִי יָּהּ, עָנָנִי בַמֶּרְחָב יָהּ. ו יהוה לִי לֹא אִירָא, מַה יַּעֲשֶׂה לִי אָדָם. ז יהוה לִי בְּעֹזְרָי, וַאֲנִי אֶרְאֶה בְשֹׂנְאָי. ח טוֹב לַחֲסוֹת בַּיהוה, מִבְּטֹחַ בָּאָדָם. ט טוֹב לַחֲסוֹת בַּיהוה, מִבְּטֹחַ בִּנְדִיבִים. י כָּל גּוֹיִם סְבָבוּנִי, בְּשֵׁם יהוה כִּי אֲמִילַם. יא סַבּוּנִי גַם סְבָבוּנִי, בְּשֵׁם יהוה כִּי אֲמִילַם. יב סַבּוּנִי כִדְבֹרִים, דֹּעֲכוּ כְּאֵשׁ קוֹצִים; בְּשֵׁם יהוה כִּי אֲמִילַם. יג דָּחֹה דְחִיתַנִי לִנְפֹּל, וַיהוה עֲזָרָנִי. יד עָזִּי וְזִמְרָת יָהּ, וַיְהִי לִי לִישׁוּעָה. טו קוֹל רִנָּה וִישׁוּעָה בְּאָהֳלֵי צַדִּיקִים, יְמִין יהוה עֹשָׂה חָיִל. טז יְמִין יהוה רוֹמֵמָה, יְמִין יהוה עֹשָׂה חָיִל. יז לֹא אָמוּת כִּי אֶחְיֶה, וַאֲסַפֵּר מַעֲשֵׂי יָהּ. יח יַסֹּר יִסְּרַנִּי יָּהּ, וְלַמָּוֶת לֹא נְתָנָנִי. יט פִּתְחוּ לִי שַׁעֲרֵי צֶדֶק, אָבֹא בָם אוֹדֶה יָהּ. כ זֶה הַשַּׁעַר לַיהוה, צַדִּיקִים יָבֹאוּ בוֹ. כא אוֹדְךָ כִּי עֲנִיתָנִי, וַתְּהִי לִי לִישׁוּעָה. כב אֶבֶן מָאֲסוּ הַבּוֹנִים, הָיְתָה לְרֹאשׁ פִּנָּה. כג מֵאֵת יהוה הָיְתָה

זֹאת, הִיא נִפְלָאת בְּעֵינֵינוּ. כד זֶה הַיּוֹם עָשָׂה יהוה, נָגִילָה וְנִשְׂמְחָה בוֹ. כה אָנָּא יהוה, הוֹשִׁיעָה נָּא, אָנָּא יהוה, הַצְלִיחָה נָּא. כו בָּרוּךְ הַבָּא בְּשֵׁם יהוה, בֵּרַכְנוּכֶם מִבֵּית יהוה. כז אֵל יהוה וַיָּאֶר לָנוּ, אִסְרוּ חַג בַּעֲבֹתִים עַד קַרְנוֹת הַמִּזְבֵּחַ. כח אֵלִי אַתָּה וְאוֹדֶךָּ, אֱלֹהַי אֲרוֹמְמֶךָּ. כט הוֹדוּ לַיהוה כִּי טוֹב, כִּי לְעוֹלָם חַסְדּוֹ.

DAY 25 / יוֹם כ״ה לַחֹדֶשׁ

קיט א אַשְׁרֵי תְמִימֵי דָרֶךְ, הַהֹלְכִים בְּתוֹרַת יהוה. ב אַשְׁרֵי נֹצְרֵי עֵדֹתָיו, בְּכָל לֵב יִדְרְשׁוּהוּ. ג אַף לֹא פָעֲלוּ עַוְלָה, בִּדְרָכָיו הָלָכוּ. ד אַתָּה צִוִּיתָה פִקֻּדֶיךָ, לִשְׁמֹר מְאֹד. ה אַחֲלַי, יִכֹּנוּ דְרָכָי לִשְׁמֹר חֻקֶּיךָ. ו אָז לֹא אֵבוֹשׁ, בְּהַבִּיטִי אֶל כָּל מִצְוֹתֶיךָ. ז אוֹדְךָ בְּיֹשֶׁר לֵבָב, בְּלָמְדִי מִשְׁפְּטֵי צִדְקֶךָ. ח אֶת חֻקֶּיךָ אֶשְׁמֹר, אַל תַּעַזְבֵנִי עַד מְאֹד.

ט בַּמֶּה יְזַכֶּה נַּעַר אֶת אָרְחוֹ, לִשְׁמֹר כִּדְבָרֶךָ. י בְּכָל לִבִּי דְרַשְׁתִּיךָ, אַל תַּשְׁגֵּנִי מִמִּצְוֹתֶיךָ. יא בְּלִבִּי צָפַנְתִּי אִמְרָתֶךָ, לְמַעַן לֹא אֶחֱטָא לָךְ. יב בָּרוּךְ אַתָּה יהוה, לַמְּדֵנִי חֻקֶּיךָ. יג בִּשְׂפָתַי סִפַּרְתִּי, כֹּל מִשְׁפְּטֵי פִיךָ. יד בְּדֶרֶךְ עֵדְוֹתֶיךָ שַׂשְׂתִּי, כְּעַל כָּל הוֹן. טו בְּפִקֻּדֶיךָ אָשִׂיחָה, וְאַבִּיטָה אֹרְחֹתֶיךָ. טז בְּחֻקֹּתֶיךָ אֶשְׁתַּעֲשָׁע, לֹא אֶשְׁכַּח דְּבָרֶךָ.

יז גְּמֹל עַל עַבְדְּךָ, אֶחְיֶה וְאֶשְׁמְרָה דְבָרֶךָ. יח גַּל עֵינַי וְאַבִּיטָה, נִפְלָאוֹת מִתּוֹרָתֶךָ. יט גֵּר אָנֹכִי בָאָרֶץ, אַל תַּסְתֵּר מִמֶּנִּי מִצְוֹתֶיךָ. כ גָּרְסָה נַפְשִׁי לְתַאֲבָה, אֶל מִשְׁפָּטֶיךָ בְכָל עֵת. כא גָּעַרְתָּ זֵדִים אֲרוּרִים, הַשֹּׁגִים מִמִּצְוֹתֶיךָ. כב גַּל מֵעָלַי חֶרְפָּה וָבוּז, כִּי עֵדֹתֶיךָ נָצָרְתִּי. כג גַּם יָשְׁבוּ שָׂרִים בִּי נִדְבָּרוּ, עַבְדְּךָ יָשִׂיחַ בְּחֻקֶּיךָ. כד גַּם עֵדֹתֶיךָ שַׁעֲשֻׁעָי, אַנְשֵׁי עֲצָתִי.

כה דָּבְקָה לֶעָפָר נַפְשִׁי, חַיֵּנִי כִּדְבָרֶךָ. כו דְּרָכַי סִפַּרְתִּי וַתַּעֲנֵנִי, לַמְּדֵנִי חֻקֶּיךָ. כז דֶּרֶךְ פִּקּוּדֶיךָ הֲבִינֵנִי, וְאָשִׂיחָה בְּנִפְלְאוֹתֶיךָ. כח דָּלְפָה נַפְשִׁי מִתּוּגָה, קַיְּמֵנִי כִּדְבָרֶךָ. כט דֶּרֶךְ שֶׁקֶר הָסֵר מִמֶּנִּי, וְתוֹרָתְךָ חָנֵּנִי. ל דֶּרֶךְ אֱמוּנָה בָחָרְתִּי, מִשְׁפָּטֶיךָ שִׁוִּיתִי. לא דָּבַקְתִּי בְעֵדְוֹתֶיךָ, יהוה אַל תְּבִישֵׁנִי. לב דֶּרֶךְ מִצְוֹתֶיךָ אָרוּץ, כִּי תַרְחִיב לִבִּי.

לג הוֹרֵנִי יהוה דֶּרֶךְ חֻקֶּיךָ, וְאֶצְּרֶנָּה עֵקֶב. לד הֲבִינֵנִי וְאֶצְּרָה תוֹרָתֶךָ, וְאֶשְׁמְרֶנָּה בְכָל לֵב. לה הַדְרִיכֵנִי בִּנְתִיב מִצְוֹתֶיךָ, כִּי בוֹ חָפָצְתִּי. לו הַט לִבִּי אֶל עֵדְוֹתֶיךָ, וְאַל אֶל בָּצַע. לז הַעֲבֵר עֵינַי מֵרְאוֹת שָׁוְא, בִּדְרָכֶךָ חַיֵּנִי. לח הָקֵם לְעַבְדְּךָ אִמְרָתֶךָ, אֲשֶׁר לְיִרְאָתֶךָ. לט הַעֲבֵר חֶרְפָּתִי אֲשֶׁר יָגֹרְתִּי, כִּי מִשְׁפָּטֶיךָ טוֹבִים. מ הִנֵּה תָּאַבְתִּי לְפִקֻּדֶיךָ, בְּצִדְקָתְךָ חַיֵּנִי.

מא וִיבֹאֻנִי חֲסָדֶךָ יהוה, תְּשׁוּעָתְךָ כְּאִמְרָתֶךָ. מב וְאֶעֱנֶה חֹרְפִי דָבָר, כִּי בָטַחְתִּי בִּדְבָרֶךָ. מג וְאַל תַּצֵּל מִפִּי דְבַר אֱמֶת עַד מְאֹד, כִּי לְמִשְׁפָּטֶךָ

יִחַלְתִּי. מד וְאֶשְׁמְרָה תוֹרָתְךָ תָמִיד לְעוֹלָם וָעֶד. מה וְאֶתְהַלְּכָה בָרְחָבָה, כִּי פִקֻּדֶיךָ דָרָשְׁתִּי. מו וַאֲדַבְּרָה בְעֵדֹתֶיךָ נֶגֶד מְלָכִים, וְלֹא אֵבוֹשׁ. מז וְאֶשְׁתַּעֲשַׁע בְּמִצְוֹתֶיךָ אֲשֶׁר אָהָבְתִּי. מח וְאֶשָּׂא כַפַּי אֶל מִצְוֹתֶיךָ אֲשֶׁר אָהָבְתִּי, וְאָשִׂיחָה בְחֻקֶּיךָ.

מט זְכָר דָּבָר לְעַבְדֶּךָ, עַל אֲשֶׁר יִחַלְתָּנִי. נ זֹאת נֶחָמָתִי בְעָנְיִי, כִּי אִמְרָתְךָ חִיָּתְנִי. נא זֵדִים הֱלִיצֻנִי עַד מְאֹד, מִתּוֹרָתְךָ לֹא נָטִיתִי. נב זָכַרְתִּי מִשְׁפָּטֶיךָ מֵעוֹלָם יהוה, וָאֶתְנֶחָם. נג זַלְעָפָה אֲחָזַתְנִי מֵרְשָׁעִים, עֹזְבֵי תוֹרָתֶךָ. נד זְמִרוֹת הָיוּ לִי חֻקֶּיךָ, בְּבֵית מְגוּרָי. נה זָכַרְתִּי בַלַּיְלָה שִׁמְךָ יהוה, וָאֶשְׁמְרָה תוֹרָתֶךָ. נו זֹאת הָיְתָה לִּי, כִּי פִקֻּדֶיךָ נָצָרְתִּי.

נז חֶלְקִי יהוה, אָמַרְתִּי לִשְׁמֹר דְּבָרֶיךָ. נח חִלִּיתִי פָנֶיךָ בְכָל לֵב, חָנֵּנִי כְּאִמְרָתֶךָ. נט חִשַּׁבְתִּי דְרָכָי, וָאָשִׁיבָה רַגְלַי אֶל עֵדֹתֶיךָ. ס חַשְׁתִּי וְלֹא הִתְמַהְמָהְתִּי, לִשְׁמֹר מִצְוֹתֶיךָ. סא חֶבְלֵי רְשָׁעִים עִוְּדֻנִי, תוֹרָתְךָ לֹא שָׁכָחְתִּי. סב חֲצוֹת לַיְלָה אָקוּם לְהוֹדוֹת לָךְ, עַל מִשְׁפְּטֵי צִדְקֶךָ. סג חָבֵר אָנִי לְכָל אֲשֶׁר יְרֵאוּךָ, וּלְשֹׁמְרֵי פִּקּוּדֶיךָ. סד חַסְדְּךָ יהוה מָלְאָה הָאָרֶץ, חֻקֶּיךָ לַמְּדֵנִי.

סה טוֹב עָשִׂיתָ עִם עַבְדְּךָ, יהוה כִּדְבָרֶךָ. סו טוּב טַעַם וָדַעַת לַמְּדֵנִי, כִּי בְמִצְוֹתֶיךָ הֶאֱמָנְתִּי. סז טֶרֶם אֶעֱנֶה אֲנִי שֹׁגֵג, וְעַתָּה אִמְרָתְךָ שָׁמָרְתִּי. סח טוֹב אַתָּה וּמֵטִיב, לַמְּדֵנִי חֻקֶּיךָ. סט טָפְלוּ עָלַי שֶׁקֶר זֵדִים, אֲנִי בְּכָל לֵב אֱצֹּר פִּקּוּדֶיךָ. ע טָפַשׁ כַּחֵלֶב לִבָּם, אֲנִי תּוֹרָתְךָ שִׁעֲשָׁעְתִּי. עא טוֹב לִי כִי עֻנֵּיתִי, לְמַעַן אֶלְמַד חֻקֶּיךָ. עב טוֹב לִי תוֹרַת פִּיךָ, מֵאַלְפֵי זָהָב וָכָסֶף.

עג יָדֶיךָ עָשׂוּנִי וַיְכוֹנְנוּנִי, הֲבִינֵנִי וְאֶלְמְדָה מִצְוֹתֶיךָ. עד יְרֵאֶיךָ יִרְאוּנִי וְיִשְׂמָחוּ, כִּי לִדְבָרְךָ יִחָלְתִּי. עה יָדַעְתִּי יהוה כִּי צֶדֶק מִשְׁפָּטֶיךָ, וֶאֱמוּנָה עִנִּיתָנִי. עו יְהִי נָא חַסְדְּךָ לְנַחֲמֵנִי, כְּאִמְרָתְךָ לְעַבְדֶּךָ. עז יְבֹאוּנִי רַחֲמֶיךָ וְאֶחְיֶה, כִּי תוֹרָתְךָ שַׁעֲשֻׁעָי. עח יֵבֹשׁוּ זֵדִים כִּי שֶׁקֶר עִוְּתוּנִי, אֲנִי אָשִׂיחַ בְּפִקּוּדֶיךָ. עט יָשׁוּבוּ לִי יְרֵאֶיךָ, וְיֹדְעֵי עֵדֹתֶיךָ. פ יְהִי לִבִּי תָמִים בְּחֻקֶּיךָ, לְמַעַן לֹא אֵבוֹשׁ.

פא כָּלְתָה לִתְשׁוּעָתְךָ נַפְשִׁי, לִדְבָרְךָ יִחָלְתִּי. פב כָּלוּ עֵינַי לְאִמְרָתֶךָ, לֵאמֹר מָתַי תְּנַחֲמֵנִי. פג כִּי הָיִיתִי כְּנֹאד בְּקִיטוֹר, חֻקֶּיךָ לֹא שָׁכָחְתִּי. פד כַּמָּה יְמֵי עַבְדֶּךָ, מָתַי תַּעֲשֶׂה בְרֹדְפַי מִשְׁפָּט. פה כָּרוּ לִי זֵדִים שִׁיחוֹת, אֲשֶׁר לֹא כְתוֹרָתֶךָ. פו כָּל מִצְוֹתֶיךָ אֱמוּנָה; שֶׁקֶר רְדָפוּנִי, עָזְרֵנִי. פז כִּמְעַט כִּלּוּנִי בָאָרֶץ, וַאֲנִי לֹא עָזַבְתִּי פִקֻּדֶיךָ. פח כְּחַסְדְּךָ חַיֵּנִי, וְאֶשְׁמְרָה עֵדוּת פִּיךָ.

פט לְעוֹלָם יהוה, דְּבָרְךָ נִצָּב בַּשָּׁמָיִם. צ לְדֹר וָדֹר אֱמוּנָתֶךָ, כּוֹנַנְתָּ אֶרֶץ

וַתַּעֲמֹד. צֹא לְמִשְׁפָּטֶיךָ עָמְדוּ הַיּוֹם, כִּי הַכֹּל עֲבָדֶיךָ. צֹב לוּלֵי תוֹרָתְךָ שַׁעֲשֻׁעָי, אָז אָבַדְתִּי בְעָנְיִי. צֹג לְעוֹלָם לֹא אֶשְׁכַּח פִּקּוּדֶיךָ, כִּי בָם חִיִּיתָנִי. צֹד לְךָ אֲנִי הוֹשִׁיעֵנִי, כִּי פִקּוּדֶיךָ דָרָשְׁתִּי. צֹה לִי קִוּוּ רְשָׁעִים לְאַבְּדֵנִי, עֵדֹתֶיךָ אֶתְבּוֹנָן. צֹו לְכָל תִּכְלָה רָאִיתִי קֵץ, רְחָבָה מִצְוָתְךָ מְאֹד.

יוֹם כ״ו לַחֹדֶשׁ / DAY 26

צֹז מָה אָהַבְתִּי תוֹרָתֶךָ, כָּל הַיּוֹם הִיא שִׂיחָתִי. צֹח מֵאֹיְבַי תְּחַכְּמֵנִי מִצְוֹתֶךָ, כִּי לְעוֹלָם הִיא לִי. צֹט מִכָּל מְלַמְּדַי הִשְׂכַּלְתִּי, כִּי עֵדְוֹתֶיךָ שִׂיחָה לִי. ק מִזְּקֵנִים אֶתְבּוֹנָן, כִּי פִקּוּדֶיךָ נָצָרְתִּי. קֹא מִכָּל אֹרַח רָע כָּלִאתִי רַגְלָי, לְמַעַן אֶשְׁמֹר דְּבָרֶךָ. קֹב מִמִּשְׁפָּטֶיךָ לֹא סָרְתִּי, כִּי אַתָּה הוֹרֵתָנִי. קֹג מַה נִּמְלְצוּ לְחִכִּי אִמְרָתֶךָ, מִדְּבַשׁ לְפִי. קֹד מִפִּקּוּדֶיךָ אֶתְבּוֹנָן, עַל כֵּן שָׂנֵאתִי כָּל אֹרַח שָׁקֶר.

קֹה נֵר לְרַגְלִי דְבָרֶךָ, וְאוֹר לִנְתִיבָתִי. קֹו נִשְׁבַּעְתִּי וָאֲקַיֵּמָה, לִשְׁמֹר מִשְׁפְּטֵי צִדְקֶךָ. קֹז נַעֲנֵיתִי עַד מְאֹד, יְהוָה, חַיֵּנִי כִדְבָרֶךָ. קֹח נִדְבוֹת פִּי רְצֵה נָא, יְהוָה, וּמִשְׁפָּטֶיךָ לַמְּדֵנִי. קֹט נַפְשִׁי בְכַפִּי תָמִיד, וְתוֹרָתְךָ לֹא שָׁכָחְתִּי. קֹי נָתְנוּ רְשָׁעִים פַּח לִי, וּמִפִּקּוּדֶיךָ לֹא תָעִיתִי. קֹיא נָחַלְתִּי עֵדְוֹתֶיךָ לְעוֹלָם, כִּי שְׂשׂוֹן לִבִּי הֵמָּה. קֹיב נָטִיתִי לִבִּי לַעֲשׂוֹת חֻקֶּיךָ לְעוֹלָם עֵקֶב.

קֹיג סֵעֲפִים שָׂנֵאתִי, וְתוֹרָתְךָ אָהָבְתִּי. קֹיד סִתְרִי וּמָגִנִּי אָתָּה, לִדְבָרְךָ יִחָלְתִּי. קֹטו סוּרוּ מִמֶּנִּי מְרֵעִים, וְאֶצְּרָה מִצְוֹת אֱלֹהָי. קֹטז סָמְכֵנִי כְאִמְרָתְךָ וְאֶחְיֶה, וְאַל תְּבִישֵׁנִי מִשִּׂבְרִי. קֹיז סְעָדֵנִי וְאִוָּשֵׁעָה, וְאֶשְׁעָה בְחֻקֶּיךָ תָמִיד. קֹיח סָלִיתָ כָּל שׁוֹגִים מֵחֻקֶּיךָ, כִּי שֶׁקֶר תַּרְמִיתָם. קֹיט סִגִים הִשְׁבַּתָּ כָל רִשְׁעֵי אֶרֶץ, לָכֵן אָהַבְתִּי עֵדֹתֶיךָ. קֹכ סָמַר מִפַּחְדְּךָ בְשָׂרִי, וּמִמִּשְׁפָּטֶיךָ יָרֵאתִי.

קֹכא עָשִׂיתִי מִשְׁפָּט וָצֶדֶק, בַּל תַּנִּיחֵנִי לְעֹשְׁקָי. קֹכב עֲרֹב עַבְדְּךָ לְטוֹב, אַל יַעַשְׁקֻנִי זֵדִים. קֹכג עֵינַי כָּלוּ לִישׁוּעָתֶךָ, וּלְאִמְרַת צִדְקֶךָ. קֹכד עֲשֵׂה עִם עַבְדְּךָ כְחַסְדֶּךָ, וְחֻקֶּיךָ לַמְּדֵנִי. קֹכה עַבְדְּךָ אָנִי הֲבִינֵנִי, וְאֵדְעָה עֵדֹתֶיךָ. קֹכו עֵת לַעֲשׂוֹת לַיהוָה, הֵפֵרוּ תוֹרָתֶךָ. קֹכז עַל כֵּן אָהַבְתִּי מִצְוֹתֶיךָ, מִזָּהָב וּמִפָּז. קֹכח עַל כֵּן כָּל פִּקּוּדֵי כֹל יִשָּׁרְתִּי, כָּל אֹרַח שֶׁקֶר שָׂנֵאתִי.

קֹכט פְּלָאוֹת עֵדְוֹתֶיךָ, עַל כֵּן נְצָרָתַם נַפְשִׁי. קֹל פֵּתַח דְּבָרֶיךָ יָאִיר, מֵבִין פְּתָיִים. קֹלא פִּי פָעַרְתִּי וָאֶשְׁאָפָה, כִּי לְמִצְוֹתֶיךָ יָאָבְתִּי. קֹלב פְּנֵה אֵלַי וְחָנֵּנִי, כְּמִשְׁפָּט לְאֹהֲבֵי שְׁמֶךָ. קֹלג פְּעָמַי הָכֵן בְּאִמְרָתֶךָ, וְאַל תַּשְׁלֶט בִּי כָל אָוֶן. קֹלד פְּדֵנִי מֵעֹשֶׁק אָדָם, וְאֶשְׁמְרָה פִּקּוּדֶיךָ. קֹלה פָּנֶיךָ הָאֵר בְּעַבְדֶּךָ, וְלַמְּדֵנִי אֶת חֻקֶּיךָ. קֹלו פַּלְגֵי מַיִם יָרְדוּ עֵינָי, עַל לֹא שָׁמְרוּ תוֹרָתֶךָ.

קֹלז צַדִּיק אַתָּה יְהוָה, וְיָשָׁר מִשְׁפָּטֶיךָ. קֹלח צִוִּיתָ צֶדֶק עֵדֹתֶיךָ, וֶאֱמוּנָה מְאֹד. קֹלט צִמְּתַתְנִי קִנְאָתִי, כִּי שָׁכְחוּ דְבָרֶיךָ צָרָי. קֹמ צְרוּפָה אִמְרָתְךָ מְאֹד,

וְעַבְדְּךָ אֲהֵבָהּ. קמא צָעִיר אָנֹכִי וְנִבְזֶה, פִּקֻּדֶיךָ לֹא שָׁכָחְתִּי. קמב צִדְקָתְךָ צֶדֶק לְעוֹלָם, וְתוֹרָתְךָ אֱמֶת. קמג צַר וּמָצוֹק מְצָאוּנִי, מִצְוֹתֶיךָ שַׁעֲשֻׁעָי. קמד צֶדֶק עֵדְוֹתֶיךָ לְעוֹלָם, הֲבִינֵנִי וְאֶחְיֶה.

קמה קָרָאתִי בְכָל לֵב, עֲנֵנִי יהוה; חֻקֶּיךָ אֶצֹּרָה. קמו קְרָאתִיךָ הוֹשִׁיעֵנִי, וְאֶשְׁמְרָה עֵדֹתֶיךָ. קמז קִדַּמְתִּי בַנֶּשֶׁף וָאֲשַׁוֵּעָה, לִדְבָרְךָ יִחָלְתִּי. קמח קִדְּמוּ עֵינַי אַשְׁמֻרוֹת, לָשִׂיחַ בְּאִמְרָתֶךָ. קמט קוֹלִי שִׁמְעָה כְחַסְדֶּךָ; יהוה, כְּמִשְׁפָּטֶךָ חַיֵּנִי. קנ קָרְבוּ רֹדְפֵי זִמָּה, מִתּוֹרָתְךָ רָחֵקוּ. קנא קָרוֹב אַתָּה יהוה, וְכָל מִצְוֹתֶיךָ אֱמֶת. קנב קֶדֶם יָדַעְתִּי מֵעֵדֹתֶיךָ, כִּי לְעוֹלָם יְסַדְתָּם.

קנג רְאֵה עָנְיִי וְחַלְּצֵנִי, כִּי תוֹרָתְךָ לֹא שָׁכָחְתִּי. קנד רִיבָה רִיבִי וּגְאָלֵנִי, לְאִמְרָתְךָ חַיֵּנִי. קנה רָחוֹק מֵרְשָׁעִים יְשׁוּעָה, כִּי חֻקֶּיךָ לֹא דָרָשׁוּ. קנו רַחֲמֶיךָ רַבִּים יהוה, כְּמִשְׁפָּטֶיךָ חַיֵּנִי. קנז רַבִּים רֹדְפַי וְצָרָי, מֵעֵדְוֹתֶיךָ לֹא נָטִיתִי. קנח רָאִיתִי בֹגְדִים וָאֶתְקוֹטָטָה, אֲשֶׁר אִמְרָתְךָ לֹא שָׁמָרוּ. קנט רְאֵה כִּי פִקּוּדֶיךָ אָהָבְתִּי; יהוה, כְּחַסְדְּךָ חַיֵּנִי. קס רֹאשׁ דְּבָרְךָ אֱמֶת, וּלְעוֹלָם כָּל מִשְׁפַּט צִדְקֶךָ.

קסא שָׂרִים רְדָפוּנִי חִנָּם, וּמִדְּבָרְךָ פָּחַד לִבִּי. קסב שָׂשׂ אָנֹכִי עַל אִמְרָתֶךָ, כְּמוֹצֵא שָׁלָל רָב. קסג שֶׁקֶר שָׂנֵאתִי וַאֲתַעֵבָה, תּוֹרָתְךָ אָהָבְתִּי. קסד שֶׁבַע בַּיּוֹם הִלַּלְתִּיךָ, עַל מִשְׁפְּטֵי צִדְקֶךָ. קסה שָׁלוֹם רָב לְאֹהֲבֵי תוֹרָתֶךָ, וְאֵין לָמוֹ מִכְשׁוֹל. קסו שִׂבַּרְתִּי לִישׁוּעָתְךָ יהוה, וּמִצְוֹתֶיךָ עָשִׂיתִי. קסז שָׁמְרָה נַפְשִׁי עֵדֹתֶיךָ, וָאֹהֲבֵם מְאֹד. קסח שָׁמַרְתִּי פִקּוּדֶיךָ וְעֵדֹתֶיךָ, כִּי כָל דְּרָכַי נֶגְדֶּךָ.

קסט תִּקְרַב רִנָּתִי לְפָנֶיךָ, יהוה; כִּדְבָרְךָ הֲבִינֵנִי. קע תָּבוֹא תְּחִנָּתִי לְפָנֶיךָ, כְּאִמְרָתְךָ הַצִּילֵנִי. קעא תַּבַּעְנָה שְׂפָתַי תְּהִלָּה, כִּי תְלַמְּדֵנִי חֻקֶּיךָ. קעב תַּעַן לְשׁוֹנִי אִמְרָתֶךָ, כִּי כָל מִצְוֹתֶיךָ צֶּדֶק. קעג תְּהִי יָדְךָ לְעָזְרֵנִי, כִּי פִקּוּדֶיךָ בָחָרְתִּי. קעד תָּאַבְתִּי לִישׁוּעָתְךָ, יהוה; וְתוֹרָתְךָ שַׁעֲשֻׁעָי. קעה תְּחִי נַפְשִׁי וּתְהַלְלֶךָּ, וּמִשְׁפָּטֶךָ יַעְזְרֻנִי. קעו תָּעִיתִי כְּשֶׂה אֹבֵד, בַּקֵּשׁ עַבְדֶּךָ; כִּי מִצְוֹתֶיךָ לֹא שָׁכָחְתִּי.

⁓{ THE SABBATH / יום השבת }⁓

יום כ"ז לחדש / DAY 27

קכב א שִׁיר הַמַּעֲלוֹת; אֶל יהוה בַּצָּרָתָה לִּי קָרָאתִי וַיַּעֲנֵנִי. ב יהוה הַצִּילָה נַפְשִׁי מִשְּׂפַת שֶׁקֶר, מִלָּשׁוֹן רְמִיָּה. ג מַה יִּתֵּן לְךָ, וּמַה יֹּסִיף לָךְ, לָשׁוֹן רְמִיָּה. ד חִצֵּי גִבּוֹר שְׁנוּנִים, עִם גַּחֲלֵי רְתָמִים. ה אוֹיָה לִי כִּי גַרְתִּי מֶשֶׁךְ, שָׁכַנְתִּי עִם אָהֳלֵי קֵדָר. ו רַבַּת שָׁכְנָה לָּהּ נַפְשִׁי, עִם שׂוֹנֵא שָׁלוֹם. ז אֲנִי שָׁלוֹם, וְכִי אֲדַבֵּר, הֵמָּה לַמִּלְחָמָה.

קכא א שִׁיר לַמַּעֲלוֹת; אֶשָּׂא עֵינַי אֶל הֶהָרִים, מֵאַיִן יָבֹא עֶזְרִי. ב עֶזְרִי מֵעִם יהוה, עֹשֵׂה שָׁמַיִם וָאָרֶץ. ג אַל יִתֵּן לַמּוֹט רַגְלֶךָ, אַל יָנוּם שֹׁמְרֶךָ. ד הִנֵּה לֹא יָנוּם וְלֹא יִישָׁן, שׁוֹמֵר יִשְׂרָאֵל. ה יהוה שֹׁמְרֶךָ, יהוה צִלְּךָ עַל יַד יְמִינֶךָ. ו יוֹמָם הַשֶּׁמֶשׁ לֹא יַכֶּכָּה, וְיָרֵחַ בַּלָּיְלָה. ז יהוה יִשְׁמָרְךָ מִכָּל רָע, יִשְׁמֹר אֶת נַפְשֶׁךָ. ח יהוה יִשְׁמָר צֵאתְךָ וּבוֹאֶךָ, מֵעַתָּה וְעַד עוֹלָם.

קכב א שִׁיר הַמַּעֲלוֹת לְדָוִד; שָׂמַחְתִּי בְּאֹמְרִים לִי, בֵּית יהוה נֵלֵךְ. ב עֹמְדוֹת הָיוּ רַגְלֵינוּ, בִּשְׁעָרַיִךְ יְרוּשָׁלָיִם. ג יְרוּשָׁלַיִם הַבְּנוּיָה, כְּעִיר שֶׁחֻבְּרָה לָּהּ יַחְדָּו. ד שֶׁשָּׁם עָלוּ שְׁבָטִים, שִׁבְטֵי יָהּ, עֵדוּת לְיִשְׂרָאֵל, לְהֹדוֹת לְשֵׁם יהוה. ה כִּי שָׁמָּה יָשְׁבוּ כִסְאוֹת לְמִשְׁפָּט, כִּסְאוֹת לְבֵית דָּוִד. ו שַׁאֲלוּ שְׁלוֹם יְרוּשָׁלָיִם, יִשְׁלָיוּ אֹהֲבָיִךְ. ז יְהִי שָׁלוֹם בְּחֵילֵךְ, שַׁלְוָה בְּאַרְמְנוֹתָיִךְ. ח לְמַעַן אַחַי וְרֵעָי, אֲדַבְּרָה נָּא שָׁלוֹם בָּךְ. ט לְמַעַן בֵּית יהוה אֱלֹהֵינוּ, אֲבַקְשָׁה טוֹב לָךְ.

קכג א שִׁיר הַמַּעֲלוֹת; אֵלֶיךָ נָשָׂאתִי אֶת עֵינַי, הַיֹּשְׁבִי בַּשָּׁמָיִם. ב הִנֵּה כְעֵינֵי עֲבָדִים אֶל יַד אֲדוֹנֵיהֶם, כְּעֵינֵי שִׁפְחָה אֶל יַד גְּבִרְתָּהּ; כֵּן עֵינֵינוּ אֶל יהוה אֱלֹהֵינוּ, עַד שֶׁיְּחָנֵּנוּ. ג חָנֵּנוּ יהוה חָנֵּנוּ, כִּי רַב שָׂבַעְנוּ בוּז. ד רַבַּת שָׂבְעָה לָּהּ נַפְשֵׁנוּ, הַלַּעַג הַשַּׁאֲנַנִּים, הַבּוּז לִגְאֵי יוֹנִים.

קכד א שִׁיר הַמַּעֲלוֹת לְדָוִד; לוּלֵי יהוה שֶׁהָיָה לָנוּ, יֹאמַר נָא יִשְׂרָאֵל. ב לוּלֵי יהוה שֶׁהָיָה לָנוּ, בְּקוּם עָלֵינוּ אָדָם. ג אֲזַי חַיִּים בְּלָעוּנוּ, בַּחֲרוֹת אַפָּם בָּנוּ. ד אֲזַי הַמַּיִם שְׁטָפוּנוּ, נַחְלָה עָבַר עַל נַפְשֵׁנוּ. ה אֲזַי עָבַר עַל נַפְשֵׁנוּ, הַמַּיִם הַזֵּידוֹנִים. ו בָּרוּךְ יהוה, שֶׁלֹּא נְתָנָנוּ טֶרֶף לְשִׁנֵּיהֶם. ז נַפְשֵׁנוּ כְּצִפּוֹר נִמְלְטָה מִפַּח יוֹקְשִׁים; הַפַּח נִשְׁבָּר וַאֲנַחְנוּ נִמְלָטְנוּ. ח עֶזְרֵנוּ בְּשֵׁם יהוה, עֹשֵׂה שָׁמַיִם וָאָרֶץ.

קכה א שִׁיר הַמַּעֲלוֹת; הַבֹּטְחִים בַּיהוה, כְּהַר צִיּוֹן לֹא יִמּוֹט, לְעוֹלָם יֵשֵׁב. ב יְרוּשָׁלַיִם הָרִים סָבִיב לָהּ; וַיהוה סָבִיב לְעַמּוֹ, מֵעַתָּה וְעַד עוֹלָם. ג כִּי לֹא יָנוּחַ שֵׁבֶט הָרֶשַׁע עַל גּוֹרַל הַצַּדִּיקִים, לְמַעַן לֹא יִשְׁלְחוּ הַצַּדִּיקִים בְּעַוְלָתָה יְדֵיהֶם. ד הֵיטִיבָה יהוה לַטּוֹבִים, וְלִישָׁרִים בְּלִבּוֹתָם. ה וְהַמַּטִּים עֲקַלְקַלּוֹתָם, יוֹלִיכֵם יהוה אֶת פֹּעֲלֵי הָאָוֶן, שָׁלוֹם עַל יִשְׂרָאֵל.

קכו א שִׁיר הַמַּעֲלוֹת; בְּשׁוּב יהוה אֶת שִׁיבַת צִיּוֹן, הָיִינוּ כְּחֹלְמִים. ב אָז יִמָּלֵא שְׂחוֹק פִּינוּ, וּלְשׁוֹנֵנוּ רִנָּה; אָז יֹאמְרוּ בַגּוֹיִם, הִגְדִּיל יהוה לַעֲשׂוֹת עִם אֵלֶּה. ג הִגְדִּיל יהוה לַעֲשׂוֹת עִמָּנוּ, הָיִינוּ שְׂמֵחִים. ד שׁוּבָה יהוה אֶת שְׁבִיתֵנוּ, כַּאֲפִיקִים בַּנֶּגֶב. ה הַזֹּרְעִים בְּדִמְעָה, בְּרִנָּה יִקְצֹרוּ. ו הָלוֹךְ יֵלֵךְ וּבָכֹה נֹשֵׂא מֶשֶׁךְ הַזָּרַע; בֹּא יָבֹא בְרִנָּה, נֹשֵׂא אֲלֻמֹּתָיו.

קכז א שִׁיר הַמַּעֲלוֹת לִשְׁלֹמֹה; אִם יהוה לֹא יִבְנֶה בַיִת, שָׁוְא עָמְלוּ בוֹנָיו בּוֹ, אִם יהוה לֹא יִשְׁמָר עִיר, שָׁוְא שָׁקַד שׁוֹמֵר. ב שָׁוְא לָכֶם מַשְׁכִּימֵי קוּם, מְאַחֲרֵי שֶׁבֶת, אֹכְלֵי לֶחֶם הָעֲצָבִים, כֵּן יִתֵּן לִידִידוֹ שֵׁנָא. ג הִנֵּה נַחֲלַת יהוה בָּנִים, שָׂכָר פְּרִי הַבָּטֶן. ד כְּחִצִּים בְּיַד גִּבּוֹר, כֵּן בְּנֵי הַנְּעוּרִים. ה אַשְׁרֵי הַגֶּבֶר אֲשֶׁר מִלֵּא אֶת אַשְׁפָּתוֹ מֵהֶם; לֹא יֵבֹשׁוּ, כִּי יְדַבְּרוּ אֶת אוֹיְבִים בַּשָּׁעַר.

קכח א שִׁיר הַמַּעֲלוֹת; אַשְׁרֵי כָּל יְרֵא יהוה, הַהֹלֵךְ בִּדְרָכָיו. ב יְגִיעַ כַּפֶּיךָ כִּי תֹאכֵל, אַשְׁרֶיךָ וְטוֹב לָךְ. ג אֶשְׁתְּךָ כְּגֶפֶן פֹּרִיָּה בְּיַרְכְּתֵי בֵיתֶךָ; בָּנֶיךָ כִּשְׁתִלֵי זֵיתִים סָבִיב לְשֻׁלְחָנֶךָ. ד הִנֵּה כִי כֵן יְבֹרַךְ גָּבֶר יְרֵא יהוה. ה יְבָרֶכְךָ יהוה מִצִּיּוֹן, וּרְאֵה בְּטוּב יְרוּשָׁלָיִם כֹּל יְמֵי חַיֶּיךָ. ו וּרְאֵה בָנִים לְבָנֶיךָ, שָׁלוֹם עַל יִשְׂרָאֵל.

קכט א שִׁיר הַמַּעֲלוֹת; רַבַּת צְרָרוּנִי מִנְּעוּרַי, יֹאמַר נָא יִשְׂרָאֵל. ב רַבַּת צְרָרוּנִי מִנְּעוּרָי, גַּם לֹא יָכְלוּ לִי. ג עַל גַּבִּי חָרְשׁוּ חֹרְשִׁים, הֶאֱרִיכוּ לְמַעֲנִיתָם. ד יהוה צַדִּיק, קִצֵּץ עֲבוֹת רְשָׁעִים. ה יֵבֹשׁוּ וְיִסֹּגוּ אָחוֹר, כֹּל שֹׂנְאֵי צִיּוֹן. ו יִהְיוּ כַּחֲצִיר גַּגּוֹת, שֶׁקַּדְמַת שָׁלַף יָבֵשׁ. ז שֶׁלֹּא מִלֵּא כַפּוֹ קוֹצֵר, וְחִצְנוֹ מְעַמֵּר. ח וְלֹא אָמְרוּ הָעֹבְרִים: בִּרְכַּת יהוה אֲלֵיכֶם, בֵּרַכְנוּ אֶתְכֶם בְּשֵׁם יהוה.

קל א שִׁיר הַמַּעֲלוֹת, מִמַּעֲמַקִּים קְרָאתִיךָ יהוה. ב אֲדֹנָי שִׁמְעָה בְקוֹלִי, תִּהְיֶינָה אָזְנֶיךָ קַשֻּׁבוֹת לְקוֹל תַּחֲנוּנָי. ג אִם עֲוֹנוֹת תִּשְׁמָר יָהּ, אֲדֹנָי, מִי יַעֲמֹד. ד כִּי עִמְּךָ הַסְּלִיחָה, לְמַעַן תִּוָּרֵא. ה קִוִּיתִי יהוה, קִוְּתָה נַפְשִׁי, וְלִדְבָרוֹ הוֹחָלְתִּי. ו נַפְשִׁי לַאדֹנָי, מִשֹּׁמְרִים לַבֹּקֶר, שֹׁמְרִים לַבֹּקֶר. ז יַחֵל יִשְׂרָאֵל אֶל יהוה; כִּי עִם יהוה הַחֶסֶד, וְהַרְבֵּה עִמּוֹ פְדוּת. ח וְהוּא יִפְדֶּה אֶת יִשְׂרָאֵל, מִכֹּל עֲוֹנוֹתָיו.

קלא א שִׁיר הַמַּעֲלוֹת לְדָוִד; יהוה, לֹא גָבַהּ לִבִּי, וְלֹא רָמוּ עֵינַי, וְלֹא הִלַּכְתִּי בִּגְדֹלוֹת וּבְנִפְלָאוֹת מִמֶּנִּי. ב אִם לֹא שִׁוִּיתִי וְדוֹמַמְתִּי נַפְשִׁי; כְּגָמֻל עֲלֵי אִמּוֹ, כַּגָּמֻל עָלַי נַפְשִׁי. ג יַחֵל יִשְׂרָאֵל אֶל יהוה, מֵעַתָּה וְעַד עוֹלָם.

קלב א שִׁיר הַמַּעֲלוֹת; זְכוֹר יהוה לְדָוִד, אֵת כָּל עֻנּוֹתוֹ. ב אֲשֶׁר נִשְׁבַּע לַיהוה, נָדַר לַאֲבִיר יַעֲקֹב. ג אִם אָבֹא בְּאֹהֶל בֵּיתִי, אִם אֶעֱלֶה עַל עֶרֶשׂ יְצוּעָי. ד אִם אֶתֵּן שְׁנַת לְעֵינָי, לְעַפְעַפַּי תְּנוּמָה. ה עַד אֶמְצָא מָקוֹם לַיהוה, מִשְׁכָּנוֹת לַאֲבִיר יַעֲקֹב. ו הִנֵּה שְׁמַעֲנוּהָ בְאֶפְרָתָה, מְצָאנוּהָ בִּשְׂדֵי יָעַר. ז נָבוֹאָה לְמִשְׁכְּנוֹתָיו, נִשְׁתַּחֲוֶה לַהֲדֹם רַגְלָיו. ח קוּמָה יהוה לִמְנוּחָתֶךָ, אַתָּה וַאֲרוֹן עֻזֶּךָ. ט כֹּהֲנֶיךָ יִלְבְּשׁוּ צֶדֶק, וַחֲסִידֶיךָ יְרַנֵּנוּ.

יּ בַּעֲבוּר דָּוִד עַבְדֶּךָ, אַל תָּשֵׁב פְּנֵי מְשִׁיחֶךָ. יאּ נִשְׁבַּע יהוה לְדָוִד, אֱמֶת לֹא
יָשׁוּב מִמֶּנָּה; מִפְּרִי בִטְנְךָ אָשִׁית לְכִסֵּא לָךְ. יבּ אִם יִשְׁמְרוּ בָנֶיךָ בְּרִיתִי,
וְעֵדֹתִי זוֹ אֲלַמְּדֵם; גַּם בְּנֵיהֶם עֲדֵי עַד, יֵשְׁבוּ לְכִסֵּא לָךְ. יגּ כִּי בָחַר יהוה
בְּצִיּוֹן, אִוָּהּ לְמוֹשָׁב לוֹ. ידּ זֹאת מְנוּחָתִי עֲדֵי עַד, פֹּה אֵשֵׁב כִּי אִוִּתִיהָ.
טוּ צֵידָהּ בָּרֵךְ אֲבָרֵךְ, אֶבְיוֹנֶיהָ אַשְׂבִּיעַ לָחֶם. טזּ וְכֹהֲנֶיהָ אַלְבִּישׁ יֶשַׁע,
וַחֲסִידֶיהָ רַנֵּן יְרַנֵּנוּ. יזּ שָׁם אַצְמִיחַ קֶרֶן לְדָוִד, עָרַכְתִּי נֵר לִמְשִׁיחִי.
יחּ אוֹיְבָיו אַלְבִּישׁ בֹּשֶׁת, וְעָלָיו יָצִיץ נִזְרוֹ.

קלג אּ שִׁיר הַמַּעֲלוֹת לְדָוִד; הִנֵּה מַה טּוֹב וּמַה נָּעִים, שֶׁבֶת אַחִים גַּם יָחַד.
בּ כַּשֶּׁמֶן הַטּוֹב עַל הָרֹאשׁ, יֹרֵד עַל הַזָּקָן; זְקַן אַהֲרֹן, שֶׁיֹּרֵד עַל פִּי
מִדּוֹתָיו. גּ כְּטַל חֶרְמוֹן שֶׁיֹּרֵד עַל הַרְרֵי צִיּוֹן; כִּי שָׁם צִוָּה יהוה אֶת הַבְּרָכָה,
חַיִּים עַד הָעוֹלָם.

קלד אּ שִׁיר הַמַּעֲלוֹת; הִנֵּה בָּרְכוּ אֶת יהוה כָּל עַבְדֵי יהוה, הָעֹמְדִים
בְּבֵית יהוה בַּלֵּילוֹת. בּ שְׂאוּ יְדֵכֶם קֹדֶשׁ, וּבָרְכוּ אֶת יהוה. גּ יְבָרֶכְךָ
יהוה מִצִּיּוֹן, עֹשֵׂה שָׁמַיִם וָאָרֶץ.

קלה אּ הַלְלוּיָהּ, הַלְלוּ אֶת שֵׁם יהוה, הַלְלוּ עַבְדֵי יהוה. בּ שֶׁעֹמְדִים בְּבֵית
יהוה, בְּחַצְרוֹת בֵּית אֱלֹהֵינוּ. גּ הַלְלוּיָהּ, כִּי טוֹב יהוה, זַמְּרוּ לִשְׁמוֹ כִּי נָעִים.
דּ כִּי יַעֲקֹב בָּחַר לוֹ יָהּ, יִשְׂרָאֵל לִסְגֻלָּתוֹ. הּ כִּי אֲנִי יָדַעְתִּי כִּי גָדוֹל יהוה,
וַאֲדֹנֵינוּ מִכָּל אֱלֹהִים. וּ כֹּל אֲשֶׁר חָפֵץ יהוה עָשָׂה; בַּשָּׁמַיִם וּבָאָרֶץ, בַּיַּמִּים
וְכָל תְּהֹמוֹת. זּ מַעֲלֶה נְשִׂאִים מִקְצֵה הָאָרֶץ; בְּרָקִים לַמָּטָר עָשָׂה, מוֹצֵא
רוּחַ מֵאוֹצְרוֹתָיו. חּ שֶׁהִכָּה בְּכוֹרֵי מִצְרָיִם, מֵאָדָם עַד בְּהֵמָה. טּ שָׁלַח אוֹתֹת
וּמֹפְתִים בְּתוֹכֵכִי מִצְרָיִם, בְּפַרְעֹה וּבְכָל עֲבָדָיו. יּ שֶׁהִכָּה גּוֹיִם רַבִּים, וְהָרַג
מְלָכִים עֲצוּמִים. יאּ לְסִיחוֹן מֶלֶךְ הָאֱמֹרִי, וּלְעוֹג מֶלֶךְ הַבָּשָׁן, וּלְכֹל
מַמְלְכוֹת כְּנָעַן. יבּ וְנָתַן אַרְצָם נַחֲלָה, נַחֲלָה לְיִשְׂרָאֵל עַמּוֹ. יגּ יהוה שִׁמְךָ
לְעוֹלָם, יהוה זִכְרְךָ לְדֹר וָדֹר. ידּ כִּי יָדִין יהוה עַמּוֹ, וְעַל עֲבָדָיו יִתְנֶחָם.
טוּ עֲצַבֵּי הַגּוֹיִם כֶּסֶף וְזָהָב, מַעֲשֵׂה יְדֵי אָדָם. טזּ פֶּה לָהֶם וְלֹא יְדַבֵּרוּ, עֵינַיִם
לָהֶם וְלֹא יִרְאוּ. יזּ אָזְנַיִם לָהֶם וְלֹא יַאֲזִינוּ, אַף אֵין יֶשׁ רוּחַ בְּפִיהֶם.
יחּ כְּמוֹהֶם יִהְיוּ עֹשֵׂיהֶם, כֹּל אֲשֶׁר בֹּטֵחַ בָּהֶם. יטּ בֵּית יִשְׂרָאֵל בָּרְכוּ אֶת
יהוה, בֵּית אַהֲרֹן בָּרְכוּ אֶת יהוה. כּ בֵּית הַלֵּוִי בָּרְכוּ אֶת יהוה, יִרְאֵי יהוה
בָּרְכוּ אֶת יהוה. כאּ בָּרוּךְ יהוה מִצִּיּוֹן, שֹׁכֵן יְרוּשָׁלָיִם, הַלְלוּיָהּ.

קלו אּ הוֹדוּ לַיהוה כִּי טוֹב, כִּי לְעוֹלָם חַסְדּוֹ. בּ הוֹדוּ לֵאלֹהֵי הָאֱלֹהִים, כִּי
לְעוֹלָם חַסְדּוֹ. גּ הוֹדוּ לַאֲדֹנֵי הָאֲדֹנִים, כִּי לְעוֹלָם חַסְדּוֹ. דּ לְעֹשֵׂה

נִפְלָאוֹת גְּדֹלוֹת לְבַדּוֹ, כִּי לְעוֹלָם חַסְדּוֹ. ה לְעֹשֵׂה הַשָּׁמַיִם בִּתְבוּנָה, כִּי לְעוֹלָם חַסְדּוֹ. ו לְרֹקַע הָאָרֶץ עַל הַמָּיִם, כִּי לְעוֹלָם חַסְדּוֹ. ז לְעֹשֵׂה אוֹרִים גְּדֹלִים, כִּי לְעוֹלָם חַסְדּוֹ. ח אֶת הַשֶּׁמֶשׁ לְמֶמְשֶׁלֶת בַּיּוֹם, כִּי לְעוֹלָם חַסְדּוֹ. ט אֶת הַיָּרֵחַ וְכוֹכָבִים לְמֶמְשְׁלוֹת בַּלָּיְלָה, כִּי לְעוֹלָם חַסְדּוֹ. י לְמַכֵּה מִצְרַיִם בִּבְכוֹרֵיהֶם, כִּי לְעוֹלָם חַסְדּוֹ. יא וַיּוֹצֵא יִשְׂרָאֵל מִתּוֹכָם, כִּי לְעוֹלָם חַסְדּוֹ. יב בְּיָד חֲזָקָה וּבִזְרוֹעַ נְטוּיָה, כִּי לְעוֹלָם חַסְדּוֹ. יג לְגֹזֵר יַם סוּף לִגְזָרִים, כִּי לְעוֹלָם חַסְדּוֹ. יד וְהֶעֱבִיר יִשְׂרָאֵל בְּתוֹכוֹ, כִּי לְעוֹלָם חַסְדּוֹ. טו וְנִעֵר פַּרְעֹה וְחֵילוֹ בְיַם סוּף, כִּי לְעוֹלָם חַסְדּוֹ. טז לְמוֹלִיךְ עַמּוֹ בַּמִּדְבָּר, כִּי לְעוֹלָם חַסְדּוֹ. יז לְמַכֵּה מְלָכִים גְּדֹלִים, כִּי לְעוֹלָם חַסְדּוֹ. יח וַיַּהֲרֹג מְלָכִים אַדִּירִים, כִּי לְעוֹלָם חַסְדּוֹ. יט לְסִיחוֹן מֶלֶךְ הָאֱמֹרִי, כִּי לְעוֹלָם חַסְדּוֹ. כ וּלְעוֹג מֶלֶךְ הַבָּשָׁן, כִּי לְעוֹלָם חַסְדּוֹ. כא וְנָתַן אַרְצָם לְנַחֲלָה, כִּי לְעוֹלָם חַסְדּוֹ. כב נַחֲלָה לְיִשְׂרָאֵל עַבְדּוֹ, כִּי לְעוֹלָם חַסְדּוֹ. כג שֶׁבְּשִׁפְלֵנוּ זָכַר לָנוּ, כִּי לְעוֹלָם חַסְדּוֹ. כד וַיִּפְרְקֵנוּ מִצָּרֵינוּ, כִּי לְעוֹלָם חַסְדּוֹ. כה נֹתֵן לֶחֶם לְכָל בָּשָׂר, כִּי לְעוֹלָם חַסְדּוֹ. כו הוֹדוּ לְאֵל הַשָּׁמָיִם, כִּי לְעוֹלָם חַסְדּוֹ.

קלז א עַל נַהֲרוֹת בָּבֶל, שָׁם יָשַׁבְנוּ, גַּם בָּכִינוּ, בְּזָכְרֵנוּ אֶת צִיּוֹן. ב עַל עֲרָבִים בְּתוֹכָהּ, תָּלִינוּ כִּנֹּרוֹתֵינוּ. ג כִּי שָׁם שְׁאֵלוּנוּ שׁוֹבֵינוּ דִּבְרֵי שִׁיר וְתוֹלָלֵינוּ שִׂמְחָה, שִׁירוּ לָנוּ מִשִּׁיר צִיּוֹן. ד אֵיךְ נָשִׁיר אֶת שִׁיר יהוה, עַל אַדְמַת נֵכָר. ה אִם אֶשְׁכָּחֵךְ יְרוּשָׁלָיִם, תִּשְׁכַּח יְמִינִי. ו תִּדְבַּק לְשׁוֹנִי לְחִכִּי, אִם לֹא אֶזְכְּרֵכִי; אִם לֹא אַעֲלֶה אֶת יְרוּשָׁלַיִם עַל רֹאשׁ שִׂמְחָתִי. ז זְכֹר יהוה לִבְנֵי אֱדוֹם אֵת יוֹם יְרוּשָׁלָיִם; הָאֹמְרִים עָרוּ, עָרוּ עַד הַיְסוֹד בָּהּ. ח בַּת בָּבֶל הַשְּׁדוּדָה, אַשְׁרֵי שֶׁיְשַׁלֶּם לָךְ אֶת גְּמוּלֵךְ שֶׁגָּמַלְתְּ לָנוּ. ט אַשְׁרֵי שֶׁיֹּאחֵז וְנִפֵּץ אֶת עֹלָלַיִךְ אֶל הַסָּלַע.

קלח א לְדָוִד, אוֹדְךָ בְכָל לִבִּי, נֶגֶד אֱלֹהִים אֲזַמְּרֶךָּ. ב אֶשְׁתַּחֲוֶה אֶל הֵיכַל קָדְשְׁךָ וְאוֹדֶה אֶת שְׁמֶךָ, עַל חַסְדְּךָ וְעַל אֲמִתֶּךָ; כִּי הִגְדַּלְתָּ עַל כָּל שִׁמְךָ אִמְרָתֶךָ. ג בְּיוֹם קָרָאתִי וַתַּעֲנֵנִי, תַּרְהִבֵנִי בְנַפְשִׁי עֹז. ד יוֹדוּךָ יהוה כָּל מַלְכֵי אָרֶץ, כִּי שָׁמְעוּ אִמְרֵי פִיךָ. ה וְיָשִׁירוּ בְּדַרְכֵי יהוה, כִּי גָדוֹל כְּבוֹד יהוה. ו כִּי רָם יהוה, וְשָׁפָל יִרְאֶה, וְגָבֹהַּ מִמֶּרְחָק יְיֵדָע. ז אִם אֵלֵךְ בְּקֶרֶב צָרָה, תְּחַיֵּנִי; עַל אַף אֹיְבַי תִּשְׁלַח יָדֶךָ, וְתוֹשִׁיעֵנִי יְמִינֶךָ. ח יהוה יִגְמֹר בַּעֲדִי; יהוה חַסְדְּךָ לְעוֹלָם, מַעֲשֵׂי יָדֶיךָ אַל תֶּרֶף.

קלט א לַמְנַצֵּחַ לְדָוִד מִזְמוֹר; יהוה, חֲקַרְתַּנִי וַתֵּדָע. ב אַתָּה יָדַעְתָּ שִׁבְתִּי וְקוּמִי, בַּנְתָּה לְרֵעִי מֵרָחוֹק. ג אָרְחִי וְרִבְעִי זֵרִיתָ, וְכָל דְּרָכַי הִסְכַּנְתָּה. ד כִּי אֵין מִלָּה בִּלְשׁוֹנִי, הֵן יהוה יָדַעְתָּ כֻלָּהּ. ה אָחוֹר וָקֶדֶם

צְרָרְתַּנִי, וַתָּשֶׁת עָלַי כַּפֶּכָה. וּפְלִיאָה דַעַת מִמֶּנִּי, נִשְׂגְּבָה לֹא אוּכַל לָהּ.
זְאָנָה אֵלֵךְ מֵרוּחֶךָ, וְאָנָה מִפָּנֶיךָ אֶבְרָח. חְאִם אֶסַּק שָׁמַיִם, שָׁם אָתָּה,
וְאַצִּיעָה שְּׁאוֹל, הִנֶּךָ. טְאֶשָּׂא כַנְפֵי שָׁחַר, אֶשְׁכְּנָה בְּאַחֲרִית יָם. יְגַּם שָׁם
יָדְךָ תַנְחֵנִי, וְתֹאחֲזֵנִי יְמִינֶךָ. יאְוָאֹמַר: אַךְ חֹשֶׁךְ יְשׁוּפֵנִי, וְלַיְלָה אוֹר בַּעֲדֵנִי.
יבְגַּם חֹשֶׁךְ לֹא יַחְשִׁיךְ מִמֶּךָ; וְלַיְלָה כַּיּוֹם יָאִיר, כַּחֲשֵׁיכָה כָּאוֹרָה. יגְכִּי
אַתָּה קָנִיתָ כִלְיֹתָי, תְּסֻכֵּנִי בְּבֶטֶן אִמִּי. ידְאוֹדְךָ עַל כִּי נוֹרָאוֹת נִפְלֵיתִי;
נִפְלָאִים מַעֲשֶׂיךָ, וְנַפְשִׁי יֹדַעַת מְאֹד. טוְלֹא נִכְחַד עָצְמִי מִמֶּךָ; אֲשֶׁר
עֻשֵּׂיתִי בַסֵּתֶר, רֻקַּמְתִּי בְּתַחְתִּיּוֹת אָרֶץ. טזְגָּלְמִי רָאוּ עֵינֶיךָ, וְעַל סִפְרְךָ
כֻּלָּם יִכָּתֵבוּ; יָמִים יֻצָּרוּ, וְלוֹ אֶחָד בָּהֶם. יזְוְלִי מַה יָּקְרוּ רֵעֶיךָ, אֵל; מֶה
עָצְמוּ רָאשֵׁיהֶם. יחְאֶסְפְּרֵם, מֵחוֹל יִרְבּוּן; הֱקִיצֹתִי וְעוֹדִי עִמָּךְ. יטְאִם
תִּקְטֹל אֱלוֹהַּ, רָשָׁע, וְאַנְשֵׁי דָמִים סוּרוּ מֶנִּי. כְאֲשֶׁר יֹמְרוּךָ לִמְזִמָּה, נָשׂוּא
לַשָּׁוְא עָרֶיךָ. כאְהֲלוֹא מְשַׂנְאֶיךָ יהוה, אֶשְׂנָא, וּבִתְקוֹמְמֶיךָ אֶתְקוֹטָט.
כבְתַּכְלִית שִׂנְאָה שְׂנֵאתִים, לְאוֹיְבִים הָיוּ לִי. כגְחָקְרֵנִי אֵל וְדַע לְבָבִי, בְּחָנֵנִי
וְדַע שַׂרְעַפָּי. כדְוּרְאֵה אִם דֶּרֶךְ עֹצֶב בִּי, וּנְחֵנִי בְּדֶרֶךְ עוֹלָם.

קמ אְלַמְנַצֵּחַ מִזְמוֹר לְדָוִד. בְחַלְּצֵנִי יהוה מֵאָדָם רָע, מֵאִישׁ חֲמָסִים
תִּנְצְרֵנִי. גְאֲשֶׁר חָשְׁבוּ רָעוֹת בְּלֵב, כָּל יוֹם יָגוּרוּ מִלְחָמוֹת. דְשָׁנְנוּ
לְשׁוֹנָם כְּמוֹ נָחָשׁ, חֲמַת עַכְשׁוּב תַּחַת שְׂפָתֵימוֹ סֶלָה. הְשָׁמְרֵנִי יהוה, מִידֵי
רָשָׁע, מֵאִישׁ חֲמָסִים תִּנְצְרֵנִי, אֲשֶׁר חָשְׁבוּ לִדְחוֹת פְּעָמָי. וְטָמְנוּ גֵאִים פַּח
לִי וַחֲבָלִים, פָּרְשׂוּ רֶשֶׁת לְיַד מַעְגָּל, מֹקְשִׁים שָׁתוּ לִי סֶלָה. זְאָמַרְתִּי
לַיהוה: אֵלִי אָתָּה, הַאֲזִינָה יהוה קוֹל תַּחֲנוּנָי. חְיֱהוִה אֲדֹנָי עֹז יְשׁוּעָתִי,
סַכֹּתָה לְרֹאשִׁי בְּיוֹם נָשֶׁק. טְאַל תִּתֵּן יהוה מַאֲוַיֵּי רָשָׁע, זְמָמוֹ אַל תָּפֶק
יָרוּמוּ סֶלָה. יְרֹאשׁ מְסִבָּי, עֲמַל שְׂפָתֵימוֹ יְכַסֵּימוֹ. יאְיִמּוֹטוּ עֲלֵיהֶם גֶּחָלִים;
בָּאֵשׁ יַפִּלֵם, בְּמַהֲמֹרוֹת בַּל יָקוּמוּ. יבְאִישׁ לָשׁוֹן בַּל יִכּוֹן בָּאָרֶץ; אִישׁ חָמָס
רָע, יְצוּדֶנּוּ לְמַדְחֵפֹת. יגְיָדַעְתִּי כִּי יַעֲשֶׂה יהוה דִּין עָנִי, מִשְׁפַּט אֶבְיֹנִים.
ידְאַךְ צַדִּיקִים יוֹדוּ לִשְׁמֶךָ, יֵשְׁבוּ יְשָׁרִים אֶת פָּנֶיךָ.

קמא אְמִזְמוֹר לְדָוִד; יהוה, קְרָאתִיךָ, חוּשָׁה לִי, הַאֲזִינָה קוֹלִי בְּקָרְאִי לָךְ.
בְתִּכּוֹן תְּפִלָּתִי קְטֹרֶת לְפָנֶיךָ, מַשְׂאַת כַּפַּי מִנְחַת עָרֶב. גְשִׁיתָה
יהוה שָׁמְרָה לְפִי, נִצְרָה עַל דַּל שְׂפָתָי. דְאַל תַּט לִבִּי לְדָבָר רָע, לְהִתְעוֹלֵל
עֲלִלוֹת בְּרֶשַׁע אֶת אִישִׁים פֹּעֲלֵי אָוֶן, וּבַל אֶלְחַם בְּמַנְעַמֵּיהֶם. הְיֶהֶלְמֵנִי
צַדִּיק חֶסֶד וְיוֹכִיחֵנִי, שֶׁמֶן רֹאשׁ אַל יָנִי רֹאשִׁי, כִּי עוֹד וּתְפִלָּתִי
בְּרָעוֹתֵיהֶם. וְנִשְׁמְטוּ בִידֵי סֶלַע שֹׁפְטֵיהֶם, וְשָׁמְעוּ אֲמָרַי כִּי נָעֵמוּ. זְכְּמוֹ

פֶּלַח וּבָקַע בָּאָרֶץ, נִפְזְרוּ עֲצָמֵינוּ לְפִי שְׁאוֹל. ז כִּי אֵלֶיךָ יֱהוִֹה אֲדֹנָי עֵינָי,
בְּכָה חָסִיתִי אַל תְּעַר נַפְשִׁי. ט שָׁמְרֵנִי מִידֵי פַח יָקְשׁוּ לִי, וּמֹקְשׁוֹת פֹּעֲלֵי
אָוֶן. י יִפְּלוּ בְמַכְמֹרָיו רְשָׁעִים, יַחַד אָנֹכִי עַד אֶעֱבוֹר.

קמב א מַשְׂכִּיל לְדָוִד, בִּהְיוֹתוֹ בַמְּעָרָה תְפִלָּה. ב קוֹלִי אֶל יֱהוִֹה אֶזְעָק,
קוֹלִי אֶל יֱהוִֹה אֶתְחַנָּן. ג אֶשְׁפֹּךְ לְפָנָיו שִׂיחִי, צָרָתִי לְפָנָיו אַגִּיד.
ד בְּהִתְעַטֵּף עָלַי רוּחִי, וְאַתָּה יָדַעְתָּ נְתִיבָתִי, בְּאֹרַח זוּ אֲהַלֵּךְ טָמְנוּ פַח לִי.
ה הַבֵּיט יָמִין וּרְאֵה וְאֵין לִי מַכִּיר, אָבַד מָנוֹס מִמֶּנִּי, אֵין דּוֹרֵשׁ לְנַפְשִׁי.
ו זָעַקְתִּי אֵלֶיךָ יֱהוִֹה, אָמַרְתִּי אַתָּה מַחְסִי, חֶלְקִי בְּאֶרֶץ הַחַיִּים. ז הַקְשִׁיבָה
אֶל רִנָּתִי כִּי דַלּוֹתִי מְאֹד, הַצִּילֵנִי מֵרֹדְפַי כִּי אָמְצוּ מִמֶּנִּי. ח הוֹצִיאָה
מִמַּסְגֵּר נַפְשִׁי, לְהוֹדוֹת אֶת שְׁמֶךָ; בִּי יַכְתִּרוּ צַדִּיקִים, כִּי תִגְמֹל עָלָי.

קמג א מִזְמוֹר לְדָוִד; יֱהוִֹה, שְׁמַע תְּפִלָּתִי, הַאֲזִינָה אֶל תַּחֲנוּנַי, בֶּאֱמֻנָתְךָ
עֲנֵנִי בְּצִדְקָתֶךָ. ב וְאַל תָּבוֹא בְמִשְׁפָּט אֶת עַבְדֶּךָ, כִּי לֹא יִצְדַּק לְפָנֶיךָ
כָל חָי. ג כִּי רָדַף אוֹיֵב נַפְשִׁי, דִּכָּא לָאָרֶץ חַיָּתִי, הוֹשִׁיבַנִי בְמַחֲשַׁכִּים כְּמֵתֵי
עוֹלָם. ד וַתִּתְעַטֵּף עָלַי רוּחִי, בְּתוֹכִי יִשְׁתּוֹמֵם לִבִּי. ה זָכַרְתִּי יָמִים מִקֶּדֶם,
הָגִיתִי בְכָל פָּעֳלֶךָ, בְּמַעֲשֵׂה יָדֶיךָ אֲשׂוֹחֵחַ. ו פֵּרַשְׂתִּי יָדַי אֵלֶיךָ, נַפְשִׁי
כְּאֶרֶץ עֲיֵפָה לְךָ סֶלָה. ז מַהֵר עֲנֵנִי יֱהוִֹה, כָּלְתָה רוּחִי; אַל תַּסְתֵּר פָּנֶיךָ
מִמֶּנִּי, וְנִמְשַׁלְתִּי עִם יֹרְדֵי בוֹר. ח הַשְׁמִיעֵנִי בַבֹּקֶר חַסְדֶּךָ, כִּי בְךָ בָטָחְתִּי;
הוֹדִיעֵנִי דֶּרֶךְ זוּ אֵלֵךְ, כִּי אֵלֶיךָ נָשָׂאתִי נַפְשִׁי. ט הַצִּילֵנִי מֵאֹיְבַי יֱהוִֹה, אֵלֶיךָ
כִסִּתִי. י לַמְּדֵנִי לַעֲשׂוֹת רְצוֹנֶךָ כִּי אַתָּה אֱלוֹהָי; רוּחֲךָ טוֹבָה תַּנְחֵנִי בְּאֶרֶץ
מִישׁוֹר. יא לְמַעַן שִׁמְךָ יֱהוִֹה תְּחַיֵּנִי, בְּצִדְקָתְךָ תּוֹצִיא מִצָּרָה נַפְשִׁי.
יב וּבְחַסְדְּךָ תַּצְמִית אֹיְבָי; וְהַאֲבַדְתָּ כָּל צֹרְרֵי נַפְשִׁי, כִּי אֲנִי עַבְדֶּךָ.

קמד א לְדָוִד, בָּרוּךְ יֱהוִֹה צוּרִי, הַמְלַמֵּד יָדַי לַקְּרָב, אֶצְבְּעוֹתַי לַמִּלְחָמָה.
ב חַסְדִּי וּמְצוּדָתִי מִשְׂגַּבִּי וּמְפַלְטִי לִי, מָגִנִּי וּבוֹ חָסִיתִי, הָרוֹדֵד עַמִּי
תַחְתָּי. ג יֱהוִֹה, מָה אָדָם וַתֵּדָעֵהוּ, בֶּן אֱנוֹשׁ וַתְּחַשְּׁבֵהוּ. ד אָדָם לַהֶבֶל דָּמָה,
יָמָיו כְּצֵל עוֹבֵר. ה יֱהוִֹה, הַט שָׁמֶיךָ וְתֵרֵד, גַּע בֶּהָרִים וְיֶעֱשָׁנוּ. ו בְּרוֹק בָּרָק
וּתְפִיצֵם, שְׁלַח חִצֶּיךָ וּתְהֻמֵּם. ז שְׁלַח יָדֶיךָ מִמָּרוֹם, פְּצֵנִי וְהַצִּילֵנִי מִמַּיִם
רַבִּים, מִיַּד בְּנֵי נֵכָר. ח אֲשֶׁר פִּיהֶם דִּבֶּר שָׁוְא, וִימִינָם יְמִין שָׁקֶר. ט אֱלֹהִים,
שִׁיר חָדָשׁ אָשִׁירָה לָּךְ, בְּנֵבֶל עָשׂוֹר אֲזַמְּרָה לָּךְ. י הַנּוֹתֵן תְּשׁוּעָה
לַמְּלָכִים, הַפּוֹצֶה אֶת דָּוִד עַבְדּוֹ מֵחֶרֶב רָעָה. יא פְּצֵנִי וְהַצִּילֵנִי מִיַּד בְּנֵי
נֵכָר; אֲשֶׁר פִּיהֶם דִּבֶּר שָׁוְא, וִימִינָם יְמִין שָׁקֶר. יב אֲשֶׁר בָּנֵינוּ כִּנְטִעִים,
מְגֻדָּלִים בִּנְעוּרֵיהֶם; בְּנוֹתֵינוּ כְזָוִיֹּת, מְחֻטָּבוֹת תַּבְנִית הֵיכָל. יג מְזָוֵינוּ
מְלֵאִים, מְפִיקִים מִזַּן אֶל זַן; צֹאנֵנוּ מַאֲלִיפוֹת, מְרֻבָּבוֹת בְּחוּצוֹתֵינוּ.

יד אַלּוּפֵינוּ מְסֻבָּלִים; אֵין פֶּרֶץ וְאֵין יוֹצֵאת, וְאֵין צְוָחָה בִּרְחֹבֹתֵינוּ. טו אַשְׁרֵי הָעָם שֶׁכֵּכָה לּוֹ, אַשְׁרֵי הָעָם שֶׁיהוה אֱלֹהָיו.

קמה א תְּהִלָּה לְדָוִד, אֲרוֹמִמְךָ אֱלוֹהַי הַמֶּלֶךְ, וַאֲבָרְכָה שִׁמְךָ לְעוֹלָם וָעֶד. ב בְּכָל יוֹם אֲבָרְכֶךָּ, וַאֲהַלְלָה שִׁמְךָ לְעוֹלָם וָעֶד. ג גָּדוֹל יהוה וּמְהֻלָּל מְאֹד, וְלִגְדֻלָּתוֹ אֵין חֵקֶר. ד דּוֹר לְדוֹר יְשַׁבַּח מַעֲשֶׂיךָ, וּגְבוּרֹתֶיךָ יַגִּידוּ. ה הֲדַר כְּבוֹד הוֹדֶךָ, וְדִבְרֵי נִפְלְאֹתֶיךָ אָשִׂיחָה. ו וֶעֱזוּז נוֹרְאֹתֶיךָ יֹאמֵרוּ, וּגְדוּלָּתְךָ אֲסַפְּרֶנָּה. ז זֵכֶר רַב טוּבְךָ יַבִּיעוּ, וְצִדְקָתְךָ יְרַנֵּנוּ. ח חַנּוּן וְרַחוּם יהוה, אֶרֶךְ אַפַּיִם וּגְדָל חָסֶד. ט טוֹב יהוה לַכֹּל, וְרַחֲמָיו עַל כָּל מַעֲשָׂיו. י יוֹדוּךָ יהוה כָּל מַעֲשֶׂיךָ, וַחֲסִידֶיךָ יְבָרְכוּכָה. יא כְּבוֹד מַלְכוּתְךָ יֹאמֵרוּ, וּגְבוּרָתְךָ יְדַבֵּרוּ. יב לְהוֹדִיעַ לִבְנֵי הָאָדָם גְּבוּרֹתָיו, וּכְבוֹד הֲדַר מַלְכוּתוֹ. יג מַלְכוּתְךָ מַלְכוּת כָּל עֹלָמִים, וּמֶמְשַׁלְתְּךָ בְּכָל דּוֹר וָדֹר. יד סוֹמֵךְ יהוה לְכָל הַנֹּפְלִים, וְזוֹקֵף לְכָל הַכְּפוּפִים. טו עֵינֵי כֹל אֵלֶיךָ יְשַׂבֵּרוּ, וְאַתָּה נוֹתֵן לָהֶם אֶת אָכְלָם בְּעִתּוֹ. טז פּוֹתֵחַ אֶת יָדֶךָ, וּמַשְׂבִּיעַ לְכָל חַי רָצוֹן. יז צַדִּיק יהוה בְּכָל דְּרָכָיו, וְחָסִיד בְּכָל מַעֲשָׂיו. יח קָרוֹב יהוה לְכָל קֹרְאָיו, לְכֹל אֲשֶׁר יִקְרָאֻהוּ בֶאֱמֶת. יט רְצוֹן יְרֵאָיו יַעֲשֶׂה, וְאֶת שַׁוְעָתָם יִשְׁמַע וְיוֹשִׁיעֵם. כ שׁוֹמֵר יהוה אֶת כָּל אֹהֲבָיו, וְאֵת כָּל הָרְשָׁעִים יַשְׁמִיד. כא תְּהִלַּת יהוה יְדַבֶּר פִּי, וִיבָרֵךְ כָּל בָּשָׂר שֵׁם קָדְשׁוֹ לְעוֹלָם וָעֶד.

קמו א הַלְלוּיָהּ, הַלְלִי נַפְשִׁי אֶת יהוה. ב אֲהַלְלָה יהוה בְּחַיָּי, אֲזַמְּרָה לֵאלֹהַי בְּעוֹדִי. ג אַל תִּבְטְחוּ בִנְדִיבִים, בְּבֶן אָדָם שֶׁאֵין לוֹ תְשׁוּעָה. ד תֵּצֵא רוּחוֹ יָשֻׁב לְאַדְמָתוֹ, בַּיּוֹם הַהוּא אָבְדוּ עֶשְׁתֹּנֹתָיו. ה אַשְׁרֵי שֶׁאֵל יַעֲקֹב בְּעֶזְרוֹ, שִׂבְרוֹ עַל יהוה אֱלֹהָיו. ו עֹשֶׂה שָׁמַיִם וָאָרֶץ, אֶת הַיָּם וְאֶת כָּל אֲשֶׁר בָּם; הַשֹּׁמֵר אֱמֶת לְעוֹלָם. ז עֹשֶׂה מִשְׁפָּט לַעֲשׁוּקִים, נֹתֵן לֶחֶם לָרְעֵבִים; יהוה מַתִּיר אֲסוּרִים. ח יהוה פֹּקֵחַ עִוְרִים, יהוה זֹקֵף כְּפוּפִים; יהוה אֹהֵב צַדִּיקִים. ט יהוה שֹׁמֵר אֶת גֵּרִים, יָתוֹם וְאַלְמָנָה יְעוֹדֵד; וְדֶרֶךְ רְשָׁעִים יְעַוֵּת. י יִמְלֹךְ יהוה לְעוֹלָם, אֱלֹהַיִךְ צִיּוֹן לְדֹר וָדֹר, הַלְלוּיָהּ.

קמז א הַלְלוּיָהּ, כִּי טוֹב זַמְּרָה אֱלֹהֵינוּ, כִּי נָעִים נָאוָה תְהִלָּה. ב בּוֹנֵה יְרוּשָׁלַיִם יהוה, נִדְחֵי יִשְׂרָאֵל יְכַנֵּס. ג הָרֹפֵא לִשְׁבוּרֵי לֵב, וּמְחַבֵּשׁ לְעַצְּבוֹתָם. ד מוֹנֶה מִסְפָּר לַכּוֹכָבִים, לְכֻלָּם שֵׁמוֹת יִקְרָא. ה גָּדוֹל אֲדוֹנֵינוּ וְרַב כֹּחַ, לִתְבוּנָתוֹ אֵין מִסְפָּר. ו מְעוֹדֵד עֲנָוִים יהוה, מַשְׁפִּיל רְשָׁעִים עֲדֵי אָרֶץ. ז עֱנוּ לַיהוה בְּתוֹדָה, זַמְּרוּ לֵאלֹהֵינוּ בְכִנּוֹר. ח הַמְכַסֶּה שָׁמַיִם בְּעָבִים, הַמֵּכִין לָאָרֶץ מָטָר; הַמַּצְמִיחַ הָרִים חָצִיר. ט נוֹתֵן לִבְהֵמָה

לַחְמָה, לִבְנֵי עֹרֵב אֲשֶׁר יִקְרָאוּ. י לֹא בִגְבוּרַת הַסּוּס יֶחְפָּץ, לֹא בְשׁוֹקֵי הָאִישׁ יִרְצֶה. יא רוֹצֶה יהוה אֶת יְרֵאָיו, אֶת הַמְיַחֲלִים לְחַסְדּוֹ. יב שַׁבְּחִי יְרוּשָׁלַיִם אֶת יהוה; הַלְלִי אֱלֹהַיִךְ, צִיּוֹן. יג כִּי חִזַּק בְּרִיחֵי שְׁעָרָיִךְ, בֵּרַךְ בָּנַיִךְ בְּקִרְבֵּךְ. יד הַשָּׂם גְּבוּלֵךְ שָׁלוֹם, חֵלֶב חִטִּים יַשְׂבִּיעֵךְ. טו הַשֹּׁלֵחַ אִמְרָתוֹ אָרֶץ, עַד מְהֵרָה יָרוּץ דְּבָרוֹ. טז הַנֹּתֵן שֶׁלֶג כַּצָּמֶר, כְּפוֹר כָּאֵפֶר יְפַזֵּר. יז מַשְׁלִיךְ קַרְחוֹ כְפִתִּים, לִפְנֵי קָרָתוֹ מִי יַעֲמֹד. יח יִשְׁלַח דְּבָרוֹ וְיַמְסֵם, יַשֵּׁב רוּחוֹ יִזְּלוּ מָיִם. יט מַגִּיד דְּבָרָו לְיַעֲקֹב, חֻקָּיו וּמִשְׁפָּטָיו לְיִשְׂרָאֵל. כ לֹא עָשָׂה כֵן לְכָל גּוֹי, וּמִשְׁפָּטִים בַּל יְדָעוּם, הַלְלוּיָהּ.

קמח א הַלְלוּיָהּ, הַלְלוּ אֶת יהוה מִן הַשָּׁמַיִם, הַלְלוּהוּ בַּמְּרוֹמִים. ב הַלְלוּהוּ כָל מַלְאָכָיו, הַלְלוּהוּ כָּל צְבָאָיו. ג הַלְלוּהוּ שֶׁמֶשׁ וְיָרֵחַ, הַלְלוּהוּ כָּל כּוֹכְבֵי אוֹר. ד הַלְלוּהוּ שְׁמֵי הַשָּׁמָיִם, וְהַמַּיִם אֲשֶׁר מֵעַל הַשָּׁמָיִם. ה יְהַלְלוּ אֶת שֵׁם יהוה, כִּי הוּא צִוָּה וְנִבְרָאוּ. ו וַיַּעֲמִידֵם לָעַד לְעוֹלָם, חָק נָתַן וְלֹא יַעֲבוֹר. ז הַלְלוּ אֶת יהוה מִן הָאָרֶץ, תַּנִּינִים וְכָל תְּהֹמוֹת. ח אֵשׁ וּבָרָד, שֶׁלֶג וְקִיטוֹר, רוּחַ סְעָרָה עֹשָׂה דְבָרוֹ. ט הֶהָרִים וְכָל גְּבָעוֹת, עֵץ פְּרִי וְכָל אֲרָזִים. י הַחַיָּה וְכָל בְּהֵמָה, רֶמֶשׂ וְצִפּוֹר כָּנָף. יא מַלְכֵי אֶרֶץ וְכָל לְאֻמִּים, שָׂרִים וְכָל שֹׁפְטֵי אָרֶץ. יב בַּחוּרִים וְגַם בְּתוּלוֹת, זְקֵנִים עִם נְעָרִים. יג יְהַלְלוּ אֶת שֵׁם יהוה, כִּי נִשְׂגָּב שְׁמוֹ לְבַדּוֹ; הוֹדוֹ עַל אֶרֶץ וְשָׁמָיִם, יד וַיָּרֶם קֶרֶן לְעַמּוֹ, תְּהִלָּה לְכָל חֲסִידָיו, לִבְנֵי יִשְׂרָאֵל עַם קְרֹבוֹ, הַלְלוּיָהּ.

קמט א הַלְלוּיָהּ, שִׁירוּ לַיהוה שִׁיר חָדָשׁ, תְּהִלָּתוֹ בִּקְהַל חֲסִידִים. ב יִשְׂמַח יִשְׂרָאֵל בְּעֹשָׂיו, בְּנֵי צִיּוֹן יָגִילוּ בְמַלְכָּם. ג יְהַלְלוּ שְׁמוֹ בְמָחוֹל, בְּתֹף וְכִנּוֹר יְזַמְּרוּ לוֹ. ד כִּי רוֹצֶה יהוה בְּעַמּוֹ, יְפָאֵר עֲנָוִים בִּישׁוּעָה. ה יַעְלְזוּ חֲסִידִים בְּכָבוֹד, יְרַנְּנוּ עַל מִשְׁכְּבוֹתָם. ו רוֹמְמוֹת אֵל בִּגְרוֹנָם, וְחֶרֶב פִּיפִיּוֹת בְּיָדָם. ז לַעֲשׂוֹת נְקָמָה בַּגּוֹיִם, תּוֹכֵחוֹת בַּלְאֻמִּים. ח לֶאְסֹר מַלְכֵיהֶם בְּזִקִּים, וְנִכְבְּדֵיהֶם בְּכַבְלֵי בַרְזֶל. ט לַעֲשׂוֹת בָּהֶם מִשְׁפָּט כָּתוּב, הָדָר הוּא לְכָל חֲסִידָיו, הַלְלוּיָהּ.

קנ א הַלְלוּיָהּ, הַלְלוּ אֵל בְּקָדְשׁוֹ, הַלְלוּהוּ בִּרְקִיעַ עֻזּוֹ. ב הַלְלוּהוּ בִגְבוּרֹתָיו, הַלְלוּהוּ כְּרֹב גֻּדְלוֹ. ג הַלְלוּהוּ בְּתֵקַע שׁוֹפָר, הַלְלוּהוּ בְּנֵבֶל וְכִנּוֹר. ד הַלְלוּהוּ בְתֹף וּמָחוֹל, הַלְלוּהוּ בְּמִנִּים וְעֻגָב. ה הַלְלוּהוּ בְצִלְצְלֵי שָׁמַע, הַלְלוּהוּ בְּצִלְצְלֵי תְרוּעָה. ו כֹּל הַנְּשָׁמָה תְּהַלֵּל יָהּ, הַלְלוּיָהּ.

מִי יִתֵּן מִצִּיּוֹן יְשׁוּעַת יִשְׂרָאֵל; בְּשׁוּב יהוה שְׁבוּת עַמּוֹ, יָגֵל יַעֲקֹב יִשְׂמַח יִשְׂרָאֵל. וּתְשׁוּעַת צַדִּיקִים מֵיהוה, מָעוּזָּם בְּעֵת צָרָה. וַיַּעְזְרֵם יהוה וַיְפַלְּטֵם; יְפַלְּטֵם מֵרְשָׁעִים וְיוֹשִׁיעֵם, כִּי חָסוּ בוֹ.

יְהִי רָצוֹן מִלְּפָנֶיךָ, יהוה אֱלֹהֵינוּ וֵאלֹהֵי אֲבוֹתֵינוּ, בִּזְכוּת

אַחֲרֵי סֵפֶר אֶחָד:

סֵפֶר רִאשׁוֹן | סֵפֶר שֵׁנִי | סֵפֶר שְׁלִישִׁי | סֵפֶר רְבִיעִי | סֵפֶר חֲמִישִׁי

שֶׁבַּתְּהִלִּים שֶׁקְּרָאנוּ לְפָנֶיךָ, שֶׁהוּא כְּנֶגֶד

סֵפֶר בְּרֵאשִׁית | סֵפֶר שְׁמוֹת | סֵפֶר וַיִּקְרָא | סֵפֶר בַּמִּדְבָּר | סֵפֶר דְּבָרִים

בִּזְכוּת מִזְמוֹרָיו וּבִזְכוּת פְּסוּקָיו וּבִזְכוּת תֵּבוֹתָיו

וּבִזְכוּת שְׁמוֹתֶיךָ הַקְּדוֹשִׁים וְהַטְּהוֹרִים הַיּוֹצְאִים מֵהֶם,

אִם לֹא אָמַר סֵפֶר שָׁלֵם, יֹאמַר זֶה:

מִזְמוֹרֵי תְהִלִּים שֶׁקְּרָאנוּ לְפָנֶיךָ, וּבִזְכוּת פְּסוּקֵיהֶם וּבִזְכוּת תֵּבוֹתֵיהֶם,

וּבִזְכוּת שְׁמוֹתֶיךָ הַקְּדוֹשִׁים וְהַטְּהוֹרִים הַיּוֹצְאִים מֵהֶם,

בְּשַׁבָּת וּבְיוֹם טוֹב:	בְּחוֹל:
שֶׁתְּהֵא נֶחְשֶׁבֶת לָנוּ אֲמִירַת מִזְמוֹרֵי תְהִלִּים אֵלּוּ, כְּאִלּוּ אֲמָרָם דָּוִד מֶלֶךְ יִשְׂרָאֵל עָלָיו הַשָּׁלוֹם בְּעַצְמוֹ, זְכוּתוֹ יָגֵן עָלֵינוּ; וְיַעֲמֹד לָנוּ לְחַבֵּר אֵשֶׁת נְעוּרִים עִם דּוֹדָהּ, בְּאַהֲבָה וְאַחֲוָה וְרֵעוּת. וּמִשָּׁם יִמָּשֵׁךְ לָנוּ שֶׁפַע לְנֶפֶשׁ רוּחַ וּנְשָׁמָה. וּכְשֵׁם שֶׁאָנוּ אוֹמְרִים לְפָנֶיךָ שִׁירָה בָּעוֹלָם הַזֶּה, כָּךְ נִזְכֶּה לוֹמַר לְפָנֶיךָ, יהוה אֱלֹהֵינוּ וֵאלֹהֵי אֲבוֹתֵינוּ, שִׁיר וּשְׁבָחָה לָעוֹלָם הַבָּא. וְעַל יְדֵי אֲמִירַת תְּהִלִּים תִּתְעוֹרֵר חֲבַצֶּלֶת הַשָּׁרוֹן לָשִׁיר בְּקוֹל נָעִים גִּילַת וְרַנֵּן, כְּבוֹד הַלְּבָנוֹן נִתַּן לָהּ, הוֹד וְהָדָר בְּבֵית אֱלֹהֵינוּ, בִּמְהֵרָה בְיָמֵינוּ, אָמֵן סֶלָה.	שֶׁתְּכַפֶּר לָנוּ עַל כָּל חַטֹּאתֵינוּ וְתִמְחָל לָנוּ עַל כָּל עֲוֹנוֹתֵינוּ, וְתִסְלַח לָנוּ עַל כָּל פְּשָׁעֵינוּ, שֶׁחָטָאנוּ וְשֶׁעָוִינוּ וְשֶׁפָּשַׁעְנוּ לְפָנֶיךָ; וְתַחֲזִירֵנוּ בִּתְשׁוּבָה שְׁלֵמָה לְפָנֶיךָ; וְתַדְרִיכֵנוּ לַעֲבוֹדָתֶךָ; וְתִפְתַּח לִבֵּנוּ בְּתַלְמוּד תּוֹרָתֶךָ; וְתִשְׁלַח רְפוּאָה שְׁלֵמָה לְחוֹלֵי עַמֶּךָ (וּלְחוֹלֶה פב״פ); וְתִקְרָא לִשְׁבוּיִם דְּרוֹר וְלַאֲסוּרִים פְּקַח קוֹחַ; וּלְכָל הוֹלְכֵי דְרָכִים וְעוֹבְרֵי יַמִּים וּנְהָרוֹת מֵעַמְּךָ יִשְׂרָאֵל, תַּצִּילֵם מִכָּל צַעַר וָנֶזֶק, וְתַגִּיעֵם לִמְחוֹז חֶפְצָם לְחַיִּים וּלְשָׁלוֹם; וְתִפְקוֹד לְכָל חֲשׂוּכֵי בָנִים בְּזֶרַע שֶׁל קַיָּמָא לַעֲבוֹדָתֶךָ וּלְיִרְאָתֶךָ; וְעֻבָּרוֹת שֶׁל עַמְּךָ בֵּית יִשְׂרָאֵל תַּצִּיל שֶׁלֹּא תַפֵּלְנָה וְלָדוֹתֵיהֶן; וְהַיּוֹשְׁבוֹת עַל הַמַּשְׁבֵּר בְּרַחֲמֶיךָ הָרַבִּים תַּצִּילֵן מִכָּל רָע, וְאֶל הַמֵּינִיקוֹת תַּשְׁפִּיעַ שֶׁלֹּא יֶחְסַר חָלָב מִדַּדֵּיהֶן;

וְאַל יִמְשׁוֹל אַסְכְּרָה וְשֵׁדִין וְכָל פְּגָעִים וּמַרְעִין בִּישִׁין בְּכָל יַלְדֵי עַמְּךָ בֵּית יִשְׂרָאֵל, וּתְגַדְּלֵם לְתוֹרָתֶךָ לִלְמוֹד תּוֹרָה לִשְׁמָהּ, וְתַצִּילֵם מֵעַיִן הָרָע וּמִדֶּבֶר וּמִמַּגֵּפָה וּמִשָּׂטָן וּמִיֵּצֶר הָרָע; וּתְבַטֵּל מֵעָלֵינוּ וּמִכָּל עַמְּךָ בֵּית יִשְׂרָאֵל בְּכָל מָקוֹם שֶׁהֵם כָּל גְּזֵרוֹת קָשׁוֹת וְרָעוֹת; וְתַטֶּה לֵב הַמַּלְכוּת עָלֵינוּ לְטוֹבָה, וְתִגְזוֹר עָלֵינוּ גְּזֵרוֹת טוֹבוֹת; וְתִשְׁלַח בְּרָכָה וְהַצְלָחָה בְּכָל מַעֲשֵׂה יָדֵינוּ; וְהָכֵן פַּרְנָסָתֵנוּ מִיָּדְךָ הָרְחָבָה וְהַמְּלֵאָה, וְלֹא יִצְטָרְכוּ עַמְּךָ יִשְׂרָאֵל זֶה לָזֶה וְלֹא לְעַם אַחֵר; וְתֵן לְכָל אִישׁ וָאִישׁ דֵּי פַרְנָסָתוֹ; וּלְכָל גְּוִיָּה וּגְוִיָּה דֵּי מַחְסוֹרָהּ; וּתְמַהֵר וְתָחִישׁ לְגָאֳלֵנוּ וְתִבְנֶה בֵּית מִקְדָּשֵׁנוּ וְתִפְאַרְתֵּנוּ. (אֵין אוֹמְרִים י״ג מִדּוֹת אֶלָּא בַצִּבּוּר וּבִזְכוּת שָׁלֹשׁ עֶשְׂרֵה מִדּוֹתֶיךָ שֶׁל רַחֲמִים הַכְּתוּבוֹת בְּתוֹרָתֶךָ – כְּמוֹ שֶׁנֶּאֱמַר: יהוה יהוה אֵל רַחוּם וְחַנּוּן אֶרֶךְ אַפַּיִם וְרַב חֶסֶד וֶאֱמֶת נֹצֵר חֶסֶד לָאֲלָפִים נֹשֵׂא עָוֹן וָפֶשַׁע וְחַטָּאָה וְנַקֵּה, שֶׁאֵינָן חוֹזְרוֹת רֵיקָם מִלְּפָנֶיךָ). עָזְרֵנוּ אֱלֹהֵי יִשְׁעֵנוּ עַל דְּבַר כְּבוֹד שְׁמֶךָ, וְהַצִּילֵנוּ וְכַפֵּר עַל חַטֹּאתֵינוּ לְמַעַן שְׁמֶךָ. בָּרוּךְ יהוה לְעוֹלָם, אָמֵן וְאָמֵן

This volume is part of
THE ARTSCROLL® SERIES
an ongoing project of
translations, commentaries and expositions on
Scripture, Mishnah, Talmud, Midrash, Halachah,
liturgy, history, the classic Rabbinic writings,
biographies and thought.

For a brochure of current publications
visit your local Hebrew bookseller
or contact the publisher:

Mesorah Publications, ltd.

4401 Second Avenue
Brooklyn, New York 11232
(718) 921-9000
www.artscroll.com